Computer Simulation for Engineers

Computer Simulation for Engineers

Robert E. Stephenson

University of Utah

 Harcourt Brace Jovanovich, Inc.

New York   Chicago   San Francisco   Atlanta

ISBN: 0-15-512646-6

Library of Congress Catalog Card Number: 75-139395

Printed in the United States of America

to FRAN

my wife, my best friend

Preface

To simulate means to model or, perhaps more accurately, to study the behavior of a model to learn more about a particular system. Simulating or modeling is more common than we might realize. For example, a little girl playing with a doll or a boy setting up his toy trains is using simulation to learn more about the real world, as is the engineer testing new devices in a wind tunnel.

Simulation, therefore, requires the creation of a model whose behavior can—often with a generous amount of imagination—be interpreted in terms of the behavior of the system being studied. In certain instances, it is appropriate to use a scale model, which may be larger than, smaller than, or equal in size to the original system or device. These scale models often yield much useful engineering information.

From a different point of view, however, a simulation model may be simply a mathematical description of the behavior of the device being studied. Manipulating this type of model according to the rules of mathematics can then produce much worthwhile information.

The simulation models we describe in this book are achieved through the use of analog, digital, or hybrid computers. Our primary emphasis is on the methods for realizing computer models. Only the simulation of continuous (and not discrete) systems is considered here. These systems may be linear or nonlinear, continuous or discontinuous, and their behavior may be described by one or more differential or algebraic equations. The behavior-describing equations may be linear or nonlinear; they may be also entirely continuous or only piecewise continuous as required to describe the system.

Chapter 1 introduces the concept of the simulation model and indicates that models can exist in a variety of forms. A block-diagram approach to simulation is developed to portray the interactive behavior of the various parts of the model and to show explicitly the various functions that the model must perform. The block diagram is used later as a tool in developing procedures for simulating on both analog and digital computers.

Chapter 2 describes a number of mathematical features that are useful in the simulation study of continuous physical systems. Many of the results developed here are used in the chapters that follow.

Chapter 3 introduces the electronic analog computer, describes the functional behavior of each of the typical components, and outlines a general procedure to be followed when using the electronic analog computer as a simulator. No attempt is made to describe the internal workings of the analog computer components. There is an appendix at the end of the book for those who want more detailed information.

This approach is something of a departure from the traditional study of analog computers. Experience has shown, however, that it is entirely practical to proceed in this manner. Considerable competence can be achieved by analog computer users who have little or no understanding of the internal workings of the machines. From this point of view, analog computers are used much like digital computers — as problem-solving tools, not as objects of study.

Chapter 4 discusses the analog computer simulation of systems whose behavior is described by linear ordinary differential equations.

Chapter 5 is devoted to the problems of time and magnitude scaling. All simulators have limitations, and scaling must be applied so that the problem and the simulator are compatible. The problem of scaling is the most troublesome aspect of analog computer use. Procedures for accomplishing both amplitude and time scaling are presented in a manner that has proved to be most easily learned by students. Two approaches in magnitude scaling are given, along with a very simple view of time scaling.

Chapter 6 deals with the simulation of more complicated systems. Here, systems whose behavior is described by sets of simultaneous ordinary differential equations or differential equations of higher order are discussed. Also considered are systems containing nonlinearities and discontinuities. The simulation of systems based on their transfer functions, a useful method for treating servomechanisms and other feedback devices, is one of the additional ideas included in this chapter.

Chapter 7 treats the simulation of systems whose behavior is described by partial differential equations. A number of vibrating and oscillating systems are presented, along with several heat-flow problems.

Chapter 8 presents the state-variable approach to system simulation. Several advantages accrue to the user of this concept of simulation. One of these advantages stems from the ease with which systems can be simulated when they are partly described by transfer functions and partly by differential equations.

Chapter 9 introduces the digital computer as a simulator of continuous physical systems, and a comparison is drawn between analog and digital computer simulators. In addition, there is a brief historical account of digital computer simulation.

Chapter 10 consists of a detailed description of how MIMIC digital computer simulation language is used. Historically, MIMIC was the first really significant and useful simulation language. It has the virtue of being easy to understand and use, and it is appropriate for many current digital computing systems.

Chapter 11 describes CSSL, the most recent digital computer simulation language. This language contains the recommendations of the Simulation Software Committee of Simulation Councils, Inc. CSSL has many features in common with other recent simulation languages, and so it is easy to understand other languages after one has learned CSSL.

Chapter 12 is a detailed account of ECAP—a special-purpose language for studying the behavior of electric circuits. ECAP is shown to be not only a simulator of electric circuits, but also a general purpose system simulator; this is done by developing an analog computer simulator in the usual way, and then using ECAP to analyze the behavior of the resulting analog computer circuit.

Chapter 13 describes another special-purpose language called COGO. This language is particularly well suited for the use of civil engineers when carrying out the calculations encountered in surveying.

Chapter 14 considers the special-purpose language called STRESS. This language is used extensively in the design and analysis of structures.

Chapter 15 introduces the reader to hybrid computers. Because of the special-purpose nature of many hybrid computing facilities, no attempt is made to present the details of programming for any particular facility. Rather, there is a general discussion of fundamental principles so that the reader may familiarize himself with some of the concepts of this subject.

In reading this book, the student may feel that undue emphasis is given to analog computers. The reason for spending so much time on analog computers is that many simulation ideas can be introduced better by this means than by means of the digital computer. However, one can implement all the ideas developed for the analog computer using the digital computer as a simulator.

It is not necessary to study all chapters in sequence, although Chapters 1, 2, 3, and 4 should be studied in that order. One could then leave analog computer simulation and move to Chapters 9 and either 10 or 11. If time permits, the student should study both Chapters 10 and 11 to obtain a firm background in general-purpose languages. Chapters 12, 13, and 14 are included to satisfy the special needs of a variety of users and may be studied independently, as desired, according to the interests and requirements of the reader.

Each chapter concludes with a group of exercises. These exercises, of varying difficulty, are intended to augment and reinforce the discussions of the chapters that precede them.

The student using this book is expected to know basic calculus and physics. In addition, it is desirable for him to have had a programming course prior to this one.

The author wishes to thank the many students and teaching assistants who worked with him throughout the period of manuscript development. Their many suggestions for improvement have been incorporated.

Appreciation is also expressed to Dr. Ralph T. Dames of Programming Sciences Corporation, Los Angeles, California, for his permission to use material from their CSSL programming manual, and to Mr. E. H. Kopf of Jet Propulsion Laboratories for allowing me to use his examples of CSSL programming.

Special thanks go to the College of Engineering of the University of Utah, and in particular to Mrs. Marian Swenson of the Electrical Engineering Department and to her secretarial staff for manuscript typing and preparation.

Robert E. Stephenson

Contents

3 The Electronic Analog Computer

4 Analog Simulation of Systems Described by Linear Ordinary Differential Equations

5 Time and Magnitude Scaling

6 The Simulation of More Complicated Systems

7 Analog Simulation Involving Partial Differential Equations

8 State Variable Approach to System Simulation

9 Digital Computer Simulation

10 MIMIC

11 Continuous System Simulation Language (CSSL)

12 Electronic Circuit Analysis Program (ECAP)

13 Coordinate Geometry (COGO)

14 Structural Engineering Systems Solver (STRESS)

15 Hybrid Computers

Appendix

Computer Simulation for Engineers

Simulation — What Is It?

1.1 Introduction

When we embark on a study of a physical system we must often rely on our knowledge of physics and mathematics to guide us. A knowledge of the physical principles involved helps in understanding why a physical system behaves the way it does, and a knowledge of mathematics helps in describing the behavior of the physical system in an organized symbolic manner. Mathematical manipulation of the resulting mathematical description of the physical system often reveals considerable information concerning the behavior of the system and permits us to express this behavior in a quantitative way.

For a variety of reasons, it is impractical to solve many problems by the direct application of mathematics. For example, suppose the following differential equation was encountered as one which describes the behavior of a physical system in which we have some interest.

$$10\frac{d^2y}{dt^2} + 5\frac{dy}{dt} + 40y = G(t) \tag{1.1}$$

Equation 1.1 looks innocent enough at first glance and we might try to solve it using the principles of mathematics which we learned during our study of differential equations. Under some rather restricted conditions, this approach might be satisfactory — or even preferable. Suppose, however, that $G(t)$ in Eq. 1.1 must assume a large number of different forms including zero, finite constants, linear and nonlinear functions of t, and nonanalytical functions of t. Now, how do we proceed under these conditions? Methods for solving some of these kinds of problems are not included in most courses in differential equations. Furthermore, it is not really a pleasant task to solve an equation many times with perhaps only a slight variation in $G(t)$ from one solution to the next. Obviously, what is needed is a device or method of solution which will permit easy handling of the many difficult forms of $G(t)$ and, at the same time, eliminate the drudgery associated with repeatedly grinding through the details of solution time after time. The answer lies in the use of computer simulation, using either the analog or the digital computer or a combination of the two. But, we may be getting ahead of ourselves. Let us continue developing our background so that computer simulation will be more meaningful.

As a help in analyzing our problem, let us rewrite the preceeding differential equation in the following form:

$$\frac{d^2y}{dt^2} = -0.5\frac{dy}{dt} - 4y + \frac{G(t)}{10} \tag{1.2}$$

Notice that all that has really been done here is to solve the behavior-describing equation explicitly for the highest-ordered derivative. After pondering over this form of the equation, we might conclude that we need five devices to enable us to solve our problem — an adder, an integrator, a sign changer, a multiplier, and a function generator.

How does an adder help? Equation 1.2 shows d^2y/dt^2 to be equal to the sum of three quantities; two are negative and one is positive. If an adder can be devised, and if the appropriate input signals can be obtained from somewhere, the adder can then be used to form the sum of the input signals and thus obtain an output signal that is representative of d^2y/dt^2. Let us just observe in passing that both analog and digital computers contain adders and so devising an adder is not a problem.

It is convenient to use a set of block diagram symbols to represent the devices as they are encountered and used. We will adopt the symbol of Fig. 1.1 to represent an adder. Later, we will modify this symbol as it is applied to a particular type of

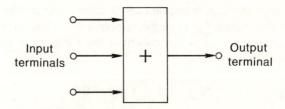

Figure 1.1 *An adder symbol.*

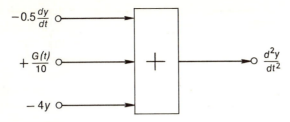

Figure 1.2 *The adder with particular inputs and output.*

computer. But, let us ignore the particular type of computer for the present and confine ourselves to the fundamentals of the analysis. The symbol of Fig. 1.1 shows the input terminals of the adder where input signals are applied representing the quantities to be added. The figure also shows an output terminal where there is a signal representing the sum of the inputs. The particular inputs and output that would be used to solve our problem are shown in Fig. 1.2.

Now, if we had an integrator that would integrate with respect to time, we could integrate d^2y/dt^2 (the output of Fig. 1.2) to obtain dy/dt. Figure 1.3 shows an integrator added to the block diagram of Fig. 1.2. Integration is possible in both analog and digital computers.

If we repeat the integration process a second time, the resulting output is y, as shown in Fig. 1.4.

So far our development has been straightforward, but now there is a problem. In all our work we have presumed that the necessary adder inputs could be found somewhere. The question is "Where?"

Observe that the output of the first integrator is dy/dt and one of the adder inputs is $-0.5\, dy/dt$. A multiplier and a sign changer can be used in combination to convert dy/dt into $-0.5\, dy/dt$. Symbols for these operations are shown in Fig. 1.5. Also shown added to Fig. 1.5 are the multiplier and sign changer needed to obtain the other adder input, $-4y$. The signal for the multiplier input is obtained from the output of the second integrator. Both multiplication and sign change can be achieved in analog and digital computers.

Since $G(t)$ might be required to assume a variety of different forms, a function generator must also be provided to generate a signal that is representative of each desired $G(t)$. A symbol for this is also given to complete the diagram of Fig. 1.5. Analog and digital computers can perform function generation.

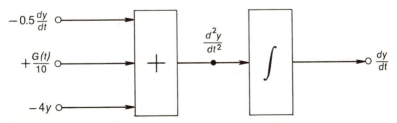

Figure 1.3 *An integrator combined with the adder of Fig. 1.2.*

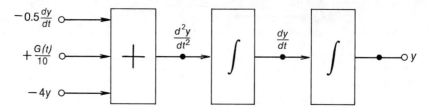

Figure 1.4 *An adder with two integrators.*

In this introduction we have indicated that the required operations of addition, integration, sign change, multiplication, and function generation can be realized through the use of either analog or digital computers. As a matter of fact, all of these operations and more can be achieved with either type of machine. This brings us to the most important decision of all. Which computer shall we use—analog or digital? We shall find that sometimes one is better and sometimes the other is. The choice must be made for each particular application, and it depends on many factors peculiar to each situation. A thorough analysis of these factors must always preceed the decision of whether to use analog or digital equipment.

Regardless of the type of implementation, analog or digital, the device selected will have behavior similar to the behavior of the original physical system. This representation of certain behavior is what we shall hereafter call *simulation.*

Our studies will explore in greater detail the principles of simulation using both analog and digital computers. We shall start with analog simulation and later turn our attention to digital simulation. At the conclusion of these studies, we should be able to make a proper decision concerning which way to go—analog or digital.

1.2 Simulating and Modeling

To simulate means to model. A simulation study of a system or device requires some type of model which assumes or has the appearance and/or behavior of the

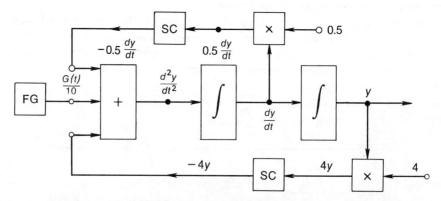

Figure 1.5 *Multipliers and sign changers and a function generator are added to Fig. 1.4.*

system or device without the reality. Engineers often use models to help them find answers to difficult problems. It is our purpose to study various ways of simulating physical systems, in order to help find answers to problems that would otherwise be difficult if not impossible to obtain.

Engineers often try to solve their problems by intuition. Although many problems have been solved that way, intuition alone is often not enough when the problem becomes extremely complex. Much time, money, and effort have been wasted by countless engineers who tried to solve their problems solely on the basis of intuition. In many of these situations, all three—time, money, and effort—could have been saved through the use of simulation.

Models for engineering use may be of several different types. Some system models, such as scale models, are very much like their counterpart systems while others are quite different. Scale models have the same structure, proportion, and appearance as the object being simulated but may be larger or smaller than the original. For example, the aerodynamic performance of a proposed airplane design can be determined from the wind tunnel performance of a small-scale model of the airplane. It would be economically unfeasible to build a wind tunnel for testing full-scale airplanes. Similarly, the expected performance of a proposed hull for a ship can be verified by constructing a small-scale model and testing it in a test tank. This kind of small-scale model testing often reveals design errors at much less expense, in much shorter time, and with much less effort than would be required for full-scale construction and testing. In some instances scale models are built to larger scales than the original, such as the model of an atom or a molecule.

Useful as the scale model may be, it does have some limitations. Scale models are not always as versatile as one would like. They are often built for a special purpose and as a result cannot be conveniently used for other purposes. Another, and perhaps more important difficulty in the use of scale models for simulation is that the scale model may not accurately represent the original system. The very fact that it is different in size may cause its operating characteristics to be quite different from those of the original system. Because of these difficulties, it is necessary to look further for other means of simulating physical systems. If a simulating scheme is to be truly useful it must be a general purpose scheme; analog and digital computers provide this generality of purpose. In some instances, useful simulators may be achieved through the use of scale models, but in other instances, simulators may only slightly resemble or even have no physical similiarity at all to the original system.

The network analyzer model of an electrical power system has very little physical resemblance to its full-scale counterpart. There exists some resemblance in that both are electrical systems. In this model, it is the electrical operating characteristics that must be preserved and physical appearance is of no consequence. A small-scale model of a power system with miniature poles, lines, transformers, etc., would have such different electrical properties as to be entirely useless as a simulator. Voltage, current, impedance, phase angles, and real and reactive power all have their respective counterparts in both the network analyzer model and the full-scale system, but here the resemblance ends. The physical appearance of the model in no way resembles the original, nor is there any need for physical resemblance. The network analyzer may be conveniently contained in a single room. The system being studied, on the other hand, may extend for hundreds of miles.

Operating conditions can be studied on a network analyzer model that would be impossible to study on the full-scale power system. For example, short circuits can be imposed on the model, but it would be disastrous to short circuit the actual system. Not only would damaged equipment result but the system would probably fail. Behavior of the model under such severe conditions can be used to determine the behavior of the larger system under corresponding conditions. This understanding of system behavior can be achieved at considerable advantage in terms of time, money, and convenience. In fact, much information concerning severe operating conditions, such as short circuits and the resulting instabilities, can be obtained from the model that would obviously be impossible to obtain on the full-scale system and still keep the system operating.

A mathematical model is yet a third type of simulator which finds engineering usefulness. If sufficiently accurate mathematical relationships can be found that properly describe the behavior of the original system, these relationships can often be manipulated according to the rules of mathematics to yield much desirable information. However, such mathematical manipulations are not always possible or even practicable and often the effort required is not justified in terms of the information obtainable. Also, nonlinearities, or time varying parameters, or uncertain boundary conditions can make mathematical manipulations undesirable or impossible. When these situations do occur, one must resort to other means of solution. It is in this kind of situation that the electronic analog computer simulation and/or the digital computer simulation are valuable. Mathematical models and analog and digital computer models usually bear no resemblance at all to the original system.

1.3 Computer Simulation

Using the mathematical model which describes the performance of a physical system, an analog computer model can be constructed. The analog computer model and the original system are related only through the fact that both are described by the same or similar mathematical relationships. The physical appearance of the two are ordinarily not even remotely similar. Furthermore, in electronic analog computers, the measurable quantities are time varying voltages, while in the system being simulated the corresponding quantities may be such diverse things as velocity, displacement, acceleration, temperature, density, stress, strain, or a myriad of other physical attributes. The voltages in an analog computer which represent these physical attributes are easily measured and recorded. The physical attributes of the original system, however, may be quite difficult to measure or to record. Time varying, nonlinear elements which may cause severe problems in analyzing the mathematical model by mathematical manipulations can be handled quite easily in either the analog or digital computer models.

It is necessary when studying system behavior by means of an analog computer model, to cause the voltages at various points in the computer model to behave in a manner analogous to the corresponding physical quantities in the original system. It is possible, as we shall learn, to have the analog computer behave more slowly or more rapidly than the original system. When this is done, the computer behavior is said to be *time scaled.* Of course, it is possible to have the computer operate at the same speed as the original system. The computer is then said to be operating in *real time.* Magnitude scaling is also possible. In fact, it is the usual situation to have both time and magnitude scaling imposed on an analog computer model. Magnitude scaling is necessary when the physical limitations of the simulator prevent a one-for-one equivalence between the magnitude of system variables and their simulator counterparts. The results of analog computer simulation are often displayed on a cathode ray oscilloscope or are plotted automatically by means of some sort of pen writing oscillograph or *xy* recorder. The mathematical relationships used for analog computer simulation can also be used for digital computer simulation. The accuracy possible and the information storage capability of the digital computer make it particularly attractive. Ease of programming is also a most desirable feature.

The digital computer must perform the required mathematical operations in a numerical manner. The results of the digital computer simulation study may be tabulated numbers which can be manually or automatically plotted to visually display the simulated performance. These plots can then be interpreted in terms of original system performance. Special languages have been developed to aid in translating the mathematical relationships describing the original system behavior into a form which the digital computer can use for simulation. Later chapters in this book are devoted to the description and utilization of some of these languages.

Most of the available general purpose digital computers have a single arithmetic unit. For this reason it is necessary that the computer perform its required mathematical operations sequentially. It is often necessary, therefore, that digital computer simulations proceed at a slowed time scale. In spite of this, however, the digital computer is a very useful and powerful tool for simulation studies.

To overcome the above problems which often force digital computer simulation studies to proceed at slowed time scale, and yet to preserve the advantages of accuracy and information storage, *hybrid computers* have been developed. The hybrid computer is a combination of both analog and digital computers. These machines provide the high speed, parallel or simultaneous processing capability of the analog computer, and the accuracy and information storage capability of the digital computer.

Since both analog and digital computer models are possible, there is always a question as to which model is better in any particular situation. Considerable personal preference is involved in making this decision. After using both kinds of computers for simulation purposes one finds that there are important differences in the two methods. A very significant advantage of the analog computer is that it can be used in a way such that there is a one-to-one correspondence between the components of the original system and those of the analog computer model. Suppose certain actions occur in the original system which are of particular interest. It is possible to arrange the analog computer so that these activities have their explicit counterparts in the analog simulator. The person using the analog computer as a simulator of a physical system can then observe, measure, and record what the system does. In this way one obtains a rather realistic feel for the actual behavior of the system being simulated.

In a digital computer simulation, information is supplied to the computer concerning the equations which describe the behavior of the system. Boundary and initial conditions, as well as procedures to be followed, are specified to the computer. The computer then manipulates this information as it has been instructed to do to produce numerical results which are tabulations of the system performance under the specified conditions. This may require hundreds of thousands or even millions of computing operations per second. Finally, the results may be produced either in tabulated form or (automatically) plotted to give a pictorial representation of the behavior of the system. As digital computers are presently constituted, there is little, if any, physical correspondence between the results obtained and the behavior of the system being studied. Hence, one does not get a good feel for the physical behavior of the simulated system from the digital computer output. The advantages of the digital computer, however, often outweigh its disadvantages and make it an entirely satisfactory and useful simulator. Because of the advantages and disadvantages of each type of simulation scheme, it is not unusual to find both types of simulators being used when studying a given problem. At the outset, when little is known about the system being studied, it is convenient to set up an analog computer model based on the scanty information available and proceed to learn as much as possible by this means. As understanding of the system increases, and as design decisions are made and incorporated, it may then be desirable to simulate the resulting system on the digital computer. The digital computer model can be used to provide greater accuracy and as a check on the previous analog computer model. The two computers working as a simulation team often give more useful information concerning a system than would either computer simulator acting alone.

1.4 Summary

There is an area of problem solving in which it is clear that the human is superior to all other means. Human intuition is often most valuable in solving engineering problems. There are also areas, however, where the human needs additional insight that often can be achieved through the use of models.

The use of scale models is one method by which this insight can be gained. Mathematical models, solved in a conventional manner or by the use of analog or digital computer simulators, are also helpful. Each method of simulation has its advantages and disadvantages and the ultimate method must be selected with full consideration given to these. The process of simulation really involves two systems—the original system being studied and the system which simulates it. These two systems are related through the similar mathematical relationships which describe both systems.

Simulation could, therefore, be described as a three step process:

(1) A mathematical model is first created to describe the behavior of the system being studied.

(2) This mathematical model is manipulated whenever possible and practicable to give the desired information concerning the system being studied.

(3) Whenever conventional mathematical manipulation is impractical the analog and/or digital computer may be used to simulate the mathematical model.

Simulation is used for two principal reasons. These are:

(1) To give greater understanding and insight into the behavior of the physical system and the principles upon which its design is based.

(2) To provide a convenient, inexpensive, and time saving means of gaining this understanding and insight under a variety of operating conditions.

It is the purpose of the remainder of this book to study the mathematics which describe the behavior of many types of physical systems, and to learn to use the analog computer and digital computer in simulating these systems.

EXERCISES

1. In your own words, define simulation.
2. Why might it be impractical to solve many problems using only mathematical methods and procedures?
3. Explain why the solution of Eq. 1.2 would be aided by the availability of an adder, an integrator, a sign changer, a multiplier, and a function generator.
4. Why are scale models not always satisfactory as simulators?
5. What advantages can one expect to realize through the use of computer simulation?
6. What is meant by "real-time simulation"?
7. How does the analog computer compare with the digital computer with regard to
   (a) Speed?
   (b) Accuracy?
   (c) Availability?
   (d) User training required?
   (e) Convenience?
   (f) Cost?
   (g) Relating the behavior of the computer model with the behavior of the system being studied?

2

Simulation Mathematics

2.1 Introduction

Two things are said to be *analogous* whenever there is an agreement, a likeness, or a correspondence between them. For our purposes we shall consider things to be analogous when they have the same mathematical description of behavior. In this sense then, there is a partial similarity among objects of study upon which the comparison of behavior can be based. The purpose of this chapter is to look at the mathematics which describe the behavior of several kinds of physical systems. The similarities and differences are considered and in this way a foundation is constructed upon which further aspects of simulation can be built. Much of the material contained in this chapter may be familiar to the reader. If so, it can be reviewed quickly. Be certain that it is well understood, however, because it will be referred to often.

2.2 Algebraic Analogies

There are many examples of physical systems, which are encountered by engineers, whose behavior can be described in part by algebraic equations of the general type

$$z = xy + k \qquad (2.1)$$

In this equation, either x or y or both may be variables or constants and k is a constant. A few examples of relationships describing physical systems which are of this form in which $k = 0$ are as follows:

From kinetics

$$F = Ma \tag{2.2}$$
$$\text{force} = \text{(mass)(acceleration)}$$

From electricity (Ohm's Law)

$$V = iR \tag{2.3}$$
$$\text{voltage} = \text{(current)(resistance)}$$

From fluid mechanics

$$Q = Av \tag{2.4}$$
$$\text{quantity of fluid per unit time} = \text{(area)(velocity)}$$

From mechanics

$$M = wx \tag{2.5}$$
$$\text{moment} = \text{(weight)(distance)}$$

From acoustics

$$F_a = pA_s \tag{2.6}$$
$$\text{force on speaker cone} = \text{(sound pressure)(area)}$$

The relationships of Eqs. 2.2–2.6 are similar in form, and there are many other equations having this same form. Equations 2.2–2.6 are only representative and the reader will surely be able to extend the list to almost any desired length.

The solutions to equations such as Eqs. 2.2–2.6 are so simple that simulation is rarely used to obtain them. Expressions such as these, however, are frequently found as part of more complicated equations for which solution by simulation might be very practical indeed.

Another type of algebraic equation that is frequently encountered is of the form

$$z = x^2 y + k \tag{2.7}$$

As before, x and y may be variables or constants and k is a constant. A few examples of this type of expression in which $k = 0$ are as follows:

From geometry

$$A = r^2 \pi \tag{2.8}$$
$$\text{area} = \text{(radius)}^2 \text{(pi)}$$

From physics

$$S = t^2(g/2) \tag{2.9}$$
$$\text{distance} = \text{(time)}^2 \text{(acceleration/2)}$$

From electricity

$$P = i^2 R \tag{2.10}$$
$$\text{power} = \text{(current)}^2 \text{(resistance)}$$

From kinetics
$$KE = v^2(M/2) \tag{2.11}$$
$$\text{kinetic energy} = (\text{velocity})^2(\text{mass}/2)$$

From electromagnetic fields
$$W = i^2(L/2) \tag{2.12}$$
$$\text{stored energy} = (\text{current})^2(\text{inductance}/2)$$

From acoustics
$$F_a = A_s^2(y/C) \tag{2.13}$$
$$\text{force on a speaker cone} = (\text{area})^2(\text{displacement}/\text{acoustical capacitance})$$

As before, these relationships are listed only as being indicative of a general class. Many more examples can readily be found.

2.3   Analogies Involving Integration and Differentiation

If mathematical expressions are included which contain integrals or derivatives, additional analogies immediately suggest themselves. Some expressions containing derivatives are of the general form

$$z = y\frac{dx}{dt} + k \tag{2.14}$$

Some examples of relationships of this type in which $k = 0$ are as follows:

From electricity
$$V = L\frac{di}{dt} \tag{2.15}$$
$$\text{voltage} = (\text{inductance})(\text{rate of change of current})$$

From kinetics (translation)
$$F = M\frac{dv}{dt} \tag{2.16}$$
$$\text{force} = (\text{mass})(\text{rate of change of velocity})$$

From kinetics (rotation)
$$T = J\frac{d\omega}{dt} \tag{2.17}$$
$$\text{torque} = (\text{moment of inertia})(\text{rate of change of angular velocity})$$

Equations 2.15–2.17 can also be written as analogous equations containing second derivatives. Equation 2.15 becomes

$$V = L\frac{d^2q}{dt^2} \tag{2.18}$$
$$\text{voltage} = (\text{inductance})(\text{second time derivative of charge})$$

Eq. 2.16 becomes

$$F = M\frac{d^2s}{dt^2}$$

(2.19)

force = (mass)(second time derivative of displacement)

and Eq. 2.17 becomes

$$T = J\frac{d^2\theta}{dt^2}$$

(2.20)

torque = (moment of inertia)(second time
derivative of angular displacement)

In a similar manner, analogous expressions containing integrals can be found such as

From kinetics

$$\omega = \int_{\theta_1}^{\theta_2} T\, d\theta + w_0$$

(2.21)

work = integral of torque over the range of θ from
θ_1 to θ_2 plus the initial work, w_0 at θ_1

From electromagnetic fields

$$\Phi = \frac{1}{N}\int_{T_1}^{T_2} V\, dt + \Phi_0$$

(2.22)

flux = integral of voltage over the range of t from
T_1 to T_2 plus the initial flux, Φ_0 at T_1

From statics

$$V = \int_{X_1}^{X_2} w\, dx + V_0$$

(2.23)

shear = integral of loading over the range of x from
X_1 to X_2 plus the initial shear V_0 at X_1

2.4 Oscillating or Vibrating Systems

The words oscillation and vibration are synonomous. Vibration is usually used to describe the behavior of mechanical systems while oscillation is used to describe the behavior of electrical systems. Oscillations or vibrations may be either desirable or undesirable in physical systems. In electrical oscillators and signal generators, they are desirable. So also, are they desirable in many vibrating mechanical tools. They are undesirable in public address systems and otherwise smoothly running internal combustion engines. Unwanted vibrations may cause disturbing noise, undue wear, severe strain on mechanical parts and failure due to fatigue in metal parts, or excessive voltage or current in electrical equipment.

Oscillations or vibrations are occurrences that repeat themselves in periodic fashion. Oscillations may be damped or undamped—free or forced. If they are damped, they change in magnitude with time; if they are undamped they continue indefinitely at fixed amplitude. A free oscillation or vibration occurs when the periodic behavior continues after the disturbing influence is removed. If the periodic behavior occurs only because of continued influence of some applied outside disturbance, the oscillations or vibrations are said to be forced.

Note that damping may be negative as well as positive. When negative damping occurs in an oscillating system, the amplitude of the oscillations increases with time. When this occurs, the system is said to be unstable, a characteristic which is usually undesirable. Unstable mechanical systems will ordinarily vibrate with increasing amplitude until breakage occurs due to the high stresses produced or until some other form of saturation causes the amplitude of the vibrations to reach some stable operating condition. A corresponding behavior occurs in an unstable electrical system.

An undamped free oscillating system has no energy loss. Such a system will oscillate at its natural frequency. The presence of damping—either positive or negative—will cause the actual frequency to depart from the natural frequency.

For purposes of this discussion, suppose that we assemble a mechanical system consisting of a spring, a body containing mass, and a dashpot as shown in Fig. 2.1.

We assume the foot-pound-second system of units. In this system,

M = mass in slugs = weight in lb/32

k = spring constant = lb/ft

c = dashpot constant = lb/ft/sec

x = displacement = ft

F = external applied force = lb

We further assume that the spring and dashpot are without mass, that the body is absolutely rigid, the spring is perfectly elastic, and that all of the damping is in the dashpot. This last feature assumes that the spring and rollers exhibit no friction. Deflection is measured from the position where the spring is exactly unstressed. This rather idealized system can only be approximated in practice but often the approximation is surprisingly good.

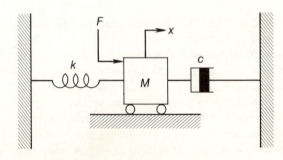

Figure 2.1 *A mechanical system.*

In a system such as that shown in Fig. 2.1, the force needed to accelerate the mass is

$$f_a = M \frac{d^2 x}{dt^2} \qquad (2.24)$$

in accordance with the principles of kinetics. The force exerted on the body by the spring is

$$f_s = kx \qquad (2.25)$$

and the force exerted on the body by the dashpot is

$$f_d = c \frac{dx}{dt} \qquad (2.26)$$

The external applied force is some function of time

$$F = f(t) \qquad (2.27)$$

and includes the possibilities of F being zero or equal to a constant. Writing an equilibrium force equation for this system gives

$$f_a + f_d + f_s = F \qquad (2.28)$$

When Eqs. 2.24–2.27 are substituted into Eq. 2.28 we obtain

$$M \frac{d^2 x}{dt^2} + c \frac{dx}{dt} + kx = f(t) \qquad (2.29)$$

The rollers of Fig. 2.1 can be eliminated from the system by arranging it so that all motion is in the vertical direction (see Fig. 2.2). In this arrangement the weight

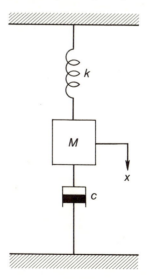

Figure 2.2 *A vertically oscillating mechanical system.*

of the body is supported by the spring; and the spring in turn will be stretched enough to support this weight. If the displacement x is measured from the resulting quiescent position, the effect of the body weight is cancelled and need no longer be considered. All physical quantities have the same meaning in the system of Fig. 2.2 as they have in the system of Fig. 2.1. Incidentally, the driving force has been set equal to zero in Fig. 2.2.

The equation describing the behavior of the system of Fig. 2.2 can be determined in exactly the same manner as for the system of Fig. 2.1. This equation is

$$M\frac{d^2x}{dt^2} + c\frac{dx}{dt} + kx = 0 \tag{2.30}$$

An analogous system can be constructed to operate in the torsional mode as shown in Fig. 2.3.

In the system of Fig. 2.3, the body has a moment of inertia J about its axis of rotation. The rotational displacement is measured from the quiescent position where the torsional support rod is untwisted. The torsional spring constant is k and the frictional coefficient is c. In much the same way that the describing equations for the translational systems of Figs. 2.1 and 2.2 were developed, a describing equation for the torsional system of Fig. 2.3 can also be developed. The resulting equation is

$$J\frac{d^2\theta}{dt^2} + c\frac{d\theta}{dt} + k\theta = 0 \tag{2.31}$$

In Eq. 2.31
J = moment of inertia = slug ft^2
k = torsional spring constant = lb ft/rad
c = torsional friction = lb ft/rad/sec
θ = angular displacement = rad

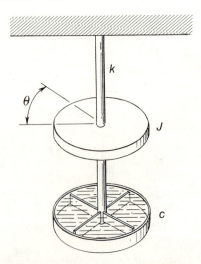

Figure 2.3 *A torsional system.*

2.5 Further Aspects of Oscillating Systems

We have seen from the foregoing sections of this chapter that the behavior of many different kinds of physical systems can be described by similar mathematical expressions or equations. It is this mathematical similarity that we use as a principal tool in the continuing study of simulation.

Let us again turn our attention to the study of a vibrating mechanical system. Because of our frequent contact with systems of this type, we have developed an almost intuitive understanding of their behavior. For this reason, it is helpful for us to use this familiar system as a specific example to study. Figure 2.2 shows a mechanical system which we will study in some detail.

Equation 2.30 is the force equilibrium equation which mathematically describes the behavior of the mechanical system of Fig. 2.2. We get a better understanding and appreciation of the details of the behavior of this system if we first solve Eq. 2.30 by employing the usual classical method of solution. Any standard book on differential equations will prove to be a valuable reference.

A consideration of Eq. 2.30 reveals that the solution, or evaluation of x, must be such that x itself, and the first and second derivatives of x with respect to time, are all of the same general form. This must be true since the sum of the three terms in Eq. 2.30 is equal to zero at all times. One function which satisfies this requirement is of the type

$$x = \epsilon^{mt} \tag{2.32}$$

where m is a constant that must be determined.

Differentiating Eq. 2.32 with respect to time gives

$$\frac{dx}{dt} = m\epsilon^{mt} \tag{2.33}$$

and

$$\frac{d^2x}{dt^2} = m^2\epsilon^{mt} \tag{2.34}$$

Substituting these results in Eq. 2.30, we obtain

$$(Mm^2 + cm + k)\,\epsilon^{mt} = 0$$

and since ϵ^{mt} cannot be zero, for finite values of m and t, the bracketed term must be zero. That is,

$$Mm^2 + cm + k = 0 \tag{2.35}$$

Equation 2.35 is called the *auxiliary* or *characteristic* equation and is a typical quadratic equation. The two values of m that satisfy Eq. 2.35 can be found by application of the familiar quadratic formula which yields

$$m = -\frac{c}{2M} \pm \sqrt{\left(\frac{c}{2M}\right)^2 - \frac{k}{M}} = -\alpha \pm \omega \tag{2.36}$$

The two values of m, m_1, and m_2, can be obtained from Eq. 2.36 and can be written as

$$m_1 = -\alpha + \omega$$

(2.37)

$$m_2 = -\alpha - \omega$$

Depending upon the values of the coefficients of Eq. 2.30, ω may be real, zero, or imaginary. The two values of m in Eq. 2.37 give rise to two solutions:

$$x_1 = \epsilon^{m_1 t}$$

and

(2.38)

$$x_2 = \epsilon^{m_2 t}$$

For physical systems the complete solution can be obtained by combining these two solutions along with two arbitrary constants and a particular integral. In this case, the particular integral or steady-state solution is zero and, therefore, the complete solution becomes

$$x = C_1 \epsilon^{m_1 t} + C_2 \epsilon^{m_2 t}$$

(2.39)

The constants C_1 and C_2 can be determined from the given boundary conditions but this is not our primary interest here. We are more interested in the nature of the roots of the characteristic equation. Suppose, for example, the parameters of the mechanical system of Fig. 2.2 were $M = 1$, $c = 3$, and $k = 2$. The characteristic equation, therefore, is

$$m^2 + 3m + 2 = 0$$

$$m = \tfrac{1}{2}(-3 \pm \sqrt{3^2 - 8}) = -2 \text{ or } -1$$

Substituting into Eq. 2.39 gives

$$x = C_1 \epsilon^{-2t} + C_2 \epsilon^{-1t}$$

This solution is a nonoscillating solution because the exponents are real. This means that the physical system behaves in such a way that if given an initial displacement from the quiescent position and released, it returns to the quiescent position with no oscillations. Depending upon the initial velocity, it may have at most one overshoot. This situation is termed the *overdamped* case. The displacement as a function of time may occur in a variety of ways, three of which are shown in Fig. 2.4.

As mentioned earlier, our everyday experience with mechanical systems gives us an intuitive understanding of their behavior. We know that if the mechanical system of Fig. 2.2 contained a large amount of friction, the system would perhaps not vibrate at all. Suppose, for example, that the dashpot was filled with a very viscous material such as molasses or honey. Under these conditions, if the system were initially displaced and released, the system would return to the quiescent position in an exponential-like manner with no oscillations. This is the physical meaning of the overdamped case. If the dashpot was filled with a slightly less viscous material to make $c = \sqrt{8}$ rather than 3 as before, the characteristic equation would then become

$$m^2 + \sqrt{8}m + 2 = 0$$

This equation has two equal roots. That is,

$$m = \tfrac{1}{2}(\sqrt{8} \pm \sqrt{8-8}) = -\sqrt{2} = -1.41$$

Under these conditions the general solution is

$$x = C_1\epsilon^{-1.41t} + C_2 t\epsilon^{-1.41t} \tag{2.40}$$

Notice the t in the second term that was not present in the earlier case.

Again, as in the overdamped case, the solution is a nonoscillating solution. If the system having these new parameters was given an initial displacement and released, it would again return to the quiescent position with no oscillations. This situation is termed the *critically damped* case and is also illustrated in Fig. 2.2. Setting $x = 0$ in Eq. 2.40 gives $t = -C_1/C_2$, which shows that there may be a time when $x = 0$. If the initial conditions are such that C_1 is negative and C_2 is positive, $t = -C_1/C_2$ is positive. In other words, there may be an overshoot in this case also. This is the situation wherein any further decrease whatsoever in the system damping, with other parameters remaining unchanged, would introduce oscillations into the system behavior. There is no essential difference between overdamped and critically damped behavior, except that if in a given system the damping was changed from overdamped to critically damped, the critically damped condition would respond more quickly.

Suppose the viscosity of the dashpot fluid was further decreased until $c = 2$. The characteristic equation then becomes

$$m^2 + 2m + 2 = 0$$

which has the solution

$$m = \tfrac{1}{2}(-2 \pm \sqrt{4-8})$$

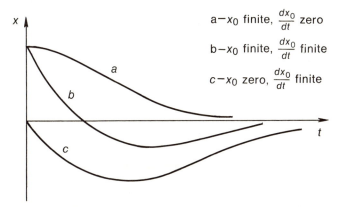

$a - x_0$ finite, $\dfrac{dx_0}{dt}$ zero

$b - x_0$ finite, $\dfrac{dx_0}{dt}$ finite

$c - x_0$ zero, $\dfrac{dx_0}{dt}$ finite

Figure 2.4 *The overdamped and critically damped cases.*

or

$$m = -1 \pm \tfrac{1}{2}\sqrt{-4} = -1 \pm j1$$

Comparing these results with Eq. 2.37 we see that we may now write

$$m = -1 \pm j1 = -\alpha \pm j\omega$$

When substituted into Eq. 2.39, these results give the complete solution of Eq. 2.41.

$$x = C_1 \epsilon^{(-\alpha + j\omega)t} + C_2 \epsilon^{(-\alpha - j\omega)t} \tag{2.41}$$

Equation 2.41 is a valid solution but is inconvenient because of the imaginary exponentials. We can rewrite 2.41 as

$$x = \epsilon^{-\alpha t} (C_1 \epsilon^{j\omega t} + C_2 \epsilon^{-j\omega t})$$

The Euler formulas state that

$$\epsilon^{j\omega t} = \cos \omega t + j \sin \omega t$$

and

$$\epsilon^{-j\omega t} = \cos \omega t - j \sin \omega t$$

Substituting these identities into the above equation gives

$$x = \epsilon^{-\alpha t}[(C_1 + C_2) \cos \omega t + j(C_1 - C_2) \sin \omega t] \tag{2.42}$$

Examination of Eq. 2.42 shows that the system will oscillate with a radian frequency of approximately ω radians per second. The amplitude of these oscillations, however, will ultimately decrease with time because of the exponential multiplier $\epsilon^{-\alpha t}$. This situation is termed the *underdamped* case and is illustrated in Fig. 2.5, where x_0 is finite and dx_0/dt is zero. In the particular case where $M = 1$, $c = 2$, $k = 2$, Eq. 2.42 becomes

$$x = \epsilon^{-t}[(C_1 + C_2) \cos t + j(C_1 - C_2) \sin t]$$

since $\alpha = -1$ and $\omega = 1$.

Reducing all friction in the mechanical system to zero results in the characteristic equation

$$m^2 + 2 = 0$$

which, when solved for m, gives

$$m = \pm j\sqrt{2}$$

or

$$m = 0 \pm j\omega$$

Setting $\alpha = 0$ in Eq. 2.42 gives

$$x = (C_1 + C_2) \cos \omega t + j(C_1 - C_2) \sin \omega t \tag{2.43}$$

as a complete solution. For the particular system where $M = 1$, $c = 0$, and $k = 2$, Eq. 2.43 becomes

$$x = (C_1 + C_2) \cos \sqrt{2}t + j(C_1 - C_2) \sin \sqrt{2}t$$

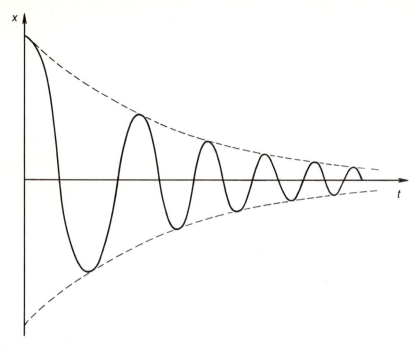

Figure 2.5 *The underdamped case.*

The foregoing discussion can be summarized by examining Eq. 2.36 and pointing out certain pertinent facts:

Overdamping occurs when

$$\frac{c^2}{4M^2} > \frac{k}{M} \qquad (2.44)$$

Critical damping occurs when

$$\frac{c^2}{4M^2} = \frac{k}{M} \qquad (2.45)$$

Underdamping occurs when

$$\frac{c^2}{4M^2} < \frac{k}{M} \qquad (2.46)$$

Zero damping occurs when

$$c = 0$$

2.6 Damping Ratio

A useful concept in the study of vibrating systems is that of the damping ratio. The *damping ratio* is defined as

$$\text{damping ratio} = \zeta = \frac{c}{c_K} \qquad (2.47)$$

where c is the actual damping in the system and c_K is the critical damping. Critical damping c_K can be found from Eq. 2.45 as

$$c_K = 2\sqrt{kM} \qquad (2.48)$$

Substituting Eq. 2.48 into Eq. 2.47 gives

$$\zeta = \frac{c}{2\sqrt{kM}}$$

A moment's consideration will show that overdamping occurs when $\zeta > 1$, critical damping occurs when $\zeta = 1$, and underdamping occurs when $\zeta < 1$.

2.7 Frequency of Oscillation

If we look at Eq. 2.36, we see that for zero damping ($c = 0$),

$$\sqrt{\frac{-k}{M}} = j\sqrt{\frac{k}{M}} = j\omega_n \qquad (2.49)$$

Here, ω_n is called the *natural* or *undamped frequency of oscillation.* By way of comparison, the "actual" frequency of oscillation in the underdamped case when $0 < c < c_k$ is given by

$$|\omega| = \sqrt{\left|\left(\frac{c}{2M}\right)^2 - \frac{k}{M}\right|} \qquad (2.50)$$

As pointed out earlier, if c is positive, the amplitude of the oscillations decreases with time. Because of this decreasing amplitude, the motion is not strictly periodic. For purposes of engineering analysis, the difference between true periodic motion and the actual nonperiodic oscillations is often ignored; this is not serious unless ζ is near unity. It can be shown that the magnitude of ω is given by

$$\omega = \omega_n\sqrt{1 - \zeta^2} \qquad (2.51)$$

2.8 A Modification of the Force Equation

Equation 2.30 can be rewritten as

$$\frac{d^2x}{dt^2} + \frac{c}{M}\frac{dx}{dt} + \frac{k}{M}x = 0 \qquad (2.52)$$

which can in turn be written as

$$\frac{d^2x}{dt^2} + 2\zeta\omega_n\frac{dx}{dt} + \omega_n^2 x = 0 \qquad (2.53)$$

Using our previous development and comparing Eqs. 2.52 and 2.53, observe that when the force equation is written in the form of Eq. 2.52:

(1) The coefficient of x is ω_n^2 and hence ω_n can be found by inspection.
(2) The coefficient of dx/dt is $2\zeta\omega_n$, and since ω_n is known, ζ can be found easily.
(3) Knowing ζ and ω_n, the "actual" frequency of oscillation can then be found from Eq. 2.51.

2.9 Exponential Decay of Oscillations

In our earlier discussion we found that the amplitude of oscillations in an underdamped oscillating system decreases exponentially as a function of time. This coincides with much of our personal everyday experience. The bouncing of a ball dropped on a hard horizontal surface or the string of a guitar plucked once and released are examples of this phenomenon. Mathematically, this exponential decay is represented in Eq. 2.42 by the inclusion of the exponential term, $\epsilon^{-\alpha t}$.

Such exponential behavior is frequently described in terms of the time constant of the system whose behavior is being studied. The *time constant* is defined as that value of time which makes the magnitude of the exponent in the exponential term equal to unity. The time constant is frequently symbolized by the Greek letter τ. Consequently

$$\alpha\tau = 1 \quad \text{or} \quad \tau = \frac{1}{\alpha} \qquad (2.54)$$

Looking back on Eq. 2.35 we see that $\alpha = c/2M$, which when substituted into Eq. 2.54 yields

$$\tau = \frac{2M}{c} \qquad (2.55)$$

Furthermore, a combination of Eq. 2.55 with parts of Eqs. 2.52 and 2.53 reveals that Eq. 2.55 can be rewritten as

$$\tau = \frac{1}{\zeta\omega_n} \qquad (2.56)$$

Equation 2.56 provides a convenient method for computing the time constant of an exponentially varying function in terms of the previously found damping ratio ζ and the natural radian frequency of oscillation ω_n. The time constant is a sort of normalized parameter that can be used for describing the behavior of exponentially varying systems in general. Table 2.1 shows how the amplitude of an exponentially decaying function varies with time, where time is measured in multiples of time constants. The same relationships are portrayed in Fig. 2.6.

A consideration of Table 2.1 and Fig. 2.6 shows the reader that the study of an underdamped system rarely, if ever, needs to be carried beyond a time of four time constants. At such time, the amplitude of the damped oscillations will have de-

Table 2.1

Exponential Magnitude Variation

t	$\epsilon^{-\alpha t}$ or $\epsilon^{-t/\tau}$
0	1
1τ	0.3679
2τ	0.1353
3τ	0.0498
4τ	0.0183
5τ	0.0067

creased to less than 2% of the amplitude they would have had if there had been no damping. Alternatively, the exponential term will have completed over 98% of its ultimate change at time equal to four time constants, and hence the study can be terminated.

2.10 Electrical Oscillations

Beginning with Section 2.5, we formulated a number of concepts based on a vibrating mechanical system. Similar concepts could have been developed using an analogous electrical system; however, our intuition serves us better in the mechanical case because our senses tell us more about the behavior of these systems. We can see and feel mechanical vibrations—this is an everyday experience. On the other hand, electrical oscillations cannot be seen or felt. They require

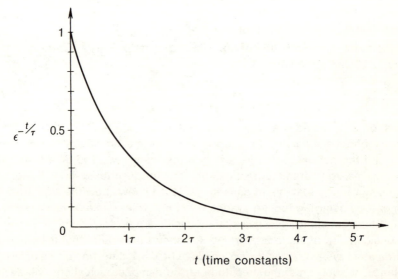

Figure 2.6 *Exponential magnitude variation.*

special equipment to detect and measure them and consequently, we are not nearly as aware of them. Nevertheless, electrical oscillations do occur and can also be described mathematically.

Consider the electrical circuit of Fig. 2.7.

The voltage drop across the inductor is

$$V_L = L\frac{di}{dt} \tag{2.57}$$

while the voltage drop across the resistor is

$$V_R = Ri \tag{2.58}$$

and the voltage drop across the capacitor is

$$V_C = \frac{1}{C}\int i \, dt \tag{2.59}$$

By definition, $i = dq/dt$. Substituting this into Eqs. 2.57–2.59 gives Eqs. 2.60–2.62.

$$V_L = L\frac{d^2q}{dt^2} \tag{2.60}$$

$$V_R = R\frac{dq}{dt} \tag{2.61}$$

$$V_C = \frac{q}{C} \tag{2.62}$$

The sum of the voltage drops around the closed circuit must equal the applied voltage in accordance with Kirchoff's voltage law. This is stated in Eq. 2.63.

$$V_L + V_R + V_C = e(t) \tag{2.63}$$

Substituting Eqs. 2.60–2.62 into Eq. 2.63 gives

$$L\frac{d^2q}{dt^2} + R\frac{dq}{dt} + \frac{q}{C} = e(t) \tag{2.64}$$

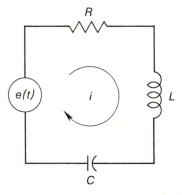

Figure 2.7 *An electrical circuit.*

The reader should take time at this point to compare Eqs. 2.64 and 2.29 and to reflect on the similarities of the derivations. In a manner similar to our earlier work, equations can be written in terms of the electrical circuit parameters to describe the electrical circuit behavior.

2.11 Higher-Order Systems

One might at first expect that systems of higher-order equations would be encountered frequently when studying complex physical systems of higher order. It is true that higher-order systems of equations can be written to describe the behavior of systems of higher order. It is also true, however, that one can write systems of equations which describe the behavior of these complex systems, but whose terms do not exceed the second order. This is not an unusual consequence either, because systems of second-order equations arise quite naturally when describing the behavior of most physical systems.

To make the point clear, let us consider a particular physical system such as the two-loop electrical circuit shown in Fig. 2.8. We will construct a mathematical model for this circuit and perform some mathematical manipulations. Application of Kirchoff's voltage law to this circuit yields the following two integro-differential equations:

$$L_a \frac{di_a}{dt} + R_a i_a + \frac{1}{C} \int (i_a - i_b) \, dt = e_a = E \sin \omega t \qquad (2.65)$$

$$L_b \frac{di_b}{dt} + R_b i_b + \frac{1}{C} \int (i_b - i_a) \, dt = 0 \qquad (2.66)$$

Taking the Laplace transform of Eqs. 2.65 and 2.66 gives Eqs. 2.67 and 2.68, if initial currents are both assumed to be zero and the initial charge on the capacitor is also assumed to be zero. Capital letters are used here to denote the Laplace transform of problem variables.

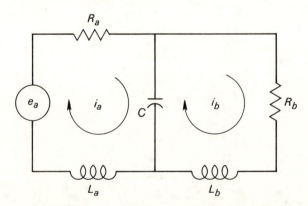

Figure 2.8 *A two-loop electrical circuit.*

$$\left(L_a s + R_a + \frac{1}{Cs}\right)I_a - \frac{1}{Cs}I_b = E_a$$

$$\left(L_b s + R_b + \frac{1}{Cs}\right)I_b - \frac{1}{Cs}I_a = 0 \qquad (2.67)$$

Rearranging terms and applying Cramer's rule yields

$$I_a = \cfrac{\begin{vmatrix} E_a & -\dfrac{1}{Cs} \\[2ex] 0 & \left(L_b s + R_b + \dfrac{1}{Cs}\right) \end{vmatrix}}{\begin{vmatrix} \left(L_a s + R_a + \dfrac{1}{Cs}\right) & -\dfrac{1}{Cs} \\[2ex] -\dfrac{1}{Cs} & \left(L_b s + R_b + \dfrac{1}{Cs}\right) \end{vmatrix}} \qquad (2.68)$$

and

$$I_b = \cfrac{\begin{vmatrix} \left(L_a s + R_a + \dfrac{1}{Cs}\right) & E_a \\[2ex] -\dfrac{1}{Cs} & 0 \end{vmatrix}}{\begin{vmatrix} L_a s + R_a + \dfrac{1}{Cs} & -\dfrac{1}{Cs} \\[2ex] -\dfrac{1}{Cs} & \left(L_b s + R_b + \dfrac{1}{Cs}\right) \end{vmatrix}} \qquad (2.69)$$

Expanding Eqs. 2.68 and 2.69 we get

$$I_a\left[\left(L_a s + R_a + \frac{1}{Cs}\right)\left(L_b s + R_b + \frac{1}{Cs}\right) - \frac{1}{C^2 s^2}\right] = E_a\left(L_b s + R_b + \frac{1}{Cs}\right) \qquad (2.70)$$

$$I_b\left[\left(L_a s + R_a + \frac{1}{Cs}\right)\left(L_b s + R_b + \frac{1}{Cs}\right) - \frac{1}{C^2 s^2}\right] = \frac{E_a}{Cs} \qquad (2.71)$$

which reduce to

$$I_a\left(L_a L_b s^2 + L_a R_b s + \frac{L_a}{C} + R_a L_b s + R_a R_b + \frac{R_a}{Cs} + \frac{L_b}{C} + \frac{R_b}{Cs} + \frac{1}{C^2 s^2} - \frac{1}{C^2 s^2}\right)$$
$$= E_a\left(L_b s + R_b + \frac{1}{Cs}\right) \qquad (2.72)$$

$$I_b\left(L_a L_b s^2 + L_a R_b s + \frac{L_a}{C} + R_a L_b s + R_a R_b + \frac{R_a}{Cs} + \frac{L_b}{C} + \frac{R_b}{Cs} + \frac{1}{C^2 s^2} - \frac{1}{C^2 s^2}\right)$$
$$= \frac{E_a}{Cs} \qquad (2.73)$$

Multiplying through by Cs and collecting terms gives

$$I_a[L_a L_b C s^3 + (L_a R_b C + L_b R_a C)s^2 + (L_a + L_b + R_a R_b C)s + R_a + R_b]$$
$$= E_a(L_b C s^2 + R_b C s + 1) \qquad (2.74)$$

$$I_b[L_aL_bCs^3 + (L_aR_bC + L_bR_aC)s^2 + (L_a + L_b + R_aR_bC)s + R_a + R_b]$$
$$= E_a \qquad (2.75)$$

If we rewrite the expression in differential equation form, we have

$$L_aL_bC\frac{d^3i_a}{dt^3} + (L_aR_bC + L_bR_aC)\frac{d^2i_a}{dt^2} + (L_a + L_b + R_aR_bC)\frac{di_a}{dt} + (R_a + R_b)i_a$$
$$= E(1 - L_bC\omega^2)\sin\omega t + ER_bC\omega\cos\omega t \qquad (2.76)$$

and

$$L_aL_bC\frac{d^3i_b}{dt^3} + (L_aR_bC + L_bR_aC)\frac{d^2i_b}{dt^2} + (L_a + L_b + R_aR_bC)\frac{di_b}{dt} + (R_a + R_b)i_b$$
$$= E\sin\omega t \qquad (2.77)$$

Equations 2.76 and 2.77 are independent, third-degree differential equations which are a mathematical model of the circuit in Fig. 2.7 and which can be solved by any method desired, including the analog or digital computer. Furthermore, all of the preceding mathematics can be avoided by simulating the system using either the analog or digital computer and basing the simulation on Eqs. 2.65 and 2.66. When proceeding in this manner it is often convenient—although not necessary—to re-write Eqs. 2.65 and 2.66 without the integrals. Differentiating these equations gives

$$L_a\frac{d^2i_a}{dt^2} + R_a\frac{di_a}{dt} + \frac{ia}{C} - \frac{ib}{C} = E\omega\cos\omega t \qquad (2.78)$$

$$L_b\frac{d^2i_b}{dt} + R_b\frac{di_b}{dt} + \frac{ib}{C} - \frac{ia}{C} = 0 \qquad (2.79)$$

A comparison of Eqs. 2.76 and 2.77 with Eqs. 2.78 and 2.79, respectively, reveals that the latter are considerably simpler than the former. By the same token, although either set of equations could be analyzed by simulation and used to determine the behavior of the circuit of Fig. 2.7, a simulator based on the latter set would be considerably simpler than one based on the former set. One would do well, therefore, to use the simpler set.

2.12 Summary

There are many physical systems which can be described by the same or similar mathematical expressions. It is frequently possible to write behavior-describing equations for a particular physical system and then, using techniques we learn later, construct either an analog or digital computer model which obeys the same mathematical behavior description. The model, so constructed, can then be studied and much can be learned from the model about the original system.

Because of the similarity of the behavior of many different systems, efforts are made to find common ways of characterizing and relating them. Such concepts as natural frequency ω_n, damping ratio ζ, and time constant τ make this comparison easier. Furthermore, from these easily computed quantities, much can be learned about the system without actually solving the behavior-describing equations in detail.

Oscillating electrical systems and vibrating mechanical systems have much in common. The study of such systems is often accomplished with rather elegant and clever mathematical manipulations. Frequently, however, the use of models or other simulators avoids the necessity of these mathematical procedures. One of our goals in the following chapters is to learn how this can be accomplished.

EXERCISES

1. List five more engineering analogies based on Eq. 2.1, in addition to those listed in Eqs. 2.2–2.6.
2. List five more engineering analogies based on Eq. 2.7, in addition to those listed in Eqs. 2.8–2.13.
3. List five more engineering analogies containing integrals and five more involving second derivatives, in addition to those listed in Eqs. 2.15–2.23.
4. Prove Eq. 2.48.
5. What is the value of the damping ratio for each of the examples in the discussion of Section 2.5.
6. Prove Eq. 2.51.
7. Prove Eq. 2.53.
8. Determine the natural frequency of oscillation, the damping ratio, the time constant, and the actual frequency of oscillation for each of the following equations:

   (a) $5\dfrac{d^2x}{dt^2} + 5\dfrac{dx}{dt} + 20x = 10$

   (b) $2\dfrac{d^2x}{dt^2} + 0.05\dfrac{dx}{dt} + 0.1x = 0$

   (c) $\dfrac{d^2x}{dt^2} + 5\dfrac{dx}{dt} + x = 0$

   (d) $2\dfrac{d^2x}{dt^2} + 5x = 20$

9. In each of the equations of Exercise 8, determine the nature of the behavior (overdamped, critically damped, underdamped, or undamped). Plot x approximately, in each case, as a function of time, if $\left.\dfrac{dx}{dt}\right|_0 = 0$ and $x_0 = 1$.
10. Write equations in terms of electrical circuit parameters analogous to Eqs. 2.36, 2.44–2.50, 2.52, and 2.53.
11. Refer to the system of Fig. 2.2. Select values of M, c, and k in the mks system of units that will result in the following performance characteristics; $\omega_n = 2$ rad/sec, $\omega = 1.32$ rad/sec, $\zeta = 0.75$, $\tau = 0.67$ sec.
12. How long would you allow the simulator of Exercise 11 to run? Explain why.

13. Refer to the system of Fig. 2.3. Select values of J, c, and k in the foot-pound-second system of units that will result in the following performance characteristics: $\omega_n = 10$ rad/sec, $\omega < 10$ rad/sec, $\zeta = 0.005$, $\tau = 20$ sec.

14. Refer to the system of Fig. 2.6. Select practical values of R, L, and C that will result in the following performance characteristics; $\omega_n = 10^4$ rad/sec, $\omega < 10^4$ rad/sec, $\zeta = 5 \times 10^{-2}$, $\tau = 2 \times 10^{-3}$ sec.

15. If a real-time simulator of the system of Exercise 14 were implemented, for how long would you expect meaningful performance signals to be produced?

16. Consider the two-loop electrical network shown in Fig. 2.9.
    (a) Develop two third-order behavior-describing differential equations for this network similar to Eqs. 2.76 and 2.77.
    (b) Write two second-order behavior-describing differential equations for this network similar to Eqs. 2.78 and 2.79.

17. Consider the mechanical system of Fig. 2.10.
    Displacements x_1 and x_2 are measured from the quiescent positions of the system. Find two behavior-describing simultaneous differential equations for this mechanical system.

18. Show that the natural frequency of oscillation of the system shown in Fig. 2.2 is given by

$$\omega_n = \frac{0.904}{\sqrt{x_{ss}}} \text{ cycles/sec}$$

where x_{ss} is the amount in feet by which the spring would be stretched by the action of the weight of the mass acting alone.

19. (a) When an automobile is lowered onto its wheels so that it is entirely supported by its springs, it is observed that the springs are compressed 6 in. Estimate the natural frequency of oscillation due to the action of the automobile on its springs.
    (b) The tires are observed to compress 1/2 in. Estimate the natural frequency of oscillation due to the action of the automobile on its tires.

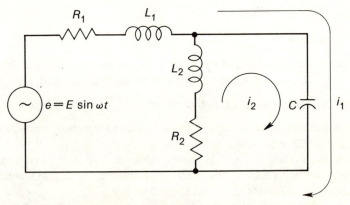

Figure 2.9

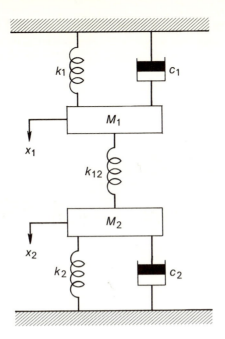

Figure 2.10

3

The Electronic Analog Computer

3.1 Introduction

Earlier we mentioned that models are used as tools in simulation studies which are designed to obtain insight into system behavior. The electronic analog computer (EAC) provides one excellent means of model building for simulation studies. What one really does when using the EAC as a simulator is to construct a model whose behavior is described by the same mathematical expressions as those describing the behavior of the original system. The behavior of the EAC model is then observed and interpreted in terms of the behavior of the original system.

The EAC is simply a device which provides all of the necessary components for model building arranged in such a way as to make the creation of a model convenient and rapid. The EAC model is created in the laboratory under carefully controlled conditions away from the distractions of the shop. In this relatively pleasant environment one can effectively concentrate on the details of the problem. With adequate instrumentation, the EAC can produce useful information relatively quickly.

We can effectively study the EAC as a simulator from several different points of view. The traditional approach is first to study the behavior of the EAC elements at a circuit level in order to understand their internal workings, and then to learn how to connect these elements together as required for the simulation of a particular system. A less traditional approach, but one that is equally effective as far as the user is concerned, is to treat the EAC as most users treat the digital computer; that is, as a tool with little or no concern or attention given to the internal workings of the machine. When following this latter approach, the EAC elements are treated simply as functional blocks that must be interconnected by wires as required by the particular problem being solved. This attitude proves to be no more of an obstacle to the users of analog computers than it does to the users of digital computers. Problems can be solved very successfully using this computer-as-a-tool point of view. This is the point of view we adopt for our work. There will, no doubt, be some readers who will not be satisfied with this approach and who will want a more detailed explanation of EAC operation. For these readers an Appendix is provided which supplies the desired explanatory details.

An EAC may be very large or very small. It may cost as little as a few hundred dollars or as much as several hundred thousand dollars (or even more). It may range in size from a portable device to a fixed installation occupying a floor area of several hundred square feet. Regardless of the size of the EAC's, however, there are certain features that are common to all. In this chapter we consider these common features and establish procedures for using EAC's as simulators.

It was pointed out in Chapter 1 that the useful signals in EAC's are voltages. These voltages may be constant, but more typically they vary with time. They may change in polarity or magnitude or both. It is the task of the EAC user to assemble the various elements of the EAC in such a way that the voltage signals at various locations throughout the EAC can be observed, recorded, and interpreted in terms of the behavior of the original system being simulated.

Voltage signals must be measured with respect to some reference. In EAC's, ground potential is ordinarily used as a common reference for all signals. We assume this common reference throughout all of the following discussion. Although this ground reference could be explicitly shown in the block diagrams which follow, it will simplify the diagrams considerably if it is omitted. This has become quite common practice in analog computer literature. The user must however, be aware that ground reference is always an inherent part of EAC use.

An individual who is using the EAC for the first time will discover two kinds of symbols that are used to represent the various elements of the EAC. One kind of symbol is used on block diagrams and a quite different kind of symbol is often used on the EAC itself. Some confusion can result from this different usage unless care is taken to correlate the two kinds of symbols. We shall discuss both kinds of symbols, and careful consideration of them will be helpful to the beginning EAC user. A fairly standard set of symbols has evolved for use on block diagrams, but the symbols used on the EAC's themselves often vary from one EAC to another. For each standard block diagram of an EAC computing element, there is also a patching diagram. The patching diagram shows the user how connections are made to connect elements together to construct the desired simulator. The examples presented here are only indicative and the user must examine the EAC that he is using to find its particular scheme.

When using an EAC to simulate a system, advanced planning is necessary. The block diagram is used to organize and aid in this planning. After the plan has been completed, the elements of the EAC must then be connected together electrically as indicated on the completed block diagram. The user must, therefore, be able to translate the block diagram symbols into equivalent EAC symbols. The user is urged to consult the operator's manual that is supplied with each EAC and which describes the details of the machine being used.

3.2 The Patch Panel

An EAC consists of a number of devices, such as adders, integrators, multipliers, and so on, that must be connected together electrically. The means for interconnecting the devices, of necessity, must be flexible so that the interconnection can be accomplished in various ways to simulate a variety of systems. A *patch panel* is provided for this purpose. The patch panel may be a fixed integral part of the machine or it may be removable. It is usually an integral part of the lower cost machines, and is removable in the more costly ones. The removable version provides for greater flexibility and utility by permitting a user to preserve a simulation setup by removing the patch panel containing all of the connecting wires, and by replacing it with another patch panel which has been connected up for a different simulation study. The removed patch panel, with all connecting wires in place, can then be stored until needed again at which time it can be reinserted in the EAC. This flexibility also allows one or more users to be setting up their patch panels at remote locations while the EAC is being used to process someone else's work.

The patch panel is simply an insulating board containing many jacks which are constructed so as to properly receive the insertion of a patch cord plug and make electrical connection with it. All connections between the patch panel and the EAC proper are through spring contacts which separate when the panel is removed. Each jack is connected internally through one of these spring contacts to a terminal of a computer element. The adders, integrators, multipliers, etc., of the EAC each have connections through these spring contacts from their inputs and outputs to jacks on the patch panel. Plugs, one on each end of a patch cord, are inserted into the proper jacks where they connect with the spring contacts to complete the desired electrical connections between the various units. Should we wish to connect the output of a potentiometer to the input of an adder, for example, we would insert the plug on one end of a patch cord into the jack that is connected internally to the potentiometer output. The plug on the other end of the patch cord would be inserted into the appropriate jack connecting to an amplifier input.

3.3 The Potentiometer

The potentiometer, commonly called a *pot*, can be thought of as a multiplier by means of which an input voltage signal can be multiplied by a fractional constant to give an output voltage signal. The fractional multiplier constant is adjustable and can be set by means of a dial to have any desired value between 0.0 and 1.0 inclusive. The output signal is always equal to or less than the input signal as determined by the potentiometer setting. The block diagram symbol for a potentiometer is shown in Fig. 3.1. In this figure, X is the input signal, Y is the output signal, and

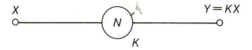

Figure 3.1 *The block diagram symbol of a potentiometer.*

K is the multiplier constant by which X is multiplied to get Y. The small circles represent the jacks through which electrical connection is made to the potentiometer, and the larger circle represents the potentiometer itself. The N in Fig. 3.1 is a number used to identify the particular potentiometer being used. Often in an EAC simulation study many potentiometers will be used. As each potentiometer is selected and incorporated into the model, its identifying number is written inside the larger circle on the block diagram. A particular potentiometer symbol might appear as shown in Fig. 3.2. In this figure, potentiometer numbered 17 is used to multiply the input X by 0.637 to obtain the output Y. Not shown in the block diagram symbol, but necessary for proper electrical behavior of the potentiometer, is an internal connection to ground. The patch panel often shows this connection schematically as indicated in Fig. 3.3. In this figure four schematic diagrams are shown. Again, the circles represent jacks into which patch cords must be inserted to complete electrical connections to the potentiometer.

The symbols associated with the jacks on the patch panel in Fig. 3.3 are electrical schematic symbols for potentiometers. It is only necessary to recognize that the upper jack in each case is the input jack and the jack next to the top is the output jack. Some of the potentiometers in Fig. 3.3 are shown with their lower ends permanently connected to ground while others are connected to ungrounded jacks. This is done to provide the user with ungrounded potentiometers should he need them. If one wishes to ground one of these latter potentiometers he can do so simply by connecting the lower end jack to a nearby grounded jack with a short patch cord. When a removable patch panel is used, the potentiometers them-

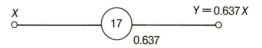

Figure 3.2 *A particular potentiometer block diagram symbol.*

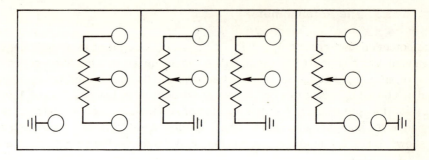

Figure 3.3 *Potentiometer jacks on a patch panel.*

selves and associated dials are located remotely from the jacks of Fig. 3.3 in a portion of the EAC which is not a part of the removable patch panel. If no patch panel is provided on a particular EAC the potentiometer, dial, and input-output jacks are often grouped together. A typical arrangement of this kind is shown in Fig. 3.4. The dials and potentiometers supplied with most EAC's are of the multiple turn type. These multiple turn dials can be read to three significant figures. It should not be inferred that the dial indicates the exact multiplier constant by which the input is multiplied to get the output. Loading effects often cause the setting as read from the dial to be quite different from the actual multiplier constant. Strictly speaking, the two will agree only when the potentiometer has nothing connected to its output. In most EAC's there are means by which the potentiometers can be accurately set independently of the dial reading. This is usually done with the potentiometer connected to its intended load. The dial is simply used as an indicator of position so that an operator can record the dial reading and can return the potentiometer to a given setting at a later time if he wishes, without repeating the more cumbersome multiplier setting procedure. The potentiometers described to this point are *linear* potentiometers. That is, if loading effects are ignored, there is a linear relationship between the potentiometer setting and the multiplying constant. For some special purposes nonlinear potentiometers are desirable. Nonlinear potentiometers can be obtained having a variety of nonlinear characteristics. One very common use of nonlinear potentiometers is for the generation of sinusoidal signals, where the potentiometer output is a sinusoidal function of the potentiometer position.

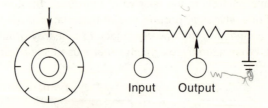

Input   Output

Figure 3.4 *A typical potentiometer and connection diagram when no patch panel is provided.*

3.4 Adders and Sign Changers

As you use the EAC to simulate physical systems you will frequently need to perform the operations of addition and sign change. The electronic circuit for adding two or more voltage signals makes use of an operational amplifier and some resistors connected together in such a way that the output voltage is, at all times, equal to, or at least proportional to, the sum of the input voltages. The input signals may have magnitudes and polarities that vary with time. The adder is constituted so that it will accept a number of time and/or polarity varying input signals and produce the time and/or polarity varying sum at the output. It has also proved convenient to have the adder perform a sign inversion as well as to perform addition.

An adder has more than one input terminal. Any one or more of these input terminals can be used as needed. If an input terminal is not used, it is as though it were not present, since it has no effect on the output. If only one input terminal is used, the adder serves only as an inverter or sign changer. Multiplication of each input signal by a constant is also provided by the typical EAC adder or sign changer. This constant can be either larger or smaller than unity in most EAC's. In some machines the multiplying factors are internally set to a few prescribed values. In other machines the operator can select the values to be any of a large number of possibilities. One must become acquainted with his machine to determine which scheme it uses.

The block diagram symbol for an adder is shown in Fig. 3.5. The adder shown here has four input terminals, but there may be more or less than four in any given machine. In Fig. 3.5, the 8 indicates that this adder makes use of amplifier 8. The other numbers in the figure are multiplying factors by which the respective input signals are multiplied. If in a particular case $A = 1$ V, $B = -3$ V, $C = 2$ V, and $D = -1$ V, the output would be

$$Z = -[10(+1) + 5(-3) + 2 + (-1)] = 4 \text{ V}$$

Figure 3.6 illustrates a typical patch panel diagram for an adder showing the input and output jacks. The multiplying constant for each input is shown along side the corresponding jack. Figure 3.6 would be the patch panel configuration for the block diagram shown in Fig. 3.5. The output jacks are all connected together. This is done because there is only one output but you may wish to connect it to several other devices. The several output jacks allow this to be done very conveniently.

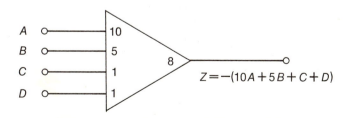

Figure 3.5 *An adder block diagram symbol.*

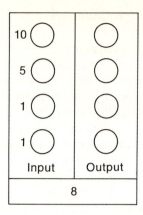

Figure 3.6 *An adder patch panel configuration.*

There is a limit to the magnitude of the output voltage of any amplifier. If this limit is exceeded, the proper behavior of the amplifier cannot be guaranteed. This limiting voltage is called the *reference voltage.* Usually, each amplifier is provided with a visual indicator which is illuminated if the reference voltage of that amplifier is exceeded. The operator must be on the alert to detect any excessive voltage indications and must take steps to modify the computer model so as to eliminate these occurrences. These procedures will be clarified as we continue our study.

3.5 Integrators

The most fundamental element in the EAC is the *integrator.* Chapter 1 explained how a system whose behavior is described by a differential equation could be simulated using integrators as parts of the simulator. One might very well ponder the possibility of constructing a simulator using differentiators rather than integrators, and might correctly conclude that this procedure is theoretically possible. However, practical difficulties are encountered when one attempts to do this. The spurious electrical noise which surrounds us, and affects all electrical equipment to some degree, is accentuated by differentiators but is subdued by integrators. For this reason, EAC's use integrators rather than differentiators.

As we have mentioned several times, the signals in EAC's are time varying voltages. These signals are integrated with respect to time by the integrators of the EAC. Since these integrators will integrate only with respect to time, it is fortunate that time is the independent variable in most physical systems. In those few systems where time is not the independent variable, a change of variable must be made so that the integration can be performed with respect to time when doing a simulation study.

An integrator functions with only a single input terminal, but it has been found to be convenient if several input terminals are provided so that addition as well as integration can be done in the same unit. Furthermore, as in the case of the

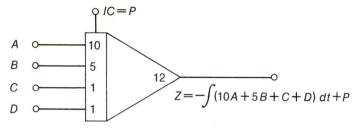

Figure 3.7 *An integrator block diagram symbol.*

adder, the integrator is equipped to multiply each input signal by a constant, and to invert the sign of the result. The block diagram symbol of an integrator using amplifier numbered 12 is shown in Fig. 3.7. The number of inputs in this diagram is four, but other integrators may have a different number. Also, the available multiplying constants may vary from one machine to another.

Integration does not always begin with the output starting from zero. The output may have some finite initial condition of either polarity when integration begins. The terminal marked *IC* in Fig. 3.7 provides this capability. In some machines the sign of the initial condition signal applied to the *IC* terminal is inverted in the output, while in other machines it is not inverted. You must ascertain how your machine behaves in this regard. In our discussions we will assume that no inversion of initial condition signals occurs.

In summary, the EAC integrator is capable of multiplying each input signal by a prescribed constant, adding the resulting products, integrating the resulting sum with respect to time, inverting the sign of the result, and adding the prescribed initial condition to produce the output. Integration begins at $t = 0$ and proceeds as time increases until stopped by the operator. The output of the integrator at any time t is the result of integrating the sum of inputs from $t = 0$ up to the given time t, and adding the given initial condition. The same reference voltage limitations apply to integrator outputs as apply to adder outputs. Figure 3.8 shows a patch panel configuration for an integrator.

3.6 Multipliers

Multiplication of a time varying voltage signal by a constant can be achieved through the use of a potentiometer only, if the constant is less than unity. If the constant is greater than unity, one can use a potentiometer in combination with the multiplier constant associated with an adder input, an integrator input, or a sign changer input. The potentiometer can be omitted entirely if the constant happens to have a value that can be achieved with the adder, integrator, or sign changer alone.

It is often the case that multiplication of two time varying voltage signals is desired. This is accomplished in a device called a *multiplier.* Multipliers have been designed to operate successfully based on a number of different principles; some

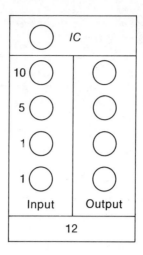

Figure 3.8 *An integrator patch panel configuration.*

are electromechanical and some are entirely electronic in operation. The user of an analog computer will do well to examine his particular machine to determine the kind of multiplier it uses and to learn its characteristics and limitations.

No attempt is made here to discuss the principles of operation of multipliers. It is sufficient to say that a multiplier is usually provided with two input terminals and one output terminal. Two time varying signals can be applied to the input terminals and a time varying signal that is proportional to the instantaneous product of the two input signals will appear at the output. The actual product of the input signals is divided by the reference voltage of the computer. Division by the reference voltage allows the two multiplier input signals to each be as large as the reference voltage, without the multiplier output voltage exceeding the reference voltage. This makes the multiplier compatible with the other units and convenient to work with.

The block diagram symbol for the multiplier is shown in Fig. 3.9. In Fig. 3.9, multiplier 6 is shown with inputs X and Y. The reference voltage is assumed to be 10 V. If at some instant X were 5 V and Y were 3 V, the output Z would be 1.5 V. The multiplier must operate so that the proper algebraic sign of the product is

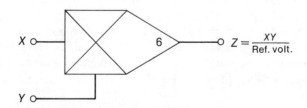

Figure 3.9 *A multiplier block diagram symbol.*

obtained. If the algebraic signs of the two input signals are different, one negative and one positive, the sign of the product should be negative. If both inputs have the same sign, the sign of the product should be positive. If the multiplier is working properly, these results will be obtained. In some types of multipliers, inversion of the otherwise correct algebraic sign of the output also occurs, as it does in the case of adders and integrators. In other types of multipliers, output sign inversion does not occur. In the multipliers in this book, it is assumed that sign inversion of the product does *not* occur.

3.7 Function Generators

Almost any user of an EAC will soon encounter the need for special functions. These functions must be generated. If the necessary function is periodic such as a sine wave, a square wave, a triangular wave, or other such repetitious function, it can often be obtained from a signal generator of the conventional type.

Special functions are often generated by special devices built by EAC manufacturers for the specific purpose. For example, some manufacturers offer devices that will generate output signals equal to the logarithms of the input signals. Devices such as these are usually subject to the same reference voltage limitations at their outputs as are other EAC components.

Often functions are needed that cannot be described by conventional mathematical expressions. Sometimes these functions can only be described in terms of tabulated data points (much experimental data is of this sort). This situation calls for general purpose equipment that is sufficiently flexible that it can be adapted to suit a wide variety of purposes. Biased diode function generators provide this needed flexibility. These devices are commonly arranged such that by means of some simple potentiometer adjustments, a wide variety of output signals can be realized as functions of the input signals. The schemes used by different EAC manufacturers to accomplish these results differ widely in their detail.

Figure 3.10 shows a block diagram symbol which is often used to represent a function generator. At times, the output of such a device may be a function of time, and under such conditions there is no input signal shown. On other occasions, the output may be a function of one of the problem variables, and under these circumstances the input must be indicated.

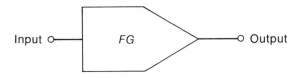

Figure 3.10 *A function generator block diagram symbol.*

3.8   The Control of the EAC

The most important feature of the control section of the EAC is the *mode switch*. This switch commonly has several positions, each of which causes the machine to behave differently.

It is obvious that there must be some way to turn the power on and off. A power control switch is provided for this purpose. The instruction manual should be consulted to learn the proper procedures for turning the EAC on; EAC's are frequently quite sensitive to variations in temperature, and must often be allowed to warm up for a considerable length of time after turning the power on. This is sometimes called the STANDBY mode and there is usually a corresponding position on the mode control switch.

It is also obvious that we must have some method to start and stop problem solutions when desired. The RESET and OPERATE mode control switch positions are for this purpose. When the switch is in the RESET position, the EAC is standing in an idle state with all integrators set to their initial output conditions. The EAC is simply in the starting condition waiting to begin the solution. When the mode control switch is moved to the OPERATE position, the problem solution begins and continues until terminated. If it is desired to repeat the solution, the mode control switch is momentarily returned to RESET, and then again to OPERATE to begin a new solution with the same initial conditions as before. The solution is repeated exactly as before each time this is done.

There is often equipment in an EAC whereby repetitive solutions can be obtained automatically. This is called the REPOP (repetitive operation) mode. When this feature is used, the initial conditions are applied and the solution is allowed to proceed as usual. However, after some predetermined time (selected by the operator) the solution is automatically terminated, the initial conditions are reestablished, and a new solution is begun. This process continues in a repetitive manner as long as desired and thus allows the operator to repeatedly observe the solution for a more careful examination of what is occurring. Also, it permits the operator to make parameter changes and to observe the effects of these changes on the solution. Should one wish to adjust the time scale such that a complete solution is obtained in a very short time, the REPOP mode allows the solution to be displayed on a cathode ray oscilloscope where the frequently repeated solution appears as a stationary image.

Often, it is desired to halt the progress of a solution at some time during the run. It may be that an exact voltage measurement is desired. For this purpose, there is often a HOLD position on the mode control switch. When the mode control switch is placed in HOLD, the progress of the solution is interrupted. All voltages are held at the values they have at the moment the mode switch is moved to the HOLD position. Any desired observations can then be made, and when they have been completed, returning the mode control switch to OPERATE will cause the solution to proceed from the conditions that prevailed at the time of the interruption. The solution does not start over from the beginning — it simply goes on from wherever it was. It is not wise to leave the EAC in the HOLD position indefinitely because voltages will change slowly with time and errors can be introduced. One should move into the HOLD position, make whatever observations are desired, and quickly get on with the solution.

An EAC usually has a POT SET mode for setting the coefficient potentiometers. When in this mode, the potentiometers can be set to the desired setting (not necessarily the same as the dial reading). This is usually accomplished with the potentiometers connected to their intended loads. A standard reference voltage source is connected to each potentiometer as it is set, with a visual indication of the output indicated by a voltmeter. The potentiometer can then be adjusted so as to have the desired multiplying factor with the loads connected just as they will be when actually running the solution.

The STATIC CHECK is the last mode to be discussed here. In some machines, STATIC CHECK and RESET mode are one and the same. When the mode control switch is placed in the STATIC CHECK position, a partial check can be made of the correctness of the computer setup. During the normal setup procedures, there are numerous chances for error. Potentiometer settings can be erroneously made; for example, amplifier input multiplier constants can be incorrectly chosen, patch cord plugs can be inserted in wrong locations, and a myriad of other errors can be inadvertently introduced. After the patching up has been completed for even a relatively simple problem, it is very confusing and quite difficult to find errors of the types mentioned. There are many wires crossing every which way connecting the various elements together and it is difficult to tell which wires are which.

With the computer in the STATIC CHECK mode, all adders, potentiometers, sign changers, multipliers, and some function generators are operational but all integrators are not. To perform a static check, initial conditions are first chosen for the outputs of all integrators. (These may or may not be the same as the initial conditions that will be used during the problem solution. If the initial conditions to be used during the problem solution are satisfactory, by all means use them. This avoids the necessity of setting the initial conditions twice. If they are not satisfactory, however, choose some that are and get on with the static check.) Depending on the values of the initial conditions that are used, the resulting outputs of all adders and sign changers are calculated, taking into account all amplifier and potentiometer multiplier constants. The corresponding voltages are then measured on the computer with a voltmeter and the measured values are compared with the calculated values. Any deviation indicates an error of some sort which must be found and corrected. Errors can be compensating and thus be overlooked during static check. This problem can be somewhat minimized by performing a static check for more than one set of integrator initial conditions.

There are some aspects of the computer setup that are not considered by the static check. Integrator multiplier constants and dynamic function generators, for example, are not verified by the static check procedure. Many errors, nevertheless, are uncovered by performing a static check. It is strongly recommended that a static check be made each time a computer setup has been completed. Much time can be saved by eliminating errors through the static check. Furthermore, satisfactory completion of a static check builds confidence in the user of the correctness of the computer solutions, and for that reason alone it is justified.

3.9 The Output Section

Depending on the sophistication of any given computer, the output section may be simple or complex. It is necessary to provide some means for connecting cathode ray oscilloscopes, pen writing oscillographs, voltmeters, and other recording and/or measuring equipment to the outputs of the various computer elements. This is frequently done on the less sophisticated machines by simply providing output jacks on the elements themselves through which connections can be made to the recording and indicating instruments. On other more sophisticated machines a special output panel is provided to which the outputs of all elements are permanently wired. A single recorder connected to this output panel can be switched, by means of a selector switch, from the output of one element to another as desired. Again, this must be checked for the particular machine.

3.10 General Procedure

Suppose that a simulation is to be done using an analog computer as a system model. Suppose further that all preliminary analysis and planning has been done and you are approaching the computer to complete the simulation study. You should have in your hand a block diagram complete in all of its detail except that it does not show the identification numbers of the elements to be used. These will be determined as the patching up proceeds. Here is the procedure to be followed.

(1) The computer will probably be turned off. If it is, turn the power switch on, place the mode control in STANDBY, go away, and come back when the computer has warmed up for the length of time recommended by the manufacturer.

(2) While the computer is warming up, you can plug up the patch board for your simulation study. It is during this process that particular elements such as amplifiers, function generators, multipliers, potentiometers, and so on are chosen. As they are selected, enter their identifying numbers into the computer block diagram.

(3) You may then place the patch board on the computer (assuming that it has warmed up sufficiently) and adjust all potentiometers and initial conditions as needed for a static check. This is usually done with the control in the reset mode.

(4) Make as many static checks as necessary to assure yourself that the computer has been set up properly.

(5) Set the mode control switch to the reset position and check all integrator initial conditions to be sure they agree with the problem requirements.

(6) Switch the mode control to the operate position and watch the overload indicators. If any of them indicate that an amplifier output voltage is exceeding the reference voltage, switch back to the reset mode, ascertain what must be done to prevent the overvoltage, implement the needed changes, record the changes carefully, and try another solution. Repeat this process until all signals are well-behaved. Be aware that signals can be too small as well as too large. Signals that are too small can only be identified by trying to measure them.

(7) Connect indicating and recording devices and make a trial run. If everything is satisfactory, make a final run obtaining the information desired.

3.11 Summary

The electronic analog computer (EAC) is a general purpose computing device that is well suited for the simulation of physical systems. It consists of a number of different kinds of elements (such as adders, integrators, multipliers, and potentiometers) which must be connected together by patch cords as required by the particular system being simulated. Once this has been done, the user has a model whose behavior should mimic that of the original system and can be so interpreted.

The basic ideas and principles of EAC design and operation are common to all machines regardless of manufacturer and they have been presented here. The details differ, however, from the machines of one manufacturer to those of another. While it is practical to discuss these fundamentals, it is not practical to discuss the details of each kind of machine simply because they are so numerous and so varied. For this reason each manufacturer provides an operator's instruction manual and an EAC user is well advised to spend some time reading the manual, to become familiar with the details of his own machine.

Once the details of the machine are known, the elements can be assembled in building block fashion to create a model of a physical system which can then be studied as desired. Some problems will be encountered in this process; the following chapters describe the solutions to many of them.

EXERCISES

In each of the following problems a partially completed block diagram of a computer element is shown. Determine the value or expression for the missing item. Assume a 100-V reference voltage in all cases. In some cases the reference voltage may be exceeded; indicate this if it occurs.

1.

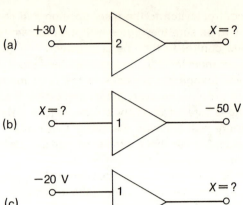

(a)

+30 V   2   X = ?

(b)

X = ?   1   −50 V

(c)

−20 V   1
+30 V   2   X = ?

(d)

−10 V   2
X = ?   5   −30 V

Figure 3.11

2.

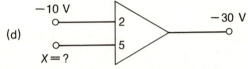

(a)

+35 V   1
X = ?   1   −50 V
−10 V   2

(b)

+10 V   1
−20 V   ?   +30 V

(c)

+10 V   ?
+15 V   ?   −40 V

(d)

+40 V   1
−10 V   2
+20 V   5   X = ?

Figure 3.12

3.

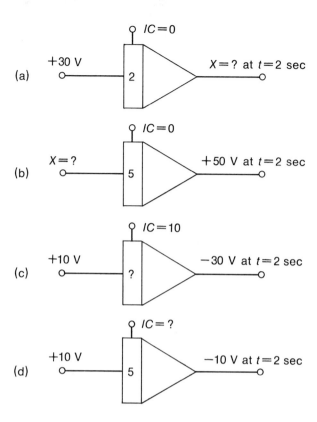

Figure 3.13

4.

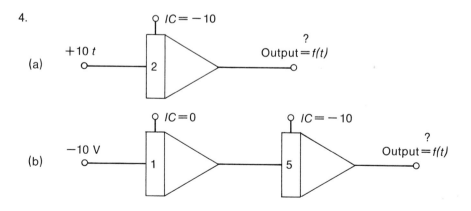

Figure 3.14

4. (cont.)

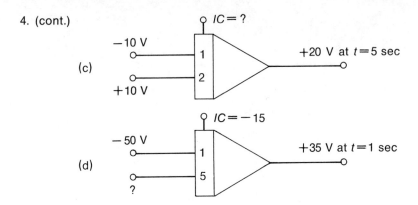

(c)   −10 V   1   IC = ?   +20 V at t = 5 sec
     +10 V   2

(d)   −50 V   1   IC = −15   +35 V at t = 1 sec
     ?   5

Figure 3.14 *(cont.)*

5.

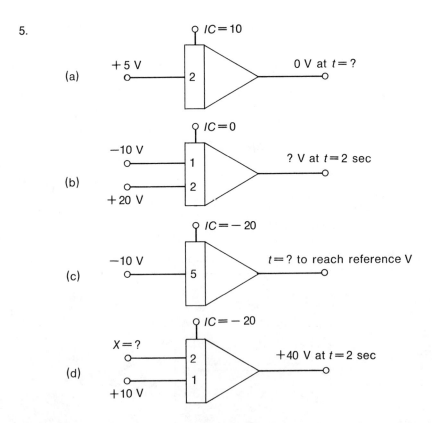

(a)   +5 V   2   IC = 10   0 V at t = ?

(b)   −10 V   1   IC = 0   ? V at t = 2 sec
     +20 V   2

(c)   −10 V   5   IC = −20   t = ? to reach reference V

(d)   X = ?   2   IC = −20   +40 V at t = 2 sec
     +10 V   1

Figure 3.15

6.

(a)
+70 V
−20 V
X = ?

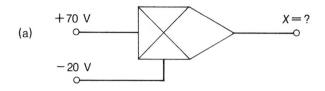

(b)
−30 V
−3 V
X = ?

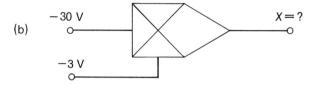

(c)
−25 V
?
+50 V

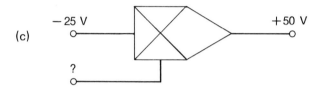

(d)
?
+20 V
+70 V

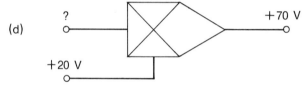

Figure 3.16

7.

(a)
$IC = −25$
+10 V
?
5
−65 V at $t = 1$ sec

(b)
−10 V
+20 V
+25 V
?
1
2
Output $= −80$ V at $t = 3$ sec

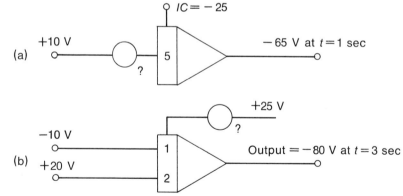

Figure 3.17

8. Explain in your own words the function and use of each of the following EAC elements:
   (a) Patch panels
   (b) Potentiometers

(c) Adders

(d) Sign changers

(e) Integrators

(f) Function generators

(g) Multipliers

(h) Control section

9. Explain in your own words the function of each of the following operating modes:

(a) RESET

(b) OPERATE

(c) POT SET

(d) HOLD

(e) REP OP

10. Explain what is meant by the STATIC CHECK of an analog computer simulator. How is it performed and what does it accomplish?

11. Outline the general procedure, step by step, in setting up an analog computer simulator and operating it to solve a problem.

4

Analog Simulation of Systems Described by Linear Ordinary Differential Equations

4.1 Introduction

In previous chapters we were introduced to the mathematics of simulation which we saw could be used to describe the behavior of several types of physical systems. We indicated that the similarity of the mathematical description of behavior of different systems is the key to simulation. Among the systems that can be described by this kind of mathematics is the electronic analog computer (EAC) and, therefore, it can be used as a simulator of other systems. It is the convenience of the EAC system which makes it superior to other systems as a simulator. What one actually does when using the EAC is to build a laboratory model of the system being studied. Since the behavior of the model and the behavior of the original system are similar, they can then be compared. Again, let us emphasize that the similar mathematical descriptions guarantee the similar behavior. The EAC equipment is convenient to assemble, flexible to apply, and practical to instrument.

EAC's function best when used to simulate systems whose behavior can be described by differential equations. Differential equations can be categorized as *ordinary differential equations* and *partial differential equations.* We shall first deal with ordinary differential equations; consideration of partial differential equations is postponed to a later chapter.

Ordinary differential equations can be further categorized as *linear* and *nonlinear*, and we shall look at both. An additional categorization of *constant coefficient* differential equations and *variable coefficient* differential equations can be made and our study will include both of these. Since some systems require more than one differential equation for their behavioral description, it is also necessary for us to consider simultaneous systems of such equations. Other terms such as *higher-order, lower-order, homogeneous, nonhomogeneous*, and so on are also applied to differential equations and they are introduced as the need arises.

4.2 First-Order Linear Ordinary Differential Equations with Constant Coefficients

The behavior of the electric circuit shown in Fig. 4.1 is given by Eq. 4.1. This is a first-order equation because the highest-ordered derivative in the equation is of degree one (the first derivative).

$$L\frac{di}{dt} + Ri = 0 \tag{4.1}$$

The circuit of Fig. 4.1 shows a constant resistance resistor in series with a constant inductance inductor. The resistance is R ohms and the inductance is L henries. The current of i amperes is shown flowing in the circuit. The influence which caused this current to flow is not shown. Equation 4.1 is a *homogeneous* equation because, when written in this form, the right-hand side of the equation is zero.

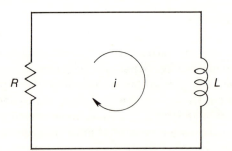

Figure 4.1 *An R-L circuit.*

Figure 4.2 shows a resistor of constant resistance R in series with a capacitor of constant capacitance C. There is some voltage across the capacitor whose source is not shown (in other words, the capacitor is charged by some unknown means). The capacitor will discharge through the resistor causing current i to flow. The homogeneous equation which describes the behavior of this circuit is

$$C\frac{dV}{dt} + \frac{V}{R} = 0 \tag{4.2}$$

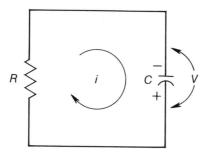

Figure 4.2 *An R-C circuit.*

Whenever a body slides with friction against a stationary surface, a frictional force is developed between the body and the surface against which it slides. The friction is said to be *viscous* friction if the frictional force is proportional to the relative velocity between the body and the stationary surface. A force due to inertia is also developed if the velocity of the moving body is changing with time.

Suppose we have a system like the one in Fig. 4.3. If the mass of the body is M and its time varying velocity is v, then the homogeneous equation describing the behavior is

$$M\frac{dv}{dt} + fv = 0 \tag{4.3}$$

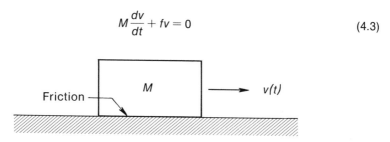

Figure 4.3 *A sliding body.*

As another example of a system whose behavior is described by a first-order differential equation, consider a tank containing G gallons of brine as shown in Fig. 4.4.

Fresh water is allowed to flow into this tank at a rate of R gallons per second. We assume that complete and instantaneous mixing occurs and that the resulting mixture is also drawn off at a rate of R gallons per second. The tank, therefore, always contains exactly G gallons of brine or diluted brine. The amount of salt in solution in the tank at any time t is designated by the symbol S and is measured in pounds. S will vary starting from some initial value and decreasing toward zero.

The concentration of the brine at any time t is given by

$$\text{concentration} = \frac{S}{G} \quad \text{(pounds per gallon)} \tag{4.4}$$

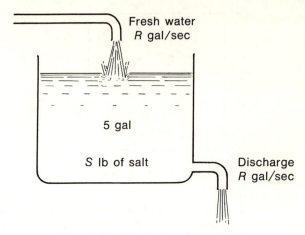

Fig. 4.4 *A brine tank system.*

Furthermore, during any differential period of time, dt, the amount of salt leaving the tank is

$$dS = \frac{-S}{G} R \, dt \quad \text{(pounds)} \tag{4.5}$$

Equation 4.5 can be rewritten as

$$\frac{dS}{dt} + \frac{R}{G} S = 0 \tag{4.6}$$

or

$$G \frac{dS}{dt} + RS = 0 \tag{4.7}$$

Equations 4.1–4.3 and 4.7 are first-order, linear, homogeneous, ordinary differential equations with constant coefficients. Equations of this sort can be solved very easily by conventional mathematical manipulations. These equations are all of the form

$$a \frac{dx}{dt} + bx = 0 \tag{4.8}$$

Solving Eq. 4.8 explicitly for the derivative gives

$$\frac{dx}{dt} = -\frac{b}{a} x \tag{4.9}$$

The solution x of this equation must be a function which differs from its derivative only by a multiplying constant. An exponential is a function which has these properties. For example, perhaps the solution could be written as an exponential function

$$x = k\epsilon^{mt} \tag{4.10}$$

where k is an arbitrary constant to be evaluated later. Differentiating Eq. 4.10 gives

$$\frac{dx}{dt} = km\epsilon^{mt} \tag{4.11}$$

Substituting Eqs. 4.10 and 4.11 in Eq. 4.9 yields

$$km\epsilon^{mt} = -\frac{b}{a} k\epsilon^{mt} \tag{4.12}$$

or

$$m = -\frac{b}{a} \tag{4.13}$$

Substituting these results into Eq. 4.10 gives

$$x = k\epsilon^{-(b/a)t} \tag{4.14}$$

This solution is not quite complete because k has not yet been evaluated. To do this, the initial value of x must be included such that x has the value x_0 when $t = 0$. Imposing these conditions gives

$$x_0 = k \tag{4.15}$$

which, when substituted into Eq. 4.14, gives

$$x = x_0\epsilon^{-(b/a)t} \tag{4.16}$$

The foregoing analytical manipulations can be simulated on an analog computer by the following procedure. Equation 4.9 shows that the first derivative of x with respect to t is equal to the negative of the product of x and a constant. If for the moment we assume that we have the derivative of x, we can integrate it with respect to t to find x itself. This is shown in Fig. 4.5. Notice that there is a sign change associated with the integrator action, and also that the integrator multiplying factor is unity. The initial condition here is zero. According to Eq. 4.9, the input for Fig. 4.5 is $-(b/a)x$. Assuming that b/a is a fraction, it can be realized with a potentiometer as shown in Fig. 4.6. The appropriate connections have been made by connecting the amplifier output to a potentiometer input and the potentiometer output to the integrator input. The correct selection for the multipliers of the integrator and potentiometer and the proper setting of the initial condition completes the simulation. The solution of Eq. 4.5 with zero initial condition is trivial,

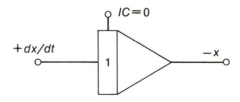

Figure 4.5 *The integrator in use.*

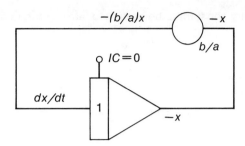

Figure 4.6 *The analog solution of Eq. 4.8*

because under these conditions the solution given by Eq. 4.16 is

$$x = 0 \qquad (4.17)$$

This is a valid solution to the equation since there is no forcing function. The solution is not very interesting, however, and more interesting results can be obtained if the initial condition is something other than zero.

To consider a particular numerical example let us assume a specific equation, Eq. 4.18. Further assume that the initial condition $x_0 = 10$.

$$5\frac{dx}{dt} + 10x = 0 \qquad (4.18)$$

The solution of Eq. 4.18 according to Eq. 4.14 is

$$x = 10\epsilon^{-2t} \qquad (4.19)$$

The analog computer solution is shown in Fig. 4.7. Notice that the integrator multiplying factor of 10 and potentiometer multiplying factor of 0.2 are used together to achieve a combined multiplying factor of 2. Also, observe that the sign of both x and dx/dt have been reversed in Fig. 4.7 from what they were in Fig. 4.6. This, of course, is permissible and makes the output of the integrator equal to x rather than its negative. This sign change is accomplished in the simulation merely by changing the sign of the initial condition voltage whose value is $+10$ V.

If the solution $x = 10\epsilon^{-2t}$ is plotted versus time, the result is the graph in Fig. 4.8. Of course, this graph can be obtained by substituting values of t into Eq. 4.19 and

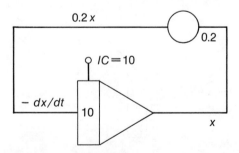

Figure 4.7 *The analog solution of Eq. 4.18.*

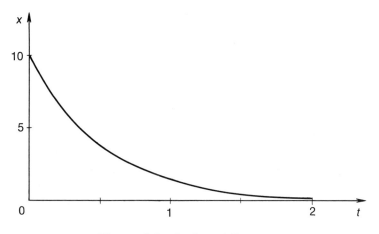

Figure 4.8 *A plot of Eq. 4.19.*

calculating and plotting the corresponding values of *x* and *t*. The same result, however, could be obtained from the analog computer by means of a pen writing oscillograph. Such a device is connected to the output terminal of the integrator and measures the voltage between this point and ground. The voltage starts with an initial voltage of +10 V and decreases exponentially toward an asymptote of zero with increasing time.

At this time, let us make a most significant observation. One might at first consider the preceding discussion as simply comprising the analog solution of a particular first-order linear differential equation. It is this, but it is more. From quite a different point of view (and incidentally, the point of view that we will stress) the above comprises the analog computer model of any physical system whose behavior can be described by a first-order linear ordinary differential equation with constant coefficients such as Eq. 4.8. We observed that the circuit of Fig. 4.1 has behavior described by Eq. 4.1, an equation which is of the type being considered. The analog computer configuration of Fig. 4.7 is, therefore, a model of Fig. 4.1. The particular circuit being simulated by Fig. 4.7 is shown in Fig. 4.9. The voltage labeled *x* in Fig. 4.7 is analogous to the current *i* in Fig. 4.9 and can be so interpreted. The behavior of voltage *x* and current *i* would be identical and the indica-

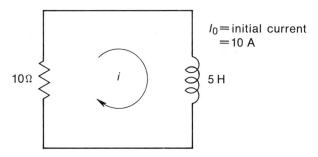

Figure 4.9 *A particular circuit simulated by Fig. 4.7.*

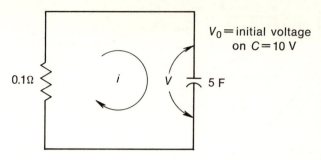

Figure 4.10 *Another particular circuit simulated by Fig. 4.7.*

tions of a voltmeter measuring voltage x in the analog computer model and an ammeter measuring current i in the circuit would be identical both initially and at any later instant.

We also observed that a similar equation — namely Eq. 4.2 describing the circuit of Fig. 4.2 — is of the same type being discussed, and therefore, the analog computer configuration of Fig. 4.7 is a model of this circuit also. In particular, the analog computer model of Fig. 4.7 would simulate the circuit of Fig. 4.10. The voltage labeled x in Fig. 4.7 is now analogous to the voltage V across the condenser in the circuit of Fig. 4.10. It begins with an initial value of 10 V and decreases exponentially toward an asymptote of zero. The initial, as well as the time variation of voltage x in the analog computer model Fig. 4.7 and voltage V in the circuit of Fig. 4.10 would be identical.

Figure 4.3 shows still another system — a mechanical system in this case — described by the same type of equation as before. Consequently, the analog computer configuration of Fig. 4.7 will serve equally well as a model for the mechanical system. The particular mechanical system that is simulated by Fig. 4.7 is shown in Fig. 4.11. The mechanical system of Fig. 4.11 has an initial velocity of 10 ft/sec. Since there is no outside force to keep the mass moving, the initial kinetic energy is dissipated by the viscous friction. The velocity decreases exponentially from its initial value of 10 ft/sec toward an asymptote of zero. The velocity v in the mechanical system is now analogous to the voltage x in the analog computer simulator. The time variation and initial value of voltage x and velocity v will be identical.

Figure 4.4 shows yet another system — a tank of brine — with the same type of behavior-describing equation. There is no reason why the analog computer of Fig. 4.7 will not suffice to simulate the behavior of this brine tank system also,

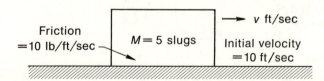

Figure 4.11 *A particular mechanical system simulated by Fig. 4.7.*

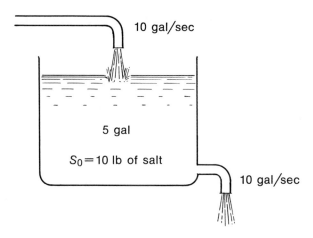

10 gal/sec

5 gal

$S_0 = 10$ lb of salt

10 gal/sec

Figure 4.12 *A brine tank system with selected parameters.*

provided the magnitudes of the system parameters are compatible. Such a selection is shown in Fig. 4.12.

If the numerical values of parameters shown in Fig. 4.12 are substituted into Eq. 4.7 the result is as shown in Eq. 4.20.

$$5\frac{dS}{dt} + 10S = 0 \tag{4.20}$$

Equation 4.20 is identical (except for the variable) with Eq. 4.18. S decreases exponentially from 10 lb toward zero; this is pictured in Fig. 4.8 in which x is first replaced by S.

Earlier we said that if the right side of a differential equation such as Eq. 4.1 is zero, the equation is said to be homogeneous. Conversely, if the right side is not zero, the equation is *nonhomogeneous*. If the circuit of Fig. 4.9 has a battery added to it, the equation describing this becomes nonhomogeneous. This modified circuit is shown in Fig. 4.13 and its analog computer simulator is shown in Figs. 4.16–4.18.

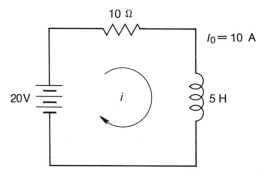

10 Ω

$I_0 = 10$ A

20V

i

5 H

Figure 4.13 *A modified R-L circuit.*

The applicable nonhomogeneous equation for the circuit of Fig. 4.13 is

$$5\frac{di}{dt} + 10i = 20 \tag{4.21}$$

Proceeding as before, this equation can be rewritten as

$$\frac{di}{dt} = -2i + 4 \tag{4.22}$$

Equation 4.22 says that the first derivative of i equals the sum of two terms. This sum could be accomplished by means of an operational amplifier adder as shown in Fig. 4.14. Notice that the adder of Fig. 4.14 incorporates the usual inherent sign change so that the output is $-di/dt$ even though the input quantities are the terms whose sum is $+di/dt$.

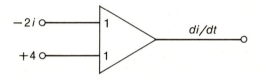

Figure 4.14 *The adder as part of a simulator.*

Integrating the output of the adder and changing sign by means of an operational amplifier integrator gives the dependent variable $+i$, as shown in Fig. 4.15. The output i of Fig. 4.15 must be multiplied by 2 and have its sign changed before connecting back to one of the adder inputs. This is accomplished by the simulator of Fig. 4.16 which is now complete.

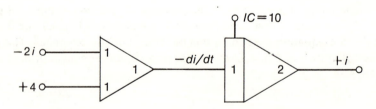

Figure 4.15 *The output of the adder is integrated.*

We can take advantage of the fact that a multiple input integrator also will add (this was pointed out in Fig. 3.7). The integrator of Fig. 4.16 can be replaced with the adder-integrator of Fig. 4.17. An equivalent solution can be obtained by the simulator shown in Fig. 4.18. A careful comparison of Figs. 4.17 and 4.18 reveals that all that is changed from one to the other are the sign of the constant input to the integrator and the sign of the initial condition voltage. The output of Fig. 4.18 is $+i$ where the output of Fig. 4.17 is $-i$.

The simplification between Fig. 4.16 and 4.17 is indicative of what can often be

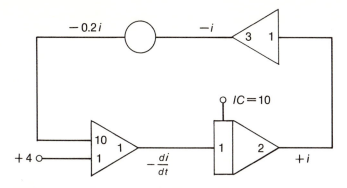

Figure 4.16 *The complete simulator of Fig. 4.13.*

achieved. Sometimes it is imperative that such simplification be accomplished. This is particularly true when a problem is so large as to require more operational amplifiers than are available. Under these conditions simplification such as that indicated here may reduce the number of amplifiers needed to a point where some problems could be solved that would otherwise be impossible.

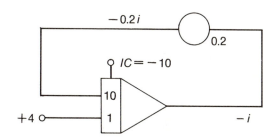

Figure 4.17 *A simpler simulator of Fig. 4.13.*

In Fig. 4.13, we modified the circuit of Fig. 4.9 by adding a voltage source. This made the describing equation nonhomogeneous (Eq. 4.21). Figure 4.19 is a plot of the solution of Eq. 4.21. Notice that the steady-state value of current is now 2 A where it previously was zero. Similar modifications in behavior would result

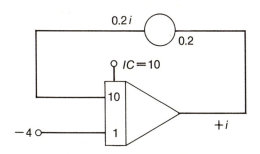

Figure 4.18 *An equivalent simulator of Fig. 4.13.*

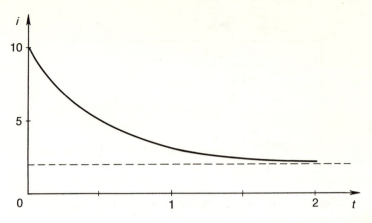

Figure 4.19 *A plot of the solution of Eq. 4.21.*

in the systems of Figs. 4.10–4.12 if they were changed as shown in Figs. 4.20–4.22 respectively. A current source of 20 A has been added to Fig. 4.10 to give Fig. 4.20. The equation describing the behavior of Fig. 4.20 is

$$5\frac{dV}{dt} + \frac{V}{0.1} = 20 \qquad (4.23)$$

A constant force of 20 lb added to the system of Fig. 4.11 results in the system of Fig. 4.21. The equation which describes the behavior of the mechanical system of Fig. 4.21 is

$$5\frac{dv}{dt} + 10v = 20 \qquad (4.24)$$

If the inflow of Fig. 4.12 is changed from fresh water to a weak brine solution containing 0.4 lb of salt per gallon (see Fig. 4.22), the amount of salt S in the tank will decrease from the initial value of 10 lb to a final steady-state value of 2 lb. This behavior is pictured in Fig. 4.19, if *i* is first replaced by S.

Under the conditions pictured in Fig. 4.22, salt is both entering and leaving the

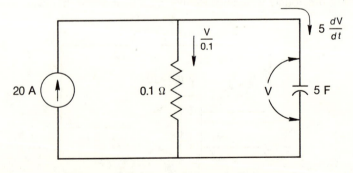

Figure 4.20 *A modified R-C circuit.*

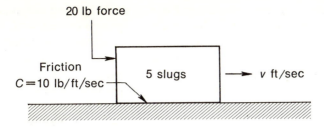

Figure 4.21 *A modified mechanical system.*

tank continuously. In time dt the amount of salt in the tank changes by an amount dS, and we have

$$dS = 0.4 \times 10 \times dt - \frac{S}{5} \times 10 \times dt \tag{4.25}$$

Equation 4.25 can be rewritten in the form

$$dS = \left(4 - \frac{10S}{5}\right) dt \tag{4.26}$$

or as

$$5\frac{dS}{dt} + 10S = 20 \tag{4.27}$$

Equation 4.27 is of the same form as Eqs. 4.21, 4.23, and 4.24 and can therefore be simulated by the simulator of Fig. 4.18.

Equations 4.21, 4.23, 4.24, and 4.27 are all very similar except for the symbols representing the dependent variables. Therefore, they have similar solutions. The graph in Fig. 4.19 which describes the behavior of the circuit of Fig. 4.13 would be identical with plots of the behavior of the systems of Figs. 4.20–4.22. Only the labeling of the ordinate would be different.

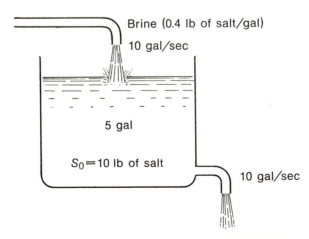

Figure 4.22 *A brine tank with inflow of weak brine.*

The analog computer simulator of Fig. 4.18 could be used without any change to study any one, or all four, of the respective systems of Figs. 4.13, 4.20, 4.21, or 4.22. The behavior of this simulator could be interpreted as current behavior if the *R-L* circuit were being studied, as voltage behavior when studying the *R-C* circuit, as velocity behavior in the case of the mechanical system, and as the amount of salt in the tank if the brine tank system were under study.

The analog computer would probably not be used in practice to study systems as simple as those of Figs. 4.13, 4.20, 4.21, or 4.22. Conventional mathematics would suffice in most cases such as these. There is educational value, however, in studying these simple situations. As systems become more complex, the mathematical operations become more difficult, and the real value of the analog computer as a simulator becomes more apparent. We look next at more complex systems where the use of the analog computer makes more sense, and then we turn our attention to situations where the analog computer becomes an almost indispensable tool.

4.3 Second-Order Linear Ordinary Differential Equations with Constant Coefficients

The electrical circuit behavior of Fig. 4.23 is given by the following integro-differential equation:

$$L\frac{di}{dt} + iR + \frac{1}{C}\int i\ dt = 0 \tag{4.28}$$

In this equation, the initial current is zero as is the initial charge on the condenser. Differentiating Eq. 4.28 with respect to *t* gives

$$L\frac{d^2i}{dt^2} + R\frac{di}{dt} + \frac{i}{C} = 0 \tag{4.29}$$

Equation 4.29 is a homogeneous equation because its right-hand side is zero. It is a second-order equation because the degree of the highest derivative is two. Similarly, the behavior of the mechanical system with zero initial conditions as

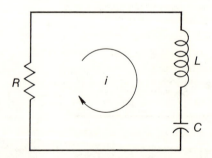

Figure 4.23 *A homogeneous electrical circuit.*

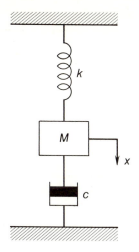

Figure 4.24 *A homogeneous mechanical system.*

shown in Fig. 4.24 can be described by a second-order homogeneous equation such as

$$M\frac{d^2x}{dt^2} + c\frac{dx}{dt} + kx = 0 \qquad (4.30)$$

Equations 4.29 and 4.30 can be used as a basis upon which to build an analog computer simulator of these systems. The procedure is the same for either equation. To be specific, let us confine our attention to the electric circuit of Fig. 4.23, and assume that $L = 2$ H, $R = 1$ Ω, and $C = 0.125$ F. Substituting these numerical values into Eq. 4.29 yields

$$2\frac{d^2i}{dt^2} + \frac{di}{dt} + 8i = 0 \qquad (4.31)$$

Solving for the highest derivative yields

$$\frac{d^2i}{dt^2} = -0.5\frac{di}{dt} - 4i \qquad (4.32)$$

The analog computer diagram of Fig. 4.25 is one possible simulator for the electrical circuit of Fig. 4.23. The behavior of this simulator would be quite uninteresting with all initial conditions at zero, but then, the original circuit behavior would also be uninteresting under similar conditions. The circuit would remain completely quiescent and undisturbed. Hence, something must be added to activate the circuit and also its simulator. A finite initial current would suffice. This could be simulated by imposing a finite initial condition on amplifier 3 in Fig. 4.25. This is shown in Fig. 4.26 for an assumed initial condition of 5 A. Initial conditions on di/dt could be imposed in a similar way.

By following this same procedure, the simulator of the mechanical system of Fig. 4.24 could be realized with initial conditions of displacement and/or velocity

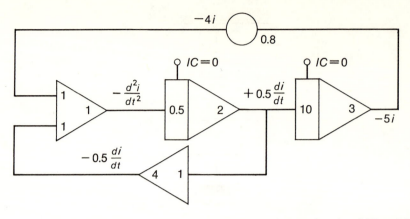

Figure 4.25 *An analog computer simulator of the circuit of Fig. 4.23.*

easily simulated. Assuming that the elements of Fig. 4.24 are mass = 2 slugs, $c = 1$ lb/ft/sec, $k = 8$ lb/ft, and $x_0 = 5$ ft; the simulator of Fig. 4.26 would serve to simulate the mechanical system also.

Adding features to the second-order systems of Figs. 4.23 and 4.24 that make them nonhomogeneous adds very little to the complexity of the simulator, while it may add considerably to the difficulty of the mathematical solution. A sinusoidally varying force is added to Fig. 4.24 to give the system of Fig. 4.27. The equation describing the behavior of the system of Fig. 4.27 is

$$2\frac{d^2x}{dt^2} + \frac{dx}{dt} + 8x = 10 \sin 2t \qquad (4.33)$$

The computer simulator for the system is shown in Fig. 4.28 for zero initial conditions. Again, we could impose other initial conditions.

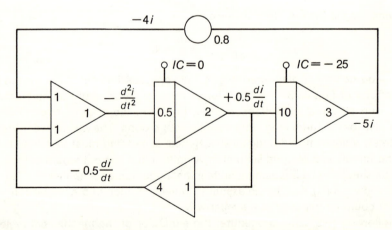

Figure 4.26 *A modification of Fig. 4.25.*

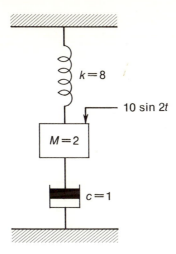

Figure 4.27 *A mechanical system with applied sinusoidal force.*

As might be expected, the diagram of Fig. 4.28 can be simplified. If it is not necessary to have the second-derivative term explicitly presented, the adding capability of the integrator can be utilized. This has been done to yield the diagram of Fig. 4.29. Notice in Fig. 4.29 how amplifier gains have been utilized to eliminate the potentiometer of Fig. 4.28.

If a sinusoidally varying voltage, $V_{max} \sin \omega t$, is added in series with the circuit of Fig. 4.23, the describing equation is nonhomogeneous:

$$L \frac{di}{dt} + Ri + \frac{1}{C} \int i \, dt = V_{max} \sin \omega t \tag{4.34}$$

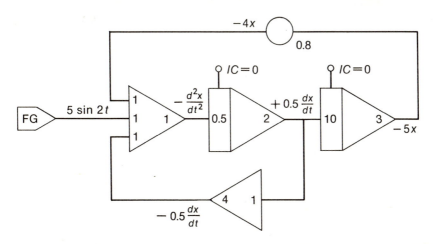

Figure 4.28 *The simulator of Fig. 4.27.*

Second-Order Linear Ordinary Differential Equations **67**

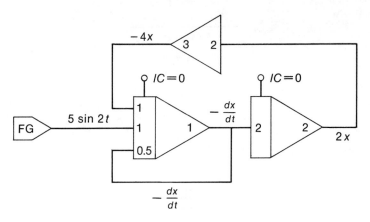

Figure 4.29 *A simplified version of Fig. 4.28.*

Differentiating Eq. 4.34 to put it into the same form as used in earlier discussions gives

$$L\frac{d^2i}{dt^2} + R\frac{di}{dt} + \frac{i}{C} = V_{max}\omega \cos \omega t \tag{4.35}$$

When numerical values are substituted, Eq. 4.36 results. It is assumed that $L = 2$ H, $R = 1\ \Omega$, $C = 0.125$ F, $V_{max} = 10$ V, and $\omega = 2$ rad/sec.

$$2\frac{d^2i}{dt^2} + \frac{di}{dt} + 8i = 20 \cos 2t \tag{4.36}$$

The analog computer simulator for this system is shown in Fig. 4.30. The point to notice here is one of contrast between Figs. 4.29 and 4.30. Observe that when the sinusoidally varying force, $F = 10 \sin 2t$ was added to the mechanical system, it was simulated by a signal of $5 \sin 2t$ in Fig. 4.29; but when the sinusoidally varying voltage, $V = 10 \sin 2t$, was added to the electrical circuit, it was simulated by

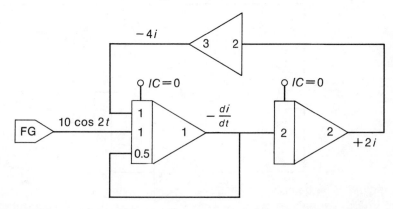

Figure 4.30 *The simulator of Fig. 4.23 with sinusoidal voltage added.*

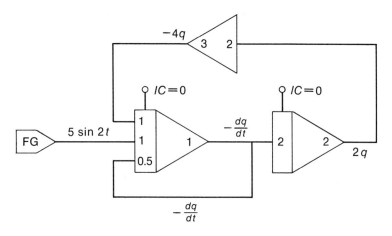

Figure 4.31 *The simulator of an electric circuit with charge as the dependent variable.*

a signal of 10 cos 2t in Fig. 4.30. Why does this apparent discrepancy exist? It occurs because displacement in the mechanical system is not directly analogous to current in the electrical circuit. A direct analogy does exist between mechanical displacement and electrical charge. If the circuit-describing equation is written in terms of charge it becomes

$$L\frac{d^2q}{dt^2} + R\frac{dq}{dt} + \frac{q}{C} = V_{max} \sin \omega t \tag{4.37}$$

Differentiation is not necessary to get the equation into proper form as was required earlier. Substitution of numerical values gives

$$2\frac{d^2q}{dt^2} + \frac{dq}{dt} + 8q = 10 \sin 2t \tag{4.38}$$

Equation 4.38 is identical with Eq. 4.33 except for the symbol used to represent the dependent variable. The simulator of Fig. 4.29 could also be used without modification, therefore, to study the electric circuit. This is shown in Fig. 4.31. Since $i = dq/dt$, the output of amplifier 1 in Fig. 4.31 could be interpreted as current and when properly scaled, it would be the same as the output of amplifier 2 in Fig. 4.30.

EXERCISES

In Exercises 1–5, determine the differential equation on which the given simulator is based. Express your answer as $d^n y/dt^n = ?$, where n is the order of the highest derivative. What are the initial conditions?

1.

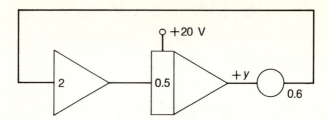

Figure 4.32

2.

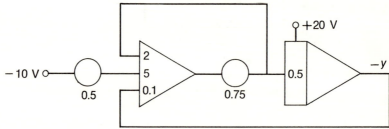

Figure 4.33

3.

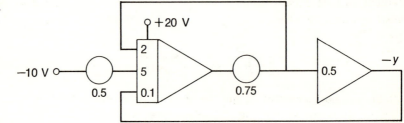

Figure 4.34

4.

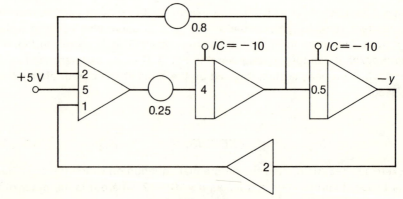

Figure 4.35

5.

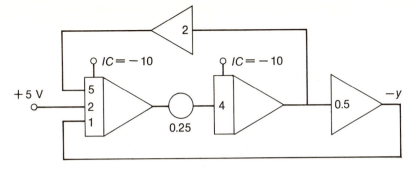

Figure 4.36

6. Consider the electric network in Fig. 4.37.

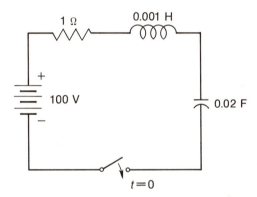

Figure 4.37

Construct an analog computer simulator that will:
(a) Determine the current in the circuit as a function of time. The initial current and the initial charge on the capacitor are zero.
(b) Determine the charge on the capacitor as a function of time.
(c) Determine the voltage across the inductor as a function of time.
7. The constant voltage source of Exercise 6 is replaced by a battery which is very old. Consequently, the voltage does not remain constant as a function of time but decays exponentially from an initial value of 100 V toward 0 V with a time constant of 0.01 sec. A plot of voltage versus time for this source is done in Figure 4.38.

Repeat Exercise 6 with this time varying voltage source in the circuit in place of the constant voltage source. [Hint: Use the circuit of Fig. 4.6 to simulate the time varying voltage source.]

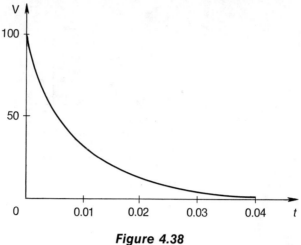

Figure 4.38

8. Consider the uniformly loaded, simply supported beam shown in Fig. 4.39.

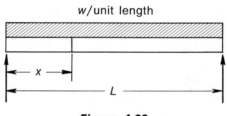

w/unit length

Figure 4.39

(a) Show that the differential equation describing the behavior of this beam is

$$EI\frac{d^2y}{dt^2} = \frac{wLx}{2} - \frac{wx^2}{2}$$

where y = deflection from the unloaded position at any point x
x = length (variable) measured from the left-hand support
L = length of the beam between supports
w = loading in weight/unit length
E = modulus of elasticity of the beam
I = moment of inertia of cross section of the beam

(b) Devise an analog computer simulator that will determine the curvature, d^2y/dx^2; the slope, dy/dx; and the deflection y all as functions of x. [Hint: A substitution of variable is required where t is substituted for x.] Note that $y_0 = y_L = 0$.

9. Repeat Exercise 8 where the uniformly loaded, simply supported beam is also subjected to an axial load P (Fig. 4.40).

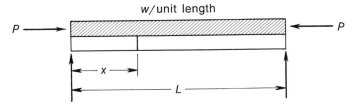

Figure 4.40

The behavior-describing equation is

$$EI\frac{d^2y}{dx^2} = -Py + \frac{wLx}{2} - \frac{wx^2}{2}$$

10. A pendulum is constructed by supporting a long slender rod having length L and weight w, from one end. It is totally immersed in a viscous fluid as shown in Fig. 4.41.

    The moment of inertia J of a long slender rod about one end is given by

$$J = \frac{wL^2}{3g}$$

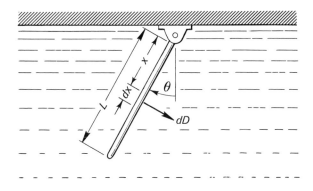

Figure 4.41

The viscous drag at any point on the rod is assumed to be proportional to the velocity at that point. Over a differential length of rod, dx, the differential drag is therefore

$$dD = cx\frac{d\theta}{dt}\,dx$$

and the differential torque resulting from the viscous drag is

$$dT = cx^2\frac{d\theta}{dt}\,dx$$

(a) Show that, in general, the behavior-describing equation is

$$\frac{d^2\theta}{dt^2} + \frac{cLg}{w}\frac{d\theta}{dt} + \frac{3g}{2L}\sin\theta = 0$$

(b) Devise an analog computer simulator for this system, assuming that θ is small, such that $\sin\theta \approx \theta$ where $L = 3$ ft and $\omega = 3$ lb.

(c) Repeat part (b) without the restriction that θ be small.

11. Determine the differential equation on which the simulator in Fig. 4.42 is based. Express your answer as

$$\frac{d^n x}{dt^n} = ?$$

where n is the order of the highest derivative.

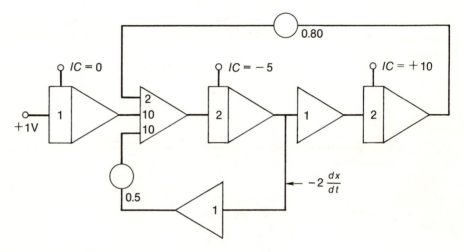

Figure 4.42

12. (a) An analog computer circuit is shown in Fig. 4.43. Find an expression for Z as a function of time. The polarity of the initial condition is not reversed by the integrator.

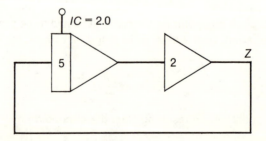

Figure 4.43

(b) Which of the amplifiers will reach reference voltage of ±10 V first?

(c) How long will it take for the amplifier of part (b) to reach reference voltage?

13. Consider the mechanical system shown in Fig. 4.44, with the following values:

$$M = 1 \text{ kg}$$
$$f = 3 \text{ N/m/sec}$$
$$K = 16 \text{ N/m}$$
$$x(0) = 2 \text{ m}$$
$$\frac{dx(0)}{dt} = -0.64 \text{ m/sec}$$

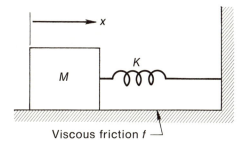

Figure 4.44

Program an EAC having a reference voltage of 100 V to verify the frequency of oscillation and the time constant as predicted from theoretical considerations.

5

Time and Magnitude Scaling

5.1   Why Is Scaling Necessary?

In EAC's, the dependent variables and their derivatives are represented by voltages, while the independent variable is represented by time. It is necessary to represent the independent variable by time because electronic integrators will only perform their function with respect to time. The signal voltages which represent the dependent variables and their derivatives, as well as the computing equipment itself, are subject to certain limitations which make scaling necessary.

One limitation is the maximum and minimum useful voltages that can be allowed. We have already mentioned that the reference voltage is the upper limit to the range of output voltage over which the performance of an operational amplifier is well-behaved. (This range depends on the design of the particular amplifier.) If the output voltage should exceed this upper limit, the behavior of the operational amplifier cannot be accurately predicted. At the other extreme is the minimum allowable voltage. There are always small errors that enter into a problem solution. Signal voltages should not be so small that they cannot be easily distinguished from these small errors.

Another limiting factor is the rate at which the signal voltages change. This rate should not exceed the frequency limitations of the computer elements or the peripheral recording equipment.

Inefficient use of the computer occurs if problem solutions take too long. In some machines, amplifier drift caused by temperature changes can be a problem during extended-time computer runs.

There is a reasonable value for the magnitude of signal voltages that is between the upper and lower practical limits. Also, there is a simulation speed that will produce the most desirable results. *Scaling* is the process which determines these values.

We have completely ignored scaling in the preceding chapters, but we can continue to ignore it no longer. It is now time to give attention to this important subject. The idea of scaling is probably the greatest source of confusion encountered in analog computer simulation. If this is so, why not steer clear of the problem? Unfortunately, the need for scaling cannot be avoided in many situations. Scaling can be made less confusing, however, if the problem is approached in a well-organized way. This is what we intend to do.

We have all had the experience of choosing scale factors when plotting tabulated experimental data. For example, suppose that you wanted to plot a curve showing the following transistor performance data on a particular piece of graph paper.

Base Current (μA)	Collector Current (mA)
0	0
50	1.10
100	1.85
150	2.50
200	3.00
250	3.40
300	3.70

When plotting this curve, you want to use the graph paper to greatest advantage. You also want to arrange the graph so that it occupies most of the space on the paper without running out into the margins. This makes the presentation most useful and its appearance most attractive also.

What one does, in this situation, is to compare the maximum value of each variable with the size limitations of the graph paper in both dimensions. An appropriate scale factor is chosen to cause the resulting graph to fit the limitations of the paper in the best fashion. If the scale is poorly chosen the graph may run off the paper as in Fig. 5.1 curve a, or it may not display the information in a useful manner as in Fig. 5.1 curves b or c. Proper choice of scale factor results in a useful result such as Fig. 5.1 curve d.

In a similar way, the computer programmer must chose scale factors so that the analog computer result is useful. If the result is too small, it may not be discernible in the background noise. If it is too large, the voltage limitations of computer elements may be exceeded. The programmer must choose his scale factors so

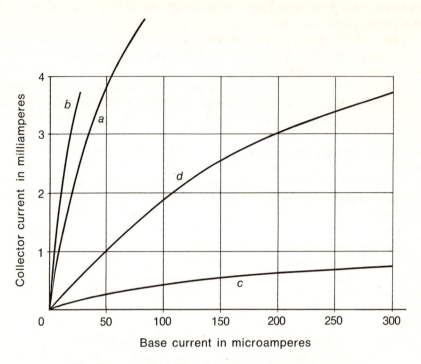

Figure 5.1 *Various plots from the same data.*

that the results best fit the performance limitations of the simulating equipment.

There are two kinds of scaling in analog computer work—time scaling and amplitude scaling. Both are usually necessary to fit the limitations of the computer and associated recording equipment to the requirements of the system being simulated.

In studying physical systems of many types, as a scientist or engineer, you may encounter parameters and performance characteristics which range over wide limits. As we mentioned before, while doing your simulation you may find that unless proper provision is made, the voltages at some points in the computer may exceed the reference or minimum allowable voltages. To further complicate the picture, the speed of response may be unsatisfactory. If the solution occurs too rapidly, you may find that the recording apparatus may not be able to follow it accurately. Suppose, for example, the solution involves the pressure versus time relationship that occurs during the passage of a bullet through a rifle barrel. This entire operation would transpire in such a short time that accurate recording might be extremely difficult if the solution were carried out in real time. Furthermore, the amplifier frequency response may be such as to introduce errors in the results.

Another difficulty could occur if high-frequency oscillations were encountered in the system behavior. In addition to being difficult to record, high frequencies cause phase shift and attenuation to occur in operational amplifiers and consequent errors result.

On the other hand, you may find the speed of response in real time to be so slow as to be unsatisfactory, also. Suppose the system being studied were a chemical reaction which required several hours or even days to come to equilibrium after being started. Obviously, it would be impractical to simulate this system in real time on an analog computer because of the excessive time involved. Furthermore, amplifier drift and imperfections in integrators become significant sources of error if lengthy solutions are attempted.

You may sometimes find it desirable to operate an analog computer on a real-time basis. It is even necessary to do so on occasion. If the operation of the computer is on a real-time scale, the occurrence of events in the computer take place at the same time as corresponding events in the system being studied. Using real-time gives you a better "feel" or acquaintance with the characteristics of the physical system. This is particularly helpful if a system is being simulated in analog form prior to the actual construction of the physical counterpart.

It is sometimes necessary to simulate only a part of a physical system, and to incorporate this simulated portion into a more complicated complete system. Under such conditions, it is obvious that the simulated portion must operate in real time so that it is compatible with the remainder of the complete physical system.

For the reasons just outlined, we must give consideration to the scaling of analog computers, both with regard to amplitude and time. Systematic methods for performing these scale changes are treated in this chapter.

5.2 Differentiating a Sinusoid

It will be helpful in understanding what follows if we digress momentarily to consider the effects of differentation on sinusoidal signals. We have seen from the earlier chapters that, under the proper conditions, some physical systems may be made to oscillate with decaying oscillations. If we ignore the exponential decrease in amplitude and consider only the oscillatory behavior, we can deduce some interesting information regarding the system behavior. Suppose that the displacement $x(t)$ of a physical system is given by

$$x(t) = C \sin \omega t \tag{5.1}$$

The velocity is then given by the first derivative of Eq. 5.1 as

$$\frac{dx(t)}{dt} = \omega C \cos \omega t \tag{5.2}$$

The acceleration is

$$\frac{d^2x(t)}{dt^2} = -\omega^2 C \sin \omega t \tag{5.3}$$

Comparing Eqs. 5.2 and 5.3 with Eq. 5.1, we note that each oscillates with the same radian frequency ω. We also observe that the amplitude of the displacement is C, the amplitude of the velocity is ωC, and the amplitude of the acceleration is $\omega^2 C$. If $\omega > 1$ the acceleration has greater numerical magnitude than the velocity, and the velocity has greater numerical magnitude than the displacement. The converse is true if $\omega < 1$. These facts are helpful in performing amplitude scaling. Similar results can be deduced for higher derivatives. Let us now return to the discussion of scaling.

5.3   Choosing the Computer Amplitude Scale Factor

When operating an analog computer, it is preferable that maximum voltages be kept at a value near to the maximum allowable so as to best use the capabilities of the equipment. This maximum voltage is ±100 V in many computers. Voltages in excess of this maximum limit cause saturation to occur in the amplifiers with consequent departure from linear operation. It is not generally possible to predict the maximum value of all voltages during a computer run and hence as a practical approach, a goal of half of the allowable voltage is frequently set as a target when planning the initial setup. If the actual voltage exceeds the target voltage it may still be within the maximum voltage allowable and if it is less than the target voltage, the actual voltage may still be large enough for satisfactory operation.

One of the advantages of the analog computer is its ability to simulate physical systems in such a way that there is a close relationship between physical system performance and computer performance. This relationship can be more or less destroyed if indiscriminate scaling is introduced. It is desirable that the scaling methods used preserve this close relationship if possible.

The dependent variables of a system are represented by voltage signals at appropriate points in the analog computer. A simple scaling method is, therefore, to let the unit of machine performance be 1 V with a scale factor relationship established between the signal in volts and the system performance in physical units. The scale factor merely indicates the number of volts in the computer simulation that represent one corresponding physical unit in the system being studied. For example, consider the amplifier of Fig. 5.2. In this figure the input to the amplifier is labeled $-4x$. In other words, the scale factor is -4. This means that if the maximum value of x at a particular time is $+2$ physical units, the maximum voltage representing this variable at the input to the amplifier would be -4 times $+2$, or -8 V. Similarly, the output is labeled $+20x$. This is correct since multiplication by

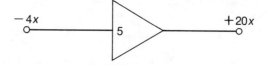

Figure 5.2   *An amplifier with scaled output and input.*

5 as well as sign change is accomplished in the amplifier. Therefore, the scale factor on the output signal is +20. Under the same conditions as before ($x = +2$ physical units), the maximum voltage at the output of the amplifier would be +20 times +2, or +40 V.

The meaning of the scale factor can be observed from a different point of view and perhaps it will clarify the meaning to do so. Suppose the voltage measured at the output is +40 V. The diagram of Fig. 5.2 shows that this is +20 times as large as x and, therefore, the corresponding value of x must be +2 physical units.

In order that the voltage levels may be properly set, it is necessary that an approximation of the magnitude of the corresponding physical quantities be known. The results of Section 5.2 are helpful in estimating the magnitude of physical quantities. Also, one should not ignore any information that is known about the performance of the system being simulated when making these estimates.

Let us again return to the mechanical system of Fig. 4.24. In particular, let us consider the system in which $M = 1$, $c = 2$, and $k = 4$. Then the equation describing the behavior of this system is

$$\frac{d^2x}{dt^2} + 2\frac{dx}{dt} + 4x = 0 \tag{5.4}$$

Applying the principles developed in Chapter 2 shows that the response of this system will be oscillatory with exponentially decreasing oscillations. The natural frequency of oscillation is $\omega_n = 2$ rad/sec and the damping ratio is 0.5. As an approximation, we will ignore the exponential decay and consider the system to oscillate with fixed amplitude at the natural frequency. We shall also assume that the initial displacement is +5 units and that the initial velocity is zero. Under these conditions, the displacement x could be described by the equation

$$x = 5 \cos 2t \tag{5.5}$$

The velocity is then

$$\text{velocity} = \frac{dx}{dt} = -10 \sin 2t \tag{5.6}$$

and the acceleration is

$$\text{acceleration} = \frac{d^2x}{dt^2} = -20 \cos 2t \tag{5.7}$$

Note that the amplitude or maximum value of x is 5, of dx/dt is 10, and of d^2x/dt^2 is 20 physical units. A computer diagram to solve Eq. 5.4 might be that of Fig. 5.3. This diagram is based on Eq. 5.8 which is merely another way of expressing Eq. 5.4.

$$\frac{d^2x}{dt^2} = -2\frac{dx}{dt} - 4x \tag{5.8}$$

Examination of Fig. 5.3 shows the output of amplifier 3 to be $+10x$; since the initial value of x was set at 5 units, the initial analogous value of $+10x$ will be +50 V. The initial condition in amplifier 3 is shown to be +50 V in the diagram.

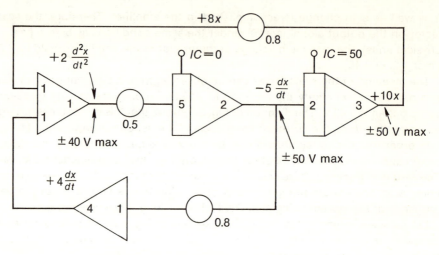

Figure 5.3 *A diagram to simulate the system described by Eq. 5.4.*

The maximum estimated value of *x* will also be +5 physical units in accordance with Eq. 5.5. Consequently, the estimated maximum analogous value of 10*x* at the output of amplifier 3 will be ±50 V. The estimated maximum value of *dx/dt* will be ±10 physical units in accordance with Eq. 5.6, and hence, the estimated maximum analogous value of 5 (*dx/dt*) at the output of amplifier 2 will be ±50 V. Similarly, the estimated maximum value of d^2x/dt^2 will be ±20 physical units in accordance with Eq. 5.7, resulting in an estimated maximum analogous value of 2 (d^2x/dt^2) at the output of amplifier 1 of ±40 V.

The previous results are only approximate, and the actual performance will surely deviate from the predicted performance. The exponential damping factor, previously ignored, will act to decrease the maximum voltages at some places in the computer. The actual frequency of oscillation will be less than the natural frequency and this will have its effect on the actual performance. Another factor which will cause the actual performance to deviate from the predicted performance is the initial condition imposed on amplifier 2. A large initial condition of either polarity impressed here may cause all signals to be different than predicted above.

In some studies it will not be possible to get good initial estimates of the magnitude of physical system quantities or of the speed of response. Do not worry too much about it. Make the best estimates you can without undue effort, determine the corresponding scale factors, and make a trial run on the computer. Realize that this first attempt will probably not be satisfactory, but appropriate changes are easily made. During the trial run, make observations of the speed of response and the magnitude of voltages throughout the computer setup. Then, change the initial settings as necessary and try again. Repeat this process until a satisfactory result is found.

Some purists might object to the foregoing procedure, but it is only making good use of the powerful tool that the computer really is. In spite of all care and sophistication one might use, mistakes will usually occur in making the original estimates. Adjustments will have to be made anyway so it is not efficient to spend time doing the computer's work! If errors are made, they will be evident when the trial is run and they can be corrected then. It is possible that combinations of initial conditions might cause the initial estimates to be wrong, but do not worry about this. Do the best you can and get on with it!

5.4 A Closer Look at Amplitude Scaling

In the preceding discussion of amplitude scaling, we assumed a reference voltage of 50 V. The maximum magnitude expected of each system variable was estimated, and a scale factor was chosen so that the product of the scale factor and expected maximum value would not exceed ±50 V. The amplitude scale factor, reference voltage, and expected maximum of a particular system variable are related by the following equation:

$$\text{amplitude scale factor} = \frac{\text{reference voltage in volts}}{\text{maximum expected value of system variable}} \quad (5.9)$$

Equation 5.9 can be used to compute the amplitude scale factors for the previously studied system as shown in Table 5.1.

Table 5.1

Problem Variable	Estimated Maximum Value	Computed Scale Factor
x	5	$\dfrac{50}{5} = 10$
$\dfrac{dx}{dt}$	10	$\dfrac{50}{10} = 5$
$\dfrac{d^2x}{dt^2}$	20	$\dfrac{50}{20} = 2.5$ (use 2)

The computed scale factor of 2.5 for d^2x/dt^2 is inconvenient to use. A more convenient scale factor is 2. This scale factor was used in Fig. 5.3. The other scale factors were found to be usable as calculated without change.

5.5 Scaled Equations

To further formalize the amplitude scaling procedure, the terms of Eq. 5.8 are each multiplied and divided by their respective scale factors to give Eq. 5.10. Hereafter, such equations are called *scaled equations*.

$$\frac{1}{2}\left(2\frac{d^2x}{dt^2}\right) = -2\left(\frac{1}{5}\right)\left(5\frac{dx}{dt}\right) - 4\left(\frac{1}{10}\right)(10x) \qquad (5.10)$$

Multiplying and dividing by the scale factors does not disturb the validity of the equation, but merely changes its appearance. This procedure is deceptive in its simplicity. Its purpose is to obtain an equation in which the scaled variables are explicitly shown. We shall refer to these scaled variables as *computer variables* because these are the quantities that appear as outputs of the various elements of the computer simulator, and are the computer signals that can be measured and recorded. The computer variables in Eq. 5.10 are enclosed in parentheses and are thus identified as $\left(2\frac{d^2x}{dt^2}\right)$, $\left(5\frac{dx}{dt}\right)$, and $(10x)$, respectively.

Equation 5.10 can be solved explicitly for the highest-ordered computer variable as shown in Eq. 5.11. Notice that the computer variables

$$-\left(2\frac{d^2x}{dt^2}\right) = 0.8\left(5\frac{dx}{dt}\right) + 0.8(10x) \qquad (5.11)$$

are preserved in this process and are again shown in parentheses. A computer simulator based on Eq. 5.11 is shown in Fig. 5.4.

A comparison of Figs. 5.3 and 5.4 shows them to be identical and it might seem that nothing has been achieved. The advantage of this later procedure, however, is that the terms in Eq. 5.11 show explicitly the computer variables, and also show the constants by which each of these terms must be multiplied. In complex problems this is a decided help in organizing one's thinking. These constant multipliers are achieved by means of appropriate potentiometer settings and amplifier gain constants.

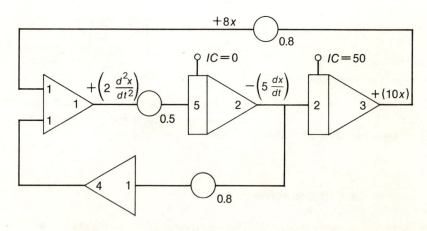

Figure 5.4 *A simulator based on Eq. 5.11.*

5.6 Scaling Applied

Another example will help to clarify the amplitude scaling procedure. Consider Eq. 5.12 which is a behavior-describing equation of a system to be simulated on a computer having a reference voltage of 10 V.

$$\frac{d^2x}{dt^2} + 3\frac{dx}{dt} + 25x = y \tag{5.12}$$

where $x(0) = 2$, $\frac{dx}{dt}(0) = -0.7$, and $y = -40$.

The natural frequency of oscillation of this system is 5 rad/sec. The constant $y = -40$ will affect the steady-state value of x by approximately 2 units. Combining this steady-state value with the initial value of $x = 2$ gives an estimated value of $x_{max} = 4$. Using the natural frequency of 5 rad/sec we estimate that $\left(\frac{dx}{dt}\right)_{max} = 20$ and that $\left(\frac{d^2x}{dt^2}\right)_{max} = 100$. The corresponding scale factors are computed as shown in Table 5.2. Equation 5.12 can be rewritten in scaled form in terms of computer variables as shown in Eq. 5.13 by multiplying and dividing by the scale factors.

Table 5.2

Problem Variable	Estimated Maximum Values	Computed Scale Factors
x	4	$\frac{10}{4} = 2.5$ (use 2)
$\frac{dx}{dt}$	20	$\frac{10}{20} = 0.5$
$\frac{d^2x}{dt^2}$	100	$\frac{10}{100} = 0.1$
y	40	$\frac{10}{40} = 0.25$

$$\frac{1}{0.1}\left(0.1\frac{d^2x}{dt^2}\right) = -3\left(\frac{1}{0.5}\right)\left(0.5\frac{dx}{dt}\right) - 25\left(\frac{1}{2}\right)(2x) + \frac{1}{0.25}(0.25y) \tag{5.13}$$

Solving for the highest-ordered computer variable gives

$$-\left(0.1\frac{d^2x}{dt^2}\right) = 0.6\left(0.5\frac{dx}{dt}\right) + 1.25(2x) - 0.4(0.25y) \tag{5.14}$$

The computer diagram based on Eq. 5.14 is shown in Fig. 5.5 where $y = -40$.

At times, we may find that all variables and their derivatives are not needed as available output signals. When this occurs a simpler computer setup can frequently be achieved. Suppose, for example, it was decided that, in Fig. 5.5, a signal

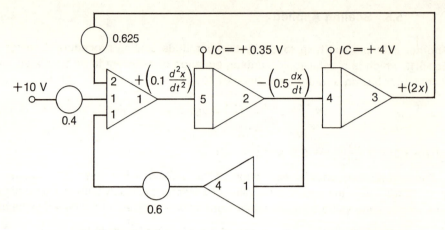

Figure 5.5 *A simulator of the system described by Eq. 5.14.*

corresponding to d^2x/dt^2 was not needed and therefore the adder, amplifier 1, could be incorporated into the first integrator, amplifier 2. Figure 5.6 illustrates a simpler simulator for this problem. A comparison of Figs. 5.5 and 5.6 reveals some differences other than the removal of amplifier 1. Amplifier 4, the sign changer, has changed location and the gains of amplifier 2, the first integrator, have also changed. The rationale behind these changes can best be understood by considering the following argument.

The output of amplifier 2 is $-\left(0.5\dfrac{dx}{dt}\right)$. Since this amplifier is used as an integrator-sign-changer, the input must be $+\left(0.5\dfrac{d^2x}{dt^2}\right)$ to give the desired output. A scaled equation displaying the components that must be combined to give $+\left(0.5\dfrac{d^2x}{dt^2}\right)$ can be obtained from Eq. 5.14 as shown in Eq. 5.15

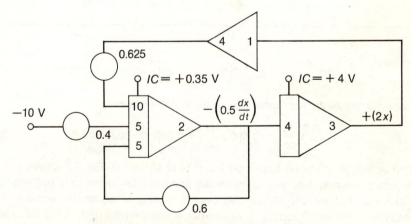

Figure 5.6 *A simpler version of Fig. 5.5.*

$$\left(0.5\frac{d^2x}{dt^2}\right) = -3\left(0.5\frac{dx}{dt}\right) - 6.25(2x) + 2(0.25y) \qquad (5.15)$$

The required computer variables with their constant multipliers and signs are explicitly shown in Eq. 5.15. It is easy to see that they have been correctly applied in Fig. 5.6. A simulator based on Eq. 5.15 as shown in Fig. 5.6 would correctly simulate the system. Notice that nowhere in Fig. 5.6 does a signal appear representing d^2x/dt^2.

In the preceding example, it was specified that the value of dx/dt was initially -0.7. The scaling procedure resulted in dx/dt having a scale factor of 0.5. The corresponding computer variable was therefore $(0.5\ dx/dt)$ and the output of amplifier 2 in Fig. 5.6 is labeled accordingly. Because of the way in which the output of amplifier 2 was determined, its sign was made negative as shown. If we then apply the scaling factor to the initial condition on the scaled value of dx/dt at the output of amplifier 2, we have

$$-(0.5\ dx/dt) = -(0.5(-0.7)) = +.35\ \text{V}$$

and the initial condition voltage of amplifier 2 is set to this value as shown.

In a similar way, since the initial value of x was set at 2, and since the output of amplifier 3 in Fig. 5.6 is labeled $+(2x)$, we have

$$+(2x) = +(2(2)) = +4\ \text{V}$$

and the initial value of voltage is shown accordingly.

5.7 Systems Other Than Second Order

The preceding discussion of magnitude scaling has only considered behavior-describing equations of the second order. It is fortunate that such equations are by far the most commonly encountered type since the procedures for amplitude scaling second-order system-describing equations are simple and direct. Some of the more discerning readers will be concerned about magnitude scaling procedures to be followed when the behavior-describing differential equations are of order other than the second. This concern is quite legitimate, so let us turn to such situations now.

Equation 5.16 is a first-order behavior-describing differential equation in which z is the dependent variable.

$$10\frac{dz}{dt} + z = 6 \qquad (5.16)$$

If the initial condition on z is $z_0 = 0$, we know from our understanding of differential equations that z increases as a function of time, from $z_0 = 0$, where $\left.\frac{dz}{dt}\right|_0 = 0.6$, toward a steady-state condition where $z = 6$ and $dz/dt = 0$. Oscillations do not occur in a system whose behavior is described by a first-order differential equation, so the maximum value of z in this case is the steady-state value of 6, and the maximum absolute value of dz/dt is the initial value of 0.6. These maximum absolute values can be used as a basis for amplitude scaling.

If the initial condition imposed on Eq. 5.16 is not zero, the maximum absolute values of z and dz/dt will be different. Suppose for example, $z_0 = -10$. The corresponding initial value of $\left.\dfrac{dz}{dt}\right|_0$ is then 1.6. In this case, the initial values of both z and dz/dt are the maximum absolute values and should be used when performing amplitude scaling.

On the other hand, if $z_0 = 4$, the corresponding initial value of $\left.\dfrac{dz}{dt}\right|_0$ is 0.2 and hence, as in the first case, the initial absolute value of $dz/dt = 0.2$ and the final absolute value of $z = 6$ should be used when performing amplitude scaling.

When one is estimating maximum absolute values of system variables, he should bring to bear all that he knows about the physics of the system being simulated, as well as his understanding of differential equations. One need not exert great effort to obtain highly accurate estimates of maximum values, but should use the best information available. One should not use estimates that are contrary to common sense knowledge. For example, a 10 V source cannot cause more than 10 mA to flow in a 1000 Ω resistor regardless of what values of inductance and capacitance may be placed in series with it. Should an estimate exceed this value, both the estimate and the procedure yielding it should be challenged.

Unfortunately, for behavior-describing differential equations above second order there is no simple relationship that always gives accurate estimates of natural frequency of oscillation. Usable estimates can often be obtained by the same procedures as used for second-order systems. In other words, Eq. 2.49 may still apply where k is the coefficient of the zero*th*-order term, and M is the coefficient of the second-order term. This will usually give results that have quite good accuracy for third-order equations, and results of at least the correct order of magnitude for fourth-order equations. Once the frequency of oscillation has been established, the earlier procedures can be used to estimate maximum values of variables and their derivatives, and amplitude scaling continues as previously described.

Forcing functions are sometimes sources of confusion when performing amplitude scaling. If these forcing functions are constants, their effects can often be estimated quite accurately.

Let us look at two equations again from Chapter 4 – Eqs. 4.20 and 4.27. Equation 4.20 describes the behavior of the system of Fig. 4.12, and Eq. 4.27 describes the behavior of the system of Fig. 4.22. Figures 4.8 and 4.19, respectively, are graphic representations of the behavior of these two systems. In the case of the system of Fig. 4.12 and Eq. 4.20, the forcing function was zero. The initial value of dS/dt was -20 lb/sec and the initial value of S was zero. In the case of the system of Fig. 4.22 and Eq. 4.27, the initial value of dS/dt was -16 lb/sec and the final value of S was 2 lb. Such effects on absolute maxima should be considered when performing amplitude scaling.

The effects of constant forcing functions on higher-ordered systems, while not so simple as for first-order systems, can usually be approximated by exerting a little effort.

Time varying forcing functions have effects which are more complex but they too can be approximated. An oscillating forcing function will have little effect if its frequency is much higher than the natural frequency of the system to which it is applied, and it will have great effect if its frequency is near the natural frequency.

A useful procedure to obtain maximum values when nonzero forcing functions are present is to estimate the absolute maximum values resulting from the initial conditions alone (forcing functions assumed equal to zero) and to add these results to an estimate of the absolute magnitudes of the corresponding values due to the forcing functions acting alone (initial conditions assumed to be zero). This gives the greatest possible estimate of the maximum absolute values. Actual maximum values are usually less than these, but you are on the safe side when using this approach.

5.8   An Outlined Procedure for Scaling

The procedural steps for determining and using amplitude scale factors are as follows:

(1) Prepare an unscaled diagram of the computer simulation showing all component interconnections. It is convenient to show a potentiometer in every operational amplifier input lead. You may not use them all, but it is better to include them and not use them than to not have them if they are needed.

(2) Estimate the expected maximum absolute values of all problem variables and their derivatives as needed in the simulation. Use whatever knowledge is available concerning the behavior of the physical system in making these estimates.

(3) Calculate the scale factors using Eq. 5.9 and adjust these calculated values to the nearest convenient value for the particular computer being used.

(4) Apply the scale factor to each variable and write scaled equations from the original equations.

(5) Label the computer diagram at appropriate locations with the scaled computer variables.

(6) Adjust potentiometer settings and amplifier multiplying constants to give proper amplifier inputs and outputs.

5.9   A Different Point of View in Scaling

Some analog computer programmers prefer to use a slightly different but equivalent amplitude scaling procedure. The method is in reality only a difference in point of view. It does, however, occasionally result in slightly different implementations. Instead of thinking of the output of an amplifier as being measured in volts, it is viewed as being measured in computer units of voltage, where one computer unit of voltage is the amplifier reference voltage. Since the maximum voltage possible at an amplifier output is the reference voltage, the maximum possible voltage is one computer unit, and any voltage less than reference voltage will be less than one computer unit. All measurements of voltage are thus equal to or less than unity when measured in computer units.

This method of scaling was invented by electric-power network-analyzer users before the advent of electronic analog computers and was called the *per-unit* system of scaling. The name per-unit was invented to contrast this approach with another commonly used system called the percent system. In the percent system, voltages are expressed as a percentage of some reference value corresponding to 100%. By contrast, in the per-unit system, voltages are expressed as a fraction of the reference value corresponding to one per-unit. In this chapter, we have chosen to call one per-unit by the name one computer unit, but they are actually the same thing (computer unit is abbreviated cu).

Using the earlier definition of scale factor as given by Eq. 5.9, and realizing that by definition, the reference voltage is one computer unit, we obtain Eq. 5.17. Scale factors defined in this manner are independent of the computer reference voltage and are the same for all computers. This is not so for the earlier method.

$$\text{amplitude scale factor} = \frac{1}{\text{maximum expected value of system variable}} \qquad (5.17)$$

Except for defining the scale factors in accordance with Eq. 5.17, the scaling procedure follows exactly the same steps as outlined in Section 5.8. Let us examine the scaling of the earlier examples using this alternate idea. Consider the example described by Eq. 5.8, whose scale factors appear in Table 5.1. When new scale factors are calculated in accordance with Eq. 5.17, Table 5.3 results.

Table 5.3

Problem Variable	Estimated Maximum Value	Computed Scale Factor
x	5	$\dfrac{1}{5}$
$\dfrac{dx}{dt}$	10	$\dfrac{1}{10}$
$\dfrac{d^2x}{dt^2}$	20	$\dfrac{1}{20}$

The scaled equation resulting from using the scale factors of Table 5.3 on Eq. 5.8 is

$$20\left(\frac{1}{20}\frac{d^2x}{dt^2}\right) = -2(10)\left(\frac{1}{10}\frac{dx}{dt}\right) - 4(5)\left(\frac{1}{5}x\right) \qquad (5.18)$$

Compare Eq. 5.18 with Eq. 5.10. Solving Eq. 5.18 explicitly for the highest-ordered computer variable gives Eq. 5.19 which should be compared with Eq. 5.11.

$$-\left(\frac{1}{20}\frac{d^2x}{dt^2}\right) = \left(\frac{1}{10}\frac{dx}{dt}\right) + \left(\frac{1}{5}x\right) \qquad (5.19)$$

A computer simulator based on Eq. 5.19 is shown in Fig. 5.7

A comparison of Fig. 5.7 with Fig. 5.4 reveals some differences. Figure 5.7 contains no potentiometers whereas Fig. 5.4 contained three. More careful consideration reveals why. When the scale factors were determined in Table 5.1, the scale factor for d^2x/dt^2 was computed as 2.5, but this was inconvenient and hence 2 was used instead. No such similar adjustment was made when computing the scale factor for d^2x/dt^2 in Table 5.3. It was computed as 1/20 and used without change. The result was the need for three potentiometers in Fig. 5.4 and none in Fig. 5.7. Otherwise, the diagrams are identical except for the initial condition on amplifier 3. This is shown as +50 V in Fig. 5.4 and +1 computer unit in Fig. 5.7. This is correct, however, because one computer unit is 50 V in this computer. The same conclusions can be drawn from either Fig. 5.4 or 5.7. For example, suppose the value of x were +4 physical units at some instant of time. What would be the corresponding voltages? In Fig. 5.4 the output of amplifier 3 would be +10x or +10(+4) = +40 V. In Fig. 5.7 the output of amplifier 3 would be +x/5 or +(+4)/5 = +0.8 computer unit. As we know, however, +0.8 computer unit is +40 V (a computer unit being 50 V) and hence both simulators give the same results.

The example of Section 5.6 could likewise be studied from this new point of view. Equation 5.12 describes the system behavior. In this case the reference voltage is 10 V and the scale factors are shown in Table 5.4. This should be compared with Table 5.2.

The scaled equation is Eq. 5.20,

$$100\left(\frac{1}{100}\frac{d^2x}{dt^2}\right) = -3(20)\left(\frac{1}{20}\frac{dx}{dt}\right) - 25(4)\left(\frac{1}{4}x\right) + 40\left(\frac{1}{40}y\right) \qquad (5.20)$$

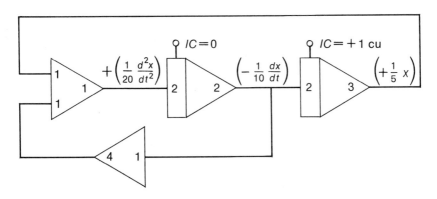

Figure 5.7 *A simulator based on Eq. 5.19.*

Table 5.4

Problem Variable	Estimated Maximum Value	Computed Scale Factors
x	4	$\dfrac{1}{4}$
$\dfrac{dx}{dt}$	20	$\dfrac{1}{20}$
$\dfrac{d^2x}{dt^2}$	100	$\dfrac{1}{100}$
y	40	$\dfrac{1}{40}$

which can be solved for the highest-ordered computer variable to give

$$-\left(\frac{1}{100}\frac{d^2x}{dt^2}\right) = +0.6\left(\frac{1}{20}\frac{dx}{dt}\right) + \left(\frac{1}{4}x\right) - 0.4\left(\frac{1}{40}y\right) \qquad (5.21)$$

The computer diagram based on Eq. 5.21 is shown in Fig. 5.8, where $y = -40$.
A comparison of Figs. 5.5 and 5.8 reveals some differences. These differences can be reconciled however, by careful consideration. This reconciliation is left for the reader.

5.10   Changing the Computer Time Scale

It has already been pointed out that it is often necessary to change the speed of operation of the analog computer to make it more suitable for the problem. Limitations of the recording equipment, the analog computer elements, and the economics of the situation dictate the necessity for time scaling.

Time scaling can be accomplished very simply in a two-step process. First, it is necessary to make a substitution of variable for t according to Eq. 5.22

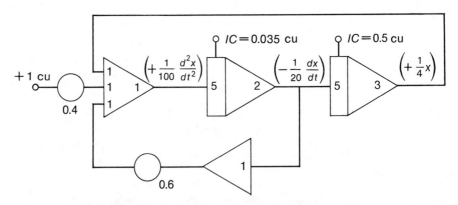

Figure 5.8   *A simulator based on Eq. 5.21.*

$$t = \frac{\tau}{a} \tag{5.22}$$

where a is the time scale factor. If $a > 1$ the simulation is slowed, if $a < 1$ it is speeded up. This substitution must be made in all functions of time, except the derivatives with respect to time, and must be done throughout the simulation equations. For example, if the expression ϵ^{-2t} appears in the simulation equations, and we are scaling down by a factor of 10, we substitute $\tau/10$ for t and the expression becomes $\epsilon^{-\tau/5}$. Second, the multiplying factors of every integrator are themselves changed by multiplying each factor by $1/a$. This causes all integrators to operate more slowly or more rapidly, depending on the magnitude of a as desired. This change can be accomplished in three ways — by changing the integrator feedback capacitor, the integrator input resistors, or by means of a coefficient potentiometer in each integrator input. Initial conditions and amplitude scaling are unaffected by this process.

5.11   A Word of Warning

The simulation of a physical system on the analog computer is deceiving in its simplicity. At least the concept is simple. When one finally gets a simulation wired up on the computer, even simple systems appear quite complicated. There are amplifiers, potentiometers, function generators, and other elements all connected together by means of patch wires. As one makes changes in the connections and settings (as one must do), especially while performing time and amplitude scaling, it is easy to make mistakes. Wrong wires can be moved, amplifier gains can be changed erroneously, and what is most serious, changes can be made and not recorded. Therefore, the user is strongly urged to keep a complete diagram of the simulation in hand and record *every* change faithfully and accurately on the diagram. If this is not done, you soon will forget some of the changes that have been made, and you will not be able to properly interpret your results.

EXERCISES

1. Show that Fig. 5.3 will simulate the system described by Eq. 5.4.

2. In the following equations, $x_0 = 10$, $\left.\dfrac{dx}{dt}\right|_0 = 0$. Determine the approximate maximum magnitudes of x and its derivatives.

(a) $\dfrac{d^2x}{dt^2} + 30x = 0$

(b) $50\dfrac{d^2x}{dt^2} + 4\dfrac{dx}{dt} + 0.5x = 20$

(c) $10\dfrac{d^2x}{dt^2} + 5\dfrac{dx}{dt} + 3x = 10\cos 2t$

3. Repeat Exercise 2 if $x_0 = 0$, $\left.\dfrac{dx}{dt}\right|_0 = 10$.

4. Devise computer diagrams for solving the equations of Exercise 2. Choose an amplitude scale that keeps all maximum voltages between ±10 and ±50 V.

5. Repeat Exercise 4 for the conditions of Exercise 3.

6. In the following behavior-describing equations, $x_0 = 0$, $\left.\dfrac{dx}{dt}\right|_0 = +10$. The computer that is to be used to simulate the systems described by these equations has a reference voltage of ±100 V. Construct a table similar to Table 5.2 for each of these equations.

   (a) $5\dfrac{d^2x}{dt^2} + 2\dfrac{dx}{dt} + 45x = 0$

   (b) $100\dfrac{d^2x}{dt^2} + 447\dfrac{dx}{dt} + 500x = 10$

   (c) $6.5\dfrac{d^2x}{dt^2} + 18\dfrac{dx}{dt} + 81x = 0$

   (d) $10\dfrac{d^2x}{dt^2} + 0.1\dfrac{dx}{dt} + 4x = 0$

   (e) $14.3\dfrac{d^2x}{dt^2} + 0.07\dfrac{dx}{dt} + 5.72x = 7.15$

7. An analog computer having a reference voltage of ±10 V is programmed to simulate a certain physical system. The output of one of the amplifiers is labeled $5\dfrac{dw}{dt}$. It is assumed that proper amplitude scaling has been performed according to the method of Section 5.4. During a simulation study, a pen writing oscillograph is used to record the signal at the output of the above-mentioned amplifier. The gain setting of this oscillograph is 0.5 V per line while making this recording.

   At a particular point in time, the resulting signal level on the recording is 13.5 lines displaced from zero. What is the corresponding value of dw/dt in the system being simulated?

8. For each of the following behavior-describing differential equations, determine the scale factors and initial conditions, and write the corresponding scaled equations. Assume a computer with a reference voltage of ±10 V.

   (a) $10^{-6}\dfrac{dV}{dt} + 10^{-4}V = 0,\qquad V_0 = +25$ V

   (b) $25\dfrac{di}{dt} + i = 10,\qquad i_0 = 2.0$ A

   (c) $10^{-7}\dfrac{d^2V}{dt^2} + 10^3V = 0,\qquad V_0 = 40$ V

   $$\left.\dfrac{dV}{dt}\right|_0 = 0$$

   (d) $5 \times 10^{-3}\dfrac{d^2q}{dt^2} + 150\dfrac{dq}{dt} + 5 \times 10^6q = 100,\qquad q_0 = 10^{-5}$ C, $\left.\dfrac{dq}{dt}\right|_0 = 0.4$ A

9. Repeat Exercise 8, except this time use a reference voltage of ±100 V.

10. The following third-order differential equation describes the behavior of a mechanical system.

$$250\frac{d^3y}{dt^3} + 1150\frac{d^2y}{dt^2} + 1100\frac{dy}{dt} + 1500y = 10,000$$

Initial conditions are

$$\frac{d^2y}{dt^2}\Big|_0 = -50, \qquad \frac{dy}{dt}\Big|_0 = 100, \qquad y_0 = 0$$

The system is experimentally tested and it is found that the maximum values are

$$\frac{d^3y}{dt^3} = 500, \qquad \frac{d^2y}{dt^2} = 100, \qquad \frac{dy}{dt} = 100, \qquad y = 100$$

Compute appropriate scale factors, write a scaled equation, and compute initial condition voltages. Assume a computer with a reference voltage of ±10 V.

11. The following differential equation describes the behavior of a system to be simulated on an EAC having a reference voltage of 10 V:

$$4\frac{d^2y}{dt^2} + 20\frac{dy}{dt} + 100\,y = 10t$$

(a) What is the natural frequency of oscillation?
(b) What is the damping ratio?
(c) Will the system actually experience oscillations?
(d) If oscillations occur, what will be their actual frequency?
(e) If the maximum estimated value of y is 2.5, what amplitude scale factor would you use on y?
(f) What time scale factor would you use?
(g) What is the time constant of the system?
(h) How long would you let the simulator run?

12. An EAC having a reference voltage of 10 V has been programmed as a simulator. In working out this program, it was necessary to apply both time scaling and amplitude scaling. The method of time scaling was to increase the gain of all integrators by a factor of 10 so that the simulator was speeded up 10 times. An integrator in that simulator is shown in Fig. 5.9(a) with its time and amplitude scaled output properly labeled. There were additional elements connected to the output and input, but these are not shown.

An oscillograph was used to record the signal at the output of the above integrator. The results are shown in Fig. 5.9(b) as an oscillating signal whose peak amplitude is 1 in and whose distance between peaks is 4 in. The sensitivity of the recorder was set at 5.0 V per inch and the paper speed was 10 in/sec. The reference voltage of the computer used was ±10 V.
(a) What is the frequency of dx/dt in the original unscaled real time system?
(b) What is the maximum value of dx/dt in the original unscaled system? Assume x to be measured in feet and t in seconds so that dx/dt is in ft/sec.

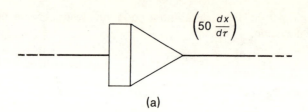

$$\left(50\,\frac{dx}{d\tau}\right)$$

(a)

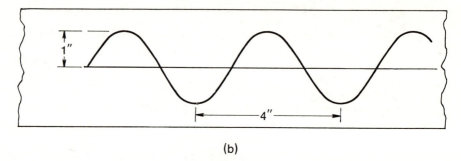

1"

4"

(b)

Figure 5.9

13. A system is described by the following differential equation. It is to be simulated on an EAC having a reference voltage of 10 V.

$$10\frac{d^2y}{dt^2} = -20\frac{dy}{dt} - 40y + 20$$

$$y(0) = +10°, \qquad \frac{dy}{dt}(0) = 0$$

(a) What is the natural frequency of oscillation?
(b) What is the actual frequency of oscillation?
(c) What is the amplitude scale factor you would use for y?
(d) What is the amplitude scale factor you would use for dy/dt?
(e) What is the amplitude scale factor you would use for d^2y/dt^2?
(f) What would be the damping ratio for this system?
(g) Write a scaled equation suitable for simulating this system.

14. (a) Devise a scaled EAC simulator for the circuit shown in Fig. 5.10 with the following values:

$$R_1 = R_2 = 500\ \Omega$$
$$L\ = 1.1\ \text{H}$$
$$E\ = 25\ \text{V}$$
$$L\frac{di}{dt} + iR = 0$$

Assume a reference voltage of 10 V. Assume also that steady-state is reached before $t = 0$.

(b) What are the original system equations?

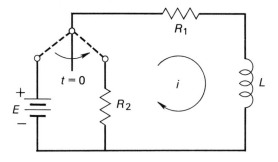

Figure 5.10

(c) What are the scaled equations?
(d) What scale factors are to be used?
(e) Show a completely labeled computer diagram to identify all signals, amplifier gains, potentiometer settings and initial conditions.
15. (a) Devise a scaled EAC simulator for the circuit shown in Fig. 5.11 with the following values:

$$R_1 = R_2 = 500 \ \Omega$$
$$C = 1 \ \mu F$$
$$E = 50 \ V$$
$$R\frac{dq}{dt} + \frac{q}{c} = 0$$

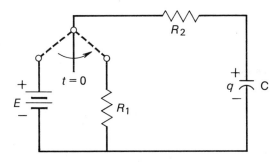

Figure 5.11

Assume a reference voltage of 100 V. Assume also that steady-state is reached before $t = 0$.
(b) What are the original system equations?
(c) What are the scaled equations?
(d) What scale factors are to be used?
(e) Show a completely labeled computer diagram to identify all signals, amplifier gains, potentiometer settings and initial conditions.

6

The Simulation of
More Complicated Systems

6.1 Introduction

The simulation of linear systems was discussed in Chapter 4. These systems, both homogeneous and nonhomogeneous, can frequently be analyzed without the use of computers, although computers may be used as labor-saving devices even when systems are simple. As systems become more and more complicated, the labor involved in analyzing their behavior by conventional mathematical procedures often becomes prohibitive. Systems can be complicated in several ways, and these complications can occur either singly or in combination. For example, some systems may require a number of simultaneous differential equations to describe their behavior. Linear simultaneous differential equations can be solved by standard means but the labor involved is ordinarily more than trivial. Other complications may arise because the describing equations are nonlinear or they have time varying parameters. Any or all of these complications may occur in a given problem. The computer becomes a necessity when analyzing such systems.

6.2 Simulation of Systems Described by Simultaneous Differential Equations

Figure 6.1 shows a mechanical system containing two masses supported by springs and coupled by a dashpot. The equations describing this system are

$$M_1 \frac{d^2x_1}{dt^2} + c_{12}\left(\frac{dx_1}{dt} - \frac{dx_2}{dt}\right) + k_1 x_1 = 0 \qquad (6.1)$$

and

$$M_2 \frac{d^2x_2}{dt^2} + c_{12}\left(\frac{dx_2}{dt} - \frac{dx_1}{dt}\right) + k_2 x_2 = 0 \qquad (6.2)$$

Let us use the following values for this example:

$$M_1 = 15 \text{ kg}$$
$$k_1 = 750 \text{ N/m}$$
$$c_{12} = 25 \text{ N/m/sec}$$
$$M_2 = 5 \text{ kg}$$
$$k_2 = 500 \text{ N/m}$$
$$x_1(0) = 0.1 \text{ m}$$
$$x_2(0) = 0.2 \text{ m}$$
$$\left.\frac{dx_1}{dt}\right|_0 = \left.\frac{dx_2}{dt}\right|_0 = 0$$

The displacements of the masses are measured from their quiescent positions. Substituting these numerical values into Eqs. 6.1 and 6.2 gives

$$15 \frac{d^2x_1}{dt^2} + 25\left(\frac{dx_1}{dt} - \frac{dx_2}{dt}\right) + 750x_1 = 0 \qquad (6.3)$$

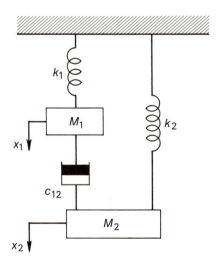

Figure 6.1 *A coupled mechanical system.*

$$5\frac{d^2x_2}{dt^2} + 25\left(\frac{dx_2}{dt} - \frac{dx_1}{dt}\right) + 500x_2 = 0 \qquad (6.4)$$

or, for our purposes

$$\frac{d^2x_1}{dt^2} + 1.67\left(\frac{dx_1}{dt} - \frac{dx_2}{dt}\right) + 50x_1 = 0 \qquad (6.5)$$

$$\frac{d^2x_2}{dt^2} + 5\left(\frac{dx_2}{dt} - \frac{dx_1}{dt}\right) + 100x_2 = 0 \qquad (6.6)$$

The unscaled computer diagram that would simulate the system of Fig. 6.1 is shown in Fig. 6.2. The structure of this diagram is based on Eqs. 6.5 and 6.6.

We must now consider the amplitude and time scaling of the simulation. The scaling procedures of Chapter 5 will be followed. The first step is to determine the approximate radian frequency of oscillation. We can use Eq. 2.49 to find the natural radian frequency of oscillation. This gives

$$\omega_{n1} = \sqrt{50} \approx 7 \text{ rad/sec}$$

$$\omega_{n2} = \sqrt{100} = 10 \text{ rad/sec}$$

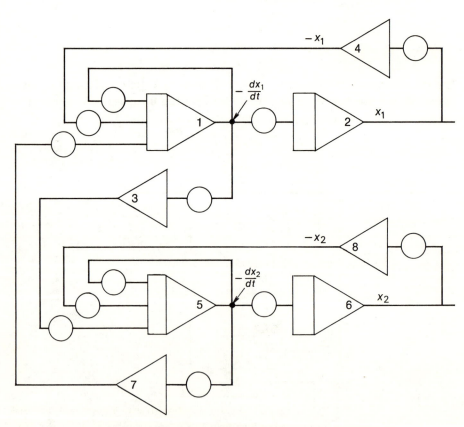

Figure 6.2 *An unscaled simulator of Fig. 6.1.*

Equations 2.47 and 2.48 are used to find the damping ratios. We obtain

$$\zeta_1 = \frac{1.67}{2 \times 7} \approx 0.12$$

$$\zeta_2 = \frac{5}{2 \times 10} = 0.25$$

The indicated frequency of oscillation comes from applying Eq. 2.51 which gives

$$\omega_1 = 7\sqrt{1 - 0.12^2} \approx 7 \text{ rad/sec}$$

$$\omega_2 = 10\sqrt{1 - 0.25^2} \approx 10 \text{ rad/sec}$$

Ignoring the coupling between the equations and the exponential decrease in amplitude, the maximum expected values of variables can be estimated. Assuming the maximum amplitude of oscillation to be equal to the initial displacement results in the following estimates:

$$(x_1)_{\max} = x_1(0) = 0.1 \text{ m}$$
$$(x_2)_{\max} = x_2(0) = 0.2 \text{ m}$$
$$\left(\frac{dx_1}{dt}\right)_{\max} = \omega_1(x_1)_{\max} = 7 \times 0.1 = 0.7 \text{ m/sec}$$

$$\left(\frac{dx_2}{dt}\right)_{\max} = \omega_2(x_2)_{\max} = 10 \times 0.2 = 2.0 \text{ m/sec}$$

It is assumed that the reference voltage in the computer being used is 10 V. The amplitude scale factors can be calculated as shown in Table 6.1.

Table 6.1

Problem Variable	Estimated Maximum Value	Computed Scale Factor	Scale Factor Used
x_1	0.1	$\frac{10}{0.1} = 100$	100
x_2	0.2	$\frac{10}{0.2} = 50$	50
$\frac{dx_1}{dt}$	0.7	$\frac{10}{0.7} = 14.3$	10
$\frac{dx_2}{dt}$	2.0	$\frac{10}{2} = 5$	5

We used Eqs. 6.5 and 6.6 to obtain the scaled equations. Solving these equations for the highest-ordered derivatives and applying the scale factor of 10 to the first and 5 to the second gives the following scaled equations:

$$\left(10\frac{d^2x_1}{dt^2}\right) = -1.67\left(10\frac{dx_1}{dt}\right) + 3.35\left(5\frac{dx_2}{dt}\right) - 5(100x_1) \tag{6.7}$$

$$\left(5\frac{d^2x_2}{dt^2}\right) = -5\left(5\frac{dx_2}{dt}\right) + 2.5\left(10\frac{dx_1}{dt}\right) - 10(50x_2) \tag{6.8}$$

The rationale behind writing the scaled equations in this form is as follows. Amplifiers 1 and 5 in Fig. 6.2 are integrator-adders. The desired scaled outputs are respectively $-\left(10\frac{dx_1}{dt}\right)$, and $-\left(5\frac{dx_2}{dt}\right)$. (See Table 6.1.) The inputs to the integrators must therefore be $+\left(10\frac{d^2x_1}{dt^2}\right)$ and $+\left(5\frac{d^2x_2}{dt^2}\right)$, respectively, so that after integration and sign change the outputs will be as desired. Equations 6.7 and 6.8 express the necessary inputs that must be supplied to the integrators so that they will have the desired outputs. The scaled diagram is shown in Fig. 6.3.

The frequencies involved in this simulation are approximately 7 rad/sec and 10 rad/sec. These frequencies are such that time scaling is not necessary. We observe

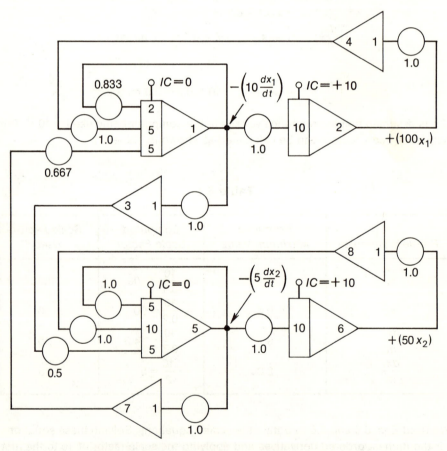

Figure 6.3 *The scaled simulator of Fig. 6.1.*

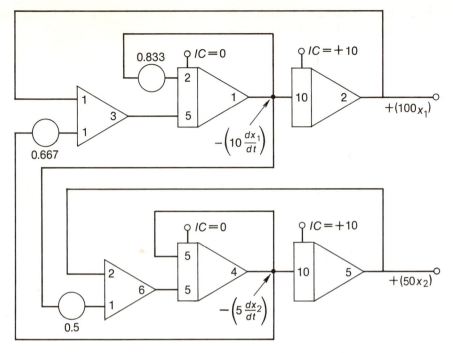

Figure 6.4 *A simplified version of Fig. 6.3.*

from Fig. 6.3 that several of the potentiometers must be set to 1.0. Whenever this occurs the corresponding potentiometer can be entirely removed unless it will be needed later to make changes in the simulator. Furthermore, a number of amplifiers are used in this setup as sign changers. Some of these can be changed to adder-sign changers with some amplifiers being eliminated as a consequence. The result of these simplifications is the diagram of Fig. 6.4.

Another example of a system which requires simultaneous differential equations to describe its behavior is the one in Fig. 6.5.

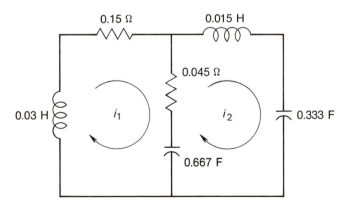

Figure 6.5 *A two-loop circuit.*

Systems Described by Simultaneous Differential Equations **103**

Loop current equations for this circuit are obtained from an application of Kirchoff's emf law. These equations are

$$0.03 \frac{di_1}{dt} + 0.195 i_1 + 1.5 \int i_1 \, dt - 0.045 i_2 - 1.5 \int i_2 \, dt = 0 \tag{6.9}$$

$$0.015 \frac{di_2}{dt} + 0.045 i_2 + 4.5 \int i_2 \, dt - 0.045 i_1 - 1.5 \int i_1 \, dt = 0 \tag{6.10}$$

Differentiating Eqs. 6.9 and 6.10 with respect to time gives

$$0.03 \frac{d^2 i_1}{dt^2} + 0.195 \frac{di_1}{dt} + 1.5 i_1 - 0.045 \frac{di_2}{dt} - 1.5 i_2 = 0 \tag{6.11}$$

$$0.015 \frac{d^2 i_2}{dt^2} + 0.045 \frac{di_2}{dt} + 4.5 i_2 - 0.045 \frac{di_1}{dt} - 1.5 i_1 = 0 \tag{6.12}$$

Equations 6.11 and 6.12 can be rewritten as

$$\frac{d^2 i_1}{dt^2} + 6.5 \frac{di_1}{dt} + 50 i_1 - 1.5 \frac{di_2}{dt} - 50 i_2 = 0 \tag{6.13}$$

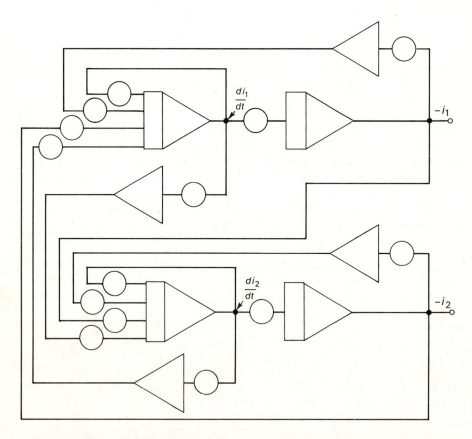

Figure 6.6 *An unscaled computer diagram for simulating Fig. 6.5.*

$$\frac{d^2i_2}{dt^2} + 3\frac{di_2}{dt} + 300i_2 - 3\frac{di_1}{dt} - 100i_1 = 0 \qquad (6.14)$$

Figure 6.6 is an unscaled diagram for simulating the system described by these equations.

As in the previous example, the natural frequencies are found by disregarding the mutual coupling terms in Eqs. 6.13 and 6.14. This gives

$$\omega_{n1} = \sqrt{50} \approx 7 \text{ rad/sec}$$

$$\omega_{n2} = \sqrt{300} \approx 17 \text{ rad/sec}$$

The system behavior is a function of the initial currents only since the circuit contains no voltage or current sources. Let us assume that $i_1(0) = 0.6$ A and $i_2(0) = 0.8$ A. Recognizing that the coupling and energy transfer may cause either current to reach a maximum somewhat larger than the initial value, we shall estimate that both currents might reach a maximum value of 1 A.

$$(i_1)_{max} = 1 \text{ A}$$

$$(i_2)_{max} = 1 \text{ A}$$

$$\left(\frac{di_1}{dt}\right)_{max} = 1 \times 7 = 7 \text{ A/sec}$$

$$\left(\frac{di_2}{dt}\right)_{max} = 1 \times 17 = 17 \text{ A/sec}$$

The amplitude scale factors are determined as shown in Table 6.2. The reference voltage is 10 V.

Applying these scale factors of Eqs. 6.13 and 6.14 and solving for the scaled value of the highest-order derivative gives

$$\left(1\frac{d^2i_1}{dt^2}\right) = -6.5\left(1\frac{di_1}{dt}\right) - 5(10i_1) + 3\left(0.5\frac{di_2}{dt}\right) + 5(10i_2) \qquad (6.15)$$

$$\left(0.5\frac{d^2i_2}{dt^2}\right) = -3\left(0.5\frac{di_2}{dt}\right) - 15(10i_2) - 1.5\left(1\frac{di_1}{dt}\right) - 5(10i_1) \qquad (6.16)$$

Table 6.2

Problem Variable	Estimated Maximum Value	Computed Scale Factor	Scale Factor Used
i_1	1	$\frac{10}{1} = 10$	10
i_2	1	$\frac{10}{1} = 10$	10
$\frac{di_1}{dt}$	7	$\frac{10}{7} = 1.4$	1
$\frac{di_2}{dt}$	17	$\frac{10}{17} = 0.6$	0.5

The scaled computer diagram is then, after simplification, the one in Fig. 6.7. If we want to apply time scaling to reduce the speed of operation by a factor of 10, we simply reduce the gain of each integrator by 10. This is most easily done in the computer by replacing each integrator capacitor by one ten times as large as originally used. Alternatively, all input resistors to the integrators could be made ten times as large as formerly or capacitors and resistors could be changed in any combination that would result in an *R-C* product that was ten times as large as formerly. The time- and amplitude-scaled diagram is shown in Fig. 6.8.

6.3 Systems Containing Discontinuities

In the system of Fig. 4.24, the dashpot was assumed to exhibit viscous friction in which the friction force was proportional to the velocity and directed opposite to it. Suppose that we now replace the dashpot with spring-held rollers as shown in Fig. 6.9. The friction force is a function of several factors in such an arrangement including the spring constant of the roller springs and the radius of the rollers.

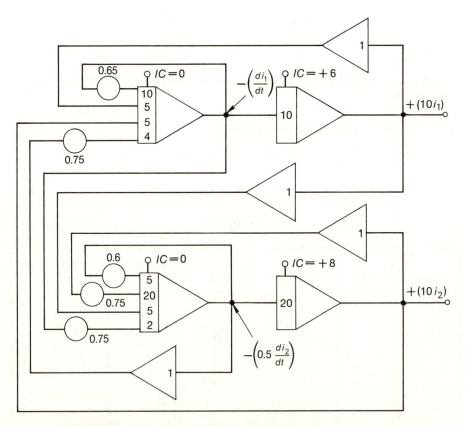

Figure 6.7 *An amplitude-scaled simulator of Fig. 6.5.*

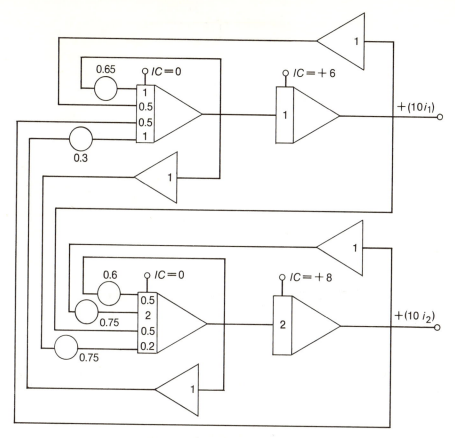

Figure 6.8 *The simulator of Fig. 6.5 after time and amplitude scaling have been applied.*

Let us assume, as is very nearly true, that the friction force in such an arrangement is independent of the velocity, but as before is directed opposite to the velocity. The magnitude of the friction force is constant but the direction changes as the direction of the velocity changes. The simulator of Fig. 6.9 must, therefore, provide for a signal representing the rolling friction which changes in sign but remains constant in amplitude. This can be achieved by a device such as that shown in Fig. A.17.

The describing equation for the system of Fig. 6.9 is

$$2\frac{d^2x}{dt^2} \pm 4 + 8x = 0 \qquad (6.17)$$

The $\pm$ sign in Eq. 6.17 indicates the discontinuous direction reversal properties of the friction force. The magnitude of the force is 4 lb and its direction is such as to always oppose the velocity. The normalized form of this describing equation is

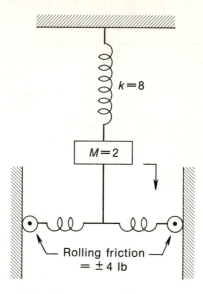

Figure 6.9 *A system with rolling friction.*

$$\frac{d^2x}{dt^2} \pm 2 + 4x = 0 \qquad (6.18)$$

The natural frequency of oscillation is $\sqrt{4} = 2$ rad/sec. Assuming an initial displacement of 1 ft and zero initial velocity, the scale factors are shown in Table 6.3. The reference voltage is 10 V.

Table 6.3

Problem Variable	Estimated Maximum Value	Computed Scale Factor	Scale Factor Used
x	1	$\dfrac{10}{1} = 10$	10
$\dfrac{dx}{dt}$	2	$\dfrac{10}{2} = 5$	5

The scaled equation becomes

$$5\frac{d^2x}{dt^2} = \mp 10 - 2(10x) \qquad (6.19)$$

Based on Eq. 6.19, a computer diagram is developed as shown in Fig. 6.10. The details of the function generator of Fig. 6.10 are shown in Fig. 6.11. The function generator of Fig. 6.11 has an inherent sign change because of the action of its operational amplifier. This requires the addition of a sign changer following the

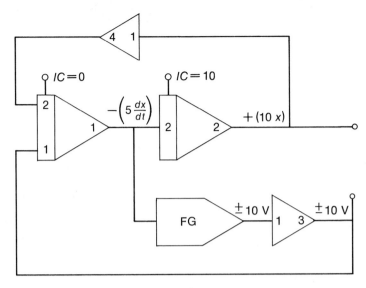

Figure 6.10 *The simulator of Fig. 6.9.*

function generator to cancel the sign change which it introduces. The need for this sign changer can be better understood by comparing Fig. 4.29 with Fig. 6.10. If the forcing function is eliminated in Fig. 4.29, the two figures are then quite similar except for the function generator and associated amplifier. Observe that the signal fed back from the output of amplifier 1 to its input is of the correct sign in Fig. 4.29. Because of the two cancelling sign changes in the function generator and sign changer of Fig. 6.10, the signal fed back will be of correct sign here also.

If the rolling friction in Fig. 6.9 is too large, it may not allow the system to move at all when released with a particular initial displacement. Another way of looking at this is that for fixed rolling friction, there is a minimum initial displacement which will result in system motion. The force due to rolling friction is discontinuous. That is, it switches instantaneously from −4 lb to +4 lb as the velocity changes direction.

In the system of Fig. 6.9, the initial displacement must be greater than a mini-

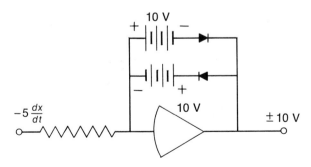

Figure 6.11 *The function generator details.*

mum of $\frac{1}{2}$ ft. This limit can be found by solving Eq. 6.18 for x with $d^2x/dt^2 = 0$. An initial displacement less than this does not produce sufficient spring force to overcome the rolling friction.

A problem that could easily be solved using computer simulation, but that would be very difficult without it is: How much initial deflection will cause the system to have a positive maximum displacement of 9 in at the end of the first cycle of oscillation? The answer can be obtained simply by varying the initial condition on amplifier 2 in Fig. 6.10 and repeating the computer solution until the desired results are achieved. This may require an initial displacement of more than 10 V. If this is the case, then the simulator in Fig. 6.10 is in trouble because the amplifier reference voltage limit of 10 V is exceeded. Rescaling is then necessary. This points up the need to estimate maximum values carefully when performing amplitude scaling so that there is some freedom to perform experiments such as the one proposed without encountering difficulties. A good way to accomplish this is to use only one-half the reference voltage when calculating amplitude scale factors. Of course, there is no rule of thumb that will give good results all of the time. The best rule is to use good judgment and keep in mind what is known about the system and the experiments to be studied on the simulator, and to use this information in performing the scaling operations.

6.4 Simulation Based on Transfer Functions

Up until now the basis for the simulation of physical systems has been the behavior-describing differential equation. In many instances, however, we do not have differential equations with which to work. This is because engineers frequently prefer to describe system behavior in terms of transfer functions rather than in terms of differential equations. One approach to the simulation of a physical system, whose behavior is described in transfer function form, is to first convert the transfer function into equivalent differential equation form, and then proceed from there in the conventional way. This conversion is often not necessary, however, because frequently it is possible to base the simulation study directly on the transfer function itself.

A comprehensive study of simulation using transfer functions is much too complex for inclusion in an introductory presentation such as this. Such a subject, treated in its entirety, could easily require an entire volume. Our purpose here is to introduce the subject and show a procedure whereby some systems can be simulated using transfer functions alone without resorting to equivalent differential equations. A more complete treatment is found in a number of text books that deal exclusively with analog computers.

Consider the transfer function of Eq. 6.20

$$\frac{X_3}{X_2} = \frac{A}{s} \tag{6.20}$$

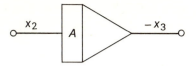

Figure 6.12 *A simulator for the system described by Eq. 6.20 or 6.24.*

in which X_3 and X_2 are functions of s and A is a constant. Cross multiplying Eq. 6.20 gives

$$sX_3 = AX_2 \qquad (6.21)$$

and taking the inverse Laplace transformation of Eq. 6.21 gives Eq. 6.22 in which x_2 and x_3 are functions of t.

$$\frac{dx_3}{dt} = Ax_2 \qquad (6.22)$$

A system described by Eq. 6.22 can be simulated, except for an inherent sign change, by the analog computer configuration of Fig. 6.12. This can be verified by separating the variables and integrating as shown in Eqs. 6.23 and 6.24.

$$dx_3 = Ax_2 \, dt \qquad (6.23)$$

or

$$x_3 = A \int x_2 \, dt \qquad (6.24)$$

Rather than laboriously going through the preceding steps each time the transfer function of Eq. 6.20 is encountered, it is much more efficient to recognize that the circuit of Fig. 6.12 accomplishes the desired simulation task and to go directly to that as a final result.

We can conduct a similar development for other transfer functions. For example, consider the transfer function

$$\frac{X_3}{X_2} = \frac{A}{1 + Bs} \qquad (6.25)$$

where X_2 and X_3 are functions of s and A and B are constants. Proceeding as before

$$(1 + Bs)X_3 = AX_2 \qquad (6.26)$$

or

$$\frac{dx_3}{dt} = \frac{A}{B}x_2 - \frac{1}{B}x_3 \qquad (6.27)$$

The system described by Eq. 6.27 can be simulated by the analog computer element of Fig. 6.13.

Again, as before, one can proceed directly from Eq. 6.25 to Fig. 6.13, once its validity has been established. A similar procedure has been pursued for a large number of other transfer functions and these are reported in several published articles and analog computer texts. Two more transfer function simulators are presented without proof in Figs. 6.14 and 6.15; the proof is left to the student.

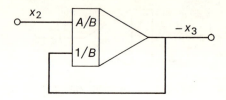

Figure 6.13 *A simulator for the system described by Eq. 6.25 or 6.27.*

6.5 Feedback Control System Simulation

As an example of the application of transfer functions in simulation, let us now turn our attention to the simulation of feedback control systems. This is an area of analog computer simulation that has proved to be extremely productive. To accomplish this development, we make use of the block diagram so familiar to the control systems engineer. Such a block diagram with a typical error detector and open-loop transfer function is shown in Fig. 6.16. One possible open-loop transfer function for Fig. 6.16 is

$$G = \frac{X_3}{X_2} = \frac{6000}{s(1 + 0.01s)(1 + 0.1s)} \tag{6.28}$$

which describes the behavior of an automatic positioning system. Furthermore, X_2, the error detector output, is given by Eq. 6.29. (X_2 is also the transfer function input.)

$$X_2 = X_1 - X_3 \tag{6.29}$$

The subtraction operation of Eq. 6.29 can be simulated by means of an analog computer adder.

The transfer function of Eq. 6.28 can be broken into three parts as shown in Eq. 6.30, and each part can be simulated separately.

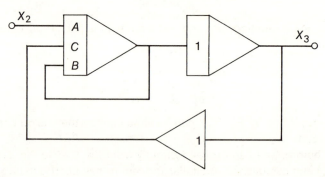

Figure 6.14 *Simulating the system where $\frac{X_3}{X_2} = \frac{A}{s^2 + Bs + C}$.*

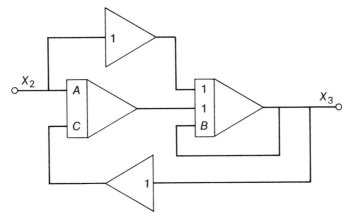

Figure 6.15 Simulating the system where $\dfrac{X_3}{X_2} = \dfrac{s + A}{s^2 + Bs + C}$.

$$\frac{X_3}{X_2} = \frac{6000}{s(1 + 0.01s)(1 + 0.1s)} = \left(\frac{6}{s}\right)\left(\frac{100}{1 + 0.1s}\right)\left(\frac{10}{1 + 0.01s}\right) \tag{6.30}$$

The term $6/s$ can be simulated by an integrator such as shown in Fig. 6.12, and the other two terms can be simulated by configurations such as the one shown in Fig. 6.13. The above division of Eq. 6.30 into the three parts may appear arbitrary but often, wherever possible, the division is done so as to preserve a close relationship with the corresponding parts of the system being simulated as shown in Fig. 6.17.

One skilled in the analysis of feedback control systems will immediately recognize that the system of Fig. 6.16, having the transfer function of Eq. 6.28, is unstable. This means that the system, as well as its simulator, oscillates with uncontrolled oscillations. One of the problems that must be solved by the control systems designer is that of stabilizing unstable systems. Some systems can be stabilized by merely reducing the gain of the system between the error signal and the con-

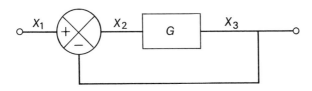

Figure 6.16 The open-loop transfer function relating X_3 and X_2 is given in Eq. 6.28.

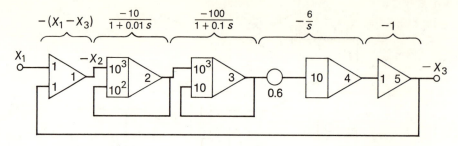

Figure 6.17 *The complete control system simulator.*

trolled quantity. This method could be used with the system of Fig. 6.16. This is often not a satisfactory solution, however, because the speed of response also decreases when the gain is reduced. Frequently more effective stabilization can be achieved by adding a series compensating network.

Figure 6.18 shows a computer element with its associated transfer function. Placing this compensating network in series with the original system which was unstable results in improved stability. The composite diagram of the complete system is shown in Fig. 6.19.

If potentiometer 1 of Fig. 6.19 is set to its highest setting (zero attenuation), the transfer function then becomes

$$\frac{X_3}{X_2} = \frac{2000}{s(1 + 0.01s)(1 + 0.02s)}$$

The system is still unstable, but adjustment of the gain to achieve stability shows the system to be stable for higher gain than before. Also, the speed of response gets better. Thus, an improvement is realized.

The advantage to be gained by using the analog computer as a simulator lies in the ability it gives the designer to quickly add the stabilizing network and try it out. Further modifications may then be indicated and they, likewise, can be quickly and easily inserted. When the desired simulated system behavior is achieved, the actual system can be constructed with assurance that it will behave properly.

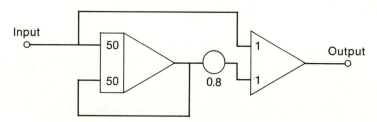

Figure 6.18 *A stabilizing network whose transfer function is* $-\dfrac{1}{5}\left(\dfrac{1 + 0.1s}{1 + 0.02s}\right)$

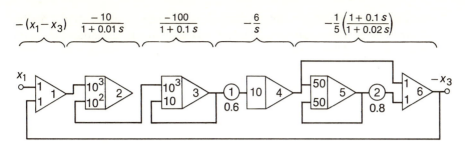

Figure 6.19 *A stabilized control system simulator.*

A practical problem may be encountered when simulating the complete system shown in Fig. 6.19. It may not be possible to realize the high gains required. Notice that amplifiers 2, 3, and 6 require gains of 100, 1000, and 50, respectively. If these gains cannot be realized in the particular computer being used, it may be necessary to apply time scaling to reduce the gains of the integrators. With rearrangement of the components and redistribution of the other gains to get them down to suitable levels, the difficulty can be overcome. Of course, the simulator will respond more slowly as a result of the time scaling, but with proper interpretation this will cause no confusion. A time-scaled simulator is shown in Fig. 6.20.

6.6 Summary

In this chapter, we have presented several examples of systems of some complexity. The components usually available in modern analog computers make it possible to simulate systems having complexities such as nonlinearities and/or discontinuities. Systems described by two or more differential equations yield to study by means of analog computer simulation using a simple extension of principles learned earlier. Systems whose behavior-describing equations are higher than second order also can be readily simulated. Amplitude scaling may not be so apparent as in second-order systems, but it still can be done.

It is also possible to work from transfer functions rather than differential equations when systems are being simulated. The procedures are quite straightforward and not difficult to apply.

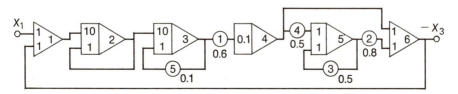

Figure 6.20 *A time-scaled simulator with stabilization.*

Complicated systems which may be difficult to analyze by conventional mathematical procedures, often can be studied by means of analog computer simulation with little, if any, additional complexity or difficulty. This fact alone makes analog computer simulation very attractive.

EXERCISES

1. Consider the system shown in Fig. 6.21.

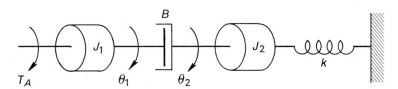

Figure 6.21

$$J_1 = 800$$
$$J_2 = 350$$
$$B = 1100$$
$$k = 1500$$
$$T_A = 90{,}000 \text{ suddenly applied at } t = 0$$

in a consistent set of units

Assume that the following equations describe the behavior of the above system.

$$J_1 \frac{d^2\theta_1}{dt^2} + B\left(\frac{d\theta_1}{dt} - \frac{d\theta_2}{dt}\right) = T_A$$

$$J_2 \frac{d^2\theta_2}{dt^2} + B\left(\frac{d\theta_2}{dt} - \frac{d\theta_1}{dt}\right) + k\theta_2 = 0$$

The initial conditions are

$$\left.\frac{d^2\theta_2}{dt^2}\right|_0 = -40, \qquad \left.\frac{d\theta_2}{dt}\right|_0 = +80$$

All other initial conditions are zero.
Assume a computer with a ±10 V reference voltage.
(a) Determine the scale factors.
(b) Write a set of properly scaled equations.
(c) Determine the initial conditions required on the scaled variables.
(d) Draw a scaled analog computer diagram for simulating this system.
2. Consider the system in Fig. 6.22.

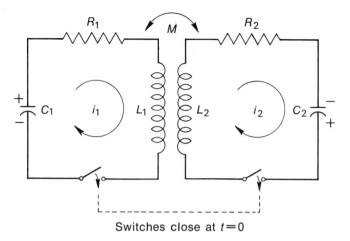

Switches close at $t=0$

Figure 6.22

The capacitors are initially charged and the switches close at $t = 0$.

$$R_1 = 200 \ \Omega \qquad L_1 = 5 \ \text{H} \qquad C_1 = 5 \ \mu\text{F}$$
$$R_2 = 2400 \ \Omega \qquad L_2 = 20 \ \text{H} \qquad C_2 = 5 \ \mu\text{F}$$
$$M = 5 \ \text{H}$$

The equations describing the circuit behavior are

$$L_1 \frac{d^2q_1}{dt^2} + M \frac{d^2q_2}{dt^2} + R_1 \frac{dq_1}{dt} + \frac{q_1}{C_1} = 0$$

$$L_2 \frac{d^2q_2}{dt^2} + M \frac{d^2q_1}{dt^2} + R_2 \frac{dq_2}{dt} + \frac{q_2}{C_2} = 0$$

The initial conditions are

$$V_{c_1}(0) = 450 \ \text{V}, \qquad V_{c_2}(0) = 650 \ \text{V}, \qquad i_1(0) = i_2(0) = 0$$

The following general relationships apply:

$$q = CV_c, \qquad i = \frac{dq}{dt}$$

Determine the following:
(a) Estimate the maximum values of the variables.
(b) Select magnitude scale factors for a computer having ±10 V reference voltage.
(c) Select an appropriate time scale factor.
(d) Show an analog computer diagram for simulating the circuit.
3. Figure 6.23 is a hydraulic system whose purpose is to maintain a constant hydraulic head. To accomplish this, a tank is provided in which the height of water h is kept as nearly as possible equal to the reference height H. The cross-sectional area of the tank is A sq ft. A float is also provided to sense the water

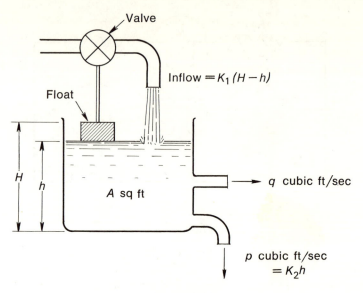

Valve

Inflow $= K_1 (H-h)$

Float

H

h

A sq ft

q cubic ft/sec

p cubic ft/sec
$= K_2 h$

Figure 6.23

level and to actuate a control valve in the supply line. The valve is constructed so that the inflow rate, in cubic feet per second, is proportional to the difference between h and H if $h < H$, and is zero if $h \geq H$.

$$\text{inflow rate} = K_1(H - h)$$

Outflow from the tank is of two kinds. Flow p, due to gravity, occurs with some restriction so that the flow is proportional to h. Flow q is a varying demand over which we have no control.

In time dt, the height changes by an amount dh and the volume changes by an amount dV where

$$dV = A \frac{dh}{dt}$$

This change in volume is equal to the difference between inflow and outflow or

$$dV = A \frac{dh}{dt} = K_1(H - h) - q - K_2 h$$

or

$$A \frac{dh}{dt} + (K_1 + K_2)h - K_1 H = q$$

(a) Select system parameters such that for $q = 0$, the error $(H - h)$ is $\frac{1}{2}$ ft or less when the inflow equals the gravity outflow of 25 ft³/sec.

(b) What will the maxim error be if q is suddenly changed from 0 to 25 ft³/sec, assuming that stable conditions have previously been obtained? What will the final steady-state error be?

(c) How could this error be reduced?

(d) Program an analog computer to permit parameter variation studies of the above system, assuming a reference voltage of ±10 V.
4. In an attempt to improve the behavior of the system of Exercise 3, some changes are made as shown in Fig. 6.24.

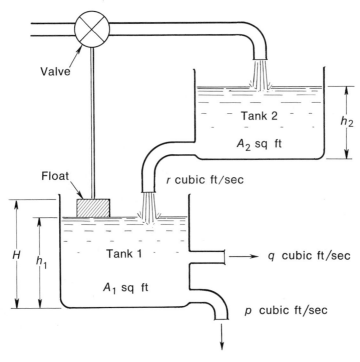

Figure 6.24

An additional tank 2, having area A_2 and water depth h_2, has been added whose discharge r is proportional to height h_2. This discharge is caught in tank 1 whose height h_1 is controlled to be as close to H as possible. The float senses the water level in tank 1, but controls the inflow rate to tank 2. Flow p is proportional to h_1 and q is a varying demand over which we have no control.
(a) Assume a set of conditions and design a control system that will meet them, based on the above configuration. Simulate your design on an analog computer to prove its performance and answer parts (b) and (c).
(b) How large can q become before the system fails by $(H - h_1)$ exceeding 1 ft?
(c) If the system is stable with $q = 50$ ft³/sec, and q is suddenly reduced to zero, how deep must tank 1 be to prevent overflow? How much time would elapse before the water depth h_1 reached a maximum?
5. A 20 ft length of chain hangs over a smooth peg, 12 ft of chain being on one side and 8 ft on the other. (See Fig. 6.25.) There is no friction and there is no initial velocity. Let p be the mass of 1 ft of chain and let x represent the displacement of either end from the equilibrium position.

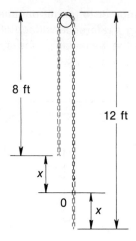

8 ft

12 ft

x

0

x

Figure 6.25

(a) Show that the behavior describing the equation is

$$20\rho \frac{d^2x}{dt^2} - 2\rho gx = 0$$

where g is the gravitational constant.

(b) Program an analog computer having a reference voltage of ±100 V to simulate this system.

6. Modify Exercise 5 so that a friction force equal to 1 ft of chain is included.

7. Refer to Exercise 4.10. A different sort of a pendulum is constructed as shown

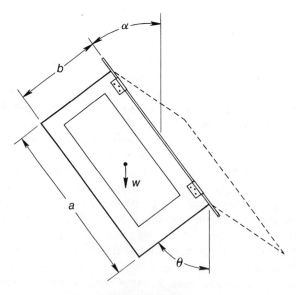

α

b

w

a

θ

Figure 6.26

in Fig. 6.26. It is a door whose axis of rotation is not vertical but rather is inclined from the vertical by angle α. There is friction in the system proportional to the square of the angular velocity.

(a) Show that the behavior-describing equation is

$$\frac{d^2\theta}{dt^2} + K\left(\frac{d\theta}{dt}\right)^2 + \frac{3g}{2b} \sin \alpha \sin \theta = 0$$

(b) Assume that

$$0 \le K \le 3, \qquad b = 5 \text{ ft}, \qquad g = 32 \text{ ft/sec}^2,$$

$$\theta_0 = 60°, \qquad \frac{d\theta}{dt}\bigg|_0 = 2\pi \text{ rad/sec}, \qquad 0 \le \alpha \le 90°$$

Program an analog computer having a ± 100 V reference voltage to simulate this system. Provide a means whereby K and α can be varied.

8. A mass M is placed at the rim of a hemispherical tank of radius R. It is allowed to start from rest and slide down into the tank. (See Fig. 6.27.)

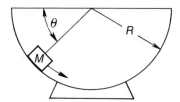

Figure 6.27

(a) Show that the behavior-describing equation is given by

$$\frac{d^2\theta}{dt^2} + \frac{g}{R}(f \sin \theta - \cos \theta) = 0$$

where

$$f = 0.005, \qquad R = 10 \text{ ft}, \qquad g = 32 \text{ ft/sec}^2$$

(b) Program an analog computer to simulate this system if the reference voltage is ± 10 V.

9. The behavior of a simple pendulum of mass M and length L (Fig. 6.28) can be expressed as

$$\frac{d^2\theta}{dt^2} + \frac{g}{L} \sin \theta = 0$$

This can also be written as

$$\frac{d\omega}{d\theta} + \frac{g}{L\omega} \sin \theta$$

where

$$\omega = \frac{d\theta}{dt}$$

Figure 6.28

(a) Show that both equations are correct.

(b) Program an analog computer to simulate the simple pendulum based on the first equation.

(c) Repeat part (b) using the second equation.

(d) Which equation is the better one on which to base a simulation study? Why?

10. A particle with mass M is attracted toward the origin with a force given by

$$F_r = \frac{mK^2}{r^3}$$

Suppose that this mass starts from location $r = a$, $\theta = 0$ with velocity $v_0 > K/a$. (See Fig. 6.29.)

(a) Show that the behavior-describing differential equations are

$$M\left[\frac{d^2r}{dt^2} - r\left(\frac{d\theta}{dt}\right)^2\right] = -\frac{mK^2}{r^2}$$

and

$$M\left[2\frac{dr}{dt}\frac{d\theta}{dt} + r\frac{d^2\theta}{dt^2}\right] = 0$$

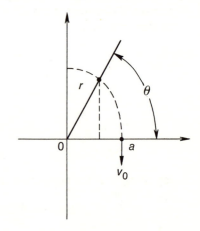

Figure 6.29

(b) Program an analog computer having a reference voltage of ± 10 V to simulate this system.

(c) Compare the results of part (b) with the theoretical result

$$r = a \sec\left[\frac{\sqrt{a^2v_0^2 - k^2}}{av_0}\theta\right]$$

11. A rocket is fired so that its motion is constrained to the horizontal. It burns 25 lb of fuel per second and expels the products of combustion directly backward giving a thrust of T lb. The rocket starts from rest with total weight of 3000 lb of which 2000 lb is fuel. Assume the friction force to be 0.01 v^2 lb where v is the velocity. Find, by analog simulation, the value of T so that the velocity of the rocket will be 5000 ft/sec at burnout.

12. (a) The behavior of the coupled mechanical system shown in Fig. 6.30 is described by a pair of simultaneous equations. Develop these equations in a form suitable for simulating the system on an EAC having a reference

voltage of 10 V. The following displacements of the system are measured from the quiescent positions:

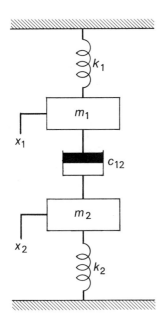

$k_1 = 70$ lb/ft
$m_1 = 1.6$ slugs
$c_{12} = 2.4$ lb/ft/sec
$k_2 = 49.8$ lb/ft
$m_2 = 0.52$ slugs
$x_1(0) = 0.12$ ft
$x_2(0) = 0.2$ ft
$$\frac{dx_1}{dt}(0) = \frac{dx_2}{dt}(0) = 0$$

Figure 6.30

(b) Design an analog computer model for simulating the system in part (a).
(c) Set up the model on the analog computer and obtain recordings of x_1, x_2, dx_1/dt and dx_2/dt.
(d) Remove the damping from the simulated system and observe the natural frequencies of the system. Compare these observations with the theoretical frequencies.

13. The mechanical system to be studied is shown in Figure 6.31.
The mass M_1 is supported on frictionless rollers. The pulley is frictionless also. The distances X_1 and X_2 are measured from the position where both springs are neither stretched nor compressed. There is no slack in the cord initially and M_2 is supported so that $X_1 = X_2 = 0$ at $t = 0$ at which time M_2 is released. We have the following values:

$$M_1 = 0.52 \text{ kg}$$
$$M_2 = 0.21 \text{ kg}$$
$$K_1 = 0.25 \text{ N/m}$$
$$K_2 = 0.78 \text{ N/m}$$
$$0 \leq C \leq 2 \text{ N/m/sec}$$
$$g = 9.8 \text{ m/sec}^2$$

Use an EAC to investigate the effect of C of $X_1(t)$ and $X_2(t)$.

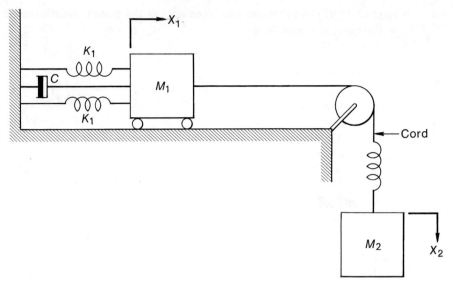

Figure 6.31

14. The system shown in Fig. 6.32 contains a nonlinear spring whose force-deflection characteristic is described by the following equation:

$$F_s = Kx + \beta x |x|$$

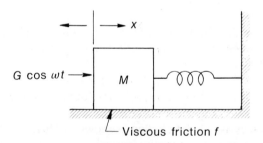

$G \cos \omega t \rightarrow$

Figure 6.32

The behavior describing equation is, therefore,

$$M\frac{d^2x}{dt^2} + f\frac{dx}{dt} + Kx + \beta x |x| = G \cos \omega t$$

Let

$$M = 20 \text{ kg}$$
$$f = 40 \text{ N/m/sec}$$
$$K = 1200 \text{ N/m}$$
$$\beta = 400 \text{ to } 800 \text{ N/m}^2 \text{ (to be varied)}$$
$$G = 80 \text{ to } 800 \text{ N (to be varied)}$$
$$\omega = 1 \text{ to } 18 \text{ rad/sec (to be varied)}$$

Use an EAC to find the combination of β, G and ω that will result in the maximum amplitude of x. Assume a reference voltage of 10 V.

15. The equations of motion of the simple pendulum in Exercise 6.9 are difficult to solve using conventional mathematics due to the presence of the $\sin \theta$ term. A simplifying assumption which is often applied to the equation is to restrict θ to small values so that $\sin \theta \approx \theta$. Apply this simplifying assumption to the equations of Exercise 6.9.

   (a) Devise a scaled EAC simulator for the simplified simple pendulum system. Assume a reference voltage of 10 V.
   (b) What is the original system equation?
   (c) What is the scaled equation?
   (d) What are the scale factors?
   (e) What is the maximum value of θ?
   (f) Show a completely labeled computer diagram identifying all signals, amplifier gains, potentiometer settings, and initial conditions.

16. Repeat Exercise 6.15 without the assumption that $\sin \theta \approx \theta$. Use a nonlinear function generator to generate $\sin \theta$.

17. Repeat Exercise 6.15 without the assumption that $\theta \approx \theta$ and with friction proportional to the angular velocity added to the system. The added term to accomplish this is $0.1\dfrac{d\theta}{dt}$.

18. Repeat Exercise 6.17 with friction proportional to the square of the angular velocity added to the system. The term to accomplish this is $0.1\left(\dfrac{d\theta}{dt}\right)^2$.

19. Show that the circuit in Fig. 6.33 can be used to generate $a \sin \theta$ and $a \cos \theta$. The reference voltage is 10 V. Assume also that $\dfrac{d\theta}{dt}$ is available as an input.

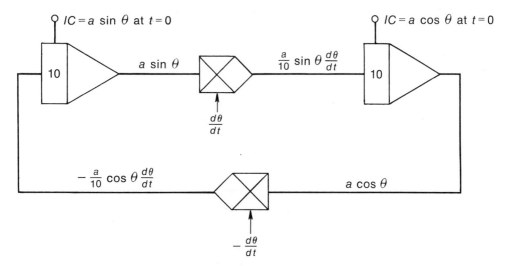

Figure 6.33

20. Repeat Exercise 6.17 using the circuit of Exercise 6.19 to generate sin θ.
21. You are requested to investigate the response of an automobile suspension system for selected disturbances using an EAC with a reference voltage of 100 V. The response of the automobile to these disturbances for various design parameters must be obtained. In particular, it is necessary to optimize the damping constant of the shock absorbers. The simplified system diagram is shown in Fig. 6.34. We have the following values:

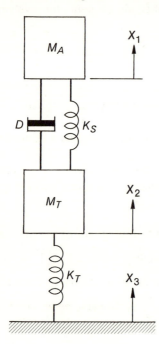

$K_S = 1000$ lb/ft
$M_A = \frac{1}{4}$ the mass of the automobile
(weight of $\frac{1}{4}$ of the auto is 960 lb)
$M_T =$ mass of the wheel and axle
(weight of the wheel and axle is 64 lb)
$K_T =$ spring constant of the tire (assumed linear)
$= 4500$ lb/ft
$D =$ damping constant of the shock absorber
$=$ variable from 0 to 200 lb sec/ft
$X_1 =$ displacement of the auto body
$X_2 =$ displacement of the wheel
$X_3 =$ road surface (variable as a function of time)
Assume all the initial conditions are zero.

Figure 6.34

(a) Write the differential equations of motion for the system by equating the sum of the forces acting on the masses involved to zero. You should obtain two simultaneous, second-order, differential equations.
(b) Scale the equations in (a) to fit the capabilities of the EAC.
(c) Design a computer set-up to solve for x_1, $\dfrac{dx_1}{dt}$, x_2 and $\dfrac{dx_2}{dt}$ when an input is applied to x_3.
(d) Set up the actual computer solution and record x_1, $\dfrac{dx_1}{dt}$, x_2, $\dfrac{dx_2}{dt}$ for various values of D for
   (1) $x_3 = 4\ \mu(t)$ in (a step function occurring at $t = 0$).
   (2) $x_3 = 4\ \mu(t) - 4\ \mu(t-0.5)$ in (an input pulse 4 in high lasting for 0.5 sec).
   (3) $x_3 =$ other inputs you may wish to examine.
(e) In your opinion, what is the best value of D? State your reasons.

22. A series circuit is comprised of a nonlinear ballast lamp, a nonlinear inductor of 1000 turns, and a sinusoidal voltage source as shown in Fig. 6.35.

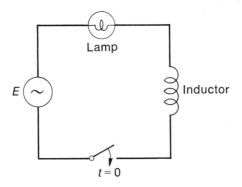

Figure 6.35

The voltage source is described as

$$E = 150 \sin (\omega t + \theta)$$

The characteristic of the ballast lamp is given by the following table. Only the positive values of data are given. The characteristic is symmetric about the origin, and it continues with the same slope as in the last interval, for values outside the tabulated range [see Fig. 6.36(a)].

VR	I
0	0.0
1	0.45
2	0.81
3	0.97
4	1.03
5	1.05
6	1.06
7	1.07
8	1.09
9	1.10
10	1.12
11	1.15
12	1.19
13	1.24
14	1.30
15	1.37

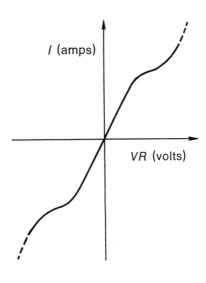

Figure 6.36(a)

The characteristic of the inductor is given by the following tabulated data. This characteristic is also symmetric about the origin [see Fig. 6.36(b)].

I	ϕ (Flux)
0.00	0
0.05	300
0.07	400
0.10	480
0.15	540
0.20	580
0.30	620
0.40	645
0.50	665
0.60	680
0.70	690
0.80	700
0.90	710
1.00	720
1.50	770

Figure 6.36(b)

(a) Find the current as a function of time over two cycles of applied voltage. $I(0) = 0$, $\phi(0) = 0$, $\theta(0) = -45°(10°) + 45°$ when the switch is closed.
(b) What is the peak value of current for each of the initial values of θ?

23. An experiment is conducted to attempt to measure the velocity of a bullet. A block of wood is suspended on a long string, the bullet is fired into the stationary block of wood, and the resulting deflection is observed. Design such an experiment by selecting:
(a) The length of the string.
(b) The size and weight of the block.
(c) The caliber of the bullet.
(d) The expected velocity of the bullet.
(e) The expected deflection of the block.
(f) Simulate your system and test its performance on an analog computer.

24. A rocket is fired from a launch pad at sea level in a vertically upward direction. The weight of the rocket itself, not including fuel, is 900 pounds. The fuel is burned at a constant rate of 100 pounds per second until all of the fuel is completely exhausted. During the burning period, the thrust developed is 7500 pounds. The aerodynamic drag on the rocket is a function of both altitude above the launch pad and velocity of the rocket, as expressed by the following equation:

$$D = K\left(\frac{dy}{dt}\right)^2$$

where K varies with altitude as given by the following tabulated data:

y (ft)	K (lbs/ft/sec)
0	0.08
5,000	0.07
10,000	0.06
20,000	0.05
35,000	0.04
60,000	0.03
200,000	0.02

The rocket is assumed to rise and fall without tumbling. Find the following using an analog computer:
(a) The amount of fuel required to achieve a maximum altitude of 200,000 feet.
(b) The time after firing that maximum altitude is achieved.
(c) The time of impact back on the earth's surface.
(d) The maximum velocity during ascent.
(e) The maximum velocity during descent.
(f) The velocity and altitude at burnout.

25. As a part of a preliminary design, you are asked to consider the magnetically coupled circuit shown in Fig. 6.37, with the following values:

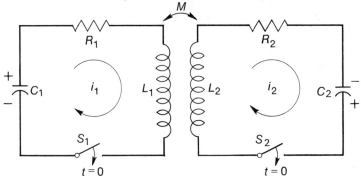

Figure 6.37

$$R_1 = 210 \ \Omega \qquad R_2 = 2300 \ \Omega$$
$$L_1 = 5.2 \ \text{H} \qquad L_2 = 1.9 \ \text{H}$$
$$C_1 = 4.8 \ \mu\text{F} \qquad C_2 = 5.2 \ \mu\text{F}$$
$$M = 5 \ \text{H}$$

Both switches are to close simultaneously at $t = 0$. Capacitor C_1 is initially charged to 400 V and capacitor C_2 is initially charged to 600 V with polarities as shown. Use an EAC to find the following information:
(a) The peak magnitude of current in both branches of the circuit.

(b) The time required for the current to reach its peak value in each branch of the circuit.
(c) The frequency of oscillation, if any.
(d) The peak voltage to which capacitor C_2 will be charged and its polarity.
(e) Repeat the problem except that S_1 closes at $t = 0$ and S_2 closes at $t = 0.1$ sec.

26. A design engineer in your group has proposed the circuit in Fig. 6.38 as a basis for a voltage doubler he has invented.

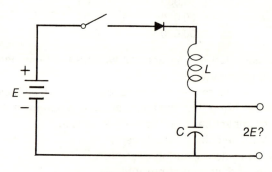

Figure 6.38

(a) Evaluate the circuit in this application.
(b) What components (diode, inductor, capacitor) would you recommend for this application if $E = 100$ V?
(c) Would you suggest the addition of other components to the circuit to make it practical?

7
Analog Simulation Involving Partial Differential Equations

7.1 Introduction

There are some types of systems described by partial differential equations which can be successfully simulated on electronic analog computers. We write differential equations in partial differential form whenever the dependent variable is a function of more than one independent variable. When simulating such systems on the electronic analog computer, the partial differential equations must be transformed into a form in which they can be handled more conveniently. This transformation is necessary because integration can be achieved in these computers only with respect to a single independent variable, namely time. One transformation scheme involves the application of the method of finite differences to convert the partial differential equations into difference differential equations.

7.2 Finite Differences

In applying the methods of numerical analysis (such as finite differences) to differential equations, it must be recognized that the methods are approximate. They may give very good results, however, if properly used. One method of analysis is called the method of *central differences*. We can best describe this method by applying it to a particular situation. Consider the curve of Fig. 7.1, which may be changing position with time, and suppose we wish to evaluate its slope at some arbitrary point p_n. The slope is given by

$$\text{slope} = \frac{\partial y}{\partial x} \qquad (7.1)$$

Equation 7.1 is written as a partial derivative because the slope is a function of both x and t (time). To use the method of central differences, we must first find the difference between two nearby values of y. One value of y, $y_{n+1/2}$, is obtained corresponding to $x = x_{n+1/2}$, which is a one-half unit of distance to the right of p_n; and another value of y, $y_{n-1/2}$, is obtained corresponding to $x_{n-1/2}$, which is a one-half unit of distance to the left of p_n. The distance between $x_{n+1/2}$ and $x_{n-1/2}$ is one unit, labeled Δx. It can be seen that if the two corresponding values of y are $y_{n+1/2}$ and $y_{n-1/2}$, respectively, the slope at point p_n (or where $x = x_n$) is approximately given by

$$\left.\frac{\partial y}{\partial x}\right|_n \approx \frac{y_{n+1/2} - y_{n-1/2}}{\Delta x} \qquad (7.2)$$

where Δx is one unit of distance in the direction of x.

An approximation to the second derivative can be obtained by following a similar argument. Now, the second derivative is really the derivative of the first derivative. If we know the first derivative at $x_{n+1/2}$ and at $x_{n-1/2}$ we can subtract the latter from the former and divide the difference by Δx to give an approximation to the second derivative. The first derivative at $x_{n+1/2}$ is given by

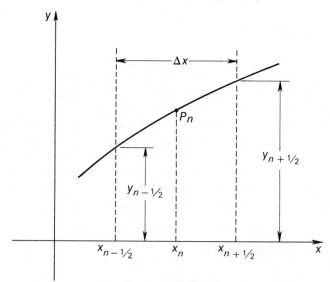

Figure 7.1 *A time-varying curve.*

$$\frac{\partial y}{\partial x}\bigg|_{n+1/2} \approx \frac{y_{n+1} - y_n}{\Delta x} \tag{7.3}$$

and the first derivative at $x_{n-1/2}$ is given by

$$\frac{\partial y}{\partial x}\bigg|_{n-1/2} \approx \frac{y_n - y_{n-1}}{\Delta x} \tag{7.4}$$

Subtracting Eq. 7.4 from 7.3 and dividing by Δx gives the expression for the second derivative as shown in Eq. 7.5:

$$\frac{\partial^2 y}{\partial x^2}\bigg|_n \approx \frac{y_{n+1} - 2y_n + y_{n-1}}{(\Delta x)^2} \tag{7.5}$$

Following similar arguments, as applied to the higher derivatives, it can be shown that

$$\frac{\partial^3 y}{\partial x^3}\bigg|_n \approx \frac{y_{n+3/2} - 3y_{n+1/2} + 3y_{n-1/2} - y_{n-3/2}}{(\Delta x)^3} \tag{7.6}$$

and that

$$\frac{\partial^4 y}{\partial x^4}\bigg|_n \approx \frac{y_{n+2} - 4y_{n+1} + 6y_n - 4y_{n-1} + y_{n-2}}{(\Delta x)^4} \tag{7.7}$$

The reader who is interested in further details regarding the methods of numerical analysis will find many references on the subject. No further attempt is made to develop the subject here. We shall apply the method to a particular situation, however.

7.3 Situations Involving Partial Differential Equations

Many physical systems are describable in terms of partial differential equations. Among these are vibrating strings, vibrating shafts, vibrating beams, and heat flow through conducting solids. Let us look at the equations which apply to each of these.

Vibrating Strings. If in considering vibrating strings we make the proper assumptions, it can be shown that

$$\frac{\partial^2 y}{\partial t^2} = \frac{Tg}{\omega(x)} \frac{\partial^2 y}{\partial x^2} = a_n \frac{\partial^2 y}{\partial x^2} \tag{7.8}$$

where y = displacement of the string
T = tension in the string
g = gravitational constant
x = distance along the equilibrium position of the string
$\omega(x)$ = distribution of weight per unit length of the
string as a function of x
t = time
a_n depends upon the particular position of x_n along the string

Vibrating Circular Shafts. An equation similar to Eq. 7.8 for torsionally vibrating circular shafts can be developed. This equation is

$$\frac{\rho}{g}\frac{\partial^2\theta}{\partial t^2} = E_s\frac{\partial^2\theta}{\partial x^2}$$

(7.9)

where θ = angular displacement in radians
g = gravitational constant
ρ = weight per unit volume
E_s = shear modulus of elasticity
x = distance along the center of the shaft
t = time

Vibrating Beams. The partial differential equation for a transversely vibrating beam is

$$\frac{Elg}{\rho A(x)}\frac{\partial^4 y}{\partial x^4} = -\frac{\partial^2 y}{\partial t^2}$$

(7.10)

where E = modulus of elasticity
I = moment of inertia of the cross section
g = gravitational constant
$A(x)$ = area of cross section as a function of x
ρ = weight per unit volume
y = displacement of the beam at any point
x = distance along the length of the undeflected beam
t = time

Heat Conduction. The equation for three-dimensional heat flow through a homogeneous conducting material is

$$\frac{\partial\mu}{\partial t} = \frac{k}{c\gamma}\left(\frac{\partial^2\mu}{\partial x^2} + \frac{\partial^2\mu}{\partial y^2} + \frac{\partial^2\mu}{\partial z^2}\right)$$

(7.11)

which for one-dimensional flow reduces to

$$\frac{\partial\mu}{\partial t} = \frac{k}{c\gamma}\frac{\partial^2\mu}{\partial x^2}$$

(7.12)

where μ = temperature
x = distance in the direction of flow
k = thermal conductivity
c = specific heat
γ = density
t = time

Electrical Transmission Line. Two equations which describe the behavior of electrical transmission lines are

$$\frac{\partial^2 e}{\partial x^2} = LC\frac{\partial^2 e}{\partial t^2} + (GL + RC)\frac{\partial e}{\partial t} + RGe$$

(7.13)

and

$$\frac{\partial^2 i}{\partial x^2} = LC\frac{\partial^2 i}{\partial t^2} + (GL + RC)\frac{\partial i}{\partial t} + RGi \tag{7.14}$$

where
$x =$ distance measured from the sending end of the line
$e =$ voltage at any point along the line as function of time
$i =$ current at any point along the line as a function of time
$R =$ resistance per unit length of line
$G =$ shunt conductance per unit length of line
$L =$ inductance per unit length of line
$C =$ shunt capacitance per unit length of line

In Eqs. 7.13 and 7.14, e and i are functions of both time and distance from the sending end. This is also true of these variables in Eqs. 7.15 and 7.16. Equations 7.13 and 7.14 reduce to Eqs. 7.15 and 7.16 if the inductance and shunt conductance are negligible.

$$\frac{\partial^2 e}{\partial x^2} = RC\frac{\partial e}{\partial t} \tag{7.15}$$

$$\frac{\partial^2 i}{\partial x^2} = RC\frac{\partial i}{\partial t} \tag{7.16}$$

Mathematically, Eqs. 7.15 and 7.16 are equivalent to Eq. 7.12.

7.4 A Vibrating String

Equation 7.8 describes in partial differential equation form the behavior of a stretched vibrating string. In this form the system *cannot* be simulated on the electronic analog computer. The equation must be transformed in order that this equipment can be used. Equation 7.5 can be substituted into Eq. 7.8 to give

$$\frac{\partial^2 y_n}{\partial t^2} = \frac{a_n}{\Delta x^2}(y_{n+1} - 2y_n + y_{n-1}) \tag{7.17}$$

Let us consider the application of Eq. 7.17 to the vibrating string shown in Fig. 7.2. This string is fixed at both ends. Suppose we designate one end of this string

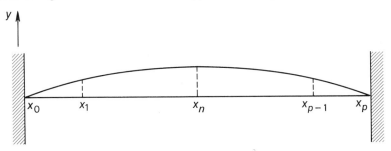

Figure 7.2 *A vibrating string.*

x_0 and the other end x_p. The point x_n is any arbitrary point between x_0 and x_p. If we consider the element of string at a particular location such as at location x_n, the partial differential equation of Eq. 7.17 can then be written as a total differential equation since the displacement of this particular element of string is a function of time only. This is expressed in Eq. 7.18.

$$\frac{d^2 y_n}{dt^2} = \frac{a_n}{\Delta x^2}(y_{n+1} - 2y_n + y_{n-1}) \tag{7.18}$$

The particular string being considered is fixed at both ends and this means that y_0 and y_p are zero at all times. If we write an equation for location x_1 similar to Eq. 7.18 we get

$$\frac{d^2 y_1}{dt^2} = \frac{a_1}{\Delta x^2}(y_2 - 2y_1 + y_0) \tag{7.19}$$

But y_0 is zero, and hence Eq. 7.19 reduces to

$$\frac{d^2 y_1}{dt^2} = \frac{a_1}{\Delta x^2}(y_2 - 2y_1) \tag{7.20}$$

Similarly, at location x_{p-1}, the equation is

$$\frac{d^2 y_{p-1}}{dt^2} = \frac{a_{p-1}}{\Delta x^2}(-2y_{p-1} + y_{p-2}) \tag{7.21}$$

Let us now consider the particular vibrating string of Fig. 7.3. This string is fixed at both ends and is divided into six equal parts, as shown. We may write equations similar to Eq. 7.19 at locations x_1, x_2, x_3, x_4, and x_5.

$$\frac{d^2 y_1}{dt^2} = \frac{a_1}{\Delta x^2}(y_2 - 2y_1) \tag{7.22}$$

$$\frac{d^2 y_2}{dt^2} = \frac{a_2}{\Delta x^2}(y_3 - 2y_2 + y_1) \tag{7.23}$$

$$\frac{d^2 y_3}{dt^2} = \frac{a_3}{\Delta x^2}(y_4 - 2y_3 + y_2) \tag{7.24}$$

$$\frac{d^2 y_4}{dt^2} = \frac{a_4}{\Delta x^2}(y_5 - 2y_4 + y_3) \tag{7.25}$$

$$\frac{d^2 y_5}{dt^2} = \frac{a_5}{\Delta x^2}(-2y_5 + y_4) \tag{7.26}$$

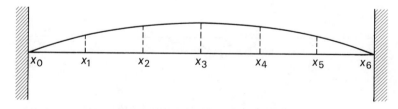

Figure 7.3 *A particular vibrating string.*

An examination of Eqs. 7.22 to 7.26 inclusive shows them to be linear, ordinary, second-order differential equations with constant coefficients. In previous chapters, we have developed methods whereby simultaneous equations such as these can be solved on the electronic analog computer. Figure 7.4 shows a computer setup for solving these equations.

As with other computer solutions, the initial conditions must be specified to obtain a particular solution. Let us assume that the string of Fig. 7.3 is initially

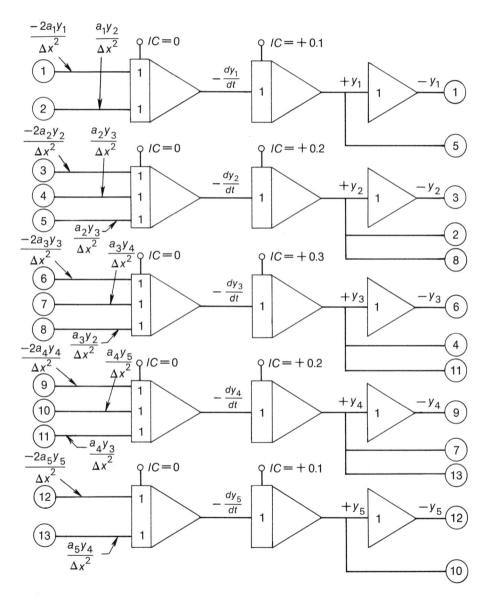

Figure 7.4 *A computer diagram for the vibrating string solution.*

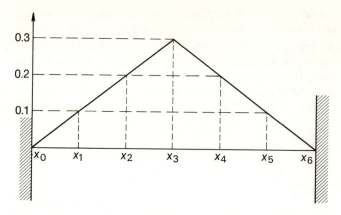

Figure 7.5 *The initial deflection of the vibrating string.*

displaced to have the shape shown in Fig. 7.5. We also assume that the string is released from this deflected position with zero initial velocity. We can see from Fig. 7.5 that the initial displacements are

$$y_1(0) = 0.1$$
$$y_2(0) = 0.2$$
$$y_3(0) = 0.3 \qquad\qquad (7.27)$$
$$y_4(0) = 0.2$$
$$y_5(0) = 0.1$$

The initial conditions of Fig. 7.4 are set in accordance with this example.

EXERCISES

1. Verify Eqs. 7.22–7.26 inclusive.
2. Verify the initial conditions shown in Fig. 7.4.
3. Figure 7.6 shows a string similar to that of Fig. 7.3 except that in this case one end is free and is given a displacement such that $y_6 = 0.3 \sin 2t$. Devise a computer diagram similar to that of Fig. 7.4. Assume the initial position to be that shown in Fig. 7.6. Specify all initial conditions. The length of the string is to be divided into six equal parts, as before.

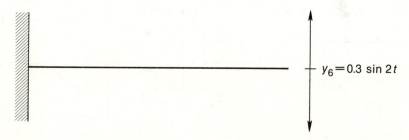

Figure 7.6 *Initial position of a vibrating string with one end fixed.*

138 *Analog Simulation Involving Partial Differential Equations*

4. Repeat Exercise 3 for the initial displacement shown in Fig. 7.7, and with y_6 constrained to move such that $y_6 = 3 \cos 2t$.

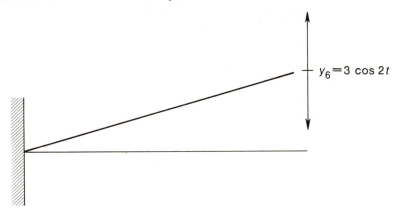

$y_6 = 3 \cos 2t$

Figure 7.7 *Another vibrating string.*

5. Repeat Exercise 3 for the string whose initial position is shown in Fig. 7.8. The initial velocity is zero.

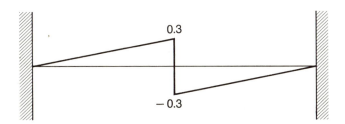

0.3

− 0.3

Figure 7.8 *Initial displacement of a string.*

6. Equation 7.9 describes the behavior of a torsionally vibrating circular shaft fixed at both ends. Devise computer diagrams for torsionally vibrating shafts having initial displacements, velocities, and end conditions analogous to those for vibrating strings shown in Figs. 7.5–7.8. Assume the shaft to be divided into six equal parts and assume the initial velocity to be zero in all cases.
7. Repeat Exercise 6 for transversely vibrating beams as described by Eq. 7.10.
8. Equation 7.12 describes the unidirectional flow of heat through a continuous homogeneous solid conductor.
   (a) Write the difference-differential equations for heat flow through a conductor between two infinite blocks. (See Fig. 7.9.) The two blocks have constant temperatures T_a and T_b, respectively. Use six points x_0, x_1, x_2, x_3, x_4, x_5 on which to base your equations. Assume an initial uniform temperature T_c throughout the conductor.
   (b) Draw a diagram similar to Fig. 7.4 for this heat flow problem.

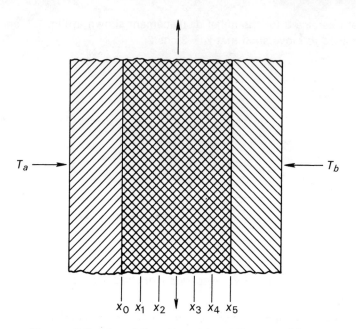

Figure 7.9 *A unidirectional heat flow problem.*

9. How would one write difference-differential equations
   (a) For a two-dimensional heat flow problem?
   (b) For a three-dimensional heat flow problem?
   (c) How would the boundary and initial conditions be fixed in the computer?

8

State Variable Approach
to System Simulation

8.1 Introduction

Systems analysts and designers often use computer simulation as a tool in their work and they are also concerned with state variable theory. A recent simulation technique that has proved useful to them in their problems is termed, quite reasonably, the *state variable approach*. Because there is this common area of application, it should not be surprising to find that state variable techniques have considerable utility in computer simulation studies. It is, therefore, advantageous for us to investigate how state variable concepts can be used in simulation applications.

A complete discussion of all of the concepts of state variable theory is beyond the scope of an introductory presentation on computer simulation such as this. Furthermore, it is unnecessary for us to treat the subject exhaustively, since not all of the ideas of state variable theory are applicable in computer simulation. We shall extract the ideas that are useful to us and use them without any attempt to present the more sophisticated concepts.

8.2   The State Variable Defined

The state of a system is so fundamental that it is difficult to define precisely. One way of getting a better feeling for the meaning of the state of a system is to think in terms of synonyms such as the instantaneous condition of the system, or the behavior of the system. As these synonyms imply, the state or condition or behavior of the system changes with respect to some independent variable which is usually time. What one tries to do, when using state variables, is to find a set (preferably a minimum set) of variables which describes the present state of the system, and which also allows one to use the past history and present state to determine the future state. The variables in such a set are called *state variables*. Often one will find that the state variables for a particular system do not form a unique set, but rather that several arbitrarily chosen sets can be found. If a set of state variables is properly chosen, however, it contains sufficient information to completely describe the transient behavior of the system being studied. In many instances the proper set of state variables occurs quite naturally as one considers the various aspects of the system which are to be characterized. We will find little difficulty in determining the proper state variables for the systems we will be studying. A general procedure for making this determination will be stated.

We have indicated several times, in earlier chapters, that the behavior of most systems encountered by engineers can be described by one or more low-order differential equations or transfer functions. Frequently these equations or transfer functions of low order can be combined so as to express the same information in a smaller number of higher-order equations or transfer functions. Although it may provide an interesting exercise in mathematical manipulation, it is not necessary, for simulation studies, to make such combinations. As we have observed, it is possible to accomplish computer simulation by working directly with the unmodified equations or transfer functions. Attractive as this procedure may be, the unmodified system equations or transfer functions frequently cause each simulation study to be unique. The state variable approach provides a more nearly uniform and foolproof procedure for simulation studies.

8.3   State Equations and Block Diagrams

Rather than combining lower-order transfer functions or equations to obtain higher-order ones, the state variable approach proceeds in quite the opposite direction. Instead of a smaller number of higher-order forms, the state variable approach uses a larger number of first-order functions or equations. The first-order forms can be programmed directly for simulation on the analog computer. When expressed in matrix form, they can be solved using the digital computer.

Returning again to the block diagrams of Chapter 1, we find in them a systematic way of obtaining the state equations of a system. The blocks presented there were of five types — integrators, adders, multipliers, sign changers, and function generators. These are pictured in Table 8.1.

It is sometimes difficult to write state equations for complex systems. The use of block diagrams, as described below, makes writing them easier.

Table 8.1

Functional Blocks

Type	Symbol[1]	Describing Equation
Adder	x_1 ... x_n → [+] → y	$y = x_1 + \cdots + x_n$
Multiplier	x_1, x_2 → [×] → y	$y = x_1 x_2$
Integrator	x → [∫] → y	$y = \int x\, dt$
Sign Changer	x → [SC] → y	$y = -x$
Function Generator	x → [FG] → y	$y = f(x)$

[1] The x's may be constants or variables.

8.4 The Generalized Differential Equation

Suppose we are given a system described in either differential equation form or in transfer function form. How are the state equations best obtained and how can these be used to simulate the given system? We now outline the procedure, keeping in mind the ideas of Chapter 1 and the functional blocks of Table 8.1.

Let us first begin with the assumption that the system behavior is described by one or more differential equations. The general nth-order differential equation can be written as

$$\frac{d^n x}{dt^n} + a_{n-1}(t)\frac{d^{n-1}x}{dt^{n-1}} + a_{n-2}(t)\frac{d^{n-2}x}{dt^{n-2}} + \cdots + a_1(t)\frac{dx}{dt} + a_0(t)x = F \qquad (8.1)$$

The method introduced in Chapter 1 suggested the following steps:
(1) Solve for the highest-ordered derivative of the dependent variable $d^n x/dt^n$.
(2) Assume that this derivative exists as the output of an adder, and pass it successively through n integrators where it is integrated n times with respect to t, the independent variable. The output of each integrator is a successively lower-ordered derivative of the dependent variable.

(3) The integrator outputs are multiplied by the appropriate coefficients, $a_i(t)$, to generate the terms comprising $d^n x/dt^n$.

(4) Sign changes are accomplished where needed. These can be included in step 3 if desired.

(5) The resulting terms are added as required to generate $d^n x/dt^n$ whose existence was assumed in step 2.

The output of each integrator in the above procedure is a state variable. From these state variables, state equations (first-order differential equations) can be written and, using these state equations, the system can be simulated on an analog computer.

Completion of the generalized example will help to clarify the procedure. Solving Eq. 8.1 for $d^n x/dt^n$ gives

$$\frac{d^n x}{dt^n} = F - a_{n-1}(t)\frac{d^{n-1}x}{dt^{n-1}} - a_{n-2}\frac{d^{n-2}x}{dt^{n-2}} - \cdots - a_1(t)\frac{dx}{dt} - a_0(t)x \qquad (8.2)$$

Figure 8.1 shows a block diagram for this generalized nth-order system. This block diagram was developed using the procedure outlined above.

The output of each integrator in Fig. 8.1 is defined and labeled as a state variable X_i. The integrator inputs are the derivatives of the integrator outputs so that

$$\frac{dX_1}{dt} = X_2$$

$$\frac{dX_2}{dt} = X_3$$

$$\vdots \qquad\qquad\qquad (8.3)$$

$$\frac{dX_{n-1}}{dt} = X_n$$

$$\frac{dX_n}{dt} = F - a_0(t)X_1 - a_1(t)X - a_{n-2}X_{n-1} - a_{n-1}(t)X_n$$

Equations 8.3 are a set of n first-order differential equations which is equivalent to Eq. 8.1. These are state equations for whatever system is described by Eq. 8.1.

It is an easily verified fact that the number of energy storage regions in a system is precisely the same as the order of the single independent equation which describes the system behavior. Consider the system of Fig. 4.27. It has two energy storage regions—the mass and the spring. Equation 4.33 describes the behavior of the system; note that it is a second-order equation. Figure 2.8 has three energy storage regions—the capacitor and the two inductors. Two independent third-order equations were developed to describe different aspects of this system (Eqs. 2.76 and 2.77). Each of the other systems that have been described in earlier chapters could be similarly examined.

If an nth-order differential equation can be expressed as n first-order differential equations, and if the behavior of a system of n energy storage regions can be expressed as an nth-order differential equation, it follows that the behavior of this system can be described by n first-order differential equations. Hence, we now have a procedure whereby we can check to see if we have the proper number of

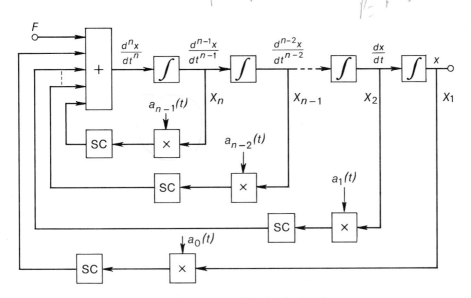

Figure 8.1 *A generalized block diagram.*

first-order equations. Simply check that the number of energy storage regions and the number of first-order equations are the same.

8.5 State Equations in Simulation

To examine how this procedure works in analog computer programming, consider the system of Fig. 4.27. With numerical values assigned to the parameters, we have Eq. 4.33 which is repeated here for convenience as Eq. 8.4.

$$2\frac{d^2x}{dt^2} + \frac{dx}{dt} + 8x = 10 \sin 2t \tag{8.4}$$

Solving for the highest-ordered derivative gives

$$\frac{d^2x}{dt^2} = 5 \sin 2t - 0.5\frac{dx}{dt} - 4x \tag{8.5}$$

The block diagram of Fig. 8.2 would perform the operations required by Eq. 8.5. Labeling the integrator outputs as state variables X_1 and X_2, we can see that Eqs. 8.6 apply.

$$\frac{dX_1}{dt} = X_2$$

$$\frac{dX_2}{dt} = 5 \sin 2t - 0.5X_2 - 4X_1 \tag{8.6}$$

These two coupled first-order equations are the state equations for the system of Fig. 4.27. If an analog computer simulator is constructed based on Eqs. 8.6,

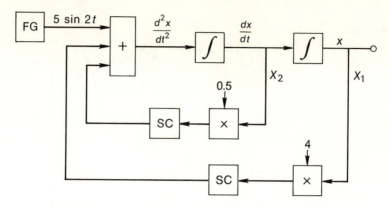

Figure 8.2 *A block diagram for the system of Fig. 4.27.*

Fig. 8.3 results. A rearrangement of the positions of the components in Fig. 8.3 gives Fig. 8.4, which is identical with Fig. 4.28, except for amplifier output labels.

We can conclude that, at least in this instance, starting with the second-order differential equation, Eq. 8.4, or with the two first-order state equations, Eqs. 8.6, yields the same final result. The conclusion is broader in scope than this. In general, this procedure can be applied to all systems that can be described in the form of Eq. 8.1.

Since the choice of state variables is not unique, neither are the state equations nor the analog computer simulator based on them. One might find, therefore, that a system simulator based on the state variable approach is quite different than the

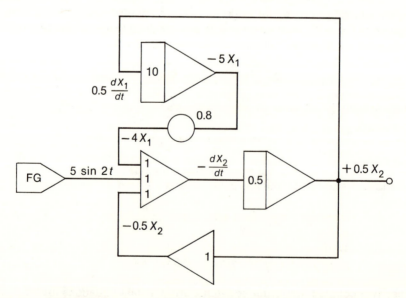

Figure 8.3 *An analog simulator based on Eqs. 8.6.*

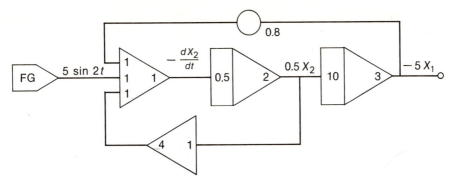

Figure 8.4 *A rearrangement of Fig. 8.3.*

simulator based on the conventional higher-order differential equation approach. If properly done, both should have the same functional behavior, however.

8.6 Advantages of State Variable Programming

One might reasonably wonder what advantages accrue from this state variable approach, if any. The advantages are subtle and will only be appreciated after some experience has been gained using the method. They can be summarized as follows:

(1) A system of n coupled first-order equations is generally easier to simulate than one nth-order equation.
(2) All states—input, intermediate, and output—are expressly formed and available for observation.
(3) The block diagram approach systematizes and simplifies the work of formulating the state equations. This is particularly useful when nonlinear and time varying situations are encountered.
(4) Systems with more than one input or output are easily included in the method.
(5) The problem of scaling is simpler because only first-order equations are involved.

8.7 Transfer Functions and State Variables

The procedure outlined above is not confined to situations where system behavior is expressed solely in differential equation form. This is fortunate because the more common situation encountered by a design engineer is to have a system specified in terms of transfer functions or perhaps a combination of differential equations, transfer functions, and experimental data.

There are two types of transfer functions usually encountered in engineering systems design or analysis. These are of the form shown in Eq. 8.7 where the denominator only is a polynomial in s,

$$\frac{X_{out}}{X_{in}} = \frac{K}{s^n + b_{n-1}s^{n-1} + b_{n-2}s^{n-2} + \cdots + b_1 s + b_0} \tag{8.7}$$

or of the form shown in Eq. 8.8, where both the numerator and denominator of the transfer function are polynomials in s. For physically realizable systems, $m \le n$.

$$\frac{X_{out}}{X_{in}} = \frac{s^m + a_{m-1}s^{m-1} + a_{m-2}s^{m-2} + \cdots + a_1 s + a_0}{s^n + b_{n-1}s^n + b_{n-2}s^{n-2} + \cdots + b_1 s + b_0} \tag{8.8}$$

For a system with zero initial conditions, the LaPlace operator s^i can be considered to be analogous to d^i/dt^i in the time domain as shown in Eq. 8.9.

$$s^i = \frac{d^n}{dt^n} \tag{8.9}$$

If Eq. 8.7 is cross multiplied, we obtain

$$KX_{in} = (s^n + b_{n-1}s^{n-1} + b_{n-2}s^{n-2} + \cdots + b_1 s + b_0)X_{out} \tag{8.10}$$

and if Eq. 8.9 is used to convert Eq. 8.10 to the time domain, the result is

$$KX_{in} = \frac{d^n X_{out}}{dt^n} + b_{n-1}\frac{d^{n-1}X_{out}}{dt^{n-1}} + b_{n-2}\frac{d^{n-2}X_{out}}{dt^{n-2}} + \cdots + b_1\frac{dX_{out}}{dt} + b_0 \tag{8.11}$$

Equation 8.11 is a typical nth-order differential equation similar to Eq. 8.1, and the techniques presented earlier will suffice to simulate it on an analog computer.

If Eq. 8.8 is rearranged, it can be written as

$$\frac{X_{out}}{s^m + a_{m-1}s^{m-1} + a_{m-2}s^{m-2} + \cdots + a_1 s_1 + a_0} = Q$$

$$\frac{X_{in}}{s^n + b_{n-1}s^{n-1} + b_{n-2}s^{n-2} + \cdots + b_1 s_1 + b_0} = Q \tag{8.12}$$

where Q is a dummy variable in s. Equation 8.12 can be written as two equations— Eq. 8.13 and Eq. 8.14.

$$X_{out} = Q(s^m + a_{m-1}s^{m-1} + a_{m-2}s^{m-2} + \cdots + a_1 s + a_0) \tag{8.13}$$

$$X_{in} = Q(s^n + b_{n-1}s^{n-1} + b_{n-2}s^{n-2} + \cdots + b_1 s + b_0) \tag{8.14}$$

Since $n \ge m$ for physically realizable systems, it follows that if the state variables in Eq. 8.14 are represented in a block diagram, all of the necessary state variables for representing Eq. 8.13 will also be available. Such a block diagram is shown in Fig. 8.5. Integration is shown here by its equivalent, $1/s$, and it is assumed that $m = n - 1$.

The output of each integrator in Fig. 8.5 is labeled with a state variable X_k. Using these variables, the state equations can be written as

$$\frac{dX_1}{dt} = X_2$$

$$\frac{dX_2}{dt} = X_3$$

$$\vdots$$

$$\frac{dX_{n-2}}{dt} = X_{n-1} \tag{8.15}$$

$$\frac{dX_{n-1}}{dt} = X_n$$

$$\frac{dX_n}{dt} = X_{in} - b_{n-1}X_n - b_{n-2}X_{n-1} - \cdots - b_1X_2 - b_0X_1$$

$$X_{out} = X_n + a_{m-1}X_{n-1} + \cdots + a_1X_2 + a_0X_1$$

and these equations could now be used as a basis for assembling an analog computer simulator.

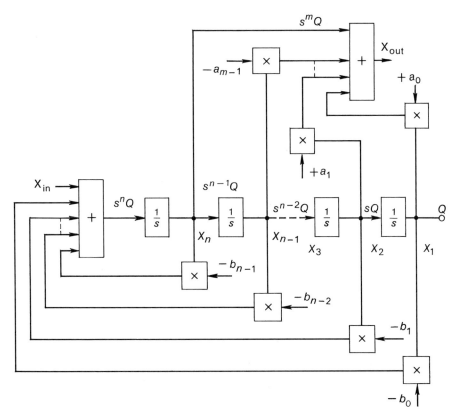

Figure 8.5 *A block diagram representation of Eq. 8.13.*

8.8 Simulating a Particular System

Let us work out an example to illustrate the use of state variables and state equations when simulating systems whose behavior is described in transfer function form.

In Chapter 6, we discussed the simulation of a feedback control system. This system was described in terms of its transfer functions, but no attempt was made to derive them. Typical transfer functions were introduced and corresponding analog computer simulators were developed. Table 8.2 shows these same transfer functions and the corresponding block diagrams.

Figure 8.6 is a diagram of the feedback control system which was discussed in Chapter 6. The error sensor in this system consists of two potentiometers which are energized from a common dc source. One of these potentiometers is connected to the input shaft and senses its position. The other is connected to the output shaft and likewise senses the position of that shaft. Whenever a difference exists between the input shaft position X_1 and the output shaft position X_3, an error voltage is produced whose magnitude is proportional to the difference between X_1 and X_3 and its polarity indicates whether X_1 is more clockwise or more counterclockwise than X_3. This error voltage is supplied to the amplifier input terminals. The error signal is amplified by the amplifier producing a proportional output voltage that is applied to the field circuit of a dc generator where it causes field current to flow. A resulting voltage is thus generated by the generator that is proportional to the field current. This generated voltage causes current to flow in the

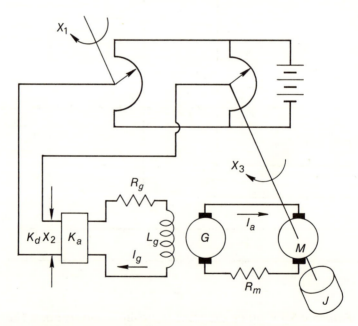

Figure 8.6 *An elementary positioning system.*

Table 8.2

Transfer Function Block Diagrams

Type	Block Diagrams
$\dfrac{X_{out}}{X_{in}} = \dfrac{A}{s}$	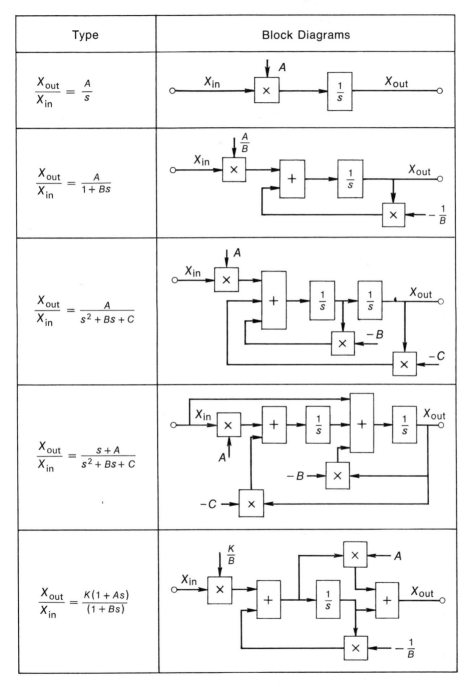
$\dfrac{X_{out}}{X_{in}} = \dfrac{A}{1+Bs}$	
$\dfrac{X_{out}}{X_{in}} = \dfrac{A}{s^2+Bs+C}$	
$\dfrac{X_{out}}{X_{in}} = \dfrac{s+A}{s^2+Bs+C}$	
$\dfrac{X_{out}}{X_{in}} = \dfrac{K(1+As)}{(1+Bs)}$	

motor armature windings which, in turn, produces torque and rotates X_3 in such a direction to cause it to more nearly agree with X_1. There are time delays in the generator field circuit and in the mechanical behavior of the motor and load which prevent instantaneous response and may cause oscillations.

The numerical values of the parameters of Fig. 8.6 are given in Table 8.3. These values were taken from an actual system.

Table 8.3

Control System Parameter Values

Symbol	Meaning	Value	Dimensions
K_d	Potentiometer constant	10	V/rad of error
K_a	Amplifier gain	100	V output/V input
R_g	Generator field resistance	100	Ω
L_g	Generator field inductance	1	H
K_g	Generator emf constant	24	V generated/amp of field current
R_m	Armature circuit resistance	0.5	Ω
K_m	Motor back emf constant	0.04	V/rad/sec
K_t	Motor torque constant	0.125	Lb-ft/amp of armature current
J	Output inertia	0.001	Slug-ft^2

The error signal is a voltage that is proportional to the difference between X_1 and X_3 as given in Eq. 8.16.

$$K_d X_2 = K_d(X_1 - X_3) \tag{8.16}$$

We observed in Chapter 6 that this system, with the numerical values of parameters given, would be unstable. To help correct this difficulty, a compensating or stabilizing network was proposed having the transfer function given in Eq. 8.17.

$$\text{transfer function} = \frac{1}{5}\left(\frac{1 + 0.1s}{1 + 0.02s}\right) \tag{8.17}$$

Not only must the control system designer determine the actual physical realization of the stabilizing network, but he must also determine its placement in the system. In theory, it can be placed anywhere between the output of the error sensor and the output of the control system. In practice, one is much more restricted as to where the stabilizing network is to be placed. We shall assume that a solution has been found that permits the network to be placed between the error sensor and the amplifier. This is a different location that was assumed in Chapter 6.

When the numerical values of Table 8.3 are used, the transfer function of the error sensor and compensating network becomes

$$\frac{\text{amplifier input}}{X_2} = \frac{K_d}{5}\left(\frac{1+0.1s}{1+0.02s}\right) = 2\left(\frac{1+0.1s}{1+0.02s}\right) \qquad (8.18)$$

Similarly, the transfer function of the amplifier and generator field circuit is

$$\frac{I_g}{\text{amplifier input}} = \frac{K_a/R_g}{1+(L_g/R_g)s} = \frac{1}{1+0.01s} \qquad (8.19)$$

Equation 8.20 gives the transfer function relating the output position X_3, and the generator field current.

$$\frac{X_3}{I_g} = \frac{K_g/K_m}{s[1+(JR_m/K_tK_m)s]} = \frac{600}{s(1+0.1s)} = \frac{6}{s}\left(\frac{100}{1+0.1s}\right) \qquad (8.20)$$

The composite transfer function relating the output shaft position X_3 and the error X_2 is obtained by combining Eqs. 8.18–8.20 to give Eq. 8.21.

$$\frac{X_3}{X_2} = \frac{1200(1+0.1s)}{s(1+0.01s)(1+0.02s)(1+0.1s)} \qquad (8.21)$$

Figure 8.7 shows a conventional block diagram for the system with the stabilizing network inserted based on the preceding discussion. From the block diagram of Fig. 8.7, the state variable block diagram of Fig. 8.8 is constructed.

From the state variable block diagram of Fig. 8.8, the state equations can be written as shown below. The reader should carefully observe the use of italicized and non-italicized symbols in these equations.

$$\frac{dX_1}{dt} = 1000X_2 - 10X_1$$

$$\frac{dX_2}{dt} = 6X_3$$

$$\frac{dX_3}{dt} = -100X_3 - 400X_4 + 1000X_1 - 1000X_1 \qquad (8.22)$$

$$\frac{dX_4}{dt} = -50X_4 + 100X_1 - 100X_1$$

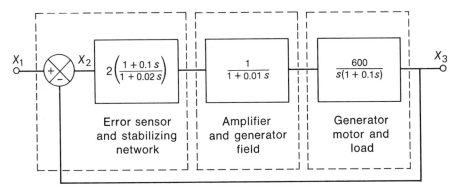

Figure 8.7 *A conventional block diagram for a feedback control system.*

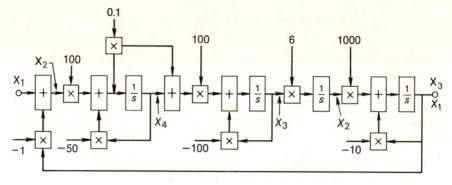

Figure 8.8 *The state variable block diagram.*

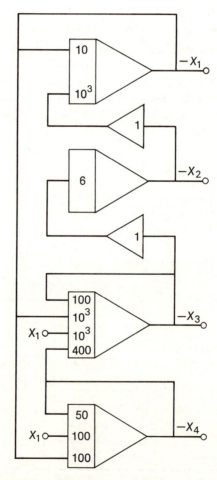

Figure 8.9 *A simulator based on Eqs. 8.22.*

The state equations, Eqs. 8.22, can now be used as a basis for programming an analog computer simulator. Such a simulator is illustrated in Figs. 8.9 and 8.10. Figure 8.9 shows a simulator without time scaling and Fig. 8.10 shows a simulator which has been slowed by a factor of 100.

8.9 Summary

The theory of state variables provides yet another approach to simulation of physical systems on the analog computer. Starting with either behavior-describing differential equations or transfer functions of higher order, the block diagram approach is a systematic procedure for developing state equations which are first-

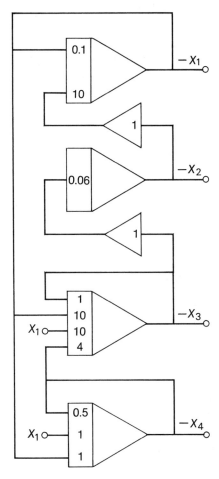

Figure 8.10 *The simulator of Fig. 8.9 which has been slowed by a factor of 100.*

order differential equations. These state equations can then be used as the basis of an analog computer simulator.

The method is straightforward and systematic. It has some subtle advantages over other methods, although there is considerable personal preference in choosing the method to be used.

One advantage of the state variable method is that it conveniently allows the simulation of systems whose behavior is partly described by transfer functions and partly described by differential equations. Since this situation is frequently encountered, the technique has considerable practical value.

EXERCISES

Note: Many of the exercises of Chapters 4 and 6 can be used as exercises to be programmed using the state variable approach. Some additional exercises are also included here.

1. A uniform bar 5 ft long is supported at its ends on springs as shown in Fig. 8.11. The bar weighs 15 lb/ft, $K_1 = 180$ lb/ft, and $K_2 = 280$ lb/ft. Motion is constrained so that the center of the bar can only move vertically. The center of the bar can translate in the vertical direction, and the bar can rotate about its center so as to give two degrees of freedom.

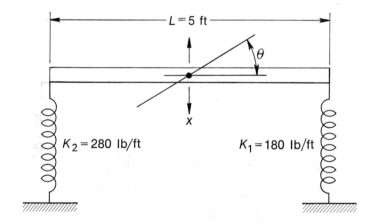

Figure 8.11

(a) Show that the equations of motion can be written as follows if θ is small so that $\sin \theta \approx \theta$:

$$\frac{w}{g}\frac{d^2x}{dt^2} = -(K_1 + K_2)x - \frac{L(K_1 - K_2)\theta}{2}$$

and

$$\frac{w}{g}\frac{L^2}{12}\frac{d^2x}{dt^2} = -\frac{L(K_1 - K_2)x}{2} - \frac{L^2(K_1 + K_2)\theta}{4}$$

(b) Program an EAC using the state variable approach to simulate this system. Assume a reference voltage of 10 V.

(c) Use the EAC to find x and θ as functions of time.

2. Rework Exercise 1 without the restriction that $\sin \theta \approx \theta$.

3. Program an EAC having a reference voltage of 100 V using the state variable approach to simulate the mechanical system shown in Fig. 8.12. Use the MKS system of units and the following set of values:

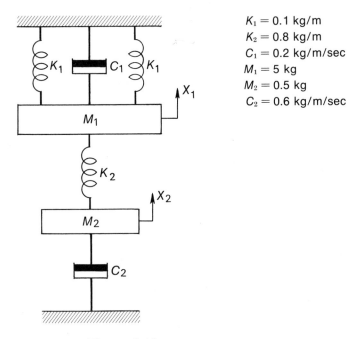

$K_1 = 0.1$ kg/m
$K_2 = 0.8$ kg/m
$C_1 = 0.2$ kg/m/sec
$M_1 = 5$ kg
$M_2 = 0.5$ kg
$C_2 = 0.6$ kg/m/sec

Figure 8.12

4. When a coil spring is stretched it tends to unwind; when it is twisted, it tends to shorten or lengthen. These characteristics allow the construction of a "tuned pendulum," as shown in Fig. 8.13. If such a device is given some initial displacement in its translational mode and released, it will begin to oscillate in an up-and-down manner. The coupling created by the previously mentioned characteristics will impart a periodic rotational torque to the pendulum and, if it is tuned properly, the pendulum will sooner or later be oscillating in the rotational mode only without any translational oscillations. This, however, creates periodic translational forces, and there is again a transfer back to the translational mode. This transfer back and forth between the two modes of oscillation continues until the original energy in the system is dissipated. The pendulum

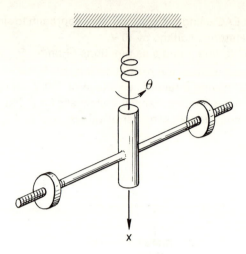

Figure 8.13

is tuned by rotating the discs on their threaded shafts causing them to move radially outward or inward until the rotational frequency of oscillation equals the translational frequency.

In the system shown, the following constants apply:

$$M = J = 1$$
$$K_x = K_\theta = 1000$$
$$K_m = 100$$

giving rise to the following equations:

$$M\frac{d^2x}{dt^2} + K_x x - K_m\theta = 0$$

$$J\frac{d^2\theta}{dt^2} + K_\theta\theta - K_m x = 0$$

or

$$\frac{d^2x}{dt^2} + 1000\,x - 100\,\theta = 0$$

$$\frac{d^2\theta}{dt^2} + 1000\,\theta - 100\,x = 0$$

Assume $x(0) = 1$, and

$$\frac{dx}{dt}(0) = \frac{d\theta}{dt}(0) = \theta(0) = 0$$

Use the state variable approach to program an EAC to simulate the tuned pendulum. Use a reference voltage of 10 V.

158   *State Variable Approach to System Simulation*

5. Figure 8.14 shows a servomechanism block diagram with a lead network compensator.

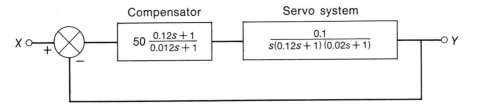

Figure 8.14

Use the state variable approach to program an EAC to simulate this servo-mechanism. Use a reference voltage of 100 V.

6. Use the state variable approach to program an EAC to simulate the servo system shown in Fig. 8.15. Assume a reference voltage of 10 V. Study the behavior of the system for a variety of inputs X.

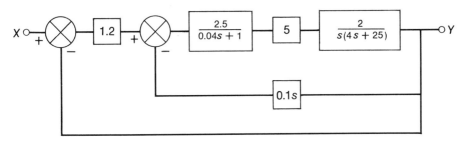

Figure 8.15

Digital Computer Simulation

9.1 Introduction

The emphasis of our study now changes abruptly from analog computer simulation to digital computer simulation. Although the change is abrupt, it is not discontinuous because much of what was done in our earlier studies will carry over and find application in this new subject matter. Of course, the basic philosophy is different, and so are the details of implementation, but many of the concepts and ideas gained from earlier chapters on analog computer simulation find useful application in this new area of study.

9.2 Why Digital Computer Simulation?

The parallel behavior of the analog computer makes it a "natural" tool for the simulation of continuous physical systems. Parallel behavior, as used here, means that, when simulating on the analog computer, the various computing operations, such as addition, integration, and multiplication, all occur simultaneously in the computer as they do in the physical system being studied. The useful analogous signals in the analog computer are time varying voltages, which change continuously. This behavior corresponds quite naturally with the behavior of physical systems in which other time varying quantities also change continuously. In some instances, systems are encountered in which the physical quantities vary discretely rather than continuously. The simulation of these discretely changing systems will not be treated here.

The behavior of a continuously varying physical system is commonly described by a system of one or more differential equations. We have seen that the ease with which such systems can be simulated on the analog computer, along with the ease with which many types of nonlinearities and nonanalytic functions can be incorporated into the simulation, make the analog computer a very powerful and useful simulation tool.

The digital computer is inherently a device which changes in discrete steps from one state to another. One might justifiably wonder why the discrete state digital computer should even be considered as a simulator of continuous systems. Why not always use the analog computer for such simulations considering that it is a "natural" kind of device to use? There are many subtle reasons involving such things as accuracy, convenience, availability, and documentation. The initial motivation for considering the digital computer for this kind of work was one of accuracy. By nature, the analog computer does not produce results that are accurate to many significant figures. The digital computer on the other hand easily produces highly accurate results.

Although improved accuracy was perhaps the initial motivation for trying digital simulation, other unsuspected advantages were also realized. Ease of programming is an obvious advantage that one using digital simulation becomes aware of immediately. A more subtle advantage occurs almost automatically. That is the complete documentation of both program and results.

The advent of digital simulation did not produce all of these advantages at once. Special simulation languages had to be conceived and developed before the potential of digital simulation could be fully realized.

9.3 Which Is Faster—Analog or Digital?

It might come as somewhat of a surprise to digital computer users to learn that the digital computer is a much *slower* simulator than is the analog computer. One ordinarily thinks of the digital computer as a high-speed device, which it truly is when performing single arithmetic operations such as addition or multiplication. A typical time for addition of two numbers, each containing several significant digits, in a modern digital machine is of the order of one microsecond, and multiplication requires only slightly longer. This certainly sounds quite fast! In simulation studies, however, many millions of such sequential operations often must be performed, and this can take considerable time. The sequential nature of the digital computer requires that all operations are done one at a time in sequence by the arithmetic unit of the computer, rather than simultaneously as in the analog computer. Given enough time, the digital computer can produce results of almost any desired accuracy but often the price is high. All things being considered, it is quite common for an analog computer solution to be several orders of magnitude faster and less costly than the corresponding digital computer solution.

In spite of the above drawbacks, the digital computer is still a powerful simulation tool for studying continuous systems. Furthermore, the advantages to be realized from digital computer simulation somewhat offset the disadvantages of relatively slow speed.

9.4   Other Attractions of Digital Simulation

There are a number of attractive features other than accuracy which make the digital computer desirable as a simulator. One of these is accessibility. The extreme popularity of digital computers during recent years has caused the number of installations to increase rapidly. The plain fact is that digital computers are ordinarily much more readily available than are analog computers. This alone makes digital computer simulation desirable. Furthermore, the programming of the digital computer, which formerly required the services of skilled programmers, has been greatly simplified by the development of problem oriented simulation languages. The existence and availability of these languages now makes it possible for persons to program quite sophisticated simulations with a modest amount of training and experience.

The most commonly used algebraic digital computer programming language for solving engineering problems is FORTRAN, of which there exist several versions. When programming a digital computer using FORTRAN, one finds that, although the basic language is not difficult to learn, considerable skill is needed to make full use of its capabilities and subtleties. To develop this skill requires time, effort, and experience, and only then does a user reach a level of ability where the language can be used to full advantage. Often, an engineer who is concerned with the engineering details of his problems is either unwilling or unable to devote the time and effort required to become a skilled digital computer programmer. If one tries to bypass doing his own programming by using a skilled programmer as an assistant, he often finds it quite frustrating to effectively communicate his thoughts to the assistant who must then in turn give them to the machine in such a way as to accomplish the desired results. A much better situation exists when the user is able to do his own programming. This is a practical approach when using one of the existing simulation languages.

One of the goals of the designers of these simulation languages was to make them simple enough so that, for the most part, they would be easy to learn and use. However, they also wanted them to have a degree of sophistication that would make them attractive and useful even to skilled programmers working on complex problems. Ideally, a simulation language should be as free as possible from bothersome restrictions and should contain adequate diagnostics to permit rapid debugging. It is also desirable that the language be based on a known algebraic language, or at least accept existing subprograms written in a known algebraic language. Many of these desirable features are realized in the languages existing today. The development of simulation languages is still being pursued and we expect that later languages will contain even more of the important features above.

We can better understand the present state of digital computer simulation by taking a brief look at the history of its development. The following account is not intended to be exhaustive, but rather includes only a selected number of simulation schemes to help the reader appreciate where digital simulation started and how it reached its present level.

9.5   Brief History of Digital Simulation

R. G. Selfridge, working on the IBM 701 at the U. S. Naval Ordnance Test Station, Inyokern, California, pioneered the development of digital simulation. Most of those who followed him devised titles or acronyms to identify their work; not so with Selfridge. His published account appeared in 1955, and even though it had no identifying name, it touched off a considerable effort in the development of digital simulation.

It must be remembered that the work by Selfridge preceded the development of algebraic languages such as FORTRAN. He managed, in spite of the difficulties of machine language programming and fixed-point arithmetic, to identify and implement many of the fundamental concepts of digital simulation as embodied in more recent simulation schemes.

California seemed to be the spawning ground for other early efforts in digital simulation. The second published account came in 1958 from H. F. Lesh at the Jet Propulsion Laboratory in Pasadena, California. He called his work Differential Equations Pseudo-code Interpreter, and gave it the abbreviation DEPI. This work was also done in machine language but this time on the Datatron 204—a decimal, fractional, fixed-point machine having a single index register. DEPI utilized a fourth-order Runge-Kutta integration procedure, and included some functional blocks not available in Selfridge's scheme.

ASTRAL (Analog Schematic Translator to Algebraic Language) also appeared in 1958, again in California. It was the work of M. L. Stein, J. Rose, and D. B. Parker working on the IBM 704 at Convair Astronautics. As a compiler, it accepted input statements which modeled an analog computer and produced a FORTRAN program which then was compiled and executed as any other FORTRAN program would be. The existence of the FORTRAN program as an intermediate step allowed modification of the program at this level. ASTRAL also provided for sorting and centralized integration. All of these features appeared again in later simulation schemes.

A parade of digital simulators proceeded after these leaders—DEPI-4 and DYANA (Dynamics Analyzer) in 1959, BLODI (Block Diagramed Compiler) and DYSAC (Digital Simulated Analog Computer) in 1961, DYNASAR (Dynamic Systems Analyzer) and PARTNER (Proof of Analog Results Through Numerically Equivalent Routine) in 1962.

A simulator which deserves special mention is DAS (Digital Analog Simulator), produced at the Martin Company in Orlando, Florida in 1963. Working with the IBM 7090, R. A. Gaskil, J. W. Harris, and A. L. McKnight developed DAS and provided the stimulation which ultimately resulted in MIDAS (Modified Integration Digital Analog Simulator) in 1963. DAS was a useful simulation language in its own right and must take a secondary place only because of the superior qualities of its descendant, MIDAS.

MIDAS was a landmark in digital simulation language development. Using the IBM 7094 at Wright–Patterson Air Base, R. T. Harnett, F. J. Sansom, and H. E. Petersen adopted the language of DAS, modified the integration scheme (thus the name), and independently incorporated many of the desirable features of other earlier languages. DAS used a rectangular integration process. MIDAS used a fifth-order predictor-corrector scheme to realize improved performance. MIDAS also included a sorting process similar to that of ASTRAL which determined the order of computation steps for proper processing. MIDAS also provided means whereby implicit equations could be solved. The success of MIDAS can be attributed to several factors — it provided sorting, it had a good integration scheme, it was written for the IBM 7090/94 which was in common use, a useful instruction manual was available, and the program was distributed free of cost to those who requested it.

PACTOLUS was developed in 1964 by R. D. Brennan for the IBM 1620 at San Jose, California. Its name is derived from Greek mythology. Midas was the king who was blessed by the gods with the gift that everything he touched would turn to gold. Unfortunately this included his food, and hence, the gift turned out to be a mixed blessing, to say the least. The story goes that Midas was told to bathe in the river Pactolus to wash away the curse which the blessing had become. In a corresponding vein, the simulation language MIDAS was also a mixed blessing. It had some very desirable features, but some undesirable ones also. Used with the 7090, it had to be handled on a closed shop basis. Analog users accustomed to open shop operation found this frustrating to say the least. PACTOLUS was an attempt to overcome the weaknesses of MIDAS. Being implemented for the small IBM 1620 allowed for open shop operation and direct interaction from the console. PACTOLUS proved to be a very useful tool for IBM 1620 users, and it was implemented on the IBM 7090 also. PACTOLUS provided the basis for the development of two other languages, DSL-90 and CSMP.

MIMIC, the successor of MIDAS, was the creation of somewhat the same team as the one that produced MIDAS. Working again at Wright–Patterson Air Force Base on the 7094, H. E. Petersen, F. J. Sansom, and L. M. Warshawsky issued the first version of MIMIC in 1965. The name MIMIC has no special meaning except that the language mimics MIDAS in many ways. As with MIDAS, MIMIC was issued to any who requested it and an excellent instruction manual was available. An improved version of MIMIC was issued in 1967. MIMIC utilizes a variable step size

Runge-Kutta integration scheme for improved performance. It has been implemented on machines other than the IBM 7090/94. In Chapter 10, we look at MIMIC in more detail.

DSL-90 (Digital Simulation Language for the 7090 class machines) was produced at IBM in San Jose, California by W. M. Lyn and D. G. Wyman in 1965 for the 7090/94 computers. DSL-90 accepts problem descriptions either in the block notation of the analog computer or as a system of differential equations. DSL-90 is a translator which converts the DSL-90 statements to a FORTRAN IV subroutine which is compiled and executed with a selected integration routine to accomplish the desired simulation. Four different integration schemes are possible. Format free input and output of data and system parameters and constants is provided.

CSMP (Continuous System Modeling Program) was developed at IBM in 1967 by R. D. Brennan. There are two versions, one for the IBM 1130 and one for the IBM 360 series of machines. CSMP is an adaptation of PACTOLUS which also incorporates the features of DSL-90 and adds some of its own. It permits the entering of statements from either punched cards or the console.

A recent attempt has been made to standardize on a single simulation language. The Simulation Softwave Committee of Simulation Councils, Inc., has introduced specifications for a new digital computer simulation language called Continuous System Simulation Language (CSSL). CSSL has been implemented for several types of existing computers and will probably be implemented for many more. CSSL is a problem oriented language for representing continuous dynamic systems that can be described by sets of ordinary differential equations. CSSL is an adjunct to Fortran IV and, in fact, since all of Fortran IV is available to the CSSL user, CSSL might be considered to be a superset of Fortran IV. It incorporates a macro-processor which effectively provides the user with a means of flexible expansion of the language. Chapter 11 is devoted to a deeper analysis of CSSL.

9.6   How Is Digital Simulation Accomplished?

The simulation of a physical system using a digital computer is somewhat dependent on the language that is employed in describing the system to the computer. Some simulation languages work only from differential equation descriptions of system behavior. Others use a block diagram description, while still others accept the system description as a number of interconnected transfer functions. A few simulation languages accept more than one kind of system description.

Regardless of the language that is used, however, it is necessary to somehow express the operations that must be performed, assign numerical values to constants and parameters, specify initial conditions or other boundary conditions, and indicate the form of the output which describes the results of the simulation study. In the chapters that follow, we describe some typical simulation languages. The procedures to be followed in each case are explained, and the capabilities and limitations of each language are clarified.

9.7 A Comparison of Analog and Digital Simulation

Regardless of whether one uses an analog computer or a digital computer to accomplish the desired simulation of a physical system, he will find that there are various kinds of operations that are common to both. These common operations have been called, by some, initializing operations, dynamic computing operations, and terminating operations.

Once the problem has been analyzed and plans for carrying out the simulation have been completed, the *initializing operations* are performed. These initializing operations are needed to get the computer ready for a particular simulation run. The details of accomplishing these operations will differ from one machine to another. For example, initial conditions must be specified to both analog and digital machines, but this is accomplished quite differently in the analog machine than in the digital machine. In the analog computer, a voltage of proper magnitude and polarity is imposed on each integrator output while in the digital computer, an instruction is provided which defines the initial conditions of each variable.

The *dynamic computing operations* are those that must occur to carry out the desired simulation processes. Addition, sign change, integration, and multiplication are some of these dynamic computing operations. Analog and digital machines must both perform these operations but, again, they do so differently.

Terminating operations are the ones which stop the simulation processes at the proper time, and produce the desired output results. These processes also may recycle the machine for another run with perhaps a change occurring in parameters or constants between runs.

Table 9.1 summarizes the operations in each category for both analog and digital simulators.

Table 9.1

	Analog Simulators	*Digital Simulators*
(A) Initializing Operations	(1) Set potentiometers. (2) Set initial conditions. (3) Set diode function generators. (4) Make static checks. (5) Check for amplifier overloads. (6) Make time and magnitude scale factor changes.	(1) Define and name problem variables. (2) Define and name functions. (3) Define and name parameters. (4) Define constants and assign values. (5) Specify initial conditions. (6) Specify integration time step size. (7) Specify time duration of run and other limits.

	Analog Simulators	*Digital Simulators*
(B) Dynamic Computing Operations	With the mode control in OPERATE the computer simultaneously carries out the required operations of addition, integration, multiplication, etc., as required to effect the desired simulated behavior of the physical system being studied.	The computer executes sequentially the required numerical operations to add, integrate, multiply, etc., as required to effect the desired simulated behavior of the physical system being studied.
(C) Terminating Operations	(1) Observe and record simulated behavior, using cathode ray oscillographs, pen-writing oscillographs, cameras, and visual observations of behavior. (2) Change mode control to RESET. (3) Change potentiometer settings, initial conditions, function generators, etc., and initiate a rerun of the simulation if applicable.	(1) Print out results or automatically plot the result of the simulation behavior (2) Change parameters, initial conditions, defined functions, etc., and initiate a rerun of the simulation if applicable.

9.8 Summary

The simulation of continuously varying physical systems can be accomplished on discretely varying digital computers using general purpose programming languages such as FORTRAN or ALGOL. The programming task can be eased, however, through the use of special simulation languages.

The development of continuous system simulation languages began in 1955 and is still going on. The goal of the developers of these languages is not only simplicity, so that beginners can program effectively, but also sophistication and power needed by skilled programmers.

Most of the simulation languages mentioned in this chapter have sufficient generality so that they can be used for simulating the behavior of a variety of physical systems. A number of special purpose languages also exist whose functions are more restricted. In the chapters that follow, we study both general and special purpose simulation languages for digital computers.

EXERCISES

1. Explain how it is possible to do simulation studies of a continuously varying physical system on a discretely varying digital computer.
2. Explain the features of analog and digital computers that cause the analog computer to be faster than the digital computer in many instances.
3. List the advantages and disadvantages of digital simulation over analog simulation.
4. Who pioneered the development of digital computer simulation of physical systems?
5. What are the meanings of the following acronyms?
   (a) DEPI
   (b) ASTRAL
   (c) DYANA
   (d) BLODI
   (e) DYSAC
   (f) PARTNER
   (g) DAS
   (h) MIDAS
   (i) MIMIC
   (j) DSL-90
   (k) CSMP
   (l) CSSL

MIMIC

10.1   Introduction

MIMIC is a programming system whose primary purpose is the simulation of physical systems on a digital computer. MIMIC can be used to simulate these systems
beginning with one or more differential equations which describe the behavior of
the system. The simulation can also be based on a block diagram of the system
which has been derived from the behavior-describing differential equations.

When using MIMIC, one can think of the digital computer as a simultaneous
parallel simulator and, in this respect, the digital computer appears to the user
much like the analog computer. The two scaling problems which cause so much
grief when using analog computers are almost eliminated by MIMIC. MIMIC utilizes
the wide dynamic range of the digital computer to virtually do away with the problem of amplitude scaling. Also, if necessary, the time step size can be controlled
to minimize the time scaling problem. Often, the time scaling problem can be completely ignored.

By standardizing the input and output procedures, and by utilizing a standard
format for all instructions, we eliminate many of the problems that plague a programmer using a more conventional algebraic language. This is accomplished in

MIMIC with little, if any, reduction in essential flexibility. There is usually a significant increase in programming efficiency achieved through the use of MIMIC. The specific time required to program a simulation study using MIMIC depends to a large extent on the problem, and on the skill of the programmer. Experience has shown that total programming and debugging time for a MIMIC program is usually about one-tenth that required for an equivalent FORTRAN program. MIMIC contains a level of sophistication of which the casual user is unaware. Repeated expressions, for example, are not redundantly calculated. Expressions containing only constants are only calculated once. Such features as these cause MIMIC programs to be very efficient. Execution time of MIMIC programs compares very favorably with FORTRAN program execution time for an equivalent program.

It is easy to learn to program in MIMIC. The nonprocedural nature of the language with its built-in sorting provision allows the user to write his instructions in a natural way without regard to sequence. The MIMIC system will reorder the instructions for proper computational sequence prior to execution.

The integration time step size is automatically adjusted by the program to keep the local relative error within a specified limit. The integration scheme used is a fourth-order variable-step Runge-Kutta method based on the following formulation.

Let y be the dependent variable and t the independent variable in the differential equation

$$\frac{dy}{dt} = f_1(t, y) \tag{10.1}$$

At some specific value of time, t_n, the value of y is

$$y(t_n) = y_n \tag{10.2}$$

For a time step size Δt, the next value of y beyond y_n at time $t_n + \Delta t$, is given by

$$y(t_n + \Delta t) = y_{n+1} \tag{10.3}$$

According to the Runge-Kutta procedures, the value of y_{n+1} at $t = t_n + \Delta t$ is

$$y_{n+1} = y_n + \frac{\Delta t}{6}(Q_1 + 2Q_2 + 2Q_3 + Q_4) \tag{10.4}$$

where

$$Q_1 = f_1(t_n, y_n) \tag{10.5}$$

$$Q_2 = f_1\left(t_n + \frac{\Delta t}{2}, y_n + \frac{Q_1}{2}\Delta t\right) \tag{10.6}$$

$$Q_3 = f_1\left(t_n + \frac{\Delta t}{2}, y_n + \frac{Q_2}{2}\Delta t\right) \tag{10.7}$$

$$Q_4 = f_1(t_n + \Delta t, y_n + Q_3\Delta t) \tag{10.8}$$

Starting from a known initial value of y_n, and for a given value of Δt, Eqs. 10.5–10.8 are evaluated in sequence. These results are substituted into Eq. 10.4 to find a next value y_{n+1}. Then, using this value as a new value of y_n, the process is repeated. This is done over and over again to obtain a series of values of y for corresponding values of t which constitute a solution to the differential equation 10.1.

The value of Δt that is used in the preceeding evaluation is determined by the values of DT, DTMIN, DTMAX, and the accuracy of the computation. The meanings of these symbols are given in Section 10.3. If the programmer does not explicitly designate DT to be otherwise, the MIMIC processor assumes DT to be 0.1. Similarly unless specifically designated to be otherwise, DTMIN is set to zero and DTMAX is set equal to DT by the processor. The step size Δt is automatically controlled by the integration routine to keep the local relative error below 5×10^{-6}. The local relative error is computed by comparing the values of y_{n+1} obtained by computing with two half-size steps in Δt and one full-sized step. The range over which Δt may vary is given by

$$\text{DTMIN} \leq \Delta t \leq \text{DTMAX} \leq \text{DT}$$

Early in Chapter 1, a differential equation was introduced and a block diagram was developed. It was assumed that the equation and block diagram described a physical system whose behavior was to be simulated. The equation was Eq. 1.1 and the complete block diagram was shown in Fig. 1.5. This equation and block diagram are repeated here and are given new numbers for convenient reference. (These new numbers are Eq. 10.9 and Fig. 10.1.)

$$10\frac{d^2y}{dt^2} + 5\frac{dy}{dt} + 40y = G(t) \tag{10.9}$$

We shall base our first digital simulator on the block diagram of Fig. 10.1. Later, we will work directly from the corresponding differential equation. An examination of Fig. 10.1 shows several symbols used to identify the problem variables. These are d^2y/dt^2, dy/dt, and y. These symbols are not available in MIMIC, and hence,

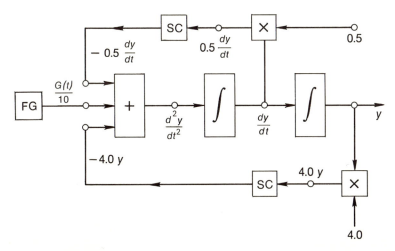

Figure 10.1 *A block diagram based on Eq. 10.9.*

new symbols (variable names) must be devised to represent the variables. Also, the examination of Fig. 10.1 reveals the need for several mathematical operations. These are addition, integration, sign change, multiplication, and function generation. The diagram also shows how the various blocks connect together. In addition to naming the variables, MIMIC must have a means whereby the required mathematical operations can be specified, and a means whereby the interconnection between these operations can be indicated. The following MIMIC program shows how these and other tasks are accomplished in the MIMIC system.

A complete MIMIC program for simulating the system shown in block diagram form in Fig. 10.1 is shown in Fig. 10.2. It is assumed that the initial conditions are $\left.\dfrac{dy}{dt}\right|_{t=0} = 0$ and $y(0) = 5.0$ units. It is also assumed that $G(t)/10 = \sin 20t$. Under these conditions the MIMIC program would be as shown in Fig. 10.2.

1	2 LCV 9	10 RESULT 18	19 EXPRESSION 72	73 80
		D2YDT2	ADD(NEG(0.5*DYDT),NEG(4.0*Y),FG)	1
		DYDT	INT(D2YDT2,0.0)	2
		Y	INT(DYDT,5.0)	3
		FG	SIN(20.0*T)	4
			FIN(T,5.0)	5
			HDR(TIME,2NDDRV,1STDRV,Y)	6
			OUT(T,D2YDT2,DYDT,Y)	7
			END	8

Figure 10.2   *A MIMIC program for the system of Fig. 10.1.*

The program of Fig. 10.2 illustrates how simple a MIMIC program can be to simulate a fairly complex system. The meaning of the various items in Fig. 10.2 must be explained in greater detail, and this is done in the sections that follow.

10.2   Instruction Format

MIMIC instructions are presented to the computer in the form of punched 80 column data processing cards. Each line in Fig. 10.2 represents a separate instruction and is punched on a separate card. The arrangement of the information on the card is shown. Each instruction is comprised of three parts: the Logical Control Variable part (LCV) punched in columns 2 through 9, the Result part (RESULT) punched in columns 10 through 18, and the expression part (EXPRESSION) punched in columns 19 through 72.

We postpone a discussion of the LCV part of an instruction to a later section of this chapter, except to say that it *must* start in column 2. The RESULT part *must* start in column 10 and the EXPRESSION part *must* start in column 19. Columns 73 through 80 are not used in MIMIC instructions, and may be ignored or used for any purpose the programmer desires. We shall use these columns to sequentially number the instructions for convenient reference. Column 1 is used to identify comment cards. Any symbol punched in column 1 causes the MIMIC system to treat the card as a comment and it is not processed. The information on such a comment card is listed in the printout but no other operations are performed.

10.3 MIMIC Instructions and Variable Names

Instruction No. 1 of Fig. 10.2 compares with the first block in the diagram of Fig. 10.1. The operation to be performed is addition. The output of the first block in Fig. 10.1 is labeled d^2y/dt^2. The equivalent of this in the MIMIC program is shown in the RESULT portion of instruction No. 1 as D2YDT2, starting in column 10. This name is arbitrary, and any other name having six or less alphameric symbols would serve just as well except that the name chosen here has the advantage that it is mnemonic. Its form is such that it suggests its own meaning and thus serves to aid the memory of the user.

The rules for selecting variable names in MIMIC are simple. MIMIC variable names may contain up to six alphameric symbols in any order. Only the letters A through Z and the decimal digits 0 through 9 are allowed. No punctuation marks or other symbols may be used in MIMIC variable names. There are six reserved names in MIMIC which must not be used for other purposes. These six names with their meanings are:

T	the independent variable
DT	the amount T changes between successive printouts
DTMAX	the maximum allowable integration step size
DTMIN	the minimum allowable integration step size
TRUE	a logical constant that is always true
FALSE	a logical constant that is always false

There are also a number of mnemonic codes for MIMIC functions that should not be used for variable names. These codes are described in detail in later material. Subject to the limitations indicated by the above rules, any name the user wishes to concoct is valid.

The EXPRESSION part of instruction No. 1 in Fig. 10.2 contains the word ADD starting in column 19. This is followed by a set of parentheses enclosing a list of items to be added. The items in this list are separated by commas. This instruction causes the listed items to be added together in the algebraic sense. That is, due regard is given to inherent algebraic signs when adding. The RESULT of this addition, in this example, is called D2YDT2 as has been explained.

The specific items to be added in instruction No. 1 of Fig. 10.2 are NEG(0.5*DYDT), NEG(4.0*Y), and FG. DYDT is the MIMIC name that was chosen for dy/dt; Y is the name chosen for y, and FG is the name chosen for the forcing function. The forcing function is produced by the function generator of the block diagram. Notice that DYDT, Y, and FG are defined in instructions No. 2, 3, and 4. To correlate the block diagram and MIMIC program, the reader should locate these various symbols and corresponding variable names in Figs. 10.1 and 10.2.

The word NEG appears twice in instruction No. 1 of Fig. 10.2. Each time NEG appears, it is followed by a set of parentheses. This indicates negation (sign change) of whatever is enclosed within the parentheses. The first occurrence of this symbol is NEG(0.5*DYDT). The asterisk (*) is one of two ways of indicating multiplication. The entire symbol therefore means that DYDT is to be multiplied by 0.5 and the result negated. In a similar manner, NEG(4.0*Y) means that Y is to be multiplied by 4.0 and the result negated. The action implemented by this process compares to the action of the multipliers and sign changers of Fig. 10.1.

The operation that is performed by instruction No. 1 of Fig. 10.2 can be expressed mathematically by Eq. 10.10.

$$\frac{d^2y}{dt^2} = -0.5\frac{dy}{dt} - 4.0y + \sin 20t \qquad (10.10)$$

One can think of the equivalent MIMIC instruction as being that shown in Eq. 10.11. Equations 10.10 and 10.11 should be carefully compared.

$$\text{D2YDT2} = \text{ADD(NEG(0.5*DYDT),NEG(4.0*Y),FG)} \qquad (10.11)$$

The equal sign (=) can actually be punched in columns 16, 17, or 18 of a MIMIC instruction card or omitted as desired by the programmer.

Instructions No. 2 and 3 in Fig. 10.2 compare with the second and third blocks of Fig. 10.1, respectively. The operation indicated in each case is that of integration. The MIMIC symbol for integration is INT starting in column 19 followed by a set of parentheses. Within the parentheses are two items separated by a comma. The first of these items indicates the name of the variable to be integrated (the integrator input) and the second item indicates the value of the initial condition to be imposed on the output of the integrator. The result of the first integration is dy/dt. In instruction No. 2 of Fig. 10.2 the corresponding result is shown as DYDT. The mathematical expression and equivalent MIMIC instruction are shown in Eqs. 10.12 and 10.13. Compare these equations term by term.

$$\frac{dy}{dt} = \int \frac{d^2y}{dt^2}\, dt + \text{Initial Condition on } \frac{dy}{dt} \text{ of } 0.0 \qquad (10.12)$$

$$\text{DYDT} = \text{INT(D2YDT2,0.0)} \qquad (10.13)$$

In a similar manner the second integration and instruction No. 3 can be compared as shown in Eqs. 10.14 and 10.15.

$$y = \int \frac{dy}{dt}\, dt + \text{Initial Condition on } y \text{ of } 5.0 \qquad (10.14)$$

$$Y = \text{INT(DYDT,5.0)} \qquad (10.15)$$

Instruction No. 4 in Fig. 10.2 provides the forcing function which in this case is assumed to be $\sin 20t$. The EXPRESSION part of this instruction is SIN(20.0*T) and the RESULT is FG. One can think of instruction No. 4 as being equivalent to

$$\frac{G(t)}{10} = \sin 20t \qquad (10.16)$$

which when written in MIMIC language is

$$FG = SIN(20.0*T) \qquad (10.17)$$

Instruction No. 5 in Fig. 10.2 tells the computer when to terminate the simulation run. The independent variable in MIMIC is always T. This variable increases from zero in increments of varying size under control of the MIMIC system. The increments by which T increases are varied in size as required by the integration process to keep the local relative error below 5×10^{-6} as has been explained earlier. In the MIMIC program of Fig. 10.2, instruction No. 5 tells the computer to stop when T becomes larger than 5.0. Any other variable can be used as a control in the FIN instruction if desired. Whenever the named variable exceeds the limit indicated, the simulation run is stopped. The RESULT part of the FIN instruction may be used as part of the logical control feature of MIMIC. This use is described in a later section.

Instruction No. 6 in Fig. 10.2 indicates the headings to be printed at the tops of the columns of output data. In this example the headings would be TIME, 2NDDRV, 1STDRV, and Y. These headings may be anything the programmer wishes that can be expressed in six characters. They may be the same as the MIMIC variable names or different, as the programmer desires. Each heading name may have up to six alphameric characters, and up to six heading names may appear in any HDR instruction. The HDR cards must precede the OUT cards in the card deck.

The HDR is used in conjunction with the OUT instruction, which is instruction No. 7 of Fig. 10.2. The values of the variables whose names are listed in parentheses in the OUT instruction will be printed on the output data sheet. They will be printed in the same order from left to right as indicated in the OUT list. The values of each dependent variable corresponding to the listed value of the independent variable will be printed out. The interval between printouts of the independent variable will be 0.1 unless explicit instructions are given to do otherwise by declaring DT to be a constant and reading in a value for it, or by including an instruction to set DT at some desired value. The variable names used in the OUT instruction must be of the same form and have the same meaning as they were assigned elsewhere in the program. Up to six items of output may be indicated by a single OUT instruction. The output format consists of up to six evenly spaced columns of numbers of the form

$$\pm X.XXXXXE \pm XX$$

The last instruction in Fig. 10.2, as in every MIMIC program, is an END instruction. Notice that it is punched starting in column 19.

10.4 Arithmetic Operators

There are four arithmetic operators in MIMIC. These are used to denote the operations of addition, subtraction, multiplication, and division. These operations are listed below along with the respective symbolic operators:

+ (plus sign)   Addition
− (minus sign)   Subtraction
⋆ (asterisk)   Multiplication
/ (slash)   Division

The preceding list of arithmetic operators is in order of *increasing* precedence except that there is no precedence of subtraction over addition nor of division over multiplication and vice versa. The following examples of MIMIC expressions and equivalent algebraic expressions should make the meaning of the precedence rule clear.

MIMIC Expression	Algebraic Expression
A+B−C	$a + b - c$
A⋆B+C	$(a{\cdot}b) + c$
A−B/C	$a - \dfrac{b}{c}$
A+B⋆C	$a + (b{\cdot}c)$
A/B−C	$\dfrac{a}{b} - c$
A⋆B/C	$\dfrac{a{\cdot}b}{c}$
A/B⋆C	$\dfrac{a{\cdot}c}{b}$

In the last two examples, which contain only ⋆ and /, since there is no precedence apparent and ambiguity can result, the precedence is established by performing the operations in sequence from left to right.

If the programmer wants to override the normal precedence of operations, he may do so by the use of parentheses. The following examples of MIMIC expressions and equivalent algebraic expressions will make the use of parentheses clear.

MIMIC Expression	Algebraic Expression
A⋆B+C	$(a{\cdot}b) + c$
A⋆(B+C)	$a(b + c)$
A/B−C	$\dfrac{a}{b} - c$
A/(B−C)	$\dfrac{a}{b - c}$
A/(B⋆C)	$\dfrac{a}{b{\cdot}c}$

The reader who is acquainted with FORTRAN programming will recognize the precedence rules as being the same in MIMIC as in FORTRAN. Also, it will be observed that MIMIC does *not* use the double asterisk for exponentiation. Exponentiation is accomplished in MIMIC by the EXP function.

10.5 MIMIC Arithmetic Functions

A number of mathematical operations have been given special attention in MIMIC. These are called functions and are each identified by a unique mnemonic code. Some of these functions were used in the MIMIC program shown in Fig. 10.2. The MIMIC arithmetic functions, with a detailed explanation of each, are shown in Table 10.1. In this table, as well as in the tables to follow, the symbols A, B, C, etc., are used to denote variable names, constants, parameters, decimal numbers with decimal points, or other MIMIC functions. Also, the underlined items are optional, and may be used as needed.

10.6 MIMIC Transcendental Functions

MIMIC provides for a number of transcendental functions. The general format is the same as that used for arithmetic functions. Table 10.2 lists the available transcendental functions.

Table 10.1

MIMIC Arithmetic Functions

Function	Form of Function	Explanation
Addition	ADD(A,B,C,D,E,F) or SUM	This function causes the values of the items listed within the parentheses to be added together. Due regard is given to inherent algebraic signs of the items when performing this addition. At least two items are required; up to six may be used. The underlined items are optional and as many as needed (up to a total of six) may be used. No comma is used after the last item.
Subtraction	SUB(A,B)	This function causes the value of B to be subtracted from A. Only two items, separated by a comma, may be listed within the parentheses.
Multiplication	MPY(A,B,C,D,E,F)	This function forms the product of the items listed within the parentheses and separated by commas. At least two items must be listed; up to six may be used. The underlined terms are optional.

Table 10.1 *(Continued)*

Function	*Form of Function*	*Explanation*
Division	DIV(A,B)	This function causes the quotient to be formed by dividing A by B. Only two items, separated by a comma, may be listed within the parentheses.
Multiply and Add	MAD(A,B,<u>C,D</u>,E,F)	This function forms a result by alternately multiplying and adding terms. The MIMIC precedence rule explained earlier applies. As many terms as are used in the function are included. The list could be thought of as $$A\star B+C\star \underline{D+E}\star F$$ The multiplications are done first to get intermediate products which are then then added. At least three items must be listed; up to six may be used.
Negation	NEG(A)	This function causes the listed variable to experience a change of algebraic sign.
Absolute Value	ABS(A)	This function produces a positive result having a value equal to the magnitude of A.
Equality	EQL(A)	This function is used to set the value of one variable equal to the value of A.

Table 10.2

MIMIC Transcendental Functions

Function	*Form of Function*	*Explanation*
Square Root	SQR(A)	This function forms the square root of A. A must have a value that is greater than or equal to zero. (Negative values of A are not allowed.)
Sine	SIN(A)	This function forms the trigonometric sine of the argument A, where A is in radians.

Cosine	COS(A)	This function forms the trigonometric cosine of the argument A, where A is in radians.
Arc Tangent	ATN(A,B)	This function forms the arc tangent of the argument A/B. The value of the result is expressed in radians. If B is not specified, it is assumed to be +1.0.
Exponential	EXP(A,B)	This function produces a result that is equal to B raised to the A power (B^A). If B is not specified, it is assumed that $B = \epsilon$. B must be positive and greater than zero.
Logarithm	LOG(A,B)	This function produces a result that is equal to the logarithm of A to the base B ($\log_B A$). If B is not specified, it is assumed that $B = \epsilon$.

10.7 Combining MIMIC Operations and Sorting

It was pointed out in Chapter 4 that analog simulators can often be simplified by combining operations. For example, the adder-integrator can frequently be used to combine both the operations of addition and integration in a single device. The price that one pays for this capability is the disappearance of one or more of the simulated physical quantities. This was illustrated in Figs. 4.28 and 4.29 wherein the number of operational amplifiers was decreased from four to three, but d^2x/dt^2 disappeared in the process.

A similar consolidating capability is available in MIMIC but one pays the same price. The program of Fig. 10.2 can be rewritten as shown in Fig. 10.3. Notice that instruction No. 1 in Fig. 10.3 is a combination of instructions No. 1, 2, and 4 of Fig.

1 2 LCV 9	10 RESULT 18	19 EXPRESSION 72	73 80
	DYDT	INT(−0.5*DYDT−4.*Y+SIN(20.0*T),0.)	1
	Y	INT(DYDT,5.0)	2
		FIN(T,5.0)	3
		HDR(TIME,1STDRV,Y)	4
		OUT(T,DYDT,Y)	5
		END	6

Figure 10.3 *A simplified version of Fig. 10.2.*

10.2. This new instruction also makes use of the arithmetic operators to reduce the amount of card punching required. This kind of combining operation can be carried to any degree desired. Notice further that in this particular example, the variable representing the second derivative (D2YDT2) has disappeared and cannot now be included in the OUT instruction.

The MIMIC processor has the capability to accept compound instructions like the first one in Fig. 10.3, and to break them up into their simpler equivalent parts. In fact, this is one of the first operations the MIMIC processor performs when simulating a system.

Another significant feature of the MIMIC processor is its built-in sorting provision. This feature allows the programmer to arrange his statements in almost any order he wishes with only minor exceptions. The processor then rearranges the operations in proper computing order so that all values of all variables are calculated before other operations are attempted which use these values. More will be said about this in a later section, when implicit functions are discussed.

10.8   Input of Constants and Parameters

Almost always, when simulating physical systems on a digital computer, one finds it necessary to supply certain numerical data. These data may be such things as the numerical equivalent of π, or the constants that apply to the particular physical system being simulated. Also, it is not uncommon to encounter a situation where one simulation study is made using one set of numerical data and another study is to follow on the same system with a different set of numerical data. The MIMIC processor has the capability to accept these data. The first kind of data are called *constants* and the second kind are called *parameters*.

There are two features of a constant or a parameter that must be supplied—its name and its numerical value. The names are supplied by means of a CON statement card for names of constants, or a PAR statement card for the names of parameters; and their numerical values are supplied by means of corresponding data cards. Up to six constants can be named in a CON or PAR statement, with as many CON or PAR statements being used as are required by the program. Corresponding to each CON statement card there must be a data card. Furthermore, there must be a one-to-one correspondence between names on the CON statement cards and the numerical values on the data cards. Corresponding to each PAR statement card there must also be at least one data card. The same one-to-one correspondence exists in the case of PAR cards and data cards also. The difference between CON and PAR functions lies in the fact that there will only be one set of data cards corresponding to the CON statements, but there will be a separate set of data cards corresponding to the PAR statements for each simulation run that is desired. If both CON and PAR functions are used, all CON cards must precede all PAR cards and the data cards must be arranged to correspond. It is good practice to arrange the card deck so that the CON cards are at the top of the deck followed by the PAR cards, followed by the other MIMIC instruction cards, followed by the data cards. Other control cards may be needed as required by the particular digital computer on which the work is being processed. These control cards may precede or follow the MIMIC cards and will differ from one machine to another.

The difference between constants, parameters, and variables should not cause confusion. Constants do not change their values from run to run. In contrast with this, parameter values may change from run to run but are constant during any given run. The values of variables, on the other hand, may change within any given run.

The input and output functions that are available in MIMIC are given in Table 10.3. The use of CFN and PFN functions is described in Section 10.9.

Table 10.3

MIMIC Input Output Functions

Function	Form of Function	Explanation
Name Constants	CON(A,B,C,D,E,F)	A,B,C,D,E, and F are programmer assigned MIMIC constant names. Each constant name may contain up to six alphameric symbols. Up to six names may be assigned in a single CON statement. As many CON statements as required to name all the constants may be used.
Name Parameters	PAR(A,B,C,D,E,F)	A,B,C,D,E, and F are programmer assigned MIMIC parameter names. Each parameter name may contain up to six alphameric symbols. Up to six names may be assigned in a single PAR statement. As many PAR statements may be used as are required to name all of the parameters.
Name Constant Function	CFN(A)	The name of the constant function is given in the RESULT portion of the CFN statement. A is the number of pairs or triples of tabulated points which define the function.

Table 10.3 *(Continued)*

Function	Form of Function	Explanation
Name Parameter Function	PFN(A)	The name of the parameter function is given in the RESULT portion of the PFN statement. A is the number of pairs or triples of tabulated points which define the function.
Print Output	OUT(A,B,C,D,E,F) or PRI	The values of the items whose MIMIC names are A,B,C,D,E, and F are printed out in the same number of columns and in the same order as the names are given in the argument list. A value of each item is printed every DT units of T. An OUT card with no items in its argument list will cause a blank line to appear on the printout sheet. As many OUT statements as needed may be used.
Print Headings	HDR(A,B,C,D,E,F) or HEA	A,B,C,D,E, and F are the names that the programmer wishes to appear at the tops of the columns of output information. These names will appear in the same order that they are given. The names may be the same as the names used in the MIMIC program or they may be different. Each HDR name may contain up to six alphameric characters, and up to six headings may appear in any HDR instruction.

The example of Fig. 10.1, whose MIMIC program was presented in Fig. 10.2, had no need to read in values of constants or parameters. The necessary numerical information to solve the problem is contained within the MIMIC expressions. Many problems cannot be programmed so simply, however. The following example will help to make the use of the CON statement clear.

Suppose, for example, that the constant coefficients of Eq. 10.9 were to be specified in different ways for different simulation studies. The equation could be rewritten as shown in Eq. 10.18, where symbols have replaced the former constant coefficients and $G(t)$ is expressed in more detail.

$$A\frac{d^2y}{dt^2} + B\frac{dy}{dt} + Cy = D \sin \omega t \qquad (10.18)$$

A MIMIC program can be written to simulate the system based on Eq. 10.18 and using MIMIC names for the symbols A, B, C, D, and ω. Before the computer simulation can be accomplished, however, numerical values must be supplied for the symbolic coefficients. One way of doing this is with a CON function. Another way is with the PAR function.

Proceeding as before, we solve for the highest-ordered derivative

$$\frac{d^2y}{dt^2} = -\frac{B}{A}\frac{dy}{dt} - \frac{C}{A}y + \frac{D}{A}\sin \omega t \qquad (10.19)$$

Let us suppose that particular numerical values for the coefficients and other constants are the same as in the earlier example. That is, $A = 10$, $B = 5$, $C = 40$, and $G(t) = 10 \sin 20t$; and where $\left.\dfrac{dx}{dt}\right|_{t=0} = 0$ and $x(0) = 5$.

A MIMIC program to accomplish this simulation based on Eq. 10.19 could be the one in Fig. 10.4. Slight variations have also been introduced in this program. The reader should carefully compare the programs of Fig. 10.4 and Fig. 10.2.

1 2 LCV 9	10 RESULT 18	19 EXPRESSION 72	73 80
		CON(A,B,C,D,OMEGA)	1
	D2YDT2	ADD(NEG(B/A*DYDT),NEG(C/A*Y),FG)	2
	DYDT	INT(D2YDT2,0.0)	3
	Y	INT(DYDT,5.0)	4
	FG	D/A*SIN(OMEGA*T)	5
		FIN(T,5.0)	6
		HDR(TIME,D2DOT,D1DOT,Y)	7
		HDR	8
		OUT(T,D2YDT2,DYDT,Y)	9
		END	10

1 12	13 24	25 36	37 48	49 60	61 72	73 80
10.0	5.0	40.0	10.0	20.0		11

Figure 10.4 *A MIMIC program for Fig. 10.1 using the CON function and a data card to supply the numerical information.*

Instruction No. 1 in Fig. 10.4 is the CON function. This is used to give names to the constants. The rules for selecting these constant names are the same as the rules for selecting variable names (up to six alphameric symbols for each name). In this example the names chosen were A, B, C, D, and OMEGA. In addition to naming the constants, they must also be given numerical values. All numbers in MIMIC must contain a decimal point; there is no provision for fixed-point (integer) arithmetic in MIMIC. The numerical values of the constants are specified on the first data card which is placed immediately following the END instruction card. This data card is card No. 11 in Fig. 10.4. Notice that the numerical information is arranged on the data card in six fields of twelve columns each. The first field is in columns 1–12 inclusive. The second field is in columns 13–24 inclusive, etc. The sixth field is in columns 61–72 inclusive. In this case only five constants are used and, hence, the sixth field is blank. All numerical data must be arranged in this manner. (Observe that each number contains a decimal point.) It is convenient to locate these numbers so that they are left-justified—that is, each number begins in the left-most column of its respective field. Leading zeros before the decimal point and trailing zeros following the decimal point may be omitted if desired. For example, 20.0 may be written 20., and 0.5 may be written .5 if desired.

MIMIC will also accept numerical data in decimal exponent form on data cards. If this form is used, the number must be right-justified. They may be left-justified also if zeros are used to fill up the unused space. For example, the number 75.618×10^{-4} could be written 75.61800E − 04 where the 7 is in the first column of the twelve column field, the 4 is in the last column, and there are two zeros added between the 8 and the E to fill the unused spaces. Blanks may be used in place of zeros to fill unused spaces if desired. If numbers are negative, the minus sign must be included in the left-most column of the field to the left of the most significant digit. If numbers are positive, the plus sign may be included or not as desired.

Instruction No. 2 of Fig. 10.4 corresponds with instruction No. 1 of Fig. 10.2, except that the numerical values have been replaced by symbols. Other changes can be observed in other instructions where symbols have replaced numbers.

Two HDR cards appear in Fig. 10.4. The first corresponds to the HDR card of Fig. 10.2 except the programmer has chosen to use different column headings this time. The second HDR card is blank. This will cause a blank line to appear between the column headings and the first number in each column of output information.

The advantage of the program of Fig. 10.4 over that of Fig. 10.2 is that now a number of different simulation runs can be made without disturbing the program instructions. Only the data card needs to be changed between runs. Let us see how the use of the PAR function even eliminates the need for changing data cards between runs.

If the programmer chose to use the PAR function instead of, or in addition to, the CON function, he would proceed in much the same way. The only difference would be that as many simulation runs would be executed as there were sets of parameter data cards provided. These runs would be executed automatically in sequence without further attention from the programmer or computer operator. The program of Fig. 10.4 could be written as shown in Fig. 10.5. It is assumed here that the coefficients A, B, and C of Eq. 10.18 are to be treated as constants, and D and ω are to be treated as parameters. Four sets of parameter data cards have been provided (one card per set) and, hence, four separate runs will be executed in sequence by the program of Fig. 10.5. The constants would be $A = 10$, $B = 5$, and $C = 40$ read from card No. 9. These values would be the same for all runs. In the first run the parameters would be $D = 10$ and $\omega = 20$ read from card No. 10; in the second run, $D = 5$ and $\omega = 20$ read from card No. 11; in the third run, $D = 10$ and $\omega = 5$ read from card No. 12; and in the fourth run, $D = 3.746$ and $\omega = 1.278$ read from card No. 13.

1	2	LCV	9	10	RESULT	18	19	EXPRESSION	72	73 80
							CON(A,B,C)			1
							PAR(D,OMEGA)			2
					DYDT		INT(−.5*DYDT−4.*Y+SIN(OMEGA*T),0.)			3
					Y		INT(DYDT,5.)			4
							FIN(T,5.)			5
							HDR(TIME,1STDRV,Y)			6
							OUT(T,DYDT,Y)			7
							END			8

1	12	13	24	25	36	37	48	49	60	61	72	73	80
10.		5.		40.								9	
10.		20.										10	
5.		20.										11	
10.		5.										12	
3.746		1.278										13	

Figure 10.5 *A program similar to Fig. 10.4 using both CON and PAR functions.*

10.9 Arbitrary Functions

Often in the simulation of physical systems one needs to incorporate one or more arbitrary functions as a part of the simulation study. It is very possible that these functions cannot be described mathematically or in terms of the functions provided in MIMIC. Frequently, the only information available is tabulated experimental data which does not lend itself to analytic expression. Rather than making it necessary to approximate such arbitrary functions by empirical expressions, as is sometimes done in simulation studies, MIMIC is capable of including arbitrary functions directly into the simulation of the system.

Just as there are constants and parameters, there are also constant functions and parameter functions. *Constant functions* are functions that do not change from run to run while *parameter functions* are functions that may change from one run to the next.

The MIMIC symbol for the constant function is CFN and the symbol for the parameter function is PFN. The tabulated data array which must be supplied to define either a constant function or a parameter function must be identified by a MIMIC name. The name of the tabulated data array is chosen by the programmer, as are the names of variable constants and parameters (up to six alphameric characters). The name of the data array is placed in the RESULT portion of the MIMIC instruction and the number of data points which define the arbitrary function is shown as the argument of the EXPRESSION portion of the CFN function or the PFN function. The CFN function and the PFN function are described in Table 10.3.

Each of the data points which define the arbitrary function is identified by a pair of numbers, one giving the value of the independent variable and one giving the corresponding value of the dependent variable. These data are arranged in sets, one set per data card, with the value of the independent variable located in columns 1 through 12 and the value of the dependent variable located in columns 13 through 24. There will therefore be as many data cards as there are points defining the arbitrary function. The data cards must be arranged in order of numerically increasing value of the independent variable.

It is also possible in MIMIC to define arbitrary functions of two independent variables. In such a situation, a triple of numbers is used on each data card to define each data point. The function is named in the RESULT portion of the CFN or PFN function with the number of triples being shown in the EXPRESSION portion. The three numbers defining each point are entered on data cards with the values of the first independent variable in columns 1 through 12, the values of the second independent variable in columns 13 through 24, and the values of the dependent variable in columns 25 through 36. (In some versions of MIMIC, the values of the dependent variable are always placed in columns 25 through 36 with 0.0 placed in columns 13 through 24 if there is only one independent variable.) The data cards must be arranged so that the values of the first independent variable form a numerically nondecreasing sequence. For each value of the first independent variable, the values of the second independent variable must be in numerically increasing order.

The arbitrary functions defined by the CFN or PFN functions and associated data, are incorporated into the MIMIC simulation program through the use of the FUN function. The FUN function is described in Table 10.6. When the FUN function is used, the variable named in the RESULT portion of the FUN statement is given the value of the particular function named as the first item in the argument list corresponding to the current value of the independent variable named as the second item in the argument list. Card No. 3 in Fig. 10.8 shows the use of the FUN function. In this case, I is given the value which is defined by the function named F for the current value of the independent variable PHI.

The use of the CFN function is illustrated by the following example. The problem is solved first by approximating the nonlinearity with an empirical expression, and then it is solved again by using the CFN function.

An electromagnetic circuit consists of a coil of 100 turns of insulated wire wound on an iron core as shown in Fig. 10.6. The resistance of the coil is 500 Ω and the coil is energized by a battery of E volts where E is either 20 V, 40 V, or 100 V. We want to find the current and flux as functions of time.

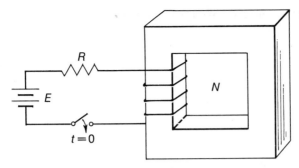

Figure 10.6

The magnetic circuit behavior has been experimentally studied and the relationship between flux in kilolines and current in amperes is given below.

Φ(kilolines)	i(amperes)
0.0	0.0
1.0	0.005
2.0	0.010
3.0	0.016
4.0	0.022
5.0	0.029
6.0	0.037
7.0	0.045
8.0	0.055
9.0	0.067
10.0	0.080
11.0	0.095
12.0	0.112
13.0	0.131
14.0	0.152
15.0	0.176
16.0	0.203
17.0	0.232
18.0	0.265
19.0	0.325
20.0	0.340

After considerable trial and error investigation, it has been found that the nonlinear relationship between current and flux can be expressed approximately as shown in the empirical equation

$$i = \frac{0.5\Phi + 0.003\Phi^3}{100} \tag{10.20}$$

where Φ is in kilolines and i is in amperes.

From Kirchoff's emf law, we can write an electric circuit equation

$$N\frac{d\Phi}{dt} \times 10^{-5} + iR = E \qquad (10.21)$$

where N is the number of turns, Φ is the flux in kilolines, i is the current in amperes, R is the resistance in ohms, t is the time in seconds, and E is the battery voltage in volts.

Solving for $d\Phi/dt$ gives

$$\frac{d\Phi}{dt} = \frac{(E - iR)10^5}{N} \qquad (10.22)$$

and substituting Eq. 10.20 for current gives

$$\frac{d\Phi}{dt} = \frac{\left(E - R\dfrac{0.5\Phi + 0.003\Phi^3}{100}\right)10^5}{N} \qquad (10.23)$$

When numerical values of $R = 500\ \Omega$ and $N = 100$ turns are substituted into Eq. 10.23 the result is

$$\frac{d\Phi}{dt} = (E - 2.5\Phi - 0.015\Phi^3)\,10^3 \qquad (10.24)$$

If time is measured in milliseconds, Eq. 10.24 reduces to

$$\frac{d\Phi}{d\tau} = E - 2.5\Phi - 0.015\Phi^3 \qquad (10.25)$$

A MIMIC program for simulating this system, based on Eq. 10.25, is shown in Fig. 10.7.

1 2 LCV 9	10 RESULT 18	19 EXPRESSION 72	73 80
		PAR(E)	1
	1DPHI	ADD(E,−2.5*PHI,−.015*PHI*PHI*PHI)	2
	PHI	INT(1DPHI,0.0)	3
	I	(0.5*PHI+0.003*PHI*PHI*PHI)/100.	4
		HDR(TIME,FLUX,CURENT)	5
		OUT(T,PHI,I)	6
		FIN(T,4.0)	7
		END	8

1 12	13 24	25 36	37 48	49 60	61 72	73 80
20.						9
40.						10
100.						11

Figure 10.7 A MIMIC program to simulate the system of Eq. 10.25.

Suppose now that the programmer wishes to use the tabulated data rather than the approximate empirical equation to describe the nonlinear relationship between flux and current. This can be done using the CFN function. If numerical values of $R = 500 \ \Omega$ and $N = 100$ turns are substituted into Eq. 10.22 the result is

$$\frac{d\Phi}{dt} = (E - 500i)\,10^3 \qquad (10.26)$$

and if time is measured in milliseconds rather than in seconds

$$\frac{d\Phi}{d\tau} = E - 500i \qquad (10.27)$$

A program to simulate the system based on Eq. 10.27 is shown in Fig. 10.8.

Suppose that it is desirable to have the arbitrary function of Fig. 10.8 change from run to run instead of being constant. To accomplish this, the PFN function must be used in place of the CFN function. Also, a different arrangement of the program cards and data cards is required.

As a general rule, all CON cards must precede all CFN cards. The CFN cards must be followed by all PAR cards and all PFN cards in that order. The data cards must also be correspondingly arranged. There must be one data card for each CON card giving the numerical value of each constant mentioned and in the same order. These cards must be followed by one set of data cards for each CFN card. These sets should each contain the proper number of cards as indicated on the CFN cards and the sets must be in the same order as the CFN cards to which they refer. The data cards for the parameters and parameter functions must follow the data cards for the constants and constant functions and be similarly arranged. There must be a complete set of data cards for the parameters and parameter functions for each run. Each set must contain the values for the parameters as indicated on the PAR cards and for the parameter functions as indicated on the PFN cards.

Refer again to Fig. 10.8. Suppose that the three values of the parameter E were to be used as before, and that three different forms of the arbitrary function F, one form corresponding to each value of E, were also to be used. The PAR card would be placed first in the program deck followed by a PFN card. The PFN card would replace the CFN card which would be removed. The data would be arranged with the first value of E on the first data card followed by 21 data cards defining the first form of the arbitrary function. This would constitute a complete set of parameter data for the first run. Another complete set of parameter data is required for each succeeding run consisting of one card containing the value of E and 21 cards defining the form of the arbitrary function. Since two additional runs were to be made in this supposed problem, two additional sets of data would be required.

With these changes, the program would produce similar results to those produced by the program of Fig. 10.8. The difference would be that the arbitrary function for each of the three runs would be different in the modified program where in the program of Fig. 10.8, the arbitrary function would be the same for each run.

1	2	9	10	18	19	72	73	80
			F		CFN(21.)		1	
					PAR(E)		2	
			I		FUN(F,PHI)		3	
			1DPHI		ADD(E,−500.*I)		4	
			PHI		INT(1DPHI,0.0)		5	
					HDR(TIME,FLUX,CURENT)		6	
					OUT(T,PHI,I)		7	
					FIN(T,4.0)		8	
					END		9	

1	12	13	24	25	36	37	48	49	60	61	72	73	80
0.0		0.0										10	
1.0		0.005										11	
2.0		0.010										12	
3.0		0.016										13	
4.0		0.022										14	
5.0		0.029										15	
6.0		0.037										16	
7.0		0.045										17	
8.0		0.055										18	
9.0		0.067										19	
10.0		0.080										20	
11.0		0.095										21	
12.0		0.112										22	
13.0		0.131										23	
14.0		0.152										24	
15.0		0.176										25	
16.0		0.203										26	
17.0		0.232										27	
18.0		0.265										28	
19.0		0.325										29	
20.0		0.340										30	
20.0												31	
40.0												32	
100.0												33	

Figure 10.8 *A program using tabulated data.*

The following example of the solution of a magnetic circuit problem is presented for further study by the reader. While it is similar in some respects to the preceding circuit, it has sufficient differences to warrant its inclusion. In the earlier problem, the energizing voltage source was a battery. In this case, it is an ac source. The circuit diagram is shown in Fig. 10.9. The numerical values we will use are

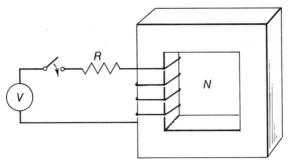

Figure 10.9 *A nonlinear magnetic circuit.*

$N = 300$ turns
Core length $= 0.45$ m
Core area of cross section $= A = 0.002$ m
$R = 7\ \Omega$
$V = 300 \sin (\omega t + \theta)$
$\omega = 377$ rad/sec

The switch can be closed at any arbitrary time during the energizing voltage cycle. The angle where this closure occurs is called θ. The current which flows in the circuit after the closure of the switch will consist of a dc transient component which will decay to zero in a short time and a steady-state ac component which will persist indefinitely after the transient component has disappeared. The result is an initial peak value of current whose magnitude and sign depend on θ. We want to find the value of θ, within one degree, that causes the peak current to have a maximum value of 6 A within 0.1 A. The waveform shown in Fig. 10.10 is typical of the behavior of such a circuit.

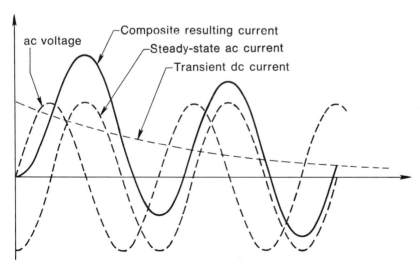

Figure 10.10 *A typical current waveform.*

In Fig. 10.10 it has been assumed that the switch was closed when θ was zero. This was the instant when the ac voltage was passing through zero in the positive direction. Also, it was assumed that the circuit parameters were such that the steady-state current was sinusoidal and lagged the voltage by approximately 90°. In a case where extreme saturation occurred in the magnetic circuit, the current waveform would be distorted. This was ignored in Fig. 10.10.

The nonlinear behavior of the magnetic core is described by the following data.

B (W/m²)	H (amp turns/m)
−2.85	−8000.
−1.96	−880.
−1.94	−800.
−1.92	−720.
−1.89	−640.
−1.85	−560.
−1.80	−480.
−1.74	−400.
−1.65	−320.
−1.47	−240.
−1.18	−160.
−0.70	− 80.
0.00	0.
0.70	80.
1.18	160.
1.47	240.
1.65	320.
1.74	400.
1.80	480.
1.85	560.
1.89	640.
1.92	720.
1.94	800.
1.96	880.
2.85	8000.

The voltage equation, summing the voltages around the closed circuit, is

$$V_L + V_R = V \tag{10.28}$$

which can be rewritten as

$$N\frac{d\phi}{dt} + Ri = V_{max} \sin{(\omega t + \theta)} \tag{10.29}$$

Solving Eq. 10.29 for the highest derivative gives Eq. 10.30.

$$\frac{d\phi}{dt} = \frac{V_{max}}{N} \sin(\omega t + \theta) - \frac{Ri}{N} \qquad (10.30)$$

Since $\phi = BA$, we can rewrite Eq. 10.30 as

$$\frac{dB}{dt} = \frac{V_{max}}{NA} \sin(\omega t + \theta) - \frac{Ri}{NA} \qquad (10.31)$$

When numerical values are substituted into Eq. 10.31 we get Eq. 10.32.

$$\frac{dB}{dt} = \frac{1}{A} \sin(377t + \theta) - \frac{7i}{300A} \qquad (10.32)$$

A MIMIC program based on Eq. 10.32 for simulating the system of Fig. 10.9 is shown in Fig. 10.11.

When the program of Fig. 10.11 is executed, a separate run will be made for eight values of θ at 5° intervals. The user can then examine these results to see which value of θ gives a maximum peak value near 6 A. Having located the 5° bracket in which the solution lies, another run can be made in which θ varies by 1° per trial, and a more precise solution can be determined.

The foregoing example will produce a satisfactory solution of a difficult problem. It does require, however, the intervention of the user to examine the results and make decisions regarding the progress of the solution. It also requires considerable card punching to prepare the data cards. If the user has available an interactive time sharing version of MIMIC, the decisions concerning the progress of the solution and the data to be supplied can be accomplished quickly to realize a very efficient and quick solution.

1 2	9 10	18 19	72 73	80
		CON(A)		
		CFN(25.)		
		PAR(THETA)		
	DT	0.0001		
	H	FUN(F,B)		
	I	H*0.0015		
	BDOT	(SIN(377.*T+THETA/57.296)−7.*I/300.)/A		
	B	INT(BDOT,0.0)		
	PHI	B*A		
		HDR(TIME,FLUX,CURENT)		
		HDR		
		OUT(T,PHI,I)		
		FIN(T,0.02)		
		END		

Figure 10.11   A MIMIC program to simulate Fig. 10.9.

Figure 10.11 *(Continued)*

1	12	13	24	25	36	37	48	49	60	61	72	73	80
0.002													
−2.85		−8000.											
−1.96		−880.											
−1.94		−800.											
−1.92		−720.											
−1.89		−640.											
−1.85		−560.											
−1.80		−480.											
−1.74		−400.											
−1.65		−320.											
−1.47		−240.											
−1.18		−160.											
−0.70		− 80.											
0.00		0.											
0.70		80.											
1.18		160.											
1.47		240.											
1.65		320.											
1.74		400.											
1.80		480.											
1.85		560.											
1.89		640.											
1.92		720.											
1.94		800.											
1.96		880.											
2.85		8000.											
0.0													
5.0													
10.0													
15.0													
20.0													
25.0													
30.0													
35.0													

10.10   Iteration, Branching, and Logical Variables

Experience has strongly established the desirability of providing iteration and branching capability in a digital computer programming language. MIMIC is no exception. Often when simulating a system using MIMIC, a programmer may wish to have the program do one thing under one set of circumstances and something quite different under another set of circumstances. Also, it is often necessary to have a program executed over and over many times with only a slight variation in data from one run to the next. This can be accomplished in MIMIC through the use of the PAR function but it usually requires the punching of many data cards. A different iterative approach is sometimes used. The *logical control variable* (LCV) and logical functions in MIMIC provide for such iteration and branching capability.

To see how branching is accomplished in MIMIC, let us turn our attention to the LCV portion of the MIMIC instruction format. The LCV was briefly mentioned in Section 10.2, but detailed discussion was deferred so that other MIMIC concepts could first be presented. Columns 2 through 9 on a MIMIC instruction card are used to indicate the name of an LCV. The logical value of an LCV is established by one of the logical functions and is always either TRUE or FALSE. If the logical value of an LCV is TRUE at execution time, any instruction containing the LCV name in columns 2 through 9 will be executed. If the logical value of an LCV is FALSE at execution time, all instructions containing the LCV name will not be executed but will be ignored. Several logical functions have been included in MIMIC and can be used with the LCV branching capability. These logical functions are shown in Table 10.4. The following examples serve to illustrate the use of the LCV and logical functions to effect iteration and branching of a simulation study.

Table 10.4

MIMIC Logical Functions

Function	Form of Function	Explanation
Function Switch	FSW(A,B,C,D)	Item A can be any valid MIMIC expression or variable name. Items B, C, and D may be any combination of arithmetic constants (numbers), logical constants (TRUE or FALSE), MIMIC expressions, or variable names. The MIMIC variable named in the RESULT portion of the FSW function is given the value of item B if item A is negative, the value of item C if item A is zero, or the value of item D if item A is positive.
Logical Switch	LSW(A,B,C)	Item A is a logical variable having a value which is logically either TRUE or FALSE. If item A is TRUE at execution time, the RESULT is given the logical value equal to the value of item B. If item A is FALSE at execution time, the RESULT is given the logical value equal to the B value of item C.

Table 10.4 *(Continued)*

Function	Form of Function	Explanation
And	AND(A,B,C,D,E,F)	The RESULT is given the logical value of TRUE if all items in the argument list are separately TRUE. If any item in the argument list is FALSE the RESULT is given the logical value of FALSE. At least two items must be included in the argument list. Up to six items may be included.
Exclusive Or	EOR(A,B)	The RESULT is given the logical value of TRUE at execution time if one of the items in the list is TRUE and the other is FALSE. If both items are TRUE or if both items are FALSE the RESULT is given the logical value of FALSE.
Inclusive Or	IOR(A,B,C,D,E,F)	The RESULT is given the logical value of TRUE if any item in the argument list is TRUE at execution time. Only if all items are FALSE is the RESULT given the logical value of FALSE. Two items must be included in the argument list; up to six items may be included.
Complement	COM(A) or NOT(A)	The RESULT is given the logical value opposite to that of item A. If item A is TRUE, the RESULT is FALSE. If item A is FALSE, the RESULT is TRUE.
Finish Simulation Run	FIN(A,B)	The FIN instruction has multiple uses. Basically it is used to indicate the conditions which cause the present simulation run to end and to commence the next run, if any. The simulation run is terminated whenever item A exceeds item B. Typically item A is a variable which varies with the simulation process and item B is a numerical quantity. Also, an LCV, if such is named in the RESULT portion of the FIN statement, is set to TRUE when the FIN statement is executed. FIN can, of course, be used without the LCV feature.

Suppose that the following branching operation is required in a simulation study.

$$y = \begin{cases} 5t, & t \le 10 \\ 50, & t > 10 \end{cases}$$

(It is assumed that this is only a part of a larger problem.) One way of coding this branching operation is with the FSW function as shown in Fig. 10.12. When the

1 2	LCV	9 10	RESULT	18 19	EXPRESSION	72 73	80
		Y		FSW(T−10.,5.*T,5.*T,50.)			

Figure 10.12 *One way of branching using FSW only.*

expression of Fig. 10.8 is evaluated the values of the subexpressions, T−10. and 5.*T, are first calculated using the current value of T. If T−10. is negative or zero, Y is set equal to the calculated value of 5.*T. If T−10. is positive, Y is set equal to 50. This accomplishes the desired branching.

Another way of accomplishing the same branching operation makes use of the logical functions and the LCV as shown in Fig. 10.13. When instruction No. 1 is executed, TLE10 is given the logical value of TRUE if T is less than or equal to 10. If T is greater than 10., TLE10 is given the logical value of FALSE. Instruction No. 2 causes TGT10 to have the opposite logical value to that of TLE10. If TLE10 is TRUE, instruction No. 3 is executed and instruction No. 4 is ignored. If TLE10 is FALSE, TGT10 is TRUE and instruction No. 3 is ignored and instruction No. 4 is executed. This causes the desired branching operation. It may appear at first glance that the procedure of Fig. 10.8 is superior to that of Fig. 10.9 but this is not necessarily so. Certainly the former requires less coding and less card punching. The expressions to be evaluated in this example are simple, however, and are therefore misleading. If the expressions to be evaluated are complicated or many in number, the method of Fig. 10.9 is superior because of the decreased amount of computer time required. The expressions in Fig. 10.12 are all evaluated every time the FSW statement is executed while in Fig. 10.13 only the expression which is needed is evaluated. The others are ignored.

Another example using LCV and logical functions will illustrate how parameters can be varied over a range. Suppose we want to evaluate the following expression

$$y = \int_0^5 \epsilon^{-at} \cos(377t + \theta)\, dt \qquad (10.33)$$

1 2	LCV	9 10	RESULT	18 19	EXPRESSION	72 73	80
		TLE10		FSW(T−10.,TRUE,TRUE,FALSE)		1	
		TGT10		NOT(TLE10)		2	
	TLE10	Y		5.*T		3	
	TGT10	Y		50.		4	

Figure 10.13 *Another way of branching using LCV.*

where *a* varies from 0 to 10 in steps of 1 and θ varies from $-45°$ to $+45°$ in steps of 1°. One way of solving this problem is shown in Fig. 10.14; this solution requires 1001 data cards. One data card is needed for each combination of A and THETA (11 values of A and 91 values of THETA).

1	2 LCV 9	10 RESULT 18	19　　　　　　　　EXPRESSIONS　　　　　72	73　80
			PAR(A,THETA)	1
		Y	INT(EXP(−A★T)★COS(377.★T+THETA/57.296),0.)	2
			FIN(T,5,0)	3
			OUT(T,Y)	4
			END	5

1　　　12	13　　　24	25　　　36	37　　　48	49　　　60	61　　　72	73　　　80
	} 1001 data cards					

Figure 10.14 *A MIMIC program to solve Eq. 10.28 with many data cards.*

This same problem as stated in Eq. 10.33 could be solved with fewer data cards by the program of Fig. 10.15. This method only requires 12 data cards.

1	2 LCV 9	10 RESULT 18	19　　　　　　　　　EXPRESSIONS　　　　　72	73　80
			CON(START)	1
START	Y		PAR(A,THETA)	2
		CHANGE	INT(EXP(−A★T)★COS(377.★T+THETA/57.296),0.)	3
		THETA	FIN(T,5.0)	4
CHANGE		START	THETA+1	5
CHANGE			FSW(THETA−45.5,FALSE,FALSE,TRUE)	6
			OUT(T,Y)	7
			END	8

1　　　12	13　　　24	25　　　36	37　　　48	49　　　60	61　　　72	73　　　80
1.0						9
0.	−45.					10
1.	−45.					11
2.	−45.					12
3.	−45.					13
4.	−45.					14
5.	−45.					15
6.	−45.					16
7.	−45.					17
8.	−45.					18
9.	−45.					19
10.	−45.					20

Figure 10.15 *Another way of solving Eq. 10.28 with fewer data cards.*

The program of Fig. 10.15 functions as follows: Instruction No. 1 causes the first data card, card No. 9, to be read giving a value of 1.0 to the logical variable START. The MIMIC system then interprets START to have a logical value of TRUE. (False values are represented by zero and true values by any nonzero value.) Instruction No. 2 is therefore executed and data card No. 10 is read, assigning values of 0.0 to A and −45 to THETA. The problem solution then proceeds in normal fashion until $T = 5$, as controlled by the FIN instruction, No. 4. At the time FIN is executed, CHANGE is given the logical value TRUE so that instructions No. 5 and 6 are executed, changing the value of THETA to −44 and the value of START to FALSE. The program then repeats in its entirety except for instruction No. 2. This instruction is not executed because now START is FALSE. For the next cycle through the program, $A = 0$ and THETA $= −44$.

The process described above continues until instruction No. 5 sets THETA to +46. At this time, instruction No. 6 sets START to TRUE so that as the next cycle begins, instruction No. 2 is executed, A is set equal to 1.0, THETA is reset back to −45, and the entire process repeats.

This routine continues until the supply of data cards is exhausted. During this entire process, A successively takes on the values of 0.0, 1.0, 2.0, 3.0, 4.0, 5.0, 6.0, 7.0, 8.0, 9.0, and 10.0. For each of these values of A, THETA ranges from −45 to +45. The result of executing the program of Fig. 10.15 is the same as for Fig. 10.14, except that only 12 data cards are needed.

10.11 Subprograms

Sometimes a situation is encountered by MIMIC users in which, for programming convenience, functions are needed that are not included in the usual MIMIC repertoire. Provision has been made in MIMIC to write such functions as subprograms and then to use them to extend the list of available functions.

A *subprogram* consists of a begin subprogram statement, a series of conventional MIMIC statements, *in sorted order*, constituting the subprogram, and an end subprogram statement. The MIMIC function code for begin subprogram is BSP, and for end subprogram the code is ESP. These functions and others are shown in Table 10.5. Each subprogram must have a MIMIC name which is created in the usual way. This name is shown in the RESULT portion of the BSP statement. The inputs to the subprogram are listed in an argument list in the BSP statement, and the outputs of the subprogram are listed in the argument list of the ESP statement.

To use a subprogram that has been named and defined by a BSP statement and an ESP statement requires a call subprogram statement followed by a return subprogram statement. These two statements must appear together and in proper sequence. The MIMIC function code for call subprogram is CSP, and for return subprogram the code is RSP. The name of the subprogram appears in the RESULT portion of the CSP statement and the inputs are listed in the CSP argument list. The outputs from the subprogram are listed in the RSP argument list.

There is a one-to-one correspondence between the items in the CSP argument list and the items in the BSP argument list. There is also a one-to-one correspondence between the items in the ESP argument list and the items in the RSP argument list. The link between the main MIMIC program and the subprogram is thus established.

The following example shows how the subprogram capability is used. Suppose

Table 10.5

MIMIC Subprogram Functions

Function	Form of Function	Explanation
Begin Subprogram	BSP(A,B,C,D,E,F)	This is the first statement in each subprogram. The name of the subprogram is an alphameric name of up to six characters and is shown in the RESULT portion of the BSP function statement. The items in the argument list are the inputs to the subprogram. Up to six items may be listed.
End Subprogram	ESP(A,B,C,D,E,F)	This is the last statement in every subprogram. The items in the argument list are the outputs from the subprogram. Up to six items may be listed.
Call Subprogram	CSP(A,B,C,D,E,F)	The name of the called subprogram appears in the RESULT portion of the CSP function statement. The inputs to the called subprogram appear in the argument list. Up to six items may be shown. There is a one-to-one correspondence between the items in the CSP argument list and the BSP argument list. A CSP statement must be immediately followed by an RSP statement.

Return Subprogram	RSP(A,B,C,D,E,F)	The outputs from the subprogram appear in the argument list. Up to six items may be shown. There is a one-to-one correspondence between the items in the RSP argument list and the ESP argument list. An RSP statement must be immediately preceded by a CSP statement.		

that a programmer finds that he repeatedly needs to solve for the roots of quadratic equations. So that we can keep the discussion simple, we assume that the equation parameters always are such that only real roots occur. The subprogram to perform the necessary operations is called ROOTS. Figure 10.16 shows how this

1 2 LCV 9	10 RESULT 18	19 EXPRESSION 72	73 80
	ROOTS	BSP(A,B,C)	
	Y1	(−B+SQR(B*B−4.*A*C))/(2.*A)	
	Y2	(−B−SQR(B*B−4.*A*C))/(2.*A)	
		ESP(Y1,Y2)	

Figure 10.16 *Defining and naming a subprogram.*

subprogram is named and defined. The subprogram defined by Fig. 10.16 would be used as shown in Fig. 10.17. It is assumed that the values of P, Q, and R have

1 2 9	10 18	19 72	73 80
	ROOTS	CSP(P,Q,R)	
		RSP(ROOT1,ROOT2)	

Figure 10.17 *Using a subprogram.*

been determined in the main program prior to the CSP function statement. Furthermore, this is only a part of the larger program. If at a later time in the main program the subprogram is needed again, it can be called as often as necessary. Perhaps the next time it is needed, the input information is given as numbers rather than as variable names and the results are called R1 and R2. The program to accomplish this is shown in Fig. 10.18.

1 2 LCV 9	10 RESULT 18	19 EXPRESSION 72	73 80
	ROOTS	CSP(2.,5.,1.)	
		RSP(R1,R2)	

Figure 10.18 *Using the subprogram again.*

10.12 Subroutines

The preceding section describes the use of MIMIC subprograms to effectively increase the number of available MIMIC functions for a given program. Now we shall consider the inclusion of other subprograms written in FORTRAN, and included as adjuncts to MIMIC main programs.

At times, a MIMIC user might find that particular computing processes can be described more conveniently in FORTRAN than in MIMIC. Also, one might already have available an existing FORTRAN program that performs some operation which is needed as part of a MIMIC program. Provision has been made in MIMIC for incorporating such FORTRAN programs as *subroutines.*

There are certain restrictions on the use of subroutines imposed by the MIMIC processor.

(1) A maximum of five FORTRAN subroutines can be incorporated into any given MIMIC program.
(2) The names of these five subroutines must be SR1, SR2, SR3, SR4, and SR5.
(3) Each subroutine may have up to six input arguments.
(4) Each subroutine may have only one output argument.
(5) The subroutine argument list must contain seven items. If fewer than seven items are needed in a particular subroutine, dummy items must be included for the unused ones to give a total of seven. The result must be returned to the main MIMIC program through the seventh item in the subroutine argument list.

The following examples illustrate the use of the subroutine feature.

Suppose that it is desired to evaluate the expressions

$$y = \begin{cases} \cos \omega t, & t \le 1.5 \\ \sin \omega t, & t > 1.5 \end{cases}$$

We will disregard the fact that this operation could be programmed using the FSW function, and use the subroutine feature instead.

```
SUBROUTINE SR1(A,B,C,D,E,F,G)
G = B
IF(A.GT.0.) G = C
RETURN
END
```

The use of the subroutine is shown in Fig. 10.19.

The limitation of returning a single argument can be lessened by calling the subroutine as many times as necessary and providing a means whereby a different

1 2 LCV 9	10 RESULT 18	19 72	73 80
	Y	SR1(T−1.5,COS(W*T),SIN(W*T))	

Figure 10.19 *Using the subroutine feature.*

result is computed each time it is called. This is illustrated by the following example. Suppose that the following three expressions are to be evaluated:

$$x = x_1 - y_1 \cos \theta$$
$$y = y_1 - x_1 \sin \theta$$
$$z = x_1^2 + y_1^2$$

The inputs to the subroutine are x_1 and y_1, and the outputs are x, y, and z. The following subroutine and the MIMIC program in Fig. 10.20 will accomplish the desired operations.

```
SUBROUTINE SR2(A,B,C,D,E,F,G)
    IF(D.EQ.2.) GO TO 5
    IF(D.EQ.3.) GO TO 6
    G = A−B*COS(C)
    RETURN
  5 G = B−A*SIN(C)
    RETURN
  6 G = A*A+B*B
    RETURN
```

1	2	9	10	18	19	72	73	80
			X		SR2(X1,Y1,THETA,1.)		1	
			Y		SR2(X1,Y1,THETA,2.)		2	
			Z		SR2(X1,Y1,THETA,3.)		3	

Figure 10.20 *Using the subroutine to produce three outputs.*

10.13 Implicit Statements

We often encounter equations in which an unknown quantity appears on both sides of the equality, in a form where the unknown cannot be solved for explicitly. These *implicit* equations usually require an iterative method of solution to determine the value of the unknown. This is particularly true if the function described by the equation does not involve integration.

There is a means in MIMIC whereby such equations can be solved; it is the implicit function, IMP. This implicit function accomplishes the desired solution by naming the unknown variable on a PAR statement, giving it an estimated initial value on the corresponding data card, and then evaluating the desired function in an iterative manner, with the IMP statement. The following example illustrates the procedure.

Suppose we wish to compute

$$y = f(y) = \cos y + \sin y \qquad (10.34)$$

In a sense, y cannot be found until y is known. The impasse can only be resolved by recourse to iterative processes. While this iteration is being executed the independent variable, which is T in MIMIC, must not be incremented. This is the purpose of the IMP function; it holds the independent variable fixed while the iterations are carried out. The MIMIC program is shown in Fig. 10.21.

1	2 LCV 9	10 RESULT 18	19 EXPRESSION	72	73 80
			PAR(Y)		
		Y	IMP(Y,SIN(Y)+COS(Y))		

1	12	13	24	25	36	37	48	49	60	61	72	73	80
1.0													

Figure 10.21   *Using the IMP function.*

The purpose of the PAR function in Fig. 10.21 is to name the variable, and to indicate its initial estimated value on the corresponding data card. In Fig. 10.21 the estimated value of y is 1.0. Starting with this original estimate, the processor computes the next approximation to y by evaluating the expressions shown in Eqs. 10.35 and 10.36.

$$y_{n+1} = (f_n - c_n y_n)/(1 - c_n) \qquad (10.35)$$

where

$$c_n = (f_n - f_{n-1})/(y_n - y_{n-1}) \qquad (10.36)$$

In Eqs. 10.35 and 10.36, f_n means $f(y_n)$, where y_n is the current approximation to the value of y; y_{n-1} is the previous value of y_n and f_{n-1} is the value of $f(y_{n-1})$. Initially, f_{n-1} and y_{n-1} are set at zero by the processor. Once a value of y_{n+1} has been determined, it is used as a new approximation of the value of y_n and the process continues repeatedly until Eq. 10.37 is satisfied.

$$|y_n - f_n| \le 5 \times 10^{-6}|y_n| \qquad (10.37)$$

at which time the value of y_n is assigned as the desired value of y and the simulation process continues.

Since the process of integration is in itself an iterative process, an unknown variable may appear on both sides of a MIMIC statement involving integration without causing difficulty. For example, the statement in Fig. 10.22 is valid where

1	2 LCV 9	10 RESULT 18	19 EXPRESSION	72	73 80
		X	INT(Y+K*X/SQR(X*X+Y*Y),5.0)		

Figure 10.22   *A valid MIMIC expression.*

the one shown in Fig. 10.23 is invalid. It was not intended that the MIMIC programs

1	2 LCV 9	10 RESULT 18	19 EXPRESSION	72	73 80
		X	Y+K*X/SQR(X*X+Y*Y)		

Figure 10.23   *An **invalid** MIMIC expression.*

of Figs. 10.22 and 10.23 produce the same result. Figure 10.23 can be made valid by changing it to Fig. 10.24. The initial value of X is 5.0 in each case.

1	2	LCV	9	10	RESULT	18	19	EXPRESSION	72	73	80
								PAR(X)			
				X				IMP(X,Y+K*X/SQR(X*X+Y*Y))			

1	12	13	24	25	36	37	48	49	60	61	72	73	80
5.0													

Figure 10.24   A valid MIMIC program (in part).

10.14   Mode Control and Limiting of Integrators

The integration statement was introduced early in this chapter as an INT function with two items in its argument list. This is the most common use of this function. The first item in the argument list indicates the integrand to be integrated and the second item is the value of the initial condition on the RESULT. The statement in Fig. 10.25 is the way one would express the following equation in MIMIC language

$$y = \int_0^t A \, dt + B \qquad (10.38)$$

1	2	LCV	9	10	RESULT	18	19	EXPRESSION	72	73	80
				Y				INT(A,B)			

Figure 10.25   The most common use of the INT function.

In Fig. 10.25 either A or B or both may be numbers, variable names, or other MIMIC expressions including other INT expressions. For example, the following equation, Eq. 10.39, could be solved as shown in Fig. 10.26.

$$\frac{d^2y}{dt^2} = \cos y^2; \quad y(0) = 2.0; \quad \frac{dy}{dt}(0) = A \qquad (10.39)$$

1	2	LCV	9	10	RESULT	18	19	EXPRESSION	72	73	80
				Y				INT(INT(COS(Y*Y),A),2.0)			

Figure 10.26   A valid MIMIC statement using compounded INT functions.

At times, when the operation of an analog computer is being simulated, it is necessary to control the mode of the integrators. The three modes available in MIMIC are OPERATE, RESET, and HOLD. These modes are invoked by adding two additional items to the INT argument list. These are treated as logical variables whose logical values are either TRUE or FALSE. These are shown in Fig. 10.27 and

1	2	LCV	9	10	RESULT	18	19	EXPRESSION	72	73	80
			Y				INT(A,B,C,D)				

Figure 10.27 *The INT function.*

in Table 10.6. If items C and D in Fig. 10.27 are both TRUE or both FALSE or are not shown at all in the argument list, the integrator is placed in the OPERATE mode. If C is FALSE and D is TRUE the integrator mode is HOLD. If C is TRUE and D is FALSE, the integrator mode is RESET.

Table 10.6

MIMIC Special Functions

Function	Form of Function	Explanation
Integration	INT(A,B,<u>C,D</u>)	The RESULT is the evaluation of the following expression $$RESULT = \int_0^t A\,dt + B$$ If C and D are both TRUE or are FALSE or are not shown the integrator is in the OPERATE mode. If C is TRUE and D is FALSE the mode is RESET. If C is FALSE and D is TRUE the mode is HOLD.
Limit Integrator	LIN(A,B,C,D)	The RESULT is set equal to zero for $$D < B < C$$ The RESULT is set equal to A for $$C \leq B \leq D$$ This function is used exclusively with an integrator, where A is the integrator input.
Limiter	LIM(A,B,C)	This function is for general limiting of variables. The RESULT is as follows: $$RESULT = \begin{cases} B, & A < B \\ A, & B \leq A \leq C \\ C, & A > C \end{cases}$$

First-Order Transfer Function	FTR(A,B)	The RESULT is the time domain evaluation of the inverse Laplace transform $$\frac{A(s)}{Bs + 1}$$ where A(s) is the variable on which $1/(Bs + 1)$ operates. The use of this function eliminates the need to express the first-order transfer function in differential equation form before programming.
Dead Space	DSP(A,B,C)	This nonlinear function simulates dead space by causing the RESULT to be as follows: $$RESULT = \begin{cases} A-B, & A < B \\ 0, & B \le A \le C \\ A-C, & A > C \end{cases}$$ The following graph illustrates the nonlinear behavior of the dead space function. 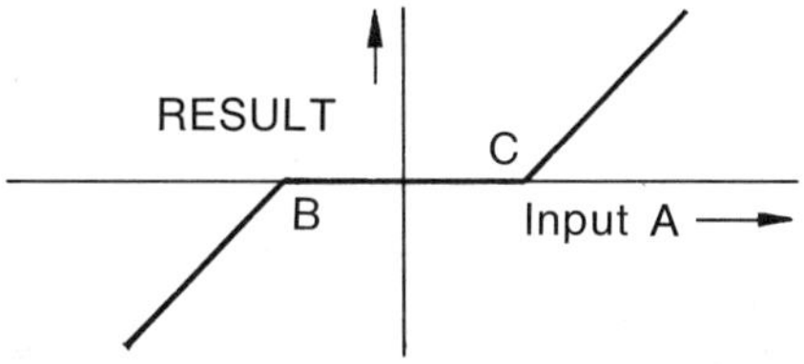
Function of One Independent Variable	FUN(A,B)	The RESULT is set equal to the value of the function whose name is A, corresponding to the current value of the independent variable B. The name of the function A must be defined and the number of pairs of points defining the function A must be given in a corresponding CFN or PFN function statement.
Function of Two Independent Variables	FUN(A,B,C)	The RESULT is set equal to the value of the function whose name is A, corresponding to the current values of the independent variables B and C. The name of the function A must be defined and the number of triples of points defining the function A must be given in a corresponding CFN or PFN function.

Table 10.6 *(Continued)*

Function	Form of Function	Explanation
Time Delay	TDL(A,B,C)	A is a MIMIC function of time. The RESULT of TDL is A delayed by B seconds. B may be variable. $$RESULT = A(t - B)$$ For $t \le$ B the RESULT is equal to the initial value of A. The number of points of A that are stored at any time is C. If C is not specified it is assumed to be 100.
Maximum	MAX(A,B,C,D,E,F)	This function compares the items listed and sets the RESULT equal to the algebraic maximum for each increment of t.
Minimum	MIN(A,B,C,D,E,F)	This function compares the items listed and sets the RESULT equal to the algebraic minimum for each increment of t.
Random Number Generator (Gaussian)	RNG(A,B,C)	The RESULT is a random sample from a Gaussian distribution with mean $=$ A and standard deviation $=$ B. C is a starting number.
Random Number Generator (Uniform)	RNU(A,B,C)	The RESULT is a random sample from a uniform distribution with lower limit A and upper limit B. C is a starting number.
Derivative	DER(A,B,C)	The RESULT is the derivative of B with respect to A. $$RESULT = dB/dA$$ where C is the value of the result at $t = 0$.
Implicit Function	IMP(A,B)	The RESULT is determined as follows: $$RESULT = A$$ where $|A-B(A)| \le 5 \times 10^{-6} \, |A|$ and where B(A) is some function of A.

At times it also becomes necessary to limit the range of variables to make them conform to physical limits imposed on the physical system being simulated. One kind of limiting is called *clipping*. In this kind of limiting, the input to the clipper is allowed to have any value while the output is only allowed to vary between certain specified limits. This is accomplished in MIMIC with the LIM function. This and other special functions are described in Table 10.6. The LIM function of Fig. 10.28 means

$$y = \begin{cases} A, & x < A \\ x, & A \le x \le B \\ B, & x > B \end{cases} \qquad (10.40)$$

1	2	LCV	9	10	RESULT	18	19	EXPRESSION	72	73	80
				Y			LIM(X,A,B)				

Figure 10.28   *The LIM function.*

When the LIM function is applied to an integrator, the RESULT of the LIM function will lie between the specified limits but the integrator will behave normally, responding to its input as though the limiter were not present.

At other times, the output of an integrator will be limited because the integrator input goes to zero. This requires a different kind of limiting. The spring, mass, damper system of Fig. 10.29 illustrates this kind of situation. Notice that there are two inelastic stops which restrain the amount of motion that is possible. When the motion attempts to exceed the limits imposed by the stops, the stops prevent this

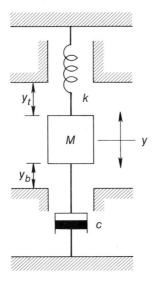

Figure 10.29   *A spring, mass, damper system with inelastic stops.*

from happening. The motion is limited by causing the velocity to be zero. This in turn causes the friction force due to the damper to become zero also, because this is present only when the velocity is finite. It is not sufficient to simply limit the displacement y with the LIM function; the velocity must be made zero also. For purposes such as this the LIN function has been provided in MIMIC. This, too, is included in Table 10.6. The equation describing the behavior of Fig. 10.29 is

$$M\frac{d^2y}{dt^2} + c\frac{dy}{dt} + ky = 0$$

(10.41)

$$\frac{dy}{dt}(0) = A, \qquad y(0) = y_0$$

Figure 10.30 shows a part of a MIMIC program that would properly simulate the system of Fig. 10.29. In Fig. 10.30 DYL is equal to DY for $YB \le Y \le YT$ and is set equal to zero for $XT < X < XL$ until the derivative of DY changes sign.

1	2	9	10	18	19	72	73	80
			2DY		(−C*DYL−K*Y)/M			
			DY		INT(2DY,A)			
			DYL		LIN(DY,Y,YB,YT)			
			Y		INT(DYL,Y0)			

Figure 10.30 *A MIMIC program using the LIN function.*

10.15 Other MIMIC Special Functions

Table 10.6 lists several other MIMIC special functions. One of these is the first-order transfer function. The MIMIC code for this function is FTR(A,B). The effect of this function is to produce a RESULT where

$$RESULT = \mathscr{L}^{-1}[A(s)/(Bs + 1)]$$

(10.42)

In Eq. 10.42, A(s) is the variable operated on by $1/(Bs + 1)$. The consequence of this is that one does need to base his simulation on the differential equation that describes the behavior of the system being simulated, as we have done heretofore, but can work directly from the corresponding transfer function. This type of function is particularly useful when the system being simulated is already described in transfer function form, because it eliminates the necessity of first writing the differential equation before the simulation can proceed.

For example, consider the R-L series circuit of Fig. 10.31. The differential equation which describes the behavior of the system of Fig. 10.31 is

$$L\frac{di}{dt} + Ri = e$$

(10.43)

One could base a simulation study on Eq. 10.43 using the methods we have pre-

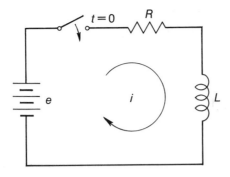

Figure 10.31 *A series R-L circuit.*

viously studied. Taking the Laplace transform of Eq. 10.43 gives

$$sLI + RI = E \qquad (10.44)$$

where E is assumed to be a constant. Solving Eq. 10.44 for I gives

$$I = \frac{E/R}{(L/R)s + 1} \qquad (10.45)$$

Equation 10.45 can be used to simulate the system using the FTR function. A part of the program which would be used is shown in Fig. 10.32. It is assumed that E, R,

1	2	LCV	9	10	RESULT	18	19	EXPRESSION	72	73	80
				I			FTR(E/R,L/R)				

Figure 10.32 *Using the FTR function.*

and L are defined and given values elsewhere in the program. If the voltage source in Fig. 10.31 had been a sinusoidal source such that

$$e = E_{\max} \sin (\omega t + \theta) \qquad (10.46)$$

the solution could have been obtained by the partial program of Fig. 10.33. It is assumed that E, R, W, THETA, and L are defined and given values elsewhere in the program.

The reader who has studied the portion of this book dealing with analog computers will recognize the similarity between the preceding discussion of the FTR function and the transfer function generation discussion concerning analog computers. See Appendix A.9 for details of analog computer transfer function generation.

1	2	LCV	9	10	RESULT	18	19	EXPRESSION	72	73	80
				I			FTR(E/R★SIN(W★T+THETA),L/R)				

Figure 10.33 *Another use of the FTR function.*

Other special MIMIC functions are shown in Table 10.6. The table is largely self-explanatory in this regard and, hence, further discussion of these functions is not included here.

10.16 Plotting

MIMIC has been designed so that plots of variables can be obtained on a conventional line printer. Table 10.7 shows the functions that can be used to obtain line printer plots. At most computer installations, plotting capabilities have been implemented that are unique with that particular computing facility and are preferred for various reasons. Should a user prefer to use his local plotting capability rather than the one furnished as a part of MIMIC, the PLO function can be utilized to call the local plot routine.

Table 10.7

MIMIC Plot Functions

Function	Form of Function	Expression
Plot	PLO(A,B,C,D,E,F)	Plots the listed items B, C, D, E, F as dependent variables versus A as the independent variable on the line printer.
Scale	SCA(A,B,C,D,E,F)	Specifies the scales to be used in units per division for each plot variable corresponding to the items in the PLO function argument list.
Zero	ZER(A,B,C,D,E,F)	Specifies the location of zero for each of the plot variables.
Page Title	TTP(up to 36 characters)	Places a title at the top of each plot page.
X Axis Title	TTX(up to 36 characters)	Places a title along the edge of each plot page.
Y Axis Title	TTY(up to 36 characters)	Places a title along the top of each plot page to identify the item plotted.

10.17 Summary

In this chapter, we have described a programming system for digital computers, named MIMIC. Using MIMIC, an analyst or designer can conveniently program a digital computer to simulate continuously varying physical systems whose behavior is described by ordinary linear or nonlinear differential equations of almost any order. Systems whose behavior is described by partial differential equations can also be studied if the procedures described in Chapter 7 are first applied. Similarly, systems whose behavior is described by simultaneous differential equations also yield to analysis through the programming capabilities of MIMIC.

The close tie that exists between analog computer programming, and digital computer programming using MIMIC, allows the individual who is familiar with the use of the analog computer to quickly learn and apply MIMIC. Essentially any problem that can be solved using the analog computer can likewise be solved using MIMIC. Real-time simulation studies are the notable exception.

The power and utility of MIMIC lies in the convenience it provides to the programmer by supplying all of the usually needed operators in a form such that they can be easily brought into use. The complexities that are often encountered with conventional programming are avoided. Such things as linkages between subroutines and the main program, memory allocation, formatting, and handling of alphabetic information are included in the MIMIC system and require no attention by the programmer. None of the capabilities of MIMIC are unique, however. They all can be achieved, although frequently with increased difficulty, through the use of more conventional languages such as FORTRAN. As stated before, it is the convenience of MIMIC that makes it so useful.

MIMIC can be quickly learned and applied to real engineering problems. It has been implemented for use on a number of different types of digital computers and has received wide acceptance by engineers and scientists.

More advanced programming systems than MIMIC have been developed, some of which are described in the following chapters. Some of these are general purpose systems and some are special purpose systems. They extend and enhance the capabilities of MIMIC but do not make MIMIC obsolete. They do possess some capabilities not included in MIMIC, and therefore find applications where MIMIC will not suffice. Nevertheless, MIMIC is still a very useful and practical system for continuous system simulation.

EXERCISES

Note: Many of the exercises of Chapters 4, 6, 7, and 8 can be used as exercises to be solved using MIMIC. Some additional exercises are included here.

1. The behavior of the feedback control system shown in the block diagram of Fig. 10.34 is described by either the transfer function shown in the block diagram or by the equation

$$B\frac{d^2x}{dt^2} + \frac{dx}{dt} = A(y - x)$$

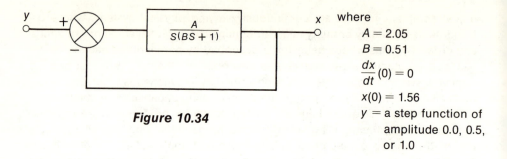

Figure 10.34

where

$A = 2.05$

$B = 0.51$

$\dfrac{dx}{dt}(0) = 0$

$x(0) = 1.56$

$y = $ a step function of amplitude 0.0, 0.5, or 1.0

Simulate the system using MIMIC programming language. Work either from the transfer function or the differential equation. Plot x as a function of time and dx/dt as a function of x.

2. (a) Make approximate plots by hand of X, Y, Z, A, and B resulting from the MIMIC program in Fig. 10.35:

```
           CON(2PI)
    DT     0.05
    Z      SIN(2PI*T)
    X      FSW(Z, −1., 0., +1.)
    Y      INT(X, 0.)
    A      Z + X
    B      X − Y + 0.25
           FIN(T, 2.0)
           HDR(T, Z, X, Y, Z, B)
           OUT(T, Z, X, Y, Z, B)
           END
6.28318
```

Figure 10.35

(b) Verify your results from part (a) by running the program on the computer.

3. When a parachutist leaves an airplane, his initial velocity is horizontal and equal to that of the plane. As a freely falling body in a resisting medium, the parachutist approaches a limiting vertical terminating velocity when the aerodynamic drag equals the weight of the parachutist. It is suspected that regardless of the initial velocity of the plane, the velocity of the parachutist will pass through a minimum value that is less than either the plane velocity or the terminal falling velocity. Since the force on the opening parachute is approximately proportional to the square of the velocity at the time of opening, it would be desirable to open the parachute at the time when the absolute free fall velocity is a minimum.

(a) Assume the drag on the parachutist with unopened chute to be proportional to the square of the velocity. Show that the equations describing his motion can be written in rectangular coordinates as

$$\frac{w}{g}\frac{dv_x}{dt} = -Kv^2\cos\theta$$

and

$$\frac{w}{g}\frac{dv_y}{dt} = w - Kv^2\sin\theta$$

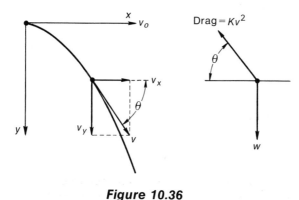

Figure 10.36

(see Fig. 10.36) where K is the constant drag coefficient in lb/ft²/sec² and w is the weight of the parachutist.

(b) Show that the motion can also be described in polar coordinates as

$$\frac{d\theta}{dt} = \frac{g\cos\theta}{v}$$

and

$$\frac{dv}{dt} = g\sin\theta - \frac{Kv^2 g}{w}$$

where

$$v = \sqrt{v_x^2 + v_y^2}$$
$$v_x = v\cos\theta$$
$$v_y = v\sin\theta$$

(c) It has been found experimentally that a freely falling parachutist reaches a limiting terminal velocity of approximately 150 ft/sec. Use either the equations for rectangular coordinates or for polar coordinates as a basis for a computer simulator. Use MIMIC to program the digital computer to simulate the system to determine the optimum time for opening the chute.

4. Figure 10.37 shows a uniform bar of weight W placed on two horizontal rollers which rotate inward in opposition to each other equally with constant angular velocity ω. The rollers are a distance l apart. The friction between the bar and the rollers is coulomb friction with coefficient f. Assume that the bar is displaced by some amount Δx and released. The bar is observed to execute horizontal oscillations.

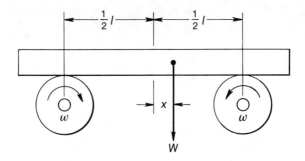

Figure 10.37

(a) Show that the equation of motion can be written as

$$\frac{d^2x}{dt^2} + \frac{2fg}{l}x = 0$$

(b) Simulate this system on the digital computer using MIMIC programming language. Assume appropriate numerical values to give a frequency of oscillation of 0.5 cycles/sec.

(c) Is it realistic that the frequency of oscillation be independent of W and ω?

5. Figure 10.38 shows a space capsule whose roll, yaw, and pitch axes are x, y, and z, respectively, about the center of mass G. During an in-flight maneuver, the position control jets are fired to create moments to position the space capsule by rotating it about each of the three axes.

(a) Show that the equations of motion are

$$J_x \frac{dw_x}{dt} + (J_z - J_y)\, w_2 w_y = M_x$$

$$J_y \frac{dw_y}{dt} + (J_x - J_z)\, w_x w_z = M_y$$

$$J_z \frac{dw_?}{dt} + (J_y - J_x)\, w_y w_x - M_z$$

where M_x, M_y, M_z are the moments about the x, y, and z axes, respectively; J_x, J_y, J_z are the moments of inertia about the x, y, and z axes, respectively;

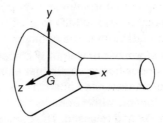

Figure 10.38

w_x, w_y, w_z are the angular velocities about the x, y, and z axes, respectively.

(b) The roll and yaw positioning jets are fired simultaneously to produce equal moments about the x and y axes. It is known that

$$J_x = 3900 \text{ slug ft}^2$$
$$J_y = J_z = 2.1\,J_x$$

The positioning moments generated by the firing of the jets are

$$M_x = M_y = 1.2 \text{ slug ft}$$
$$M_z = 0$$

These jets are fired for 0.1 sec. Assume instantaneous turn-on and turn-off. Simulate the behavior of the space capsule under these conditions using MIMIC programming language.

6. A block of iron of weight W lies on a horizontal surface under the attractive pull of a permanent magnet M (see Fig. 10.39).

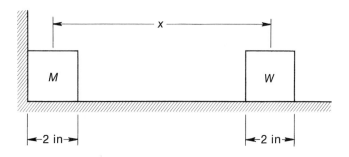

Figure 10.39

The distance between the centers of mass of the block and magnet is x. The magnet M is restrained so that it cannot move. The coefficient of coulomb friction between the block W and the surface is f. The force exerted on the block by the magnet varies inversely as the square of the distance between their centers of mass as given by K/x^2.

(a) Show that the behavior-describing equation is

$$\frac{d^2x}{dt^2} = fg - \frac{Kg}{Wx^2}$$

(b) Assume that $f = 0.1$, $g = 32.2$ ft/sec^2, $K = 0.066$ lb/ft^2, $W = 1$ lb, $x(0) = 1$ ft. Simulate the system using MIMIC programming language.

(c) How long will it take for the block and magnet to collide?

(d) Repeat parts (b) and (c) except that the surface is inclined 30° with W lower than M.

7. Repeat Exercise 6 if the entire system is immersed in a viscous fluid adding

viscous friction. This viscous friction is given by

$$\text{viscous friction} = f_v \frac{dx}{dt}$$

where $f_v = 0.25$ lb/ft/sec.

8. In the study of why materials fracture, use is made of an electron paramagnetic resonance spectrum. Data is observed in the laboratory for a particular specimen. Observations are made of electric field intensity and corresponding magnetic field intensity. Let y be the electric field intensity and x be the magnetic field intensity. The data is given in the following tabular form where $y = f(x)$:

x	y
−80	−0.5
−75	−1.5
−70	−5.0
−65	−9.2
−60	−12.7
−55	−16.5
−50	−19.5
−45	−21.3
−40	−22.9
−35	−23.4
−30	−23.5
−25	−22.5
−20	−21.2
−15	−18.0
−10	−13.0
−5	−7.5
0.0	0.0
5	4.6
10	12.4
15	16.3
20	18.5
25	20.7
30	22.0
35	22.5
40	22.5
45	21.5
50	19.5
55	16.6
60	13.9
65	10.2
70	5.5
75	0.6
80	0.0

When plotted, the data yields the curve in Fig. 10.40.

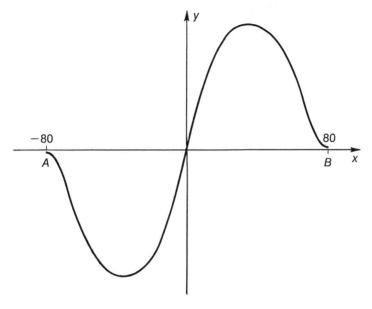

Figure 10.40

Use MIMIC programming language to write a program to find the following:

$$v = \int_A^B \int_A^B y \, dx dx$$

$$w = \int_A^B xy \, dx$$

$$u = \int_A^B y \, dx$$

$$z = xy$$

Plot u, v, w, y, z as functions of x as x varies from -80 to $+80$. [*Hint:* Let $x = t - 80$.]

9. Use MIMIC programming language to write a program to generate
   (a) a rectangular wave
   (b) a triangular wave
   (c) a sawtooth wave
   (d) a half sine wave
   (e) a half cosine wave
   In each case, make the amplitude 10 units and the period 0.01 sec.

10. The incandescent lamp whose characteristic is given in the table below is placed in series with another nonlinear resistor whose characteristic is to be found. The two nonlinear resistors are to have a combined constant resistance of 200 Ω. Use MIMIC programming language to write a program to simulate

this system and to tabulate and plot the characteristic of the lamp, the unknown resistor, and the combination.

V	I
5	0.157
10	0.227
20	0.336
30	0.403
40	0.468
50	0.525
60	0.578
70	0.627
80	0.672
90	0.714
100	0.755
110	0.796
120	0.833
130	0.867
140	0.902
150	0.935

11

Continuous System
Simulation Language (CSSL)

11.1 Introduction

The primary purpose of the early digital computer simulation languages was to provide a means for programming the digital computer in such a way that it would appear to the user to be similar to the analog computer. It soon became apparent, however, that the digital computer could be used as a simulator in its own right without any ties to the analog computer. The inherent accuracy and information storage capability of digital computers gave them a new dimension of utility, and the ease of programming gave them a new dimension of convenience.

As more and more workers became interested in digital computer simulation, the close ties with analog computers became loosened, the number of simulation languages grew and their characteristics changed. This development continued until in 1965 there were more than 20 different simulation schemes extant for the simulation of the dynamics of continuous physical systems on the digital computer. This proliferation of languages occurred with a complete absence of control—no centralized guidance directed the development. As a result, much unnecessary and wasteful duplication of effort occurred. Many good features of earlier languages were omitted from later ones, and on more than one occasion the same idea was conceived by more than one independent worker. Clearly, it was necessary for someone to provide the necessary guidance and correlation.

In 1965, under the auspices of Simulation Councils Inc., a meeting was called to draw together those workers having an interest in an orderly development of future simulation languages. An ad hoc committee was formed to become known as *The Simulation Software Committee of Simulation Councils Inc.* This committee attacked the problem and in late 1967 produced a report which defined a new language called *Continuous System Simulation Language.* This language, referred to as CSSL, has been implemented on a number of different computers. Today, programs for running CSSL simulation studies are available from several software producers.

By design, CSSL contains all of the good features of the earlier languages and provides new capabilities that are also desirable but which did not appear in earlier languages. CSSL, therefore, represents the most recent and up-to-date thinking concerning what should constitute an ideal simulation language. For these reasons, CSSL is presented here for study and consideration. CSSL is not yet available for all machines and it probably never will be. Nevertheless, since CSSL embodies most of the ideas contained in other simulation languages, those users who do not have CSSL available for their particular computer will still find a study of CSSL helpful in understanding whatever simulation scheme is available to them.

The CSSL committee began with MIMIC as a foundation language with which to work and as a starting point for committee discussions. The material of Chapter 10 which describes the features and use of MIMIC is consequently a good background for our study of CSSL here.

The procedural language for which this version of CSSL is an adjunct, is FORTRAN IV. A prior knowledge of that language would be helpful although not essential in gaining a better understanding of CSSL.

11.2   A General Description of CSSL

CSSL is a nonprocedural language whose primary purpose is the representation and simulation of continuous dynamic systems. It provides a clear, obvious, and unambiguous form for describing such systems using easily understood statements. Continuous dynamic system behavior is usually represented by one or more differential and/or algebraic equations; CSSL contains all of the necessary operators which one ordinarily needs when solving such systems of equations.

As with other simulation languages, one of the goals of CSSL is a reduction of the programming effort needed to accomplish meaningful simulation studies. Consequently, CSSL has been implemented with built-in processes for integration and with easily used input and output procedures.

Often in simulation studies, it is desirable to alter certain features of the model or its parameters between successive simulation runs. CSSL provides such capability in a natural, easily implemented way.

Errors often occur in digital computer programs during compilation as well as during execution. A complete set of problem-oriented diagnostics have been designed into CSSL. The diagnostics are very helpful in enabling the CSSL user to quickly find his errors.

For a variety of reasons, a simulation user may wish to use an expression-based representation of a system at one time, and a block-oriented representation at another time. He may also find it desirable to define new operators and proceed in a quite different manner in obtaining his solution. Such wide flexibility in approach to system simulation is possible with CSSL.

The desirable features of earlier languages that have proven their worth and have withstood the test of time have been retained in CSSL. Among these desirable features is the automatic sorting of operations into proper computational sequence. This allows the CSSL user considerable freedom in arranging his statements and consequently relieves him of one of the major concerns of digital computer programmers. This automatic sorting guarantees that no computation is attempted until all of the necessary information is available to make that computation. If it is required that calculations be performed in a particular sequence, CSSL determines this sequence. Sorting may be overridden if desired.

Simplicity is a virtue in a programming language. A simple language that is easy to learn will find a receptive audience among those users who cannot devote large amounts of time and effort to the learning and remembering of subtle and sophisticated complex languages. However, attractive as it may be, simplicity is not the only consideration of a good simulation language. The language should be readily adaptable to various levels of problem and programmer sophistication. Skilled programmers will want great flexibility and power when faced with the major task of simulating complex systems. CSSL has been designed in such a way that it can be used not only by casual, inexperienced, and infrequent users, but also by skilled, experienced programmers. This sophistication has been accomplished, in the version of CSSL described here, by allowing for a programmable flow or structure of a program and by providing a simple procedure for generating an open-ended set of programmer-defined operators. Also, clever, inventive programmers need the flexibility of CSSL and an associated procedural language. The particular procedural language to be used was not specified by the committee that designed CSSL and hence, it may vary for different versions of CSSL. Such languages as ALGOL or PL/1 could be used; however, as mentioned before, FORTRAN IV was chosen as the procedural language with which this version of CSSL acts as an adjunct.

Both implicit and explicit modes of programming are available in CSSL. The implicit mode is customarily used by unskilled programmers. In many ways, the implicit mode is similar to MIMIC, since it permits one to solve problems of considerable significance with a minimum of training and experience. When using the implicit mode, only those structure, data, and control statements need be written that are necessary to define the mathematical model of the system being simulated and to supply the input information and indicate the desired output. Statements that are oriented toward the procedural FORTRAN language are

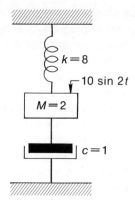

Figure 11.1 *A mechanical system.*

eliminated as are statements such as DIMENSION and FORMAT. In this way, simplicity is achieved in implicit mode CSSL programs.

The explicit mode of CSSL programming is customarily used by programmers who are more skilled. This mode allows the full capabilities and power of FORTRAN IV, combined with those of CSSL, to be applied in obtaining a problem solution. In the explicit mode, the programmer can exercise complete control of all execution logic should he desire to do so.

11.3 An Example of Implicit CSSL Programming

As an example of how CSSL can be used in the implicit mode, we will reprogram a simulator for the mechanical system of Fig. 11.1. This is the same system as shown in Fig. 4.27, and described by Eq. 4.33. A CSSL program to simulate this system is given in Fig. 11.2.

```
PROGRAM SPRING MASS DAMPER SYSTEM
    COMMENT AN EXAMPLE OF IMPLICIT CSSL PROGRAMMING
    TITLE M, C, K, F, W
    OUT M, C, K, F, W $ PAGE SKIP 1
    ALGORITHM IA = 8, JA = 8 $ CINTERVAL CI = 0.2
    XDOT = INTEG ((−C*XDOT−K*X+F*SIN(W*T))/M,0.0)
    X = INTEG (XDOT, 0.0) $ TERMT (T.GT.20.)
    CONSTANT M = 2.0, C = 1.0, K = 8.0, F = 10.0, W = 2.0
    OUTPUT XDOT, X
END
```

Figure 11.2 *A CSSL program to simulate the system of Fig. 11.1.*

The CSSL program of Fig. 11.2 is prepared by punching each line on a separate 80-column data processing card. The punched cards are then assembled to form a source program deck. When considering the following explanation of this program, you should be aware that CSSL allows a free format. Statements are not restricted to particular columns or locations. Furthermore, CSSL permits more than one statement to be placed on a single card. When this is done, a dollar sign ($) is used to indicate the end of a statement. The last statement on any card is terminated by column 72 if no indication of continuation is given.

With these ideas in mind, consider the CSSL program of Fig. 11.2. The first statement in any CSSL program must begin with the word PROGRAM. This may be followed by any other desired information which serves as a program title. Here the title chosen was SPRING, MASS, DAMPER SYSTEM. Comments can be inserted anywhere in a CSSL program by writing the word COMMENTS and following this with whatever remarks are desired. Comments have no effect on the program operation. The second line of Fig. 11.2 shows a typical comment. The next two lines illustrate one method of printing out information. The statement TITLE M, C, K, F, W causes these variable names to be printed out at the top of the output listing and OUT M, C, K, F, W causes the values previously read in to be printed out in a standard FORTRAN output format of E12.5. Up to six items of information can be printed out on each line. PAGE SKIP 1 causes one line to be skipped before the next printing. ALGORITHM IA = 8, JA = 8 indicates that the method of integration to be used is the Adams-Moulton method with error control and variable step size. CINTERVAL CI = 0.2 causes a printout to occur at 0.2 sec intervals of system time. The statement XDOT =INTEG ((−C∗XDOT−K∗X+F∗SIN(W∗T))/M,0.0) is a CSSL expression for computing values of dx/dt as based on Eq. 4.33. This is similar to the way such an instruction would be written in MIMIC. Similarly, X=INTEG(XDOT,0.0) is a statement to compute values of X. The initial conditions are set equal to 0.0 in both cases in exactly the same way as in MIMIC. TERMT (T.GT.20.) causes the simulator to stop when time is greater than 20 sec of system time. The next card, CONSTANT M = 2.0, C = 1.0, K = 8.0, F = 10.0, W = 2.0 assigns values to the various coefficients and constants. OUTPUT XDOT, X causes values of T, XDOT, and X to be printed out at each communication interval, and also causes the columns to be properly headed. END must be the last statement of every CSSL program.

Figure 11.3 shows the output that would result from executing the program of Fig. 11.2. Only that part of the output up to T = 10 is given.

M	C	K	F	W
.20000+01	.10000+01	.80000+01	.10000+02	.20000+01

T	XDOT	X
0.000000	0.000000	0.000000
.200000	.188361	1.279918−02
.400000	.671360	9.515728−02
.600000	1.26492	.288715
.800000	1.74514	.593426

Figure 11.3 *Output produced by the program of Fig. 11.2.*

Figure 11.3 *(Continued)*

T	XDOT	X
1.000000	1.90545	.965218
1.20000	1.60887	1.32489
1.40000	.824635	1.57602
1.60000	−.358532	1.62798
1.80000	−1.74522	1.41898
2.00000	−3.06960	.934120
2.20000	−4.04813	.214386
2.40000	−4.43808	−.645628
2.60000	−4.09047	−1.51138
2.80000	−2.98659	−2.23112
3.00000	−1.25076	−2.66369
3.20000	.864077	−2.70608
3.40000	3.01586	−2.31565
3.60000	4.83143	−1.52234
3.80000	5.97284	−.428316
4.00000	6.20018	.805513
4.20000	5.41915	1.98419
4.40000	3.70468	2.91067
4.60000	1.29533	3.41958
4.80000	−1.44101	3.40699
5.00000	−4.06526	2.85079
5.20000	−6.13936	1.81784
5.40000	−7.30058	.456271
5.60000	−7.32522	−1.02623
5.80000	−6.17043	−2.39483
6.00000	−3.98675	−3.42554
6.20000	−1.09837	−3.94243
6.40000	2.04598	−3.84787
6.60000	4.94405	−3.14066
6.80000	7.12151	−1.91863
7.00000	8.21038	−.365047
7.20000	8.01149	1.27925
7.40000	6.53028	2.75370
7.60000	3.97976	3.81983
7.80000	.749475	4.30020
8.00000	−2.65471	4.10812
8.20000	−5.69074	3.26312
8.40000	−7.86746	1.88949
8.60000	−8.82463	.197884
8.80000	−8.39275	−1.54732
9.00000	−6.62272	−3.06965

9.20000	−3.78034	−4.12469
9.40000	−.306026	−4.53961
9.60000	3.25397	−4.24153
9.80000	6.33405	−3.27031
10.00000	8.43962	−1.77329

Figure 11.4 is an example of an explicit CSSL program to simulate the system of Fig. 11.1. The most obvious characteristic of the explicit program is the way in which it is partitioned into parts. Each of these parts begins with a key word such as PROGRAM, INITIAL, DYNAMIC, DERIVATIVE, or TERMINAL and each part ends with END. The indentations of the various parts help to identify them. The entire program begins with PROGRAM and ends with the final END. The INITIAL part does exactly what the name implies, namely, it performs operations which normally must be done before the simulation study can begin. A typical activity here might be setting initial conditions or doing preliminary calculations that only need to be done once. The initial part ends with its own END before the DYNAMIC part begins. Among other things, the dynamic part contains the termination procedure and also includes, as a subpart, the DERIVATIVE portion. The derivative portion is given a name for reference purposes and contains statements which represent the system being studied and also contains some control statements. The function of the derivative section is to describe the dynamics of the system to be simulated. Both this section and the dynamic portion end with an END. The TERMINAL statement initiates the terminal portion in which the statements pertaining to problem termination are included. The terminal region ends with an END, as does the program itself.

Most of the statements in Fig. 11.4 are similar to those in Fig. 11.2 and the same

```
PROGRAM AN EXAMPLE OF EXPLICIT CSSL PROGRAMMING
  INITIAL $ C1=C/M $ K1=K/M $ F1=F/M
  END
    DYNAMIC
      DERIVATIVE DER
      ALGORITHM IA=8, JA=8 $ CINTERVAL CI=0.2
      XDOT=INTEG(−C1*XDOT−K1*X+F1*SIN(W*T),0.0)
      X=INTEG(XDOT,0.0) $ OUTPUT XDOT, X
      CONSTANT M=2.0, C=1.0, K=8.0, F=10.0, W=2.0
      END
    IF(T.GT.20.) GO TO FIN
    END
  TERMINAL $ FIN.. CONTINUE
  END
END
```

Figure 11.4 An explicit CSSL program to simulate the system of Fig. 11.1.

explanations apply. The principal difference is in the manner of terminating the two programs. In the implicit program of Fig. 11.2, the TERMT statement was used to terminate the program. In the explicit program of Fig. 11.4, the problem is terminated by the IF statement in the DYNAMIC portion, which directs the termination by an unconditional GO TO statement which passes control to the TERMINAL portion of the program. One other slight difference exists in that the program of Fig. 11.4 does not cause values of the various constants to be printed out. Except for these differences, the two programs are similar and would produce similar results.

When using CSSL in the implicit mode, we see from the example of Fig. 11.2 that the analyst must describe the system to be simulated, the input information, and the results desired; in terms of a number of data, structure, and control statements. The data statements are used to give numeric values to such things as constants, parameters, initial conditions, and functions defined by tabulated data. The structure statements describe the way in which the various elements of the model function together and assign CSSL names to the simulated variables. The control statements specify such things as run time, method of integration, integration interval, communication interval, and items of output desired. The programmer, when preparing an implicit mode CSSL program, will make use of symbolic names, numeric constants, and various kinds of CSSL operators and functions.

Constants are numeric quantities whose values do not change throughout a simulation study. The numeric value of a constant in CSSL must be expressed in floating point form (with a decimal point) and is supplied by means of a data statement.

Parameters are numeric quantities whose values do not change during a given simulation run, but may be changed from one run to the next. As with constants, the numeric value of a parameter must be expressed with a decimal point. Data statements are used to supply numeric values of parameters also.

Variables are quantities whose numeric values may change during a simulation run. Consequently, variables cannot be identified by their numeric values and must therefore be identified by variable names. The discussion which follows will indicate the CSSL rules for assigning variable names, for assigning numeric values to constants and parameters, and for changing the values of parameters between simulation runs.

As has been mentioned, the adjunct standard programming language, to the version of CSSL described here, is FORTRAN IV. There are differences, however, between FORTRAN IV compilers as they have been implemented for various computer systems. The CSSL user must expect, therefore, to encounter slight variations in the implementation of CSSL according to the idiosyncrasies of the particular computer and compiler he is using. The information presented here applies to the version of CSSL which operates on the UNIVAC 1108 computing system. This system was developed by Programming Services Corporation, Los Angeles, California, and is included with their permission. Differences between this version of CSSL and versions for other computing systems will be found to be minor and needed adjustments, if any, will be easy to make.

11.4   Names of Constants, Variables, and Parameters

The distinction between constants, variables, and parameters is not nearly as explicit in CSSL as in MIMIC. The distinction is more by implication than by explicit designation. Hereafter, we shall refer only to variable names, but the reader should interpret these references as applying to the names of parameters and constants also.

The rules for assigning names to variables are simple. Such names must consist of from one to six alphameric characters of which only the first must be alphabetic. The others may be alphabetic or numeric in any combination. Variable names must not contain embedded blanks or other characters of any kind. Regardless of the names given, all variables are assumed to be floating point type unless specifically declared to be otherwise.

Certain reserved words have special meanings in CSSL and/or in FORTRAN, and may cause confusion to either the CSSL system or programmer if used for CSSL variable names. Therefore, such use should be avoided. The CSSL system reserves the following special names:

>   DERIV
>   NST
>   CINT
>   IALGOR
>   JALGOR
>   HMINT
>   NIST
>   ITER
>   IERR
>   T
>   ZXXXX (where XXXX are numerals)

In addition, the relational operators, logical operators, and simulation operators of CSSL should not be used for variable names. These CSSL operators will be described later. The following are examples of valid CSSL variable names:

>   BOY
>   GIRL
>   N2
>   N3QZ
>   DT2DX2
>   X2DOT

and the following are examples of *invalid* CSSL variable names:

>   MISSISSIPPI   (too many characters)
>   24D   (begins with a numeric)
>   N(2)   (parentheses not allowed)
>   READ   (has special meaning in FORTRAN)
>   DELAY   (has special meaning in CSSL)

Constants and parameters are often named for programming convenience. They must also be given numerical values, which must be expressed with a decimal point and with or without a decimal exponent. The following numbers are valid in CSSL:

10.5
.52
0.436
30.2E–3
41E2
.16E12

The decimal exponent form of numbers (in the FORTRAN sense) is acceptable. Up to eight digits are allowed in a number, not including the exponent digits. Exponents larger than +38 or less than −38 are not permitted. The following are *invalid* CSSL numbers:

10E47   (exponent too large)
−1.23456789E15   (too many digits)

11.5 CSSL Operators

There are four kinds of operators available to the CSSL user. These are arithmetic operators, relational operators, logical operators, and simulation operators.

The arithmetic operators are the same in CSSL as in FORTRAN. They are shown below in decreasing order of execution precedence along with their accepted symbols.

** (exponentiation)
−   (unary minus)
*/ (multiplication and division)
+− (addition and subtraction)

There is no precedence of division over multiplication or vice versa. Likewise, there is no precedence of addition over subtraction. As in FORTRAN, the usual precedence can be overcome with parentheses. Whatever is enclosed in parentheses is evaluated before that which is not enclosed in parentheses. If parentheses are nested, the contents of the innermost parentheses are evaluated first.

The relational operators in CSSL are the same as in FORTRAN. These operators and their meanings are:

.LT.   (less than)
.LE.   (less than or equal to)
.EQ.   (equal to)
.GT.   (greater than)
.GE.   (greater than or equal to)
.NE.   (not equal to)

See Table 11.2 for further discussion of the relational operators.

The logical operators available in CSSL are:

.AND.   (logical and)
.OR.   (logical inclusive or)
.NOT.   (logical not)

The logical operators are described in greater detail in Table 11.3.

CSSL is capable of simulating systems containing NAND, AND, and OR logic gates. Operators have been included for this purpose. The most commonly used symbols for NAND, AND, and OR gates are shown in Fig. 11.5. The CSSL logic gate operators for simulating systems containing such gates are explained in detail in Table 11.4.

There are many other simulation operators available in CSSL. These operators are listed below in functional categories and are described in detail in Table 11.5.

A. Mathematical Operators
   (1) Derivative (DERIVT)
   (2) First-order transfer function (REALPL)
   (3) Second-order transfer function (CMPXPL)
   (4) Lead Lag function (LEDLAG)
   (5) Integrator (INTEG)
   (6) Single step delay (SDELAY)
   (7) Multiple step delay (DELAY)
   (8) Resolver (PTR), (RTP)
   (9) Zero-order hold (ZHOLD)
  (10) Implicit iterative function (IMPL)
B. Switching Function Operators
   (1) Comparator (COMPAR)
   (2) Function switch (FCNSW)
   (3) Input switch (SWIN)
   (4) Output switch (OUTSW)
   (5) RST flip flop (LOGIC)
C. Function Generator Operators
   (1) Dead space (DEAD)
   (2) Hysteresis (HSTRSS)
   (3) Limiter (BOUND)
   (4) Quantizer (QNTZR)
   (5) Integrator limiter (LIMINT)

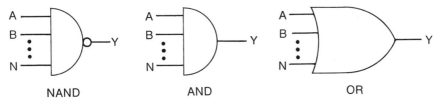

Figure 11.5 Logic gate symbols.

D. Signal Source Operators
  (1) Harmonic wave (HARM)
  (2) Ramp function (RAMP)
  (3) Step function (STEP)
  (4) Pulse generator (PULSE)
  (5) Exponential function (EXPF)
  (6) Uniform distribution random number generator (UNIF)
  (7) Gaussian distribution random number generator (GAUSS)
  (8) Ornstein–Uhlenbeck band limited noise generator (OU)
E. Input-Output Operators
  (1) Card read (CARDS)
  (2) Title (TITLE)
  (3) Line spacing (PAGE SKIP)
  (4) Page spacing (PAGE EJECT)
  (5) Printer output (OUT)
  (6) Printer output (OUTPUT)
  (7) Data input (INPUT)
  (8) Data input (CONSTANT)
  (9) Header (HDR)
 (10) Debug (DEBUG)
 (11) Range (RANGE)
 (12) Prepare for plotting (PREPAR)
 (13) Label plots (LABEL)
 (14) Subtitle plots (TAG)
 (15) Arbitrary functions (TABLE)
F. Fortran Operators
  The more common FORTRAN operators are shown below. See any FORTRAN manual for a detailed explanation of these operators.
  (1) Exponential, ϵ^x, EXP(X)
  (2) Natural logarithm, $\log_e x$, ALOG(X)
  (3) Common logarithm, $\log_{10} x$, ALOG10(X)
  (4) Trigonometric sine, $\sin x$, SIN(X)
  (5) Trigonometric cosine, $\cos x$, COS(X)
  (6) Hyperbolic tangent, $\tanh x$, TANH(X)
  (7) Square root, $x^{1/2}$, SQRT(X)
  (8) Arctangent, $\arctan x$, ATAN(X)
  (9) Absolute value, $|x|$, ABS(X)
  Only the more commonly used FORTRAN operators are shown. All of FORTRAN IV is an adjunct to CSSL.

11.6 CSSL Expressions—Free Format

Communication with the CSSL processor is commonly accomplished by means of punched 80-column data processing cards for input information, and by means of the line printer for output information. Input information, punched on data processing cards, is in the form of various kinds of statements. These statements are read by a card reader and constitute the information needed by the CSSL processor to produce the desired results.

One of the required CSSL statements is the CSSL expression. A CSSL expression may be thought of as a rule of computation whose execution produces a single-valued result. CSSL expressions are written in terms of variables, constants, functions, and operators; in this regard, CSSL expressions are similar to FORTRAN expressions. The formulation of expressions in both languages is essentially the same. CSSL, however, unlike FORTRAN, has a "free format" which allows CSSL statements to be placed on a card starting in any column and continuing on as many additional cards as desired up to a total of 19. A statement is terminated either by a dollar sign ($) terminator or by column 72 of the card if no continuation is indicated. The continuation onto subsequent cards is indicated by a symbol consisting of a series of three periods (...). This symbol, placed anywhere in a CSSL statement, causes the information on the succeeding card to be incorporated as part of the same statement. The last of the three periods must appear in or before column 72.

If a dollar sign is used to terminate a statement, another statement can be started on the same card. As many statements as desired can be placed on a single card within the space limitations of the first 72 columns, providing that each statement is separated from the following one by a dollar sign.

CSSL statements may have identifying statement labels of up to six alphameric characters. These labels are used for reference purposes as are the statement numbers in FORTRAN. The first character of a label may be either numeric or alphabetic. Furthermore, the statement label must preceed the statement which it identifies and be separated from it by a series of two periods (..). In any event, whatever label is used, it must not appear elsewhere in the program except in a proper reference statement. For example, it would be incorrect to label a statement with a number and then to have that number appear elsewhere as part of some other statement. Such a situation, as illustrated below, is not permitted.

$$21.. \quad \text{(Any CSSL statement)} \qquad \textit{Invalid}$$
$$J = J + 21$$

Also if an alphameric symbol is used as a label which could also be used as a variable name, it must not be so used. Such a situation is shown below.

$$X2.. \quad \text{(A CSSL statement)} \qquad \textit{Invalid}$$
$$Y1 = X2 \star 12.5$$

Logical control variables are statement labels of a special kind. They must precede the statements to which they apply and be separated from them by a single period (.). The logical control variable in CSSL is analogous to the LCV in MIMIC.

Comments may be inserted anywhere in a CSSL program by preceding them by the separator COMMENT, which in turn will normally be preceded by a statement terminator.

As a general rule, blanks are ignored in all CSSL program statements, including FORTRAN statements, that are a part of the CSSL program. Blanks cannot be inserted in Hollerith fields as they can in conventional FORTRAN statements because the CSSL processor will remove them.

11.7 Simulation Operators

Simulation operators are needed for implicit mode simulation when using CSSL. These operators are similar in form and purpose to the various MIMIC functions and are described in detail in Table 11.5. The explanations given in the table are complete and require no further clarification or elaboration here. Simulation operators use the values of their input arguments to produce a single output. Through the use of the macro capability of CSSL, to be described later, operators can be defined that will produce multiple outputs.

In the explanations in Tables 11.4 and 11.5, Y is used as an identifier to indicate the result produced by the simulation operator. Any valid CSSL name may be used in place of Y. The items A, B, C, etc., are either CSSL names, numbers, or expressions. T is the name of the independent variable, time. If the VARIABLE statement is used to indicate an independent variable other than time, that name should be substituted for T in all statements in which T appears.

Table 11.1

CSSL Arithmetic Operators

Operator	Explanation
Exponentiation A ** B	This operator causes A to be raised to the B*th* power. A and B may be numbers, variable names, or expressions of the same type. If A and B are of floating point type, A must be positive but B may be positive or negative. If A and B are of integer type, A and B may be positive or negative in any combination.
Multiplication A * B	This operator causes A to be multiplied by B. A and B must both be of the same type—floating point or integer. A and B may be variable names, numbers, or expressions in any combination.
Division A/B	This operator causes A to be divided by B. A and B must both be of the same type—floating point or integer. A and B may be variable names, numbers, or expressions in any combination.

Addition A + B	This operator causes A and B to be added together. A and B must both be of the same type—floating point or integer. A and B may be variable names, numbers, or expressions in any combination.
Subtraction A − B	This operator causes B to be subtracted from A. A and B must both be of the same type—floating point or integer. A and B may be variable names, numbers, or expressions in any combination.

Table 11.2

CSSL Relational Operators

Operator	*Explanation*
Less than A.LT.B	This operator produces a logical result which is TRUE only when A is less than B. Otherwise, the logical result is FALSE when A is equal to or greater than B.
Less than or equal to A.LE.B	This operator produces a logical result which is TRUE only when A is less than or equal to B in the algebraic sense. Otherwise, the logical result is FALSE when A is greater than B.
Equal A.EQ.B	This operator produces a logical result which is TRUE only when A is equal to B. Otherwise, the logical result is FALSE when A is not equal to B.
Greater than A.GT.B	This operator produces a logical result which is TRUE only when A is greater than B. Otherwise, the logical result is FALSE when A is less than or equal to B.
Greater than or equal to A.GE.B	This operator produces a logical result that is TRUE only when A is greater than or equal to B. Otherwise, the logical result is FALSE when A is less than B.
Not equal A.NE.B	This operator produces a logical result that is TRUE only when A is not equal to B. The logical result is FALSE only when A is equal to B.

Table 11.3

CSSL Logical Operators

Operator	Explanation
And A.AND.B	This operator produces a logical result which is TRUE only when A and B are both TRUE. Otherwise, the logical result is FALSE when either A or B or both are FALSE.
Inclusive or A.OR.B	This operator produces a logical result which is TRUE whenever A or B or both are TRUE. Otherwise, the logical result is FALSE only when both A and B are FALSE.
Not .NOT. A	This operator produces a logical result that is opposite to that of A. If A is TRUE, the result is FALSE. If A is FALSE, the result is TRUE.

Table 11.4

CSSL Logic Gate Operators

Operator	Explanation
Nand Gate Y = NANDL (A,B,C,...)	This operator simulates the action of a NAND gate. Any number of inputs are permitted but they must be single variables, not expressions. Positive logic is assumed so that true is represented by one and false by zero. An input greater than 0.5 is considered to be one, otherwise it is zero. The output Y is zero only when all inputs are one according to the following truth table for two inputs, otherwise Y is one. A B Y 0 0 1 0 1 1 1 0 1 1 1 0 The inverter, NOT A or $\overline{A}$, can be generated by a NANDL with a single input A.

| And Gate

Y = ANDL (A,B,C,...) | This operator simulates the action of an AND gate. Any number of inputs are permitted but they must be single variables, not expressions. Positive logic is assumed as for the NANDL operator.
    The output Y is one only when all inputs are one according to the following truth table for two inputs, otherwise Y is zero.

A B Y
0 0 0
0 1 0
1 0 0
1 1 1 |
| Or Gate

Y = ORL (A,B,C,...) | This operator simulates the action of an OR gate. Any number of inputs are permitted but they must be single variables, not expressions. Positive logic is assumed as for the NANDL operator.
    The output Y is zero only when all inputs are zero according to the following truth table. Otherwise, Y is one.

A B Y
0 0 0
0 1 1
1 0 1
1 1 1 |

Table 11.5

CSSL Simulation Operators

A. Mathematical Operators

Operator	Explanation
Derivative Y = DERIVT (YIC,X,T, TS)	This operator is used to approximate the first derivative $$Y = \frac{\Delta X}{\Delta T} \approx \frac{dX}{dT}$$ YIC is the initial condition on Y, X is the dependent variable, T is the independent variable, and TS is a storage variable which must be given a unique name. Because of the inherent noise problems in differentiators, this operator is not recommended and can usually be avoided.

Table 11.5 *(Continued)*

Operator	Explanation
First-Order Transfer Function Y = REALPL(P,X,YIC)	Item YIC is the initial condition on Y and may be a variable name or a constant. P and X are defined by the following differential equation. $$P\frac{dY}{dT} + Y = X$$ P is a constant and X may be a variable or a constant. $$Y = \begin{cases} \text{YIC}, & T = 0.0 \\ \text{Solution of the differential equation}, & T > 0.0 \end{cases}$$ $$\frac{Y(s)}{X(s)} = \frac{1}{Ps + 1}$$ The integration method used is that specified in the derivative section.
Second-Order Transfer Function Y = CMPXPL(P,Q,X, DYIC, YIC)	Item DYIC is the initial condition on dY/dT and YIC is the initial condition on Y. Both DYIC and YIC may be variable names or constants. P, Q, and X are defined by the differential equation. P and Q are constants; X may be a variable or a constant. $$P\frac{d^2Y}{dT^2} + Q\frac{dY}{dT} + Y = X$$ $$Y = \begin{cases} \text{YIC}, & T = 0.0 \\ \text{Solution of the differential equation} \\ \text{for each time step}, & T > 0.0 \end{cases}$$ $$\frac{Y(s)}{X(s)} = \frac{1}{Ps^2 + Qs + 1}$$ The integration method used is that specified in the derivative section.
Lead-Lag Y = LEDLAG(P,Q,X, YIC)	$$Y = \begin{cases} \text{YIC}, & T = 0 \\ \text{Solution of the differential equation} \\ Q\frac{dY}{dT} + Y = P\frac{dX}{dT} + X, & T > 0.0 \end{cases}$$ $$\frac{Y(s)}{X(s)} = \frac{Ps + 1}{Qs + 1}$$ Integration method used is that specified in the derivative section.

Integrator Y = INTEG(X, YIC)	$$Y = \int_0^t X dt + YIC$$ where X is a constant, arithmetic expression, or variable name. YIC is the initial condition on Y and may be a constant or a variable name but must not be another INTEG statement. INTEG statements can be nested to any desired depth. If not explicitly specified, the integration method used is Runge–Kutta–Gill fourth order.
Single Step Delay Y = SDELAY(YIC,X,TS)	This operator causes the value of X to be delayed one time step. $$Y = \begin{cases} YIC, & T = 0.0 \\ \text{Previous valid value of X,} & T > 0.0 \end{cases}$$ YIC = initial condition on Y X = input TS = a storage area having a unique name.
Variable Delay Y = DELAY(YIC,N,X,TS)	This operator is the same as SDELAY except the delay is N time steps. N is the number of time steps of delay desired and must be an integer.
Resolver X,Y = PTR(R,ANG) (polar to rectangu- lar) R,ANG = RTP(X,Y) (rectangular to polar)	X and Y are the abscissa and ordinate of a point, respectively, in a rectangular coordinates. R and ANG are the radius vector and vectorial angle in radians of a point, respectively, in polar coordinates. $$X = R*COS(ANG)$$ $$Y = R*SIN(ANG)$$ $$R = \sqrt{X^2 + Y^2}$$ $$ANG = ARCTAN (Y/X)$$
Zero-Order Hold Y = ZHOLD(YIC,P,X)	When P goes to zero, the hold operates and Y has the last value of X when P was one. YIC is the initial value of Y which is the initial output if the initial value of P is zero and must be a floating point constant or variable name. $$\frac{Y(s)}{X(s)} = \frac{1 - \epsilon^{-st}}{s}$$

Table 11.5 *(Continued)*

Operator	*Explanation*
Implicit Iterative Function Y = IMPL(Y1,E,M,FL, FY,Y2)	Y1 is the first trial value for Y. E is the error bound and must also be a floating point constant or variable name. M is the maximum number of iterations wanted and is an integer constant or variable. FL is an error flag. FY is an expression for the function of Y. Y2 is the first trial value for the next value of Y. The Newton–Raphson method is used to find Y. $$Y_{n+1} = (f_n - C_n Y_n)/(1 - C_n)$$ where $$C_n = (f_n - f_{n-1})/(Y_n - Y_{n-1})$$ and where $$f_n = FY \text{ evaluated at } Y_n$$ At the start, $$Y_{n-1} = Y1$$ $$Y_n = (1.0 + Y2) \star Y1$$ If Y2 is not specified, a value of 0.0001 is assumed. The error criterion is $$|Y_{n+1} - Y_n| \leq |Y_{n+1}| \star E$$ If this criterion is satisfied, FL is made nonzero; otherwise, FL is zero. If the variables representing Y and Y1 are the same, the iteration will use the current value of Y for the next trial. If the variables are different, Y1 will always be used as the next trial value. If M is a variable it must be declared to be an integer by PROCEDURAL $ INTEGER M $ END

B. Switching Operators

Operator	*Explanation*
Comparator Y = COMPAR(A,B)	Items A and B can be any combination of valid CSSL expressions, variable names, or arithmetic constants. $$Y = \begin{cases} 0.0, & A < B \\ 1.0, & A \geq B \end{cases}$$

Function Switch Y = FCNSW(A,B,C,D)	Item A may be any valid CSSL expression or variable name. Items B,C, and D may be any combination of arithmetic constants (numbers), logical constants (TRUE or FALSE), CSSL expressions, or variable names. $$Y = \begin{cases} B, & A < 0.0 \\ C, & A = 0.0 \\ D, & A > 0.0 \end{cases}$$
Input Switch Y = SWIN(A,B,C)	Item A may be any valid CSSL expression or variable name. Items B and C may be any combination of arithmetic constants (numbers), logical constants (TRUE or FALSE), CSSL expressions, or variable names. $$Y = \begin{cases} B, & A < 0.0 \\ C, & A \geq 0.0 \end{cases}$$
Output Switch X,Y = OUTSW(A,B)	Items A and B may be any combination of valid CSSL expressions or variable names. $$X = B;\ Y = 0.0,\ A < 0$$ $$X = 0.0;\ Y = B,\ A \geq 0$$
RST Flip Flop Y = RST(A,B,C,YP)	Items A,B, and C are the reset, set, and trigger inputs, respectively. YP is the state of the flip flop prior to the action of the RST operator. YP can be set initially by the programmer and is updated by the RST operator. $$Y = 0.0 \begin{cases} A > 0.0,\ B \leq 0.0,\ C \leq 0.0 \\ A \leq 0.0,\ B \leq 0.0,\ C \geq 0.0,\ YP > 0.0 \\ A \leq 0.0,\ B \leq 0.0,\ C \leq 0.0,\ YP \leq 0.0 \end{cases}$$ $$Y = 1.0 \begin{cases} A \leq 0.0,\ B > 0.0,\ C \leq 0.0 \\ A \leq 0.0,\ B \leq 0.0,\ C > 0.0,\ YP \leq 0.0 \\ A \leq 0.0,\ B \leq 0.0,\ C \leq 0.0,\ YP > 0.0 \end{cases}$$ Y is undefined for all other combinations of A,B,C, or YP.

Table 11.5 *(Continued)*

Operator	Explanation
RS/T Flip Flop Y = LOGIC(RST, 14, YIC, RD, SD, RC, SC, C)	This model is based upon a standard microcircuit ac coupled binary and has both clocked (synchronous) and direct (asynchronous) inputs. The clocked inputs take effect on the *falling* edge of the clock signal, while the direct inputs take effect when applied and *override* the clocked inputs. Y = Output RD = Direct reset SD = Direct set RC = Clocked reset SC = Clocked set C = Clock input YIC = Initial state (0. or 1.) RST informs the logic processor which subroutine to call and the integer 14 reserves storage; these must not be omitted. The CSSL logic convention is Y = 0.0 (False) Y = 1.0 (True) Inputs greater than 0.5 are considered one and less than or equal to 0.5 are considered zero. The direct inputs can be used alone and any input not being used should be set to 1. The direct input truth table is RD SD Y 1 0 1 0 1 0 1 1 ⋆ 0 0 E ⋆ = The state is controlled by the clocked inputs. E = Improper use of device, both set and reset triggered. Y = 1. The clocked input truth table is RC SC Y 1 0 1 0 1 0 1 1 QL 0 0 E QL = Same state as at last clock time. Clocking occurs when C goes from greater than 0.5 to less than 0.5.

	Note: This device may have its output connected back into its input through other devices, just as the actual hardware can be so connected. No sort errors or running problems will occur if the actual hardware configuration is stable.

C. Function Generators

Operator	Explanation
Dead Space Y = DEAD(A,B,X)	Item A and B are constants. X is the input. $$Y = \begin{cases} 0.0, & A \le X \le B \\ X - B, & X > B \\ X - A, & X < A \end{cases} \quad A \le B$$ Y is undefined for A > B.
Hysteresis (Type 1) Y = HSTRSS(YIC,A,B,X)	This operator simulates the common backlash type of hysteresis. It has four arguments. Y = Output YIC = Initial condition on Y A = Leftmost intercept on X axis B = Rightmost intercept on X axis X = Input

Table 11.5 *(Continued)*

Operator	*Explanation*
Hysteresis (Type 2) Y = HSTRSS(XIC,A,B, S,X)	This type of hysteresis is described by five arguments. $\quad$ Y = Output XIC = Initial condition on X $\quad$ A = Leftmost intercept on X axis $\quad$ B = Rightmost intercept on X axis $\quad$ S = Slope of the transition region $\quad$ X = Input
Limiter Y = BOUND(A,B,X)	A and B are constants. X is the input. $$Y = \begin{cases} A, & X < A \\ B, & X > B \\ X, & A \le X \le B \end{cases} \quad A \le B$$ Y is undefined for A > B.

Quantizer Y = QNTZR(P,X)	P is a constant. X is the input. K is an integer given by $$\left(\frac{X}{P} - \frac{1}{2}\right) \leq K < \left(\frac{X}{P} + \frac{1}{2}\right)$$ Y = P * K, therefore, Y = 0, ±P, ±2P, ±3P, etc. 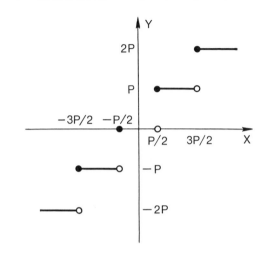
Integrator Limiter Y = LIMINT(D,YIC,LB, UB)	This operator is used to limit the output of an integrator in place of the BOUND operator. This is required because when an output variable from an integrator is held constant, the derivative of that variable (integrator input) necessarily becomes zero. It is not sufficient to simply limit the integrator output variable as the BOUND operator would do. D = Derivative of Y YIC = Initial value of Y LB = Lower bound on Y UB = Upper bound on Y

Table 11.5 *(Continued)*

D. Signal Sources

Operator	Explanation
Harmonic Wave Y = HARM(A,B,C,T)	A,B, and C are constants. A = delay in seconds, B = radian frequency, C = phase shift in radians. $$Y = \begin{cases} 0.0, & T < A \\ SIN(B{\star}(T{-}A) + C), & T \geq A \end{cases}$$
Ramp Function Y = RAMP(P,T)	P is a constant. $$Y = \begin{cases} 0.0, & T < P \\ T{-}P, & T \geq P \end{cases}$$
Step Function Y = STEP(P,T)	P is a constant. $$Y = \begin{cases} 0.0, & T < P \\ 1.0, & T \geq P \end{cases}$$

Pulse Generator Y = Pulse(TS,P,W,T)	This operator is used to simulate the generation of repeated uniform pulses. TS = Starting time W = Pulse width P = Pulse period T = Time, the independent variable 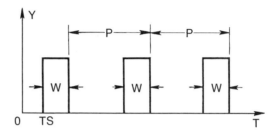
Exponential Rise and Fall Y = EXPF(YIC,TAU, T,ON)	This operator simulates an exponential rise or an exponential fall of a signal. YIC = Initial value on Y TAU = Exponential time constant T = Time, the independent variable ON = A switch. If ON > 0.5, the exponential increases. If ON < 0.5, it decreases. For example, ON = STEP(1,T) − STEP(2,T) Y = 10.∗EXPF(0., 0.1, T, ON) produces the result shown below: 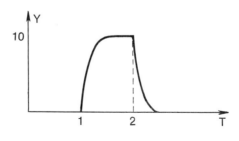

Table 11.5 *(Continued)*

Operator	Explanation
Uniform Distribution Noise Generator Y = UNIF(A,B)	Y is a uniformly distributed random number between A and B. The UNIF process is initialized by CALL UNIFI(N) in the initial section of an explicit program where N is an odd integer. If this feature is not used, the process is self-initializing, but it always starts with the same initializing integer.
Normal Distribution Noise Generator Y = GAUSS(U,SIGMA)	Y is a number with a Gaussian probability density, U is the mean, and SIGMA is the standard deviation. The GAUSS process is initialized by CALL GAUSI(N) in the initial section of an explicit program where N is an odd integer. If this feature is not used, the process is self-initializing, but it always starts with the same initializing integer.

Band Limited Noise Generator	The random number generators are of only limited practicality in digital simulation of continuous systems. They have the effect of sampled white noise and approximate an infinite bandwidth process when used with adaptive integration techniques. A more practical process is the finite energy Ornstein–Uhlenbeck process. It can be thought of as the output signal which results when Gaussian white noise is passed through a first-order lag network.
Y = OU(TAU,T,SIGMA, MEAN)	In this operator, Y is the band limited Gaussian noise, TAU is the time constant of the first-order lag with the noise spectrum break frequency of 1/TAU rad/sec, SIGMA is the standard deviation, and MEAN is the mean.
	The OU process is initialized by
	CALL OUI(N)
	in the INITIAL section of an explicit program where N is an odd integer. If this feature is not used the process is self-initializing, but it always starts with the same initializing integer.

E. Input–Output Operators

Operator	Explanation
Card Read	N_1, N_2, etc., represent CSSL variable names for which numerical values are to be read from data cards. Up to six variables may be named per CARDS statement. As many CARDS statements may be used as desired. The numerical data on the corresponding data cards must be punched in an E12.5 format. There must be one-for-one vertical and horizontal correspondence between variable names on the CARDS statements and the numerical values on the data cards. The CARDS operator is normally executed only once per problem execution. It may, however, be used with a REPEAT statement.
CARDS N_1,N_2,N_3,N_4,N_5	

Table 11.5 *(Continued)*

Operator	Explanation
Title TITLE C_1,C_2,C_3,C_4,C_5,T	C_1, C_2, etc., represent character strings to be printed on the line printer. TITLE may be used to cause page titles and column headings to be printed on the output pages. To print page titles, only one character string is used. For example: TITLE DIFFERENTIAL EQUATION SOLUTION When used to print column headings, up to six characters may be in each string. For example, TITLE VOLTS, CURENT, WATTS, HEAT, LIGHT, SOUND. The TITLE operator is normally executed only once per problem execution. If, however, an optional argument T is included, as shown, the TITLE operator is executed once for each communication interval.
Line Spacing PAGE SKIP,N,T	This operator is used to make the printer skip lines. N is an integer which indicates the number of lines to be skipped. PAGE SKIP is normally executed once per problem execution. If, however, an optional argument T is included, as shown, the PAGE SKIP operator is executed once for each communication interval.
Page Spacing PAGE EJECT	This operator causes the printer to skip to the top of the next page.
Printer Ouput (Type 1) OUT $N_1,N_2,N_3,N_4,N_5,N_6,T$	Using this operator causes the printer to print out the current values of specified variables. N_1 and N_2, etc., represent the names of the variables to be printed out. The numerical values of the variables will be printed on one line in the same order as the variable names. Up to six names may be shown per OUT statement. The output format is fixed. It results in up to six evenly spaced columns. OUT is normally executed once per problem execution. If, however, an optional T argument is included, as shown, the OUT operator is executed once per communication interval.

Printer Output (Type 2) OUTPUT N,A,B,C,...	This operator causes values of the nonsubscripted variables A, B, C, . . . to be printed out at each print interval. If N is included, it must be an integer constant and it will cause the print interval to be N communication intervals. If N is not explicitly given, the print interval will be every communication interval. Values of the independent variable, which normally is time, are printed out automatically without specific request in the OUTPUT statement. Any number of variable names not exceeding 200 may be included in a single OUTPUT statement. If the number of variables is five or less, the output format is columnar, with the variable names appearing as column headings. If the number of variables exceeds five, the output format will automatically shift to equation form. In this equation form, the output will appear as follows: $T_1 = \underline{\hspace{1cm}} \quad A = \underline{\hspace{1cm}} \quad B = \underline{\hspace{1cm}} \quad C = \underline{\hspace{1cm}}$ $\phantom{T_1 = \underline{\hspace{1cm}} \quad} D = \underline{\hspace{1cm}} \quad E = \underline{\hspace{1cm}} \quad F = \underline{\hspace{1cm}}$ $\phantom{T_1 = \underline{\hspace{1cm}} \quad} \text{etc.}$ $T_2 = \underline{\hspace{1cm}} \quad A = \underline{\hspace{1cm}} \quad B = \underline{\hspace{1cm}} \quad C = \underline{\hspace{1cm}}$ $\phantom{T_2 = \underline{\hspace{1cm}} \quad} D = \underline{\hspace{1cm}} \quad E = \underline{\hspace{1cm}} \quad F = \underline{\hspace{1cm}}$ $\phantom{T_2 = \underline{\hspace{1cm}} \quad} \text{etc.}$ This is repeated for each print interval. Only one OUTPUT statement will be recognized per simulation run.
Data Input (Type 1) INPUT A=X,B=Y, C=Z,...	This statement is used to replace the current values of the variables, A, B, C, etc., respectively, by the new values X, Y, Z, etc. Any number of variables and corresponding values may appear on a card or on a continuation card. As many INPUT statements as necessary may be included. The variables appearing on an INPUT card may be: (1) Variables initiated by a constant statement (2) Variables appearing in parallel or derivative sections (3) Variables appearing in the integration control statements, or (4) Variables appearing in the error control statements. The INPUT statement may be used to introduce new data values for any specific simulation run.

Table 11.5 *(Continued)*

Operator	Explanation
Data Input (Type 2) CONSTANT A=X,B=Y, C=Z,...	The reader is referred to Table 11.6A for an explanation of the CONSTANT statement.
Header HDR S	This statement is used to print headings at the top of printed output listings. Each HDR statement will cause a line, consisting of the character string S, to be printed at the top of each page of output. Up to five HDR statements may be used in a single program. In order for HDR to be effective, there must also be an accompanying OUTPUT statement in the program.
Debug DEBUG M,XT	The DEBUG statement will cause the values of all variables appearing in the derivative section to be printed out for the next M communication intervals, once the value of the independent variable becomes greater than XT. Only one DEBUG statement may be used per simulation run. M must be an integer constant and XT must be a floating point constant.
Range RANGE A,B,C,...	The RANGE statement causes the minimum and maximum values, reached during a simulation run, for the specified variables, to be printed out at the end of the run when the terminal condition has been met. The times at which these ranges occurred is also printed out. The number of variables specified in a RANGE statement cannot exceed 200. Only one RANGE statement will be recognized per program.
Prepare for Plotting PREPAR N,A,B,C,...	The PREPAR statement causes the values of the nonsubscripted variables whose names are listed to be collected and saved at each communication interval during the simulation run for possible future plotting. Up to ten variables, not including the independent variable T, may be specified. Values of T are automatically saved. Up to 1000 values of each variable may be saved. N is an integer indicating the maximum number of variables to be plotted.
Label Plots LABEL S	The LABEL statement functions in exactly the same way for plotting as HDR does for printing. The character string S is limited to 60 characters. Only one LABEL statement may be used per graph.

Subtitle Plots TAG S	The TAG statement provides a subtitle capability for graphs. It is used in conjunction with the LABEL statement. The character string S is limited to 24 characters.

Arbitrary Functions TABLE A,N,DIM,DATA	This statement defines arbitrary functions, assigns names, and specifies values. A is a variable name assigned by the programmer to identify the arbitrary function. N is an integer constant equal to either 1, 2, or 3, which indicates the number of independent variables. DIM gives the dimensions of the discrete data array which describes the arbitrary function. DATA consists of all the discrete data points of each independent variable, followed by the discrete data points of the function. The data must be specified in floating point constant form. The discrete data points of the independent variables must be in monotonically increasing order. The discrete points of the function may be in any order. A function of one independent variable follows the form: TABLE NAME,1,k,x_1,x_2,...,x_k,$f(x_1)$,$f(x_2)$,...,$f(x_k)$ where x is the independent variable. A function of two independent variables follows the form: TABLE NAME,2,j,k,x_1,x_2,...,x_j,y_1,y_2,...,y_k,$f(x_1,y_1)$, $f(x_2,y_1)$,...,$f(x_j,y_1)$,$f(x_1,y_2)$,$f(x_2,y_2)$, ...,$f(x_j,y_2)$,...,$f(x_1,y_k)$,$f(x_2,y_k)$,..., $f(x_j,y_k)$ where x and y are the two independent variables. A function of three independent variables follows the form: TABLE NAME,3,i,j,k,x_1,x_2,...,x_i,y_1,y_2,...,y_j,z_1,z_2,...,z_k, $f(x_1,y_1,z_1)$,$f(x_2,y_1,z_1)$,...,$f(x_i,y_1,z_1)$, $f(x_1,y_2,z_1)$,$f(x_2,y_2,z_1)$,...,$f(x_i,y_2,z_1)$,..., $f(x_i,y_j,z_1)$,$f(x_i,y_j,z_2)$,...,$f(x_i,y_j,z_k)$ where x, y, and z are the three independent variables. Once a function has been defined with its name and tabular data, its name may be used as if it were any other available function. For example, a function of two independent variables may be written:

Table 11.5 *(Continued)*

Operator	Explanation
	TABLE ZENITH 2,4,2,0.0,.79,1.57,3.14,1.1,2.2 　　　　　　　−1.1,−2.2,3.4,4.3,7.3,0.0,.34,1.5 One could picture this function as the following two-dimensional array:

Y X	1.1	2.2
0.0	−1.1	7.3
.79	−2.2	0.0
1.57	3.4	.34
3.14	4.3	1.5

Once the function ZENITH has been defined by the preceding TABLE statement, it could be used as follows:

Y = COS(ZENITH(ALPHA,GAMMA)) + SIN(THETA)

The functions will be extrapolated if the independent variable falls outside the tabulated range.

11.8　Control Statements

When a computer processes a CSSL program, some instructions are needed to tell it how to proceed. These instructions are provided by the programmer using three types of control statements — translator control statements, integration control statements, and error control statements.

As the name indicates, the translator control statements supply information to the translator regarding constants, arrays, definition of variables, termination conditions, and repetition conditions. The translator controls are fully explained in Table 11.6A.

The integration control statements supply information to the centralized integration system regarding the independent variable, the particular integration algorithm to be used, the duration of the communication interval, the number of calculation intervals in each communication interval, and the number of times the initialization algorithm is to be used for calculating history information. The integration control statements are explained in Table 11.6B.

The error control statements described in Table 11.6C are optional. If used, they apply only to the Adams–Moulton method or to the Milne method, both with error control. In all other methods, fixed-size calculation intervals are used. The error control statements specify the relative and absolute error tolerances to be applied, and cause the step size to be varied so as to keep the error within the specified bounds.

When the Adams–Moulton or the Milne integration method is specified with error control, each calculated result is subjected to an error test at each integration step to ascertain the proper size of the integration time step. Both the Adams–Moulton method and the Milne method of integration employ a predictor-corrector technique. The method for controlling the error in both procedures is similar. Having found a predicted value, X_P, of a state variable as a result of executing an INTEG statement, and a corrected value, X_C, for the same state variable, a test is made to see if Eq. 11.1 is satisfied.

$$\frac{|X_P - X_C|}{W} < \text{MERROR } |X_C| + \text{XERROR} \qquad (11.1)$$

In Eq. 11.1, W is a weighting factor — a number whose value depends on the integration method being employed. MERROR is the relative error constant and XERROR is the absolute error constant. These constants are described in Table 11.6C. Equation 11.1 is an empirical equation that experience has proved to be useful for error control purposes.

If Eq. 11.1 is not satisfied, time, which is the usual independent variable, backs up, and a new trial is made at one-half the former step size. This is repeated until Eq. 11.1 is satisfied. When causing time to back up as described, it is important that functions with memory behave properly. Such functions as hysteresis, zero-order hold, and all random number generators could cause difficulty if not properly implemented. CSSL has provided proper behavior of such functions when time is backed up.

If Eq. 11.1 is satisfied, and if every state variable error is less than 1/32 of the error criterion, then the time step is doubled and a new trial is calculated. In this way, the largest possible integration time step is used consistent with error control.

Before halving the calculation interval, a check is made to see if the reduced calculation interval will be less than or equal to the minimum calculation interval as specified on the MINTERVAL statement. If it is, an error flag is set and the calculation interval is held at the MINTERVAL value. The error flag specified by the ERRTAG statement may then be checked elsewhere in the program. The value assigned to the error flag will be either the integer 0 or the integer 1. A 0 means the flag is not set; a 1 means it is set.

Similarly, before doubling the calculation interval, a check is made to see if the increased calculation interval will be greater than or equal to the communication interval as specified on the CINTERVAL statement. If it is, the calculation interval is held at the CINTERVAL value.

Table 11.6

CSSL Control Statements

A. Translator Controls

Statement	Explanation
Array Dimensions ARRAY V1(D1), V2(D2), ..., VN(DN)	This statement of CSSL is similar to the DIMENSION and COMMON statements of FORTRAN. V1, V2, . . . , VN are variable names and D1, D2, . . . , DN are dimensions. Each dimension may be one, two, or three unsigned integer numbers separated by commas. For example, ARRAY A(10), B(7,5,6), C(3,5) Up to three dimensions and associated subscripts may be used with array variables in CSSL. Subscripted variables, which appear in a parallel or in a derivative section of an explicit mode program, must appear in an ARRAY statement and the subscripts of such variables must be unsigned integer constants. If subscripted variables appearing in a parallel or in a derivative section are to be used in statements that are to be sorted, they must be declared in an ARRAY statement.
Constant Values CONSTANT V1=N1, V2=N2, ... or CONSTANT (V1=N1, V2=N2, ...) or ARRAY A(N) CONSTANT A=(N values of A separated by commas)	This statement is functionally the same as the DATA statement of FORTRAN. V1, V2, etc., are variable names and N1, N2, etc., are the respective numerical or logical values. These values may be floating point, fixed point, or logical type. The values are assigned to the respective variables and are so stored in memory. If a variable is assigned a logical value, that variable name must appear as a logical control variable in some derivative or parallel section, or in a FORTRAN type logical expression. Properly constructed integer or floating point variable names must be used with corresponding integer or floating point values. Either a CSSL CONSTANT statement. or a FORTRAN DATA statement may be used for introducing constants. For sorting purposes, however, the CONSTANT statement must be used for all nonstate variable constants in derivative or parallel sections. Elsewhere, the FORTRAN DATA statement may be used.

Define Variables DEFINE A,B,C,...	The DEFINE statement is used only in the dynamic region of an explicit mode CSSL program. It serves to indicate to the translator that the variable names A, B, C, etc., have been introduced in another region or section and for sorting purposes have already been so defined. The use of the DEFINE statement is optional and may be omitted.
Terminate Run TERMT(E)	This statement is used only in implicit mode programs to indicate terminating conditions. E is a relational or logical expression which must be satisfied before the simulation run is terminated. E is evaluated once each communication interval and when satisfied, terminates the run. E may be a single logical variable if it is also used as a logical control variable or was expressly typed logical by a TYPE declaration statement elsewhere in the program. In explicit mode programs, the termination logic must be explicitly programmed.
Repeat Run with New Parameters REPEAT (E)	This statement is used only in implicit mode programs in place of a TERMT statement. Its function is to cause reruns of the same program with new values of parameters being read in before the rerun occurs. E is a relational or logical expression which is tested once each communication interval. If the condition of E is met, the current run is terminated and another set of parameters is read in and the run repeated. The REPEAT statement must be used, therefore, with some input statement such as CARDS. When the data cards are exhausted, the program will terminate without the need for a TERMT statement.

Table 11.6 *(Continued)*

B. Integration Controls

Statement	*Explanation*
Independent Variable VARIABLE V = X	This statement is used to declare the independent variable to be something other than time, and to assign an initial value to the independent variable. In the sample statement shown, V is the name of the independent variable and X is its initial value. For example, VARIABLE A = 10.0 In the derivative section in which the above statement appears, X is considered to be the independent variable and may be referred to as such whenever desired. Statement labels may not be used in conjunction with the VARIABLE statement. If the VARIABLE statement is omitted, T is assumed to be the independent variable and its initial value is taken as 0.0. Once the independent variable is assigned by a VARIABLE statement (or is assumed to be T because of the absence of a VARIABLE statement) it retains that name and initial value until explicitly changed by another VARIABLE statement.

Communication Interval CINTERVAL V = X	This statement assigns a name and value to the communication interval for each derivative section in which it appears. In the sample statement shown, V is the name of the communication interval and X is its value. The CINTERVAL statement causes an output to occur at each X units of the independent variable. For example, CINTERVAL CI = 0.01 would cause an output of 0.01 units of the independent variable. The name of the communication interval (CI in this case) can be referenced whenever desired. Statement labels may not be used in conjunction with the CINTERVAL statement. If the CINTERVAL statement is omitted, CINT is assumed to be the name of the communication interval and its value is taken as 1.0. Once the communication interval has been established either by a CINTERVAL statement or assumed to be CINT because of the absence of a CINTERVAL statement, it retains that name and value until explicitly changed by another CINTERVAL statement.
Number of Calculation Steps per Communication Interval NSTEPS V = K	This statement is used to specify the number of calculation steps in each communication interval. In the sample statement, V is a nonsubscripted variable name and K is its value which must be an integer greater than zero. If the NSTEPS statement is omitted, NST is assumed to be the variable name with value 1.

Table 11.6 *(Continued)*

Statement	Explanation
Integration Method ALGORITHM V1 = N1, V2 = N2	This statement specifies the integration method to be used in the derivative section in which the statement appears. The value of N1 assigned to the variable V1 specifies the integration method as follows:

Value of N1	Method Used	Calculation Interval	Number of Previous Values Required
1	Euler	Fixed	0
2	Trapezoidal	Fixed	1
3	Four-point predictor	Fixed	4
4	Adams–Moulton	Fixed	4
5	Runge–Kutta–Gill (fourth-order)	Fixed	0
6	User supplied	–	–
7	User supplied	–	–
8	Adams–Moulton with error control	Variable	4
9	Milne with error control	Variable	4

The value N2 assigned to V2 specifies the initialization method to be used to calculate the previous values required by the particular integration method N1.

If the ALGORITHM statement is not specified, V1 is assumed to be IALGOR, V2 is assumed to be JALGOR, N1 is assumed to be 5, and N2 is assumed to be 5 which specifies the Runge–Kutta–Gill fourth-order fixed interval method.

In the ALGORITHM statement the variable names and values must be integer type. The variable names must be nonsubscripted. For example, the statement

ALGORITHM I = 4, J = 1

specifies that the integration method used will be the Adams–Moulton method and the initialization method will be the Euler method.

Number of Initialization Steps NISTEPS V = K	This statement specifies the number of times the initialization method is to be used for calculating the previous values required by the integration method specified in the ALGORITHM statement. In the sample statement shown, V is a nonsubscripted integer variable name and K is an integer value. If this statement is omitted, it is assumed that the variable name is NIST and its value is 1. For example, the two statements NISTEPS K = 4 ALGORITHM I = 4, J = 1 specify the Adams–Moulton integration method, the Euler initialization method, and that the Euler method be used four times to provide the four previous values required by the Adams–Moulton method.

C. Error Controls

Statement	*Explanation*
Absolute and Relative Errors XERROR name, V = K MERROR name, Z = N	These statements apply only to the methods of integration with error control. The XERROR statement specifies an absolute error tolerance on the output variable of an INTEG operation. This output variable is identified by "name." V is a real variable name and K is its real value. Similarly, the MERROR statement specifies a relative error tolerance on the same output variable "name." Z is the name of a real variable and N is its real value. For example, Y = INTEG (YDOT, 0.0) XERROR Y, XER = 10E − 5 MERROR Y, ERR = 5E − 4 The error tolerances specified by the XERROR and MERROR statements are used with the error control procedure described in Section 11.8.

Table 11.6 *(Continued)*

Statement	Explanation
Minimum Calculation Interval MINTERVAL V = K	This statement applies only to the methods of integration with error control. V is a real variable name and K is its real value. K specifies the minimum value to which the calculation interval can be reduced. If the calculation interval is set to this minimum, the system error flag IERR is set for future reference, and calculation proceeds as though the error tests were satisfied. If the MINTERVAL statement is omitted, the CSSL system assumes V to be HMINT and K to be 0.000001. If specified, K must be such that $$0. < K < (CINTERVAL/NSTEP)$$
Error Flag ERRTAG V	This statement applies only to the methods of integration with error control. Its purpose is to give an integer name V to the error flag variable. The error flag variable is set when the calculation interval is reduced to the minimum value specified by the MINTERVAL statement. If the statement is omitted, the system assumes the name of V to be IERR. Whether assigned or assumed, the error flag can be examined by the program. For example, ERRTAG NTAG IF(NTAG .EQ.1), etc.

11.9 Detailed Program Structure

In an earlier section, we indicated briefly that a CSSL program consists of a number of source statements structured either implicitly or explicitly. The implicit structure allows the novice user of CSSL to define his problem and to solve it quickly without being burdened with the details of programming. The explicit structure provides the skilled programmer with the added capability of manipulating and controlling his simulation study.

An implicit program contains a PROGRAM statement to begin the program and an END statement to end it. The entire program between these two statements is considered to be a single derivative section. All controls are automatic except for the TERMT statement which terminates a simulation run or the REPEAT statement which reinitiates a new simulation run. An implicit program must not contain other structure statements. Segments and multiple derivative sections are not allowed.

Input and output are accomplished by judicious use of CONSTANT, INPUT, CARDS, OUT, or OUTPUT statements as explained in Table 11.5.

An explicit CSSL program is subdivided into parts or blocks somewhat reminiscent of ALGOL. The highest-order CSSL block is the PROGRAM block and is procedural in nature. Inside the PROGRAM block may be one or more *segment* blocks which are further divided into blocks called the *initial* region, the *dynamic* region, and the *terminal* region. The dynamic region may be further subdivided into one or more *derivative* and/or *parallel* sections. Explicit programs are subdivided into these various blocks by appropriate structure statements.

The block structure of CSSL programs is shown in Fig. 11.6.

The first statement of any CSSL program is the PROGRAM statement of the form:

PROGRAM NAME

A card containing this statement should be the first card in the program source deck. The last card in the source deck is the END card corresponding to the PROGRAM card. All statements in between are structure, representation, and FORTRAN statements. The program name is optional. It is used only for documentation purposes.

Segment statements are of the form:

SEGMENT NAME or SEGMENT NAME (A,B,C,...)

The name of the segment is an identifier. It serves to identify particular segments if there are more than one. If a program contains only one segment, the SEGMENT

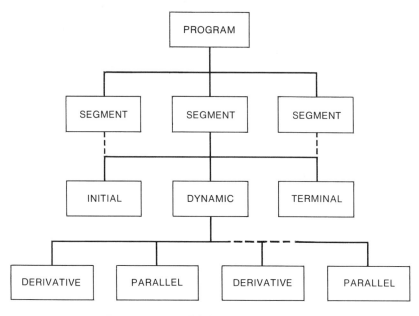

Figure 11.6 *CSSL block structure.*

statement may be omitted. The second form of the SEGMENT statement is used if parameters are to be passed to the segment in a manner analogous to passing parameters to a FORTRAN subroutine. Segments are also called by a CALL statement in a manner analogous to calling a FORTRAN subroutine. For example see Fig. 11.7.

As with FORTRAN subroutines, one segment may call another.

The INITIAL statement is of the form:

INITIAL

This statement is followed by whatever procedural FORTRAN statements are required to accomplish the one-time initial calculations or initial assignment of values to constants. Every segment must contain an initial region. Every initial region must end with an END.

Each segment must also contain a terminal region. This region contains the statements relating to the simulation termination. The statement of the form:

TERMINAL

commences this region and END ends it. The statements in between are FORTRAN procedural type statements.

Between the initial and terminal regions is the dynamic region which begins with a statement of the form:

DYNAMIC

and ends with an END statement. The control statements for one pass through the communication interval are contained in the dynamic region. This includes the logic relating to the termination procedure, and also includes the derivative section(s).

The derivative section(s) begins with the statement of the form:

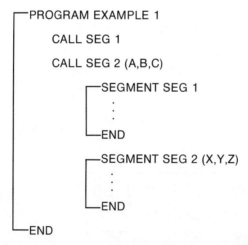

Figure 11.7 *The block structure of segments within a program.*

DERIVATIVE NAME

and ends with an END statement. For example, see Fig. 11.8.

The function of the derivative section is to describe the dynamic system being simulated. The CSSL translator generates, from the representation statement in the derivative section, a derivative subroutine which is identified by the name given in the DERIVATIVE statement. The function of this subroutine is to calculate the values of the state variables for a given value of the independent variable. Depending on which integration algorithm is used, the derivative section will be executed repeatedly at fixed or at varying intervals of the independent variable. The output is produced at fixed intervals, the communication interval, regardless of the integration method used. Multiple derivative sections are allowed in a single dynamic region.

The statements in the derivative section are nonprocedural. That is, they may be written in any order. These statements are sorted by the processor into proper computational sequence without attention by the programmer.

Parallel regions are identified by the statement:

PARALLEL NAME

at the start of a parallel region and end with an END. Parallel regions are in every way but one similar to derivative regions. The one difference is that parallel regions may not contain INTEG statements.

At times it is necessary to include some FORTRAN procedural statements in a derivative section. This is accomplished by the statement:

PROCEDURAL (Output variable list = Input variable list)

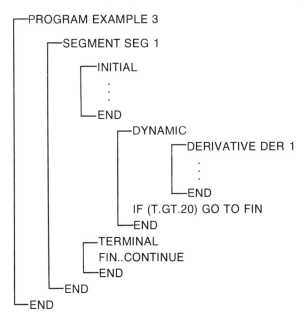

Figure 11.8 *Further details of CSSL block structure.*

The word SEQUENTIAL may be used in place of the word PROCEDURAL if desired. The input and output variable lists are lists of variable names separated by commas. The lists may contain nothing at all if there are no input or output variables in the procedural. In this case, the statement is simply

PROCEDURAL

to indicate its beginning. The list may contain no input variables; then the statement is

PROCEDURAL (Output variable list =)

or it may contain no output variables, in which case the statement is

PROCEDURAL (= Input variable list)

All outputs in the variable list must be variable names only. The inputs may be either numeric constants or variable names, but must not be expressions.

When a procedural or sequential region is defined as described above, it is sorted as a single representation statement. That is, the statements in the region are sorted as a group on the basis of the input and output variables in the structure statement. The individual statements are not sorted, however, with respect to each other.

Let us look at the system shown in block diagram form in Fig. 11.9 as an example of a system to be simulated using CSSL. The values are:

$$J = 340 \text{ slug ft}$$
$$KG = 1600 \text{ V/rad/sec}$$
$$DB = 0.98 \text{ V}$$
$$N = 0.153 \text{ lb ft}$$
$$T1 = 8 \text{ msec}$$
$$\zeta = 0.35$$
$$\omega_n = 88 \text{ rad/sec}$$
$$TX(0) = 0.0 \text{ rad}$$
$$TXD(0) = 0.05236 \text{ rad/sec}$$

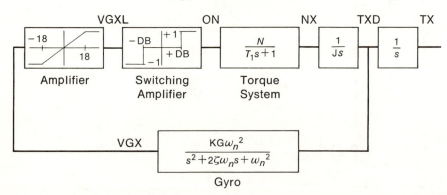

Figure 11.9 *A nonlinear system.*

For purposes of illustration, the program is written to make use of the procedural capability of CSSL.

The input to the gyro block in Fig. 11.9 is TXD and the output is VGX. As a transfer function we can write

$$\frac{VGX}{TXD} = \frac{-KG\omega_n{}^2}{s^2 + 2\zeta\omega_n s + \omega_n{}^2} \tag{11.2}$$

Equation 11.2 can be rewritten as

$$-TXD(KG\omega_n{}^2) = (s^2 + 2\zeta\omega_n s + \omega_n{}^2)\ VGX \tag{11.3}$$

which, when written as a time domain solution for the highest derivative, becomes

$$\frac{d^2VGX}{dt^2} = -2\zeta\omega_n \frac{dVGX}{dt} - \omega_n{}^2\ (VGX + KG(TXD)) \tag{11.4}$$

Integrating Eq. 11.4 gives Eq. 11.5

$$\frac{dVGX}{dt} = \int \left(-2\zeta\omega_n \frac{dVGX}{dt} - \omega_n{}^2\ (VGX + KG(TXD)) \right) dt \tag{11.5}$$

and integrating again gives

$$VGX = \int \frac{dVGX}{dt}\ dt \tag{11.6}$$

Equations 11.5 and 11.6 are the basis for writing part of the program shown in Fig. 11.10.

In the initial region of the program of Fig. 11.10, some preliminary calculations are performed prior to entering the dynamic region. By doing these calculations in the initial region, it is necessary to do them only once. If they were part of the derivative section, as they could be, they would be done repeatedly over and over again at each calculation time step. By following the procedure shown here, some computer time is saved.

The third line in the derivative section of Fig 11.10 is written

VGXD=INTEG(−TZWN*VGXD−WNSQ*(VGX+KG*TXD),0.)

which is the CSSL equivalent of Eq. 11.5. Similarly,

VGX=INTEG(VGXD,VGXI)

is the CSSL equivalent of Eq. 11.6. The next line in Fig. 11.10 is written

VGXL=BOUND(−18.,+18.,VGX)

which simulates the behavior of the saturating amplifier whose input is VGX, whose output is VGXL, and whose limits are ±18 V.

The procedural section simulates the action of the switching amplifier. The output of the procedural section is named ON and its inputs are VGXL and DB. ON is set equal to 0.0 if the absolute value of VGXL is less than DB and is 1.0 otherwise. ON is used as an input to the REALPL operator which simulates the torque system.

```
PROGRAM NONLINEAR SYSTEM
    INITIAL $ WNSQ=WN*WN $ TZWN=2.*ZETA*WN $ VGXI=-KG*TXDI
    END
        DYNAMIC
            DERIVATIVE DER $ ALGORITHM IA=8,JA=8 $ MINTERVAL MI=1.E-9
            CINTERVAL CI=2.5
            VGXD=INTEG(-TZWN*VGXD-WNSQ*(VGX+KG*TXD),0.)
            VGX=INTEG(VGXD,VGXI)
            VGXL=BOUND(-18.,+18.,VGX)
                PROCEDURAL(ON=VGXL,DB)
                ON=0.
                IF(ABS(VGXL) .LT. DB) GO TO L1
                ON=SIGN(1.,VGXL)
                L1..CONTINUE
                END
            NX=N*REALPL(0.008,ON,0.)
            TXD=INTEG(NX/J,TXDI)
            TX=INTEG(TXD,TXI)
            OUTPUT 4,VGXL,TX,TXD,NX,ON
            PREPAR VGXL
            CONSTANT N=0.153,J=340.,KG=1600.,DB=0.98,WN=88., ...
            ZETA=0.35,TXI=0.,TXDI=0.05236
            END
        IF(T .GT. 140.) GO TO FIN
        END
    TERMINAL $ FIN.. CONTINUE
    END
END
```

Figure 11.10 *A program to simulate the system of Fig. 11.9.*

The output of REALPL is NX. NX/J is integrated to give TXD, and this in turn is integrated to give TX. The statement

OUTPUT 4, VGXL, TX, TXD, NX, ON

causes the values of the mentioned variables to be printed out at every four communication intervals. The statement

PREPAR VGXL

causes the values of this variable to be accumulated at each communication interval for future plotting. The statement

CONSTANT

assigns numerical values to various symbolic names. Notice that this statement is continued onto the next card by the three consecutive periods. The dynamic region includes the statement

IF(T. GY. 140.) GO TO FIN

which terminates the simulation run after T reaches 140 sec of system time by branching to the terminal region.

The reader should take particular notice in Fig. 11.10 that the procedural section is written in FORTRAN and will not be sorted. The statement label, L1, is alphameric. This is allowed in CSSL programs even though it would not be permitted in ordinary FORTRAN programs.

11.10   User Defined Additions to CSSL

In the introduction to this chapter, we discussed why simplicity in a simulation language is attractive. Such simplicity allows for easy man-machine interaction. Also, if a language is to be convenient to use, it must be application-oriented. The designers of CSSL have attempted to satisfy both of these goals by providing an implicit program structure feature, a free format capability, and a rich repertoire of simulation operators. Nevertheless, since CSSL is a general purpose simulation language, users may sometimes find that the available operators in the CSSL repertoire are not adequate to properly represent the particular system being simulated. It then becomes desirable to have an expansion capability for including additional user-generated syntactical statements as these new requirements arise. The procedural or sequential capability of CSSL described in the preceding section gives some ability in this direction, but a more powerful tool is provided by the CSSL *macro processor.*

The term *macro* identifies a group of one or more coded instructions which is generated apart from a main program and is used to perform some desired operation. The group of instructions comprising the macro is inserted into the main program in its entirety without modification whenever the operation performed by the macro is needed. The macro instructions thus become a part of the main program and are compiled and executed with it. By this process, macro instructions lose their identity as part of a macro and become part of a main program. They are then indistinguishable from other main program instructions.

The macro processor of CSSL consists of a *macro definition processor* and a *macro call processor.* Both are used to preprocess source programs prior to entering the FORTRAN compiler. Once a macro has been defined, it may be called any number of times within the simulation structure statements as the programmer finds need for it. The macro then becomes available to the programmer as an additional CSSL operator. The macro processor translates the macro call into a set of FORTRAN statements as defined by the macro definition. These FORTRAN statements are properly inserted into the main FORTRAN program which the CSSL system generates for simulating the desired problem, and thus they become a part of the main program.

There are several salient features of the CSSL macro processor:

(1) A set of directives controls the sequence of statements generated. This minimizes memory requirements and execution time.

(2) Variable and statement labels may be generated locally within the macro.

(3) Input arguments to a macro may be constants, variables, statement labels, expressions, or FORTRAN procedural statements.

(4) The number of arguments in a macro is not fixed.

(5) Automatic substitution of standard values is permitted.

(6) Macros may be nested. One macro may call another.

(7) Diagnostics are provided for the macro definition.

(8) Macros can be defined any place within a program. Due to the method used for processing macro definitions, a macro can be used before it is defined. It is not necessary, therefore, for macro definitions to appear at the beginning of the program in which they are used.

(9) A macro definition can be changed any place within a program. The macro processor always uses the most recent macro definition.

A macro definition is introduced by a macro definition directive and is terminated by a macro end directive. The name following the macro directive assigns a name to the macro which identifies it for calling purposes. A macro call consists of the macro name followed by a list of arguments separated by commas. The maximum number of characters in the macro argument list, including commas, must not exceed 9000.

The CSSL free coding format is used for defining a macro. The exceptions to this are that all macro directives must be preceded by the mnemonic MACRO, and COMMENT statements are not permitted.

Within the macro definition, two types of statement labels may appear. Local labels are used according to standard FORTRAN coding procedures and must be declared in the RELABEL macro directive. Macro directive labels provide branching capabilities within the macro to facilitate conditional code generation. In general, macro directive labels consist of from one to four alphameric characters, preceded by the mnemonic MACRO and at least one blank. Both local labels and macro directive labels must be separated from the statement body by two consecutive periods (..) in the usual CSSL manner.

Special attention must be given to those macros that will be called in derivative or parallel sections. In these cases, statements in the macro definition that contain no equal sign or that are not to be sorted should be grouped in a procedural block. This avoids sorting conflicts when the macros are invoked and the sections containing them are processed.

The macro directives used in the macro procedure are explained in Table 11.7.

Table 11.7

MACRO Directives

Directive	Explanation

Macro Directive
 	
MACRO NAME
P,Q,R,S
	This statement introduces the macro. All statements following this constitute a macro definition until terminated by a MACRO END statement. The name, chosen in the usual way, identifies the macro for future reference. P is a dummy reference parameter that identifies elements of the macro call argument list. Q is the first dimension of arrays in the argument list, R is the second dimension, and S is the third dimension.
	
	For example, if the macro directive is written:
	
	MACRO MACRO ARC P,Q,R,S
	
	and if in the main program the following statements are found:
	
	ARRAY A(10,15), B(5), C(3,6,8)
	ARC A,B,C
	
	Upon invocation of the macro, the following meanings will be applied:
	
	P(1) = A R(1) = 15
	P(2) = B R(2) = undefined
	P(3) = C R(3) = 6
	Q(1) = 10 S(1) = undefined
	Q(2) = 5 S(2) = undefined
	Q(3) = 3 S(3) = 8
	
	As a further example, consider the following:
	
	MACRO MACRO PROD E,F
	MACRO RELABEL L1
	    DO L1 K=1, F(1)
	    L1..E(1)(K)=E(2)(K)*E(3)(K)
	MACRO END
	
	When the above macro is invoked by
	
	ARRAY X(10),Y(10),Z(8),W(3)
	PROD Z,X,Y
	
	The generated FORTRAN code would be
	
	DO 10000 K=1,8
	10000 Z(K)=X(K)*Y(K)

Table 11.7 *(Continued)*

Directive	Explanation
Relabel RELABEL L1,L2,...,LN	In this directive, the symbols L1, L2, . . . , LN are alphameric identifiers in the usual CSSL sense. This directive specifies that all labels in the list are locally defined within the macro. Each of these labels is replaced by a unique label by the processor each time the macro is called. The unique labels always begin with 1 and contain 5 digits. This directive avoids multiple-defined statement labels when the macro is called more than once by a single program. The use of this directive is illustrated in the first section of Table 11.7.

Redefine
 	
REDEFINE A,B,C,...
	In this directive, A, B, C, . . . , etc. are variable names which, by the action of this directive, are identified as being locally defined. The variable names listed are replaced by the macro processor by unique variable names of the form ZXXXX where the X's represent decimal digits. For example,
	
	<pre>MACRO MACRO SUM A
	MACRO REDEFINE B
	MACRO RELABLE L5
	    B=A(1) + A(2)
	L5..A(3)=A(1)**B
	MACRO END</pre>
	When the above macro is invoked by the statement
	
	SUM X, Y, Z
	
	the generated FORTRAN code is
	
	$Z0001 = X + Y$
	$10000\ Z = X**Z0001$

Standard Value
 	
STANDVAL P1=e1,
    P2=e2,...,Pn=en
	This directive is used to provide standard values for the arguments of a macro. The symbols P1, P2, . . . , Pn represent the elements of the dummy reference parameter in the macro definition. The symbols e1, e2, . . . , en represent standard values to be used for the respective parameters. When used, the STANDVAL directive must immediately follow the macro name definition directive. To use the STAND-VAL directive, the position of an input variable, which is to have a standard value substituted for it, is left empty in the statement invoking the macro. For example,
	
	    MACRO MACRO ABC X
	    MACRO STANDVAL X(2)=3.0, X(4)=5.0
	      X(1)(1) = X(2)
	      X(1)(2) = X(3)
	      X(1)(3) = X(4)
	      X(1)(4) = X(5)
	    MACRO END
	
	When the above macro is invoked by
	
	    ARRAY RED(4)
	    ABC RED, P,D,Q,R
	
	the FORTRAN code generated would be
	
	    RED(1) = P
	    RED(2) = D
	    RED(3) = Q
	    RED(4) = R
	
	If, however, the macro were invoked by
	
	    ARRAY BLUE (4)
	    ABC BLUE, ,D, ,R
	
	the FORTRAN code generated would be
	
	    BLUE (1) = 3.0
	    BLUE (2) = D
	    BLUE (3) = 5.0
	    BLUE (4) = R
	
	with the standard values inserted in the place of the missing arguments.

Table 11.7 *(Continued)*

Directive	Explanation

Assign
 	
ASSIGN N
INCREMENT
DECREMENT
	The ASSIGN directive assigns to N the number of elements in the argument list of a macro call. The number assigned to N is an integer. N is any identifier. This identifier can then be used as the variable subscript of the dummy reference parameter in the macro name definition directive. INCREMENT increases N by 1 and DECREMENT decreases N by 1 each time they are used. For example,
	
	      MACRO MACRO ZERO A
	      MACRO ASSIGN J
	      MACRO 10.. IF J=0 20
	                 A(J)=0.0
	      MACRO DECREMENT
	      MACRO GOTO 10
	      MACRO 20.. EXIT
	      MACRO END
	
	If the above macro is invoked by
	
	    ZERO W,X,Y,Z
	
	the generated FORTRAN code would be
	
	    Z = 0.0
	    Y = 0.0
	    X = 0.0
	    W = 0.0

Conditional Branch If E1=E2 L	The IF directive is the conditional branching instruction. If the relation E1=E2 holds, the processor will go to the directive or statement bearing the label L for the next instruction. Otherwise, the statements following the IF directive are generated until another macro directive is encountered. The parameters E1 and E2 can be subscripted dummy reference parameters, integer constants, character strings, or the identifier used in the ASSIGN directive. E1 and E2 must not be expressions.
Unconditional Branch GOTO L	This is the unconditional branching directive to the macro directive or statement labeled L. Note there is no space between the O and T.

Continue CONTINUE	The CONTINUE directive has the same use when writing macros as it has when writing FORTRAN programs. It does nothing but provide a convenient executable statement to branch to.
Local Termination EXIT	The EXIT directive designates local termination of a macro. It is similar to the RETURN statement in a FORTRAN subroutine. Any number of EXIT directives may be used (including none at all).
Macro Termination END	This directive terminates the MACRO definition. It is similar to the END statement in a FORTRAN program. There must be one and only one END per macro definition.
Print PRINT S	This directive causes the character string S to be printed out. S may be continued onto additional cards, but is limited to the number of characters that can be printed on one line by the line printer.
Macro Call NAME A, B, C, . . . or Output variable list = NAME (input variable list)	This directive is used to invoke a macro. The name is that given in the macro definition directive. There are two forms of the macro call. In the first form, A, B, C, . . . are the macro call arguments corresponding to the variables implied by the dummy reference parameter in the macro definition directive. In the second form, the output variables are listed to the left of the equal sign with the macro name and input variable list to the right. The elements in the argument list may be constants, variables, expressions, statement labels, or FORTRAN statements.

The program of Fig. 11.11 is an extension of that of Fig. 11.10 which was explained previously. Figure 11.11 is different, however, because it contains two procedural sections rather than just one. The reason for the second procedural is to make the system more nearly like reality by allowing an exponential buildup and decay of NX instead of a rather idealized step function buildup applied to a first-order lag transfer function (REALPL).

The first procedural of Fig. 11.11 is identical with the one in Fig. 11.10. The second procedural makes use of the EXPF operator to produce the desired exponential behavior. The output of this procedural is NX which was the output of the first-order lag in Fig. 11.10.

The program of Fig. 11.12 is an alternate method of writing the same program as that of Fig. 11.11, except this new program makes use of the CSSL macro capability. The FORTRAN code generated by either the program of Fig. 11.11 or Fig. 11.12 would be equivalent, as a careful comparison will reveal.

```
PROGRAM NONLINEAR SYSTEM
    INITIAL $ WNSQ=WN*WN $ TZWN=2.*ZETA*WN $ VGXI=-KG*TXDI
    END
        DYNAMIC
            DERIVATIVE DER $ ALGORITHM IA=8,JA=8 $ MINTERVAL MI=1.E-9
            CINTERVAL CI=2.$
            VGXD=INTEG(-TZWN*VGXD-WNSQ*(VGX+KG*TXD),0.)
            VGX=INTEG(VGXD,VGXI)
            VGXL=BOUND(-18.,+18.,VGX)
                PROCEDURAL (ON=VGXL,DB)
                ON=0.
                IF(ABS(VGXL) .LT. DB) GO TO L1
                ON=SIGN(1.,VGXL)
                L1.. CONTINUE
                END
                PROCEDURAL (NX=ON)
                ONP=0.
                ONN=0.
                IF(ABS(ON) .LT. 0.5) GO TO LZ
                IF(ON .GT. 0.1) GO TO LP
                ONN=1.
                GO TO LZ
                LP.. ONP=1.
                LZ.. NXP=N*EXPF(0.,0.008,T,ONP)
                NXN=N*EXPF(0.,0.008,T,ONN)
                NX=NXP-NXN
                END
            TXD=INTEG(NX/J,TXDI)
            TX=INTEG(TXD,TXI)
            OUTPUT 4,VGLX,TX,TXD,NX,ON
            PREPAR VGXL
            CONSTANT N=0.153,J=340.,KG=1600.,DB=0.98,WN=88., ...
            ZETA=0.35,TXI=0.,TXDI-0.05236
            END
        IF(T .GT. 140.) GO TO FIN
        END
    TERMINAL $ FIN.. CONTINUE
    END
END
```

Figure 11.11 *A CSSL program with two procedurals.*

```
PROGRAM NONLINEAR SYSTEM
MACRO MACRO SAM P
MACRO RELABEL L1,LZ,LP
MACRO REDEFINE ON
PROCEDURAL (P(1),P(2)=P(3),P(4))
ON=0.
IF(ABS(P(3)) .LT. P(4)) GO TO L1
ON=SIGN(1.,P(3))
L1.. CONTINUE
P(1)=0.
P(2)=0.
IF(ABS(ON) .LT. 0.5) GO TO LZ
IF (ON .GT. 0.1) GO TO LP
P(2)=1.
GO TO LZ
LP.. P(1)=1.
LZ.. CONTINUE
END
MACRO END
    INITIAL $ WNSQ=WN*WN $ TSWN=2.*ZETA*WN $ VGXI=-KG*TXDI
    END
        DYNAMIC
            DERIVATIVE DER $ ALGORITHM IA=8,JA=8 $ MINTERVAL MI=1.E-9
            CINTERVAL CI=2.5
            VGXD=INTEG(-TZWN*VGXD-WNSQ*(VGX+NG*TXD), 0.)
            VGX=INTEG(VGXD,VGXI)
            VGXL=BOUND(-18.,+18.,VGX)
            ONP,ONN=SAM(VGXL,DB)          (TRANSLATES INTO) ─────────┐
            NXP=N*EXPF(0.,0.008,T,ONP)                               │
            NXN=N*EXPF(0.,0.008,T,ONN)                               │
            NX=NXP-NXN                                               │
            TXD=INTEG(NX/J,TXDI)                                     │
            TX=INTEG(TXD,TXI)                                        │
            OUTPUT 4,VGLX,TX,TXD,NX,ON                               │
            PREPAR VGXL                                              │
            CONSTANT N=0.153,J=340.,KG=1600.,DB=0.98,WN=88., ...     │
            ZETA=0.35,TXI=0.,TXDI=0.05236                            │
            END                                                      │
        IF(T .GT. 140.) GO TO FIN                                    │
        END                                                          │
    TERMINAL $ FIN.. CONTINUE                                        │
    END                                                             │
END                                                                 │
```

Figure 11.12 *A CSSL program utilizing the macro capability.*

Figure 11.12 *(Continued)*

```
      Z0000=0.
      IF(ABS(VGXL).LT.DB) GO TO 10003 ⎤
      Z0000=SIGN(1.,VGXL)              │
10003 CONTINUE                         │
      ONP=0.                           │
      ONN=0.                           │
      IF(ABS(Z0000).LT.0.5) GO TO 10002 ⎬ ────────────────
      IF(Z0000.GT.0.1) GO TO 10001     │
      ONN=1.                           │
      GO TO 10002                      │
10001 ONP=1.                           │
10002 CONTINUE                         ⎦
```

11.11 Summary

This chapter has presented the essential features of CSSL simulation language. This is the most recent of a long line of continuous system simulation languages. Where earlier languages were constructed almost independently, CSSL resulted from the recommendations of the Simulation Software Committee of Simulation Councils, Inc. As a result, CSSL incorporates the desirable features of earlier languages that have proved to be useful and also adds some features not found in the earlier languages.

CSSL generates a FORTRAN program which is compiled and executed in the usual manner. This avoids the slowness of many previous languages which were essentially assemblers. It also allows the programmer to intervene at the FORTRAN program level should that prove to be desirable. CSSL and FORTRAN IV act as adjuncts to each other, providing flexibility, power, and convenience to the skilled programmer. However, this also provides a simple implicit structure for the less skilled user.

CSSL is in a dynamic state. Changes and improvements are constantly being made. The user will do well to become acquainted with the details of the particular version of CSSL with which he is supplied.

CSSL is a powerful and convenient tool for the simulation of continuous systems. Its use should enable the individual to solve system simulation problems of great detail and complexity.

Other simulation languages such as CSMP and DSL-90, while not as powerful as CSSL, are nevertheless quite similar. A study of this presentation of CSSL will help in the understanding of these other languages. The user should have little trouble transferring from one language to another.

EXERCISES

Note: Most of the exercises of Chapters 4, 6, 7, 8 and 10 are applicable as exercises in the use of CSSL. Some additional exercises are included here.

1. The block diagram shown in Fig. 11.13 represents a feedback control system. Block A in Fig. 11.13 is a block to be assigned various functions. Use CSSL to simulate the system and determine the behavior where $dX/dt(0) = 0, X(0) = 1.45$ and where

(a) $A = 1.0$

(b) $A = $ relay such that

$$Z = \begin{cases} 1.0, & E > 0.0 \\ 0.0, & E = 0.0 \\ -1.0, & E < 0.0 \end{cases}$$

(c) $A = $ the switching amplifier shown in Fig. 11.8 with DB $= \pm 0.25$ and a saturation level of ± 1.0.

(d) $A = $ a switching amplifier with saturation such that

$$Z = \begin{cases} 0.5, & E > 0.5 \\ E, & -0.5 \le E \le +0.5 \\ -0.5, & E < -0.5 \end{cases}$$

(e) A relay with hysteresis as shown in Fig. 11.14 where $A = -0.1, B = 0.1, Z(0) = 0.3$.

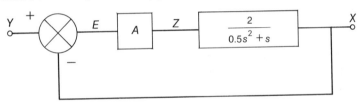

Figure 11.13

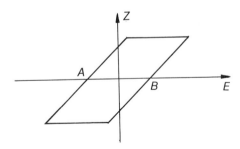

Figure 11.14

2. A thin metallic circular ring of radius $R = 0.1$ m is charged with Q C of positive charge uniformly distributed over its surface (see Fig. 11.15). An electron is released from rest at point P on the axis of the ring.

(a) Find the differential equation that describes the behavior of the electron as a function of time where the electric field intensity is given by

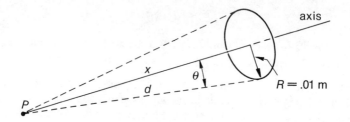

Figure 11.15

$$\mathscr{E} = \frac{Q\cos\theta}{4\pi\epsilon d^2}$$

It is given that

$$Q = 12 \times 10^{-18} \text{ C}$$
$$\epsilon = 8.85 \times 10^{-12} \text{ C}^2/\text{Nm}^2$$
$$x(0) = 0.15 \text{ m}$$
electron mass $= 9.11 \times 10^{-31}$ kg
electron charge $= 1.6 \times 10^{-19}$ C

(b) Use CSSL to simulate the behavior of the system.
(c) What is the frequency of oscillation?
(d) How long does it take the electron to reach the plane of the coil?
(e) What is the velocity of the electron when it reaches the plane of the coil?

3. Figure 11.16 shows two circular discs attached to the ends of a circular rod. The rod is twisted and released. It is known that the polar moments of inertia are $J_1 = 2.0$ lb ft sec^2, $J_2 = 1.5$ lb in sec^2, and the torsional spring constant K_1 is 4×10^5 lb in/rad.
(a) Develop the behavior describing differential equations.
(b) Simulate the system using CSSL.

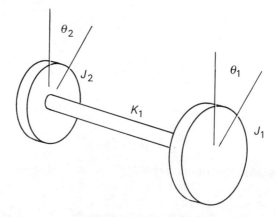

Figure 11.16

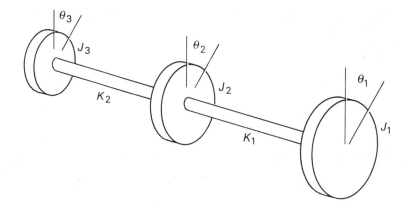

Figure 11.17

4. A third disc is added to the system of Exercise 3 as shown in Fig. 11.17, having a moment of inertia $J_3 = 0.63$ lb in sec². J_1, J_2, and K_1 are the same as in Exercise 3, but $K_2 = 3 \times 10^5 |\alpha|^{1.67}$ where α is the twist in radians in rod 2. Therefore, $|\alpha| = |\theta_2 - \theta_3|$.
   (a) Write the behavior describing differential equations.
   (b) Simulate the system using CSSL.

5.

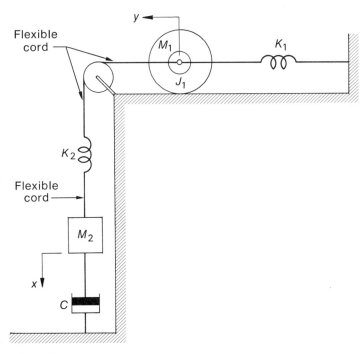

Figure 11.18

In Fig. 11.18, the cylinder has mass $M_1 = 2.5$ lb/ft/sec² and moment of inertia $J_1 = 1.2$ lb ft sec². The cylinder rolls without slipping or friction. The dashpot generates coulomb friction with a friction coefficient of $C = 10^{-2}$ lb/ft/sec. The pulley is frictionless. The suspend weight has mass $M_2 = 1.8$ lb/ft/sec². The radius of the cylinder is 10 in. Spring 1 is nonlinear, its characteristic being given by $K_1 = 250 \; d_1|d_1|$ where d_1 is the deflection of spring 1 from its unstretched position. Spring 2 is also nonlinear such that $K_2 = 175(d_2)^3$ where d_2 is the deflection of spring 2 from its unstretched position. Spring 1 is attached rigidly to its support and to the cylinder, but spring 2 is attached to the cylinder and M_2 by means of a flexible cord. The system is set in motion by releasing M_2 from rest with no slack in the cord and no stretch in the springs.

(a) Simulate the behavior of the system using CSSL. [*Hint:* Do not overlook the fact that spring 2 can only exert force when the cord is taut.]

(b) Find the value of M_2, if one exists, that will cause x to become zero once after M_2 is released, but such that x will never become negative.

(c) Find the value of M_2, if one exists, that will cause the tension in the cord to become zero once after M_2 is released without the cord ever becoming slack.

12

Electronic Circuit Analysis Program (ECAP)

12.1   Introduction

Chapters 10 and 11 introduced us to MIMIC and CSSL, two general purpose digital computer simulation languages. These languages can be used to simulate the behavior of physical systems with the only provision being, in general, that the system behavior can be described in terms of differential equations, difference equations, algebraic equations, transfer functions, and/or block diagrams.

Often however, engineers find themselves faced with the task of repeatedly simulating a particular kind of system for which general purpose simulation languages such as MIMIC or CSSL prove to be cumbersome. The analysis of structures, the calculations performed by surveyors and construction engineers, or the problems done by electronic circuit designers are typical of such situations. For performing tasks of this kind a number of special purpose, problem oriented, simulation languages have been designed. STRESS is a language which was developed for the use of structural designers, COGO is designed expressly for surveyors' use, and ECAP is meant to aid electric circuit designers in solving some of their problems.

ECAP is studied in more detail here as an example of one of these special simulation languages. The objective of ECAP is to help the circuit designer in the analysis of electric and electronic circuits. ECAP is designed so that the user can supply information about the simulated circuit to the computer and, then, request information about the performance of the simulated circuit from the computer in a systematic, simple, and natural way. ECAP performs dc, ac, or transient analyses of electric networks as requested by the programmer. The type of analysis desired, the topology of the network to be analyzed, the circuit elements comprising the network, the nature of the network excitation, and the output desired constitute the elements of an ECAP program. Networks containing as many as 50 nodes, in addition to the reference node, and as many as 200 branches can be analyzed utilizing ECAP for either dc or transient analysis. The same maximum number of nodes and branches can be accommodated during ac analysis, except when performing worst-case or sensitivity calculations. In these cases, a maximum of 25 nodes and 100 branches can be accommodated.

Chapter 1 indicated that engineers frequently use models to aid in the design process. A typical model used by electronic circuit designers has been called by some a "breadboard model." A breadboard model of a circuit is often assembled on a flat board of insulating material which is constructed so as to conveniently accept the placement of the various components of the circuit and to retain them in whatever position they are placed. The breadboard model thus contains all of the components of a proposed circuit but it is put together without the careful permanent wiring or placement of components that is required for a finished product. This rather crude breadboard model is often wired by means of clip-leads, at a workbench, in hastily assembled form. Because of the accessibility of the components, the circuit can be easily tested to determine if it has the desired behavior. Should the behavior prove unsatisfactory, modifications can be quickly and easily made until ultimately the desired behavior is achieved.

ECAP allows a circuit designer to readily simulate a model of a proposed circuit in an economical and efficient manner using a digital computer rather than a breadboard. There are several advantages of the computer simulation approach. During the various states of design development, circuit parameters can be changed with corresponding variations in circuit behavior being quickly apparent. Components that are difficult to obtain or that are expensive can be simulated and included in the proposed circuit easily, and without significant expense, thus saving time and money. Severe operating conditions can be studied safely and measurements can be made that might be difficult or dangerous to do in an actual circuit. Destructive testing of circuits containing expensive or hard to replace components is practical and feasible, since there is no danger to these components when using simulation.

Limited only by the previously stated maximum numbers of nodes and branches, any electrical network that can be assembled from any combination of the allowable standard elements can be analyzed. The standard elements do not include electronic components explicitly, but frequently these electronic devices can be replaced by their equivalent circuits which in turn are composed of standard elements.

ECAP is easy to use. The user need not know how the ECAP system functions internally, but he must understand how to communicate with it. He must know how to describe the circuit to be analyzed, how to specify the type of analysis desired, and how to interpret the results. Electrical engineers who use ECAP will find that it utilizes the language of their profession, hence, making communication with the ECAP system natural and very easy for them.

The ECAP system accepts statements, in the form of prepared 80 column data processing cards, which describe the network to be analyzed. These statements are interpreted, the network topology is deduced, the corresponding network equations are formulated, the desired analysis is made, and the requested output is generated all without further attention from the user.

12.2   ECAP dc Analysis

ECAP will perform the dc analysis of an electric circuit comprised of some combination of resistors, fixed voltage sources, fixed current sources, and/or dependent current sources. The dc analysis of networks containing electronic components can be accomplished if these components are first replaced by their equivalent circuits which in turn are comprised of resistors, fixed voltage sources, fixed current sources, and dependent current sources. Capacitors and inductors are not allowed in networks on which an ECAP dc analysis is to be performed. The steady-state dc analysis of such networks can be achieved by replacing all inductors with short circuits and all capacitors with open circuits.

A nominal solution is made of all networks being analyzed by dc analysis. In addition to the nominal solution, the user can specify that he wants separate solutions in which some of the parameters of the circuits are varied in some prescribed way. For each combination of the parameters, a separate solution will be made. In addition, the circuit designer may need to know how changes in circuit parameters affect the voltages throughout the network. This can be determined by specifying the calculations of partial derivatives and sensitivity coefficients. If the user supplies tolerance data on each circuit parameter, worst-case calculations can be made. The standard deviation of all node voltage can be calculated for a circuit whose parameters are assumed to be random, statistically independent, and normally distributed about their nominal values. A Monte Carlo analysis of a network can be made where the network elements are selected from appropriately specified distributions.

The nominal solution determines the behavior of the specified network. If requested by the programmer, all node voltages (NV), branch voltages (BV), element voltages (EV), branch currents (BC), element currents (EC), and/or element power losses (EP) can be calculated and printed out. Figure 12.1 shows the meaning of each of these symbols in a standard branch.

The dependent current sources of Fig. 12.1 (only one dependent source is shown) connect across the element of the branch. This branch is called the *to* branch. The currents in these dependent current sources depend on currents or

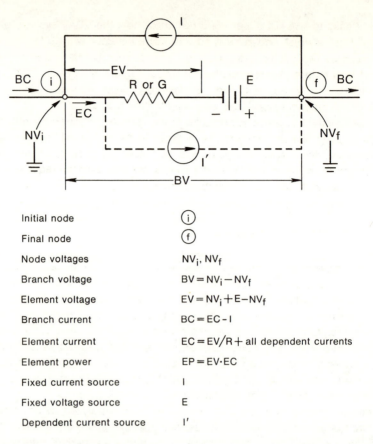

Initial node	(i)
Final node	(f)
Node voltages	NV_i, NV_f
Branch voltage	$BV = NV_i - NV_f$
Element voltage	$EV = NV_i + E - NV_f$
Branch current	$BC = EC - I$
Element current	$EC = EV/R +$ all dependent currents
Element power	$EP = EV \cdot EC$
Fixed current source	I
Fixed voltage source	E
Dependent current source	I'

Figure 12.1 *A standard branch with elements and polarities defined and indicated.*

voltages elsewhere in the network. Each dependent current source is specified by means of a current gain BETA, or a transconductance GM from the other branch called the *from* branch. The dependent current source across the to branch will have a value of current that is BETA times as large as the element current in the from branch or a value of current that is GM times the element voltage in the from branch. In general GM = BETA/R_{from}. Any branch may be used as many times as desired as a from branch or as a to branch. Some examples will help to make these details easily understood.

Suppose it is desired to perform a dc analysis of the circuit shown in Fig. 12.2. The first step to be taken by an ECAP user is to consecutively number the nodes, other than the reference node, and branches of the network. The nodes and branches may be numbered in any arbitrary order but the numbers must form consecutive sets, each set starting with number 1. Every branch must contain a resistor and may also contain a fixed voltage source, a fixed current source, and/or one or more dependent current sources. Figure 12.2 does not contain a dependent

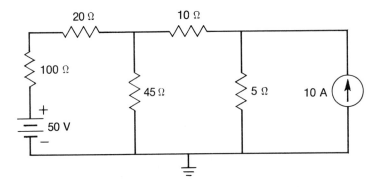

Figure 12.2 *A simple dc circuit to be analyzed.*

current source. Dependent current sources will be treated in the next example. The nodes and branches of the circuit of Fig. 12.2 have been arbitrarily numbered and these numbers are given in Fig. 12.3. The node numbers are shown encircled and the branch numbers are shown in arrowed flags. There are three nodes other than the reference node and there are five branches. The reference node is always assumed to be node zero. The arrowed flags in addition to showing the branch numbers, also show, by means of the arrows, the assumed directions of positive current flow. Should any of these assumed directions be incorrect, the signs of the computed values of current in such branches will be negative.

Once the nodes and branches have been arbitrarily but consecutively numbered, the ECAP user is in a position to describe the network topology and assign values to the circuit parameters. These tasks are accomplished by means of branch cards or more simply B-cards. The B-card information for the circuit of Fig. 12.3 is illustrated in Fig. 12.4. The information shown in this figure would be punched in 80 column data processing cards, one card for each line. Only 30 of the 80 columns are shown in Fig. 12.3.

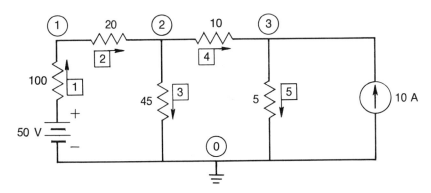

Figure 12.3 *The circuit of Fig. 12.2 with node and branch numbers indicated.*

	1	2	3	4	5	6	7	8	9	10	11	12	13	14	15	16	17	18	19	20	21	22	23	24	25	26	27	28	29	30
1			B	1			N	(	0	,	1	)	,	R	=	1	0	0	,	E	=	5	0							
2		B		2				N	(	1	,	2	)	,		R	=		2	0										
3	B			3			N	(	2		0	)	,				R	=			4	5								
4		B		4				N	(	2	,	3	)			R		=		1	0									
5		B		5			N	(	3	,	0	)	,	R	=	5	,	I	=	1	0									
6																														

Figure 12.4 *B-card information for the circuit of Fig. 12.3.*

The columns of the B-card are divided into four fields. Columns 1 through 5 form the first field, column 6 forms the second field, columns 7 through 72 form the third field, and columns 73 through 80 form the fourth field. The first field (columns 1 through 5) is used for branch number identification as shown. Branch identification is written as a B followed by the branch number. Any arrangement of spaces or placement within this field is acceptable. The second field (column 6) is the continuation field. A continuation of the preceding card is indicated by an asterisk in column 6. The third field (columns 7 through 72) is used to indicate data subgroups. One such data subgroup consists of an N followed by some parentheses containing the node numbers in sequence from the initial node to the final node corresponding to the assumed current flow direction. The node numbers are separated by commas. This field is also used to contain other data subroups whose purpose is to assign values to the circuit parameters as they relate to the branch being described by the B-card. The data subgroups are themselves separated by commas. The fourth field (columns 73 through 80) is not used by ECAP and may be used by the programmer in any way he desires.

Other than the field limitations indicated, there are no restrictions regarding the presentation of information on the B-cards. There is no prescribed order or sequence of presentation. Decimal points may be included in numbers or not as desired whenever the correct meaning is clear. Exponential form (in the FORTRAN sense) of numerical values is acceptable. Figure 12.5 shows another set of B-cards that would also suffice for the circuit of Fig. 12.3. In spite of the flexibility available, users will find an orderly arrangement of information helpful in presenting B-card data so that it can be easily scanned by eye. Figure 12.6 shows one acceptable and orderly presentation of the same information as in Fig. 12.5, both of which describe the circuit shown in Fig. 12.2.

All that is needed in addition to the B-card information to effect a nominal solu-

	1	2	3	4	5	6	7	8	9	10	11	12	13	14	15	16	17	18	19	20	21	22	23	24	25	26	27	28	29	30
1		B	1						N	(	0	,	1		)	,	R	=	1	0	0	.	0	,	E	=	5	E	1	
2		B				2		R	=	2	0	,		N	(	1	,	2	)											
3			B	3			N	(	2	,	0	)	,	R	=	4	5	.	0											
4	B			4				N	(	2	,	3	)	,	R	=	1	0												
5		B	5				I	=	1	0	0	E	−	1	,	R	=	5	,	N	(	3	,	0	)					
6																														

Figure 12.5 *Other ways of presenting B-card information.*

	1	2	3	4	5	6	7	8	9	10	11	12	13	14	15	16	17	18	19	20	21	22	23	24	25	26	27	28	29	30
1	B	1					N	(	0	,	1	)	,	R	=	1	0	0	,	E	=	5	0							
2	B	2					N	(	1	,	2	)	,	R	=	2	0													
3	B	3					N	(	2	,	0	)	,	R	=	4	5													
4	B	4					N	(	2	,	3	)	,	R	=	1	0													
5	B	5					N	(	3	,	0	)	,	R	=	5	,	I	=	1	0									
6																														

Figure 12.6 *An orderly presentation of B-card information.*

tion are a card to indicate that dc analysis is to be performed, a card to indicate what output is to be printed out, and an execute card to indicate the end of the program and to signal the computer that the solution is to proceed. Figure 12.7 shows a complete ECAP program to obtain a nominal dc solution for the circuit of Fig. 12.2.

Some additional features are shown in Fig. 12.7 which we have not yet discussed. The line numbers at the extreme left are shown here for convenient reference only, and do not appear on the actual program cards. Notice that a C in column 1 causes that card to be treated as a comment card. The information on comment cards is printed out on the program listing but is not processed in any other way and has no effect on the analysis. Lines 1, 2, 4, 10, and 12 represent comment cards. Some of the comment cards are blank and serve only to separate the parts of the program for ease of scanning by eye.

Line 3 in Fig. 12.7 represents a card which says that a dc analysis is desired. The letters DC must appear first in columns 7 to 72. Anything else may appear on the card without effect. The word ANALYSIS on this card does nothing and could just as well be omitted.

Lines 5, 6, 7, 8, and 9 signify B-cards which give the circuit topology and indicate values of parameters. Line 11 represents a card which specifies the desired output. The letters PR must appear first in columns 7 to 72 on this card. The other symbols

	1	2	3	4	5	6	7	8	9	10	11	12	13	14	15	16	17	18	19	20	21	22	23	24	25	26	27	28	29	30
1	C		A	N	A	L	Y	S	I	S		O	F		A		S	I	M	P	L	E		C	I	R	C	U	I	T
2	C																													
3							D	C		A	N	A	L	Y	S	I	S													
4	C																													
5		B	1				N	(	0	,	1	)	,	R	=	1	0	0	,	E	=	5	0							
6		B	2				N	(	1	,	2	)	,	R	=	2	0													
7		B	3				N	(	2	,	0	)	,	R	=	4	5													
8		B	4				N	(	2	,	3	)	,	R	=	1	0													
9		B	5				N	(	3	,	0	)	,	R	=	5	,	I	=	1	0									
10	C																													
11							P	R	I	N	T	,		B	V	,		E	V	,		B	C	,		E	C	,		E	P
12	C																													
13							E	X	E	C	U	T	E																	

Figure 12.7 *A complete program for dc analysis of the circuit of Fig. 12.2.*

indicate that the node voltages (NV), branch voltages (BV), element voltages (EV), branch currents (BC), element currents (EC), and element power losses (EP) are to be printed out.

Line 13 represents a card which is the signal that this is the end of the program, and that the solution is to proceed. The letters EX must appear first in columns 7 to 72 on this card. Additional characters are meaningless to the ECAP processor.

The handwritten program of Fig. 12.7 illustrates the form in which one usually writes an ECAP program preparatory to punching the program onto 80-column data processing cards. Once these cards have been punched they are submitted to the computer for processing. The results of processing the cards is printed out on the line printer. Figure 12.8 shows a reproduction of the line printer output when cards, prepared in accordance with Fig. 12.7, are processed.

Note that the program as read from the prepared punched cards is printed out first in Fig. 12.8. Should any punching errors occur when preparing the cards, the listing will help in finding them.

Following the listing of the program, Fig. 12.8 shows the requested output information. Note that each category of information is separated from the body of information by a clear and appropriate title. The order of presentation of output information is determined by the ECAP system and is not necessarily the same as the order requested on the PRINT card. No confusion exists, however, because of the clarity of the labels.

A careful study of Fig. 12.8 reveals several interesting features about the circuit being studied. Observe that the branch voltages in branches 1 and 4 are negative. This is interpreted as meaning a net voltage *rise* occurs, in the amount indicated and in the direction of assumed current, in each branch where the minus sign appears. Similarly, when the signs of the branch voltages are positive, there is a voltage *drop* in each such branch of the amount indicated and in the direction of assumed current. (See the flags in Fig. 12.3 for the assumed current directions.)

The sign of the element current in branch 4 in Fig. 12.8 is negative. This means that the direction of the actual current in element 4 is opposite to the assumed direction. In all of the other branches, the actual directions of element current agree with the assumed directions.

12.3   Dependent Current Sources

At times, particularly when analyzing electronic circuits, current gain and/or transconductance between various parts of a circuit occur. Currents resulting from such effects are simulated in the ECAP model by dependent current sources as shown in Fig. 12.1. Information concerning dependent current sources is conveyed to the ECAP processor by means of *transfer* cards or, more simply, T-cards. Let us look at an example to illustrate the use of T-cards.

Suppose that the circuit of Fig. 12.3 is modified so that a current gain from branch 3 to branch 5 occurs with a BETA (current gain) of 10. This is illustrated in

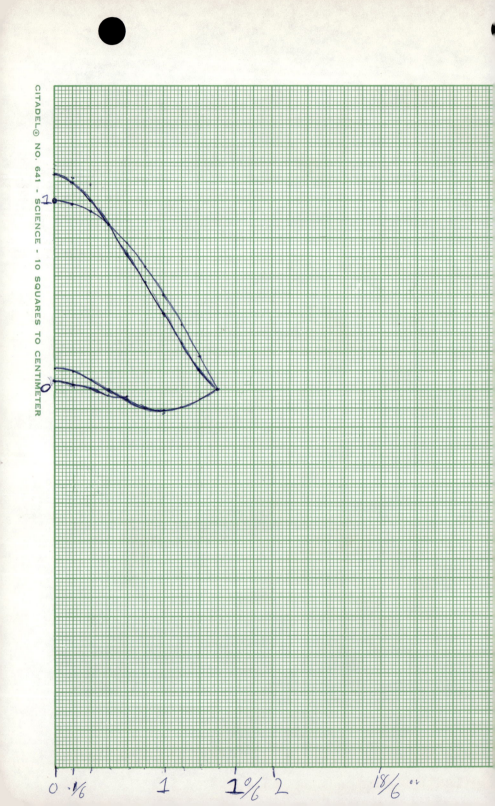

1

0

0 1/6   1   1 6/6 2   18/6 00

```
C   ANALYSIS OF A SIMPLE CIRCUIT
C
            DC ANALYSIS
C
    B1      N(0,1),R=100,E=50
    B2      N(1,2),R=20
    B3      N(2,0),R=45
    B4      N(2,3),R=10
    B5      N(3,0),R=5,I=10
C
            PRINT,BV,EV,BC,EC,EP
C
            EXECUTE
```

BRANCH VOLTAGES

BRANCHES
    1 – 4   –.40476189+02   .19047627+01   .38571426+02   –.76190486+01
    5 – 5   .46190475+02

ELEMENT VOLTAGES

BRANCHES
    1 – 4   .95238109+01   .19047627+01   .38571426+02   –.76190486+01
    5 – 5   .46190475+02

ELEMENT CURRENTS

BRANCHES
    1 – 4   .95238107–01   .95238136–01   .85714280–00   –.76190485–00
    5 – 5   .92380949+01

ELEMENT POWER LOSSES

BRANCHES
    1 – 4   .90702972–00   .18140605–00   .33061220+02   .58049901+01
    5 – 5   .42671199+03

BRANCH CURRENTS

BRANCHES
    1 – 4   .95238107–01   .95238136–01   .85714280–00   –.76190485–00
    5 – 5   –.76190507–00

Figure 12.8   *A computer printout of the program of Fig. 12.7 with output.*

Fig. 12.9. A dependent current source, T1, is connected across branch 5 having a value of ten times the element current in branch 3.

Figure 12.10 is a reproduction of a computer listing of an ECAP program written to simulate the behavior of the dc circuit of Fig. 12.9 which contains a dependent current source.

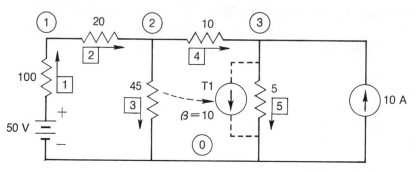

Figure 12.9 *A circuit with a dependent current source.*

Dependent current sources also may be specified in terms of transconductance. The symbol for transconductance in ECAP is GM. It is used on a T-card in much the same way as current gain (BETA) is used. In the case of transconductance, however, the magnitude of the dependent current source across the to branch will be GM times the element voltage in the from branch. Figure 12.12 is a reproduction of a program to simulate the behavior of the circuit of Fig. 12.11 which contains a transconductance from branch 3 to branch 5. A current source is connected across branch 5 having a value of 0.2 times the element voltage in branch 3.

12.4 Algebraic Signs and Other Conventions

Let us pause here in our study of ECAP dc analysis to review and reinforce our understanding of the conventions that have been adopted for numbering nodes and branches, and for assigning polarities and algebraic signs to circuit parameters.

One node in the network being studied is selected as the reference node and is given the number zero. For convenience, this is often the electrical ground of the circuit. The other nodes are arbitrarily numbered in consecutive order beginning with number 1. There must not be more than 50 nodes other than the reference node. These node numbers are shown encircled on a circuit diagram.

Similarly, the branches are also arbitrarily numbered in consecutive order beginning with number 1. There must not be more than 200 branches. In addition, an assumed direction of current flow must be assigned to the current in each branch. The branch numbers are indicated in arrowed flags on the circuit diagram. The arrows point in the assumed direction of positive current flow in each branch. A typical circuit with node numbers, branch numbers, and assumed directions of positive current flow is shown in Fig. 12.3. Within any branch, the positive current direction is from the initial node to the final node. Node numbers, branch numbers, and assumed directions for positive current flow are needed so that the network topology can be accurately described to the computer.

Each branch in a network to be analyzed by dc analysis must contain a nonzero passive resistor. In addition, each branch may also contain a constant voltage

```
C  DC ANALYSIS WITH A DEPENDENT CURRENT SOURCE
C
        DC ANALYSIS
C
  B1    N(0,1),R=100,E=50
  B2    N(1,2),R=20
  B3    N(2,0),R=45
  B4    N(2,3),R=10
  B5    N(3,0),R=5,I=10
C
  T1    B(3,5),BETA=10
C
        PRINT,BV,EV,BC,EC,EP
C
        EXECUTE
```

BRANCH VOLTAGES

BRANCHES

| 1 – 4 | –.26576576+02 | .46846846+01 | .21891891+02 | –.25225236+01 |
| 5 – 5 | .24414415+02 | | | |

ELEMENT VOLTAGES

BRANCHES

| 1 – 4 | .23423424+02 | .46846846+01 | .21891891+02 | –.25225236+01 |
| 5 – 5 | .24414415+02 | | | |

ELEMENT CURRENTS

BRANCHES

| 1 – 4 | .23423424–00 | .23423422–00 | .48648647–00 | –.25225236–00 |
| 5 – 5 | .97477477+01 | | | |

ELEMENT POWER LOSSES

BRANCHES

| 1 – 4 | .54865679+01 | .10973134+01 | .10650109+02 | .63631254–00 |
| 5 – 5 | .23798556+03 | | | |

BRANCH CURRENTS

BRANCHES

| 1 – 4 | .23423424–00 | .23423422–00 | .48648647–00 | –.25225236–00 |
| 5 – 5 | –.25225234–00 | | | |

Figure 12.10   *A computer listing of a program to simulate the circuit of Fig. 12.9.*

source, a constant current source, and one or more dependent current sources as required. A standard branch containing these features is shown in Fig. 12.1. The reader should carefully note the directions of positive current in the constant current source and the dependent current source, with respect to the initial and

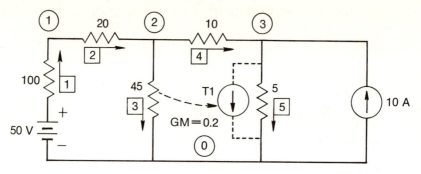

Figure 12.11 *A circuit with transconductance.*

final nodes. Positive current from the constant current source is directed from the final node toward the initial node. Positive current in the dependent current source is directed from the initial node toward the final node. The polarity of the constant voltage source is considered to be positive when the source is connected from minus to plus in the direction from the initial node toward the final node. That is, when a voltage rise occurs, the polarity of the voltage source is positive.

The topology of the circuit and the makeup of each branch are conveyed to the computer by means of B-cards and T-cards. The B-cards describe branches and the T-cards describe dependent current sources.

The letter B, followed by the branch number of the branch being described, must be punched in the first five columns of a B-card. Between columns 7 and 72 inclusive, in data subfields, are punched other items of information concerning the branch. Each data subfield is separated from the following one by a comma. The assumed direction of positive current flow is indicated by punching an N followed by a set of parentheses containing the numbers of the initial node and final node, in sequence, with the initial node number first and separated from the final node number by a comma.

If the constant source current enters at the initial node, it is given the plus sign and if it enters at the final node it is given the minus sign. This information is fed to the computer on a B-card using the letter I followed in sequence by an equal sign, a plus or a minus sign for polarity, and the value of the constant current in amperes. The plus sign can be omitted if desired.

Similarly, the polarity of the constant voltage source is given the plus sign if connected so that the negative terminal is on the initial node side and the positive terminal is on the final node side. If the constant voltage source is reversed, its polarity becomes minus. Such information is conveyed to the computer on a B-card by an E followed in sequence by an equal sign, a plus sign or a minus sign (for polarity), and the value of the constant voltage in volts. Again, the plus sign for polarity can be omitted if desired. The values of current and voltage can be expressed as numbers with or without decimal points and with or without powers of 10 multipliers.

Dependent current sources are described by means of T-cards. These sources are arbitrarily numbered in sequence beginning with number 1. The letter T, fol-

```
C   DC ANALYSIS WITH A DEPENDENT CURRENT SOURCE
C
         DC ANALYSIS
C
  B1       N(0,1),R=100,E=50
  B2       N(1,2),R=20
  B3       N(2,0),R=45
  B4       N(2,3),R=10
  B5       N(3,0),R=5,I=10
C
  T1       B(3,5),GM=0.2
C
         PRINT,BV,EV,BC,EC,EP,NV
C
         EXECUTE
```

NODE VOLTAGES

```
 NODES
  1 - 3      .27401129+02    .22881356+02    .25706215+02
```

BRANCH VOLTAGES

```
 BRANCHES
  1 - 4     -.27401129+02    .45197737+01    .22881356+02   -.28248596+01
  5 - 5      25706215+02
```

ELEMENT VOLTAGES

```
 BRANCHES
  1 - 4      .22598871+02    .45197737+01    .22881356+02   -.28248596+01
  5 - 5      .25706215+02
```

ELEMENT CURRENTS

```
 BRANCHES
  1 - 4      .22598871-00    .22598869-00    .50847457-00   -.28248596-00
  5 - 5      .97175141+01
```

ELEMENT POWER LOSSES

```
 BRANCHES
  1 - 4      .51070895+01    .10214177+01    .11634587+02    .79798317-00
  5 - 5      .24980051+03
```

BRANCH CURRENTS

```
 BRANCHES
  1 - 4      .22598871-00    .22598869-00    .50847457-00   -.28248596-00
  5 - 5     -.28248584-00
```

Figure 12.12   *A program to study the circuit of Fig. 12.11.*

lowed by the dependent source number, must be punched in the first five columns
of the T-card. The from and to branches are indicated in columns 7 through 72 by

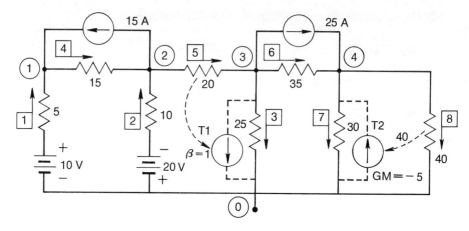

Figure 12.13 *A circuit to emphasize polarities.*

punching a B followed by a set of parentheses containing the from and to branch numbers in sequence separated by a comma. The current gain (BETA) or trans-conductance (GM) must also be shown on the T-card. This is accomplished by punching either BETA or GM followed by an equal sign, a plus or minus sign to indicate polarity, and the appropriate numerical value. If the dependent current source produces current directed toward the final node, the polarity of BETA or GM is positive, otherwise it is negative.

Figure 12.13 shows a circuit which incorporates each of the previously mentioned features. Figure 12.14 shows a portion of an ECAP program designed to accomplish a dc analysis of the circuit of Fig. 12.13.

```
C  DC ANALYSIS OF A CIRCUIT TO EMPHASIZE POLARITIES
        DC ANALYSIS
C
    B1      N(0,1),R=5,E=10
    B2      N(0,2),R=10,E=−20
    B3      N(3,0),R=25
    B4      N(1,2),R=15,I=15
    B5      N(2,3),R=20
    B6      N(3,4),R=35,I=−25
    B7      N(4,0),R=30
    B8      N(4,0),R=40
C
    T1      B(5,3),BETA=1
    T2      B(8,7),GM=−5
C
            PRINT,NV,EC,BC
            EXECUTE
```

Figure 12.14 *A program to illustrate polarities and notation*

12.5 Modification of Circuit Parameters

Often the need arises to study a single circuit configuration with a number of different sets of parameters. The creators of ECAP include a means for accomplishing this kind of modification easily and naturally.

After a nominal solution has been found, this feature of ECAP allows for as many as 50 of the branch parameters to be changed to new values, and then an entirely new solution can be found. To do this, one uses a modify routine which follows the EXECUTE card in the program for finding a nominal solution. The modify routine begins with a MODIFY card and ends with another EXECUTE card. Between the MODIFY and EXECUTE cards of any modify routine are cards which explicitly assign new values to those parameters whose values should be changed. The programmer indicates the branches to be changed on appropriate B-cards, and then lists the specific changes to be made. All parameters remain the same unless explicitly changed, and once changed, retain the new values until again changed.

Consider the three versions of the same circuit shown in Figs. 12.15 (a), (b), and (c). The modify routine permits these three versions to be studied with a nominal circuit description and two modifications of the nominal circuit. The applicable program is shown in Fig. 12.16. A careful consideration of the circuit of Fig. 12.15 and the program of Fig. 12.16 reveals the following:

(1) All parameter values remain the same from one modify solution to the next unless the modify routine explicitly changes them. For example, in Fig. 12.16(a), the resistor in branch 1 remains at 10 Ω throughout because no instruction is given to modify it. The resistor in branch 3 is changed by the first modify routine from 5 Ω to 10 Ω, at which value it remains for the second modify routine.

(2) A branch may be modified to include a nonzero voltage or current source even though it originally contained none. For example, notice the addition of a voltage source to branch 3 in Fig. 12.15(c). Also note the elimination of a voltage source in branch 5 in Fig. 12.15(b).

(3) If the PRINT instruction is modified, it can only be done by adding to earlier PRINT instructions. For example, in the nominal solution and first modification of Fig. 12.16, node voltages, element currents, and branch currents will be printed out. In the second modification these same items will be printed out and element power losses will also be printed out.

12.6 Single Parameter Modification

The modify routine may be used in a slightly different manner to study the effect of varying a single circuit parameter over a range of values. We could do this by using the modify routine as has been explained previously; however, this would require a separate modify routine for each desired value of the parameter being changed. Essentially the same result can be achieved more simply using a special feature of ECAP.

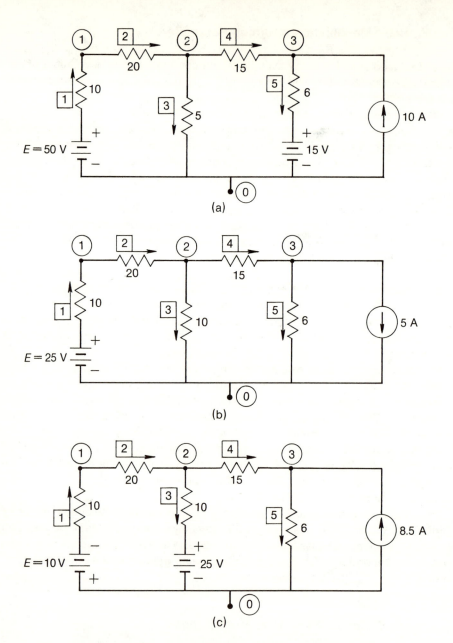

Figure 12.15 *Three variations of the same circuit.*

Suppose that after a nominal solution has been obtained in the usual way, we wish to modify one of the circuit parameters to have many additional values and we want to obtain a separate solution for each separate value of the parameter. Hence, for this problem, we use a variation of the modify routine which is more

```
C   USING THE MODIFY ROUTINE
        DC ANALYSIS
C
   B1   N(0,1),R=10,E=50
   B2   N(1,2),R=20
   B3   N(2,0),R=5
   B4   N(2,3),R=15
   B5   N(3,0),R=6,E=−15,I=10
C
        PRINT,NV,EC,BC
        EXECUTE
C
        MODIFY

   B1   E=25
   B3   R=10
   B5   E=0,I=−5
        EXECUTE
C
        MODIFY
C
   B1   E=−10
   B3   E=−25
   B5   I=8.5
        PRINT,EP
        EXECUTE
```

Figure 12.16   *A program using the modify routine to analyze the circuits in Fig. 12.15.*

efficient. Rather than indicating a single value which the parameter being modified is to assume, the programmer indicates in a *single* modify routine, that the parameter is to be varied over a range of values in steps of equal size. This is accomplished by entering the initial value of the parameter, the final value of the parameter, and the number of parameter values desired. This information is presented as shown in Eq. 12.1, as a data subgroup on a B-card or a T-card, whichever is appropriate, as part of a modify routine.

$$X = A(B)C \qquad (12.1)$$

In Eq. 12.1, X is the name of the parameter to be modified, A is the initial value of the parameter, C is the final value, and B is the number of desired incremental intervals of equal size between A and C. The size of these incremental intervals is computed as $(C - A)/B$. We can also think of B as the total number of values desired of the parameter, not including the initial value.

An example will serve to make this feature of ECAP clear. Consider the circuit of Fig. 12.15(a). Suppose we want to obtain an analysis of this circuit for numerous values of constant voltage in branch 1. Suppose further that after the nominal solution is found for the values of circuit parameters shown, a separate solution is desired for values of constant voltage in branch 1, at 10 V intervals, between 0 and 100 V inclusive. A program that can be used for this is shown in Fig. 12.17.

The first part of the program in Fig. 12.17 which produces a nominal solution is exactly like the corresponding portion of the program in Fig. 12.16. The difference here lies in the modify routine. The nominal solution obtained by the program of Fig. 12.17 will have the value of constant voltage in branch 1 set equal to 50 V. The modify routine, with voltage being modified as a parameter, will give separate solutions, in addition to the nominal solution, with this voltage source set equal to 0, 10, 20, 30, 40, 50, 60, 70, 80, 90, and 100 V, respectively. Notice that there are ten intervals in this range of parameter variation which means 11 values of the parameter. Notice also that one of the parameter values, 50 V, is equal to the nominal solution value. This unnecessary duplication could have been avoided by using some other arrangement such as letting the nominal solution be calculated for 0 V and having the parameter range from 10 to 100 V.

Any other single parameter could have been chosen as the one to vary. The procedure would have been the same except for the identification of the parameter and the manner in which it should vary.

12.7 Abbreviated ECAP Words and Phrases

Occasionally, in the preceding discussion, we indicated that some words and phrases in ECAP could be abbreviated without causing misunderstanding or confusion. Figure 12.18 shows all of the ECAP words and phrases that can be abbre-

```
C   A PROGRAM TO ILLUSTRATE SINGLE PARAMETER MODIFICATION
        DC ANALYSIS
C
    B1    N(0,1),R=10,E=50
    B2    N(1,2),R=20
    B3    N(2,0),R=5
    B4    N(2,3),R=15
    B5    N(3,0),R=6,E=-15,I=10
C
        PRINT,NV,EC,BC
        EXECUTE
C
        MODIFY
    B1    E=0(10)100
        EXECUTE
```

Figure 12.17 *A single parameter modification program.*

AC (ANALYSIS)
BE(TA)
DC (ANALYSIS)
EQ(UILIBRIUM)
EX(ECUTE)
FI(NAL TIME)
FR(EQUENCY)
IN(ITIAL TIME)
MI(SCELLANEOUS)
MO(DIFY)
OP(EN)
OU(TPUT INTERVAL)
PR(INT)
SE(NSITIVITIES)
SH(ORT)
TI(ME STEP)
TR(ANSIENT ANALYSIS)
WO(RST CASE)
1E(RROR)
2E(RROR)

Figure 12.18 *Words and phrases which can be abbreviated.*

viated, many of which have yet to be introduced and explained. In general, the first two letters of these expressions must be explicitly shown, and the remaining letters can be omitted or not as the programmer wishes. The portions of the words that can be omitted are shown enclosed in parentheses in Fig. 12.18. Only the words shown in Fig. 12.18 may be abbreviated; all other words must be spelled out completely.

The program of Fig. 12.16 is repeated in Fig. 12.19 except that wherever possible words and phrases have been abbreviated. The advantage of this feature is that it permits some reduction in the amount of card punching that is required. The disadvantage is that the meanings of the abbreviated words are not as easily understood by one who is unfamiliar with ECAP.

12.8 Miscellaneous Output

The word miscellaneous is ordinarily used to represent a heterogeneous collection of bits and pieces of things. It has a much more precise meaning in ECAP. A feature has been incorporated in ECAP to provide more of an insight into the analysis of a circuit than is possible to obtain from a line printer listing of current, voltage, and power. This is done by means of a special output instruction which, for want of a better name, is called *miscellaneous* output. When performing a dc analysis using ECAP, an instruction to PRINT, MISCELLANEOUS or more simply, PRINT,MI will result in a line printer listing of the nodal conductance matrix, the nodal impedance matrix, and the equivalent current vector. Let us look at an example to clarify the use of miscellaneous output.

Consider again the circuit of Fig. 12.2. This simple circuit could be redrawn as shown in Fig. 12.20 in which the constant voltage source of 50 V and series resistor of 100 Ω have been replaced by an equivalent consisting of a constant current source of 0.5 A and a shunt resistor of 100 Ω. Node voltage equations for the circuit of Fig. 12.20 are shown in Eqs. 12.2.

$$V_1\left(\frac{1}{100} + \frac{1}{20}\right) - V_2\left(\frac{1}{20}\right) \qquad - V_3(0) \qquad = 0.5$$

$$-V_1\left(\frac{1}{20}\right) \qquad + V_2\left(\frac{1}{20} + \frac{1}{45} + \frac{1}{10}\right) - V_3\left(\frac{1}{10}\right) \qquad = 0 \qquad (12.2)$$

$$-V_1(0) \qquad - V_2\left(\frac{1}{10}\right) \qquad + V_3\left(\frac{1}{10} + \frac{1}{5}\right) = 10$$

```
C   USING THE MODIFY ROUTINE
        DC
C
    B1   N(0,1),R=10,E=50
    B2   N(1,2),R=20
    B3   N(2,0),R=5
    B4   N(2,3),R=15
    B5   N(3,0),R=6,E=−15,I=10
C
        PR,NV,EC,BC
        EX
C
        MO
C
    B1   E=25
    B3   R=10
    B5   E=0,I=−5
        EX
C
        MO
C
    B1   E=−10
    B3   E=−25
    B5   I=8.5
        PR,EP
        EX
```

Figure 12.19 *The program of Fig. 12.16 rewritten using abbreviations.*

Equations 12.2 can be rewritten as

$$0.06V_1 - 0.05V_2 \quad - 0.0V_3 = 0.5$$
$$-0.05V_1 + 0.1722V_2 - 0.1V_3 = 0.0 \quad\quad (12.3)$$
$$-0.0V_1 \quad - 0.1V_2 \quad + 0.30V_3 = 10.0$$

Equation 12.3 can be expressed in matrix notation as shown in Eq. 12.4. The coefficients of the voltages are the nodal conductances.

$$\begin{bmatrix} 0.06 - 0.05 & -0.0 \\ -0.05 + 0.1722 & -0.1 \\ 0.0 - 0.1 & +0.3 \end{bmatrix} \begin{bmatrix} V_1 \\ V_2 \\ V_3 \end{bmatrix} = \begin{bmatrix} 0.5 \\ 0.0 \\ 10.0 \end{bmatrix} \quad\quad (12.4)$$

The square matrix of Eq. 12.4, whose terms are the nodal conductances, is called the *nodal conductance matrix.* This is one of the results produced by the miscellaneous output capability of ECAP. The column matrix on the right-hand side of Eq. 12.4 is called the *equivalent current vector.* This is another output produced by the miscellaneous output capability. The inverse of the nodal conductance matrix is called the *nodal impedance matrix.* This is the other result produced by the miscellaneous output capability. Equation 12.5 shows the nodal impedance matrix which the student can verify is the inverse of the nodal conductance matrix of Eq. 12.4.

$$\begin{bmatrix} 23.8 & 8.6 & 2.9 \\ 8.6 & 10.3 & 3.4 \\ 2.9 & 3.4 & 4.5 \end{bmatrix} \quad\quad (12.5)$$

An ECAP program to analyze the circuit of Fig. 12.20 is shown in Fig. 12.21. This program specifies a miscellaneous output and a NV output. Any other desired outputs could also have been requested. A comparison between values in the nodal conductance matrix of Fig. 12.21 and those of Eq. 12.4 shows reasonable correspondence, allowing for machine round-off. Also, the nodal impedance matrix of Fig. 12.21 agrees quite well with the values shown in Eq. 12.5. Perhaps no better correspondence should be expected since the values in Eqs. 12.4 and 12.5 were

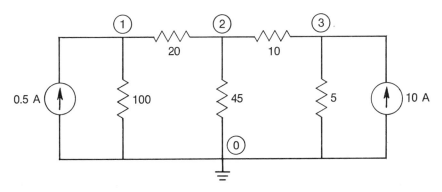

Figure 12.20 *A circuit equivalent to Fig. 12.2.*

```
C   PROGRAM TO ILLUSTRATE MISCELLANEOUS OUTPUT
C
        DC ANALYSIS
C
  B1      N(0,1),R=100,E=50
  B2      N(1,2),R=20
  B3      N(2,0),R=45
  B4      N(2,3),R=10
  B5      N(3,0),R=5,I=10
C
        PRINT,NV,MI
C
        EXECUTE
```

NODAL CONDUCTANCE MATRIX
ROW   COLS

1	1 – 3	.59999999—01	—.50000000—01	.00000000
2	1 – 3	—.50000000—01	.17222222—00	—.99999999—01
3	1 – 3	.00000000	—.99999999—01	.30000000—00

EQUIVALENT CURRENT VECTOR
NODE NO.   CURRENT

1	.49999999—00
2	.00000000
3	.10000000+02

NODAL IMPEDANCE MATRIX
ROW   COLS

1	1 – 3	.23809524+02	.85714283+01	.28571428+01
2	1 – 3	.85714284+01	.10285714+02	.34285713+01
3	1 – 3	.28571428+01	.34285713+01	.44761904+01

NODE VOLTAGES

NODES

| 1 – 3 | .40476189+02 | .38571426+02 | .46190475+02 |

Figure 12.21   *A program with MISCELLANEOUS output.*

calculated using a slide rule. The equivalent current vector of Fig. 12.21 also agrees
reasonably well with that of Eq. 12.4.

12.9   ECAP ac Analysis

The preceding discussion of the ECAP system was confined entirely to its dc
analysis feature. This is by no means the entire capability of the ECAP system. It

can also perform both ac and transient analyses. Rather than repeat those aspects of ECAP dc analysis that are common to ac analysis and transient analysis, we shall discuss only the differences. Let us first turn our attention to ac analysis.

The first and perhaps most obvious difference between dc and ac analysis is the declaration of which kind of analysis is to be performed. This is accomplished in ac analysis by a command card, placed at the start of the program, with the letters AC as the first information on the card. The word ANALYSIS may follow this if desired, but is not required.

The next difference to observe between dc and ac analysis is that passive elements such as capacitors and inductors as well as resistors are permitted as circuit elements in ac analysis. The values of capacitance are stated in farads, the values of inductance are stated in henries, and the values of resistance are stated in ohms or conductance in mhos as before. These elements and their values are specified as data subgroups on B-cards. Only one passive element is contained in any single branch. We use the letter C to identify capacitors, L to identify inductors, and R or G to identify resistors or conductors, respectively.

Constant voltage sources and constant current sources require special attention in ECAP ac analysis. Since all voltages and currents are treated as phasors, they must be given not only an rms magnitude but also a relative phase position. This is done in a data subgroup as in dc analysis, except that in this case the rms magnitude of the voltage or current source is followed by a slash followed by the phase position in degrees relative to some reference position (for example, I/θ_1). An ac analysis is meaningless without specifying the frequency at which the analysis is made. Therefore, a frequency declaration must be a part of every ECAP ac analysis program. A solution control card containing at least the letters FR must be included with an equal sign and the frequency in hertz (cycles per second) in that order.

The output specification in ac analysis is quite similar to that in dc analysis. The only difference is in the more limited output that can be requested. In ac analysis it is valid to request node voltages (NV), element currents (EC), element voltages (EV), branch currents (BC), branch voltages (BV), element power losses (EP), and miscellaneous (MI). These outputs have similar meaning to those corresponding outputs of dc analysis.

12.10 Mutual Inductance

The ECAP system has been designed to accommodate mutual inductance between branches of the circuit. In addition to the B-cards and T-cards of dc analysis, there are M-cards by means of which mutual inductance is specified. Mutual inductances may occur between branches containing self-inductance, and up to 50 branches containing self-inductance may be mutually coupled in pairs. A maximum of 25 mutual inductive couplings can be used. Each coupling is identified on an M-card by an M followed by an identifying number between 1 and 25 in columns 1 through 5. The M-cards must be numbered sequentially beginning with number 1. Columns 7 to 72 inclusive of the M-card are used to identify the coupled branches with a data subgroup consisting of a B followed by the numbers of the coupled branches enclosed in parentheses and separated by a comma. The value of the mutual inductance is indicated in a separate subgroup by an L followed by an equal sign, with the value of mutual inductance in henries.

The value of mutual inductance must be such that the coupling coefficient is less than unity. The coupling coefficient is defined by

$$k_{ab} = \frac{M_{ab}}{\sqrt{L_a L_b}} \tag{12.6}$$

where k_{ab} is the dimensionless coupling coefficient, M_{ab} is the mutual inductance between branches a and b, L_a is the self-inductance of branch a, and L_b is the self-inductance of branch b. All inductances must be expressed in the same units, preferably in henries because these are the units of inductance in ECAP.

The sign of M is related to the assumed direction of positive current in the coupled branches. If positive current in one branch causes voltage to be induced in the other branch in the positive current direction, M is positive; otherwise, M is negative. When polarity marks are shown, positive currents entering at both polarity marked terminals result in M being positive.

12.11   The ac Standard Branch

Figure 12.22 shows a standard branch for ECAP ac analysis. Notice that the current and voltage sources are alternating sources, and that the passive element may be either a resistor (R or G), an inductor (L), or a capacitor (C). All voltages and currents are treated as rms phasor quantities.

The circuit of Fig. 12.23 illustrates an ac circuit containing representative elements that may be included in ECAP ac analysis. Node and branch numbers have been indicated in the figure. A program to analyze the circuit of Fig. 12.23 is shown in Fig. 12.24.

12.12   Parameter Modification in ac Analysis

Parameters can be changed in ECAP ac analysis by using the modify routine in much the same way as for dc analysis. After a nominal solution has been found, any of the circuit parameters can be modified and a new solution obtained. A MODIFY card follows the EXECUTE card of the nominal solution, and this is followed by B-cards, T-cards, and M-cards which specify the new values of the parameters to be changed. An EXECUTE card ends the modify routine as before. As many modify routines as desired may be used.

The modify routine permits not only the modification of those parameters which have dc counterparts, but also applies to the modification of fixed voltage source phase angles, fixed current source phase angles and frequency which are unique

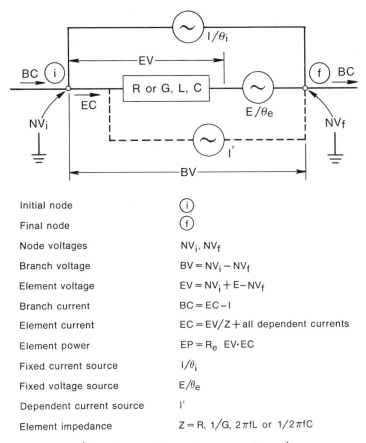

Initial node	(i)
Final node	(f)
Node voltages	NV_i, NV_f
Branch voltage	$BV = NV_i - NV_f$
Element voltage	$EV = NV_i + E - NV_f$
Branch current	$BC = EC - I$
Element current	$EC = EV/Z +$ all dependent currents
Element power	$EP = R_e\ EV \cdot EC$
Fixed current source	I/θ_i
Fixed voltage source	E/θ_e
Dependent current source	I'
Element impedance	$Z = R,\ 1/G,\ 2\pi fL$ or $1/2\pi fC$

(all voltages and currents are rms phasors)

Figure 12.22 *The ac standard branch.*

with ac analysis. Magnitude and phase or a fixed voltage or current source may be varied in a single modification or either one may be modified individually. When modifying fixed voltage sources or fixed current sources both magnitude and phase angle must be specified in the modification even though only one is being modified.

The program in Fig. 12.25 illustrates the use of the modify routine and shows several ways in which the voltage source of Fig. 12.23 can be varied.

The first modification in Fig. 12.25 changes only the magnitude of the voltage source from the value of the nominal solution while keeping the phase angle unchanged at zero degrees. The second modification changes the phase angle from that of the nominal solution while keeping the magnitude unchanged. The third modification changes both the magnitude and the phase angle. The fourth modification changes the magnitude over a range of five values while the phase angle remains unchanged, and the last modification changes both magnitude and phase

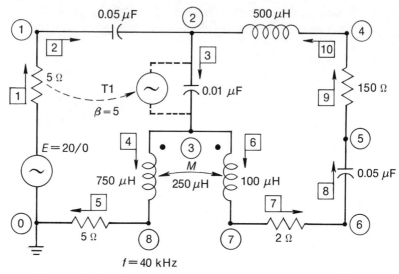

Figure 12.23 *An ac circuit to be analyzed using ECAP.*

angle over a range of ten values each. The last modification would produce ten separate solutions with the following values of voltage: 1/0, 2/5, 3/10, 4/15, 5/20, 6/25, 7/30, 8/35, 9/40, and 10/45.

12.13 Modification of Frequency in ac Analysis

The modification of frequency over a specified range of values can be accomplished in two different ways—logarithmically or linearly. In logarithmic variation, the frequency is successively multiplied by a specified multiplying factor for each successive solution. Figure 12.26 shows logarithmically varying frequency of the program of Fig. 12.24 in which the frequency is doubled for each succeeding solution. The values of frequency that would be used would be 10 000, 20 000, 40 000, 80 000, 160 000, and 320 000 Hz. The multiplying factor for logarithmic frequency need not be an integer and can be fractional if desired. Logarithmic frequency variation provides the data usually required for a frequency response study of a circuit.

Frequency may also be varied linearly over a specified range of values. Figure 12.27 shows how linear variation of frequency is accomplished. In this solution the frequency values would be 10 000, 20 000, 30 000, 40 000, and 50 000 Hz, respectively, for each solution. Notice the + sign in the frequency modification statements to indicate linear variation.

If another modify section were added to the program of Fig. 12.26 which did not contain a frequency indication, the problem would be solved using the last value of frequency determined for the preceding modify section. If we wanted to include another logarithmic frequency variation in the added MODIFY section, this must be completely specified as before.

```
C   PROGRAM TO ILLUSTRATE AC ANALYSIS NOMINAL SOLUTION
        AC ANALYSIS
C
    B1    N(0,1),R=5,E=20/0
    B2    N(1,2),C=5E-8
    B3    N(2,3),C=1E-8
    B4    N(3,8),L=750E-6
    B5    N(8,0),R=5
    B6    N(3,7),L=1E-4
    B7    N(7,6),R=2
    B8    N(6,5),C=5E-8
    B9    N(5,4),R=150
    B10   N(4,2),L=500E-6
C
    T1    B(1,3),BETA=5
C
    M1    B(4,6),L=250E-6
          FREQUENCY = 40E3
          PRINT,NV,EC
          EXECUTE
```

Figure 12.24   *A program to analyze the circuit of Fig. 12.23.*

12.14   ECAP Transient Analysis

We can use ECAP to find the transient behavior of an electric circuit in much the same way that we used it to obtain dc analysis and ac analysis. There are, of course, some features of transient analysis that are unique, and some features that are common to the other methods. These similarities and differences will now be explained.

The first two letters of the first card must be TR to indicate that a transient analysis is desired. Transient analyses can be obtained using ECAP for circuits comprised of resistors, capacitors, and inductors as static elements, fixed or time-dependent voltage and current sources and dependent current sources as active elements, and switches. Mutual inductance is *not* allowed in ECAP transient analysis. A maximum of 200 branches can be accommodated with up to 50 nodes in addition to the reference node. Each of the 200 branches must contain a single passive element and may contain one fixed or time-dependent voltage source and one fixed or time-dependent current source. Any given circuit must not contain more than five time-dependent voltage sources and five time-dependent current sources, but as many as 200 dependent current sources may be included. These current sources may be distributed among the branches in any desired combination. Any given branch may act as the from or to branch of none or up to all of the possible dependent current sources.

C   PROGRAM TO ILLUSTRATE FIXED SOURCE MODIFICATIONS
          AC ANALYSIS

```
B1      N(0,1),R=5,E=20/0
B2      N(1,2),C=5E—8
B3      N(2,3),C=1E—8
B4      N(3,8),L=750E—6
B5      N(8,0),R=5
B6      N(3,7),L=1E—4
B7      N(7,6),R=2
B8      N(6,5),C=5E—8
B9      N(5,4),R=150
B10     N(4,2),L=500E—6
T1      B(1,3),BETA=5
M1      B(4,6),L=250E—6
        FREQUENCY = 40E3
        PRINT,NV,EC
        EXECUTE
        MODIFY
B1      E=40/0
        EXECUTE
        MODIFY
B1      E=20/30
        EXECUTE
        MODIFY
B1      E=30/45
        EXECUTE
        MODIFY
B1      E=10(4)50/0(4)0
        EXECUTE
        MODIFY
B1      E=1(9)10/0(9)45
        EXECUTE
```

Figure 12.25   *Fixed source modifications.*

We can do two types of transient analysis using ECAP. One of these is an *equilibrium solution* and the other is a *transient response.* The equilibrium solution is also frequently called the *steady-state solution.* The steady state is the condition which occurs after all transients have decayed to zero. Furthermore, we can obtain the equilibrium or steady-state solution by a direct method, rather than simply waiting for the simulated circuit to reach steady state. More will be said about this later.

The output of ECAP transient analysis is limited to node voltage, element currents, and switch actuation times. Values of the node voltages and element currents are determined at the start of the transient analysis when $t = 0$ and at uniform

C   LOGARITHMIC FREQUENCY VARIATION
            AC ANALYSIS
C
    B1   N(0,1),R=5,E=20/0
    B2   N(1,2),C=5E−8
    B3   N(2,3),C=1E−8
    B4   N(3,8),L=750E−6
    B5   N(8,0),R=5
    B6   N(3,7),L=1E−4
    B7   N(7,6),R=2
    B8   N(6,5),C=5E−8
    B9   N(5,4),R=150
    B10   N(4,2),L=500E−6
C
    T1   B(1,3),BETA=5
C
    M1   B(4,6),L=250E−6
            FREQUENCY = 40E3
            PRINT,NV,EC
            EXECUTE
            MODIFY
            FREQUENCY = 10E3(2)32E4
            EXECUTE

Figure 12.26   *Logarithmic frequency variation.*

time intervals thereafter until the indicated time period has elapsed, at which time the solution is terminated. Also, the values of node voltages and element currents are determined immediately before and immediately after the operation of each switch.

The modification capability of ECAP transient analysis using the modify routine is more restricted than in either dc analysis or ac analysis. A group of one or more parameters may be modified, after a nominal solution has been found, thus obtaining an entirely new solution with the new values of the modified parameters replacing the former values. The time step is one of the parameters that may be changed in this manner. Iterative parameter modifications are *not* permitted in ECAP transient analysis.

As one would expect, some input information is required for transient analysis that is different from that needed for either dc analysis or ac analysis. Also, some solution control information must be supplied that is unique with transient solutions.

The input data which describes the network topology is handled by means of B-cards and T-cards in the same way as for the other analyses we discussed. However, M-cards are not allowed. Switch location and operation is handled by means of S-cards, the use of which is described in greater detail later. Initial conditions

```
C   LINEAR FREQUENCY VARIATION
         AC ANALYSIS
C
   B1    N(0,1),R=5,E=20/0
   B2    N(1,2),C=5E−8
   B3    N(2,3),C=1E−8
   B4    N(3,8),L=750−6
   B5    N(8,0),R=5
   B6    N(3,7),L=1E−4
   B7    N(7,6),R=2
   B8    N(6,5),C=5E−8
   B9    N(5,4),R=150
   B10   N(4,2),L=500E−6
C
   T1    B(1,3),BETA=5
C
   M1    B(4,6),L=250E−6
         FREQUENCY = 40E3
         PRINT,NV,EC
         EXECUTE
         MODIFY
         FREQUENCY = 10E3(+4)50E3
         EXECUTE
```

Figure 12.27   *Linear frequency variation.*

are an important part of transient analysis and provision has been made to set the initial conditions at whatever values are needed. The time step size between successive calculations is under the control of the programmer since it may vary widely from one circuit to another. Special functions must sometimes be included and their generation is a part of ECAP transient analysis. Nonlinear functions of some kinds can be incorporated into circuits being analyzed by this technique.

Figure 12.28 shows a standard circuit branch for ECAP transient analysis.

12.15   Time in Transient Analysis

As has been pointed out in earlier chapters, whenever a time-dependent system is studied by computer simulation techniques, two measures of time are involved. One measure of time is taken from the point of view of the system being simulated. The other is from the point of view of the computer that is doing the simulating. In other words, we have system time and computer time, and the two may or may not be equivalent. The computer may perform more rapidly, at equal speed, or less rapidly than the system being simulated. As we mentioned in Sections 1.3 and 5.1, if events in the computer simulated model occur at the same time as would

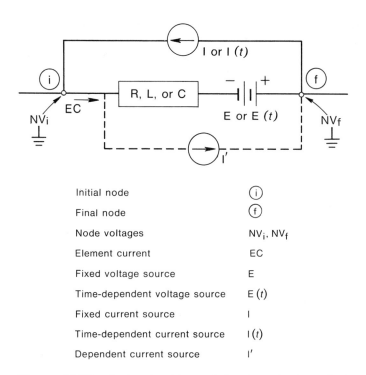

Initial node	ⓘ
Final node	ⓕ
Node voltages	NV_i, NV_f
Element current	EC
Fixed voltage source	E
Time-dependent voltage source	$E(t)$
Fixed current source	I
Time-dependent current source	$I(t)$
Dependent current source	I'

Figure 12.28 *A standard branch for transient analysis.*

corresponding events in the system being simulated, the computer is said to be operating in real time. More often, however, the system time and computer time differ, and a possible source of confusion results. In order to avoid any misunderstanding, the references to time which occur on ECAP transient solution control cards are always in terms of system time. The corresponding computer time may be longer or shorter than the system time.

An ECAP transient analysis program ordinarily requires a minimum of three solution control cards—the TIME STEP card, the OUTPUT INTERVAL card, and the FINISH TIME card. The program of Fig. 12.30 shows these three cards in use. If the OUTPUT INTERVAL and FINISH TIME are not specified, the ECAP system assumes the values as explained in Section 12.28.

When simulating the transient behavior of an electric circuit, the digital computer must compute the results successively at prescribed values of time. The time interval between these computations, in seconds, is called the *time step* and is defined by the TIME STEP card. In Fig. 12.30, the time step is 0.1 msec. Notice that the computations are performed at uniform intervals of time and that the user must give thoughtful consideration to the assignment of the time step interval. Too large a time step will not produce an accurate solution, and one that is too small will waste computer time.

Depending on the requirements of each particular problem, the user may wish to have the results of the simulation study printed out at time intervals equal to or greater than the time step. ECAP allows for output to occur at any even multiple of the time step. The OUTPUT INTERVAL card indicates the number of time steps between successive printouts. In Fig. 12.30 there are ten time steps between printouts, and, therefore, the printouts will occur every millisecond of system time.

In general, different systems operate at different speeds and require different lengths of time to produce their useful outputs. The FINISH TIME card permits the ECAP user to have flexible control over the length of time the simulation study will run. The number of seconds of system time which the simulated system will be allowed to run is indicated on the FINISH TIME card. In Fig. 12.30 the finish time is 50 msec. Since only the first two letters are significant, this may also be written as FINAL TIME.

Figure 12.29 shows a circuit to be studied using ECAP transient analysis. The quantities we want to find are the voltage across the 10 kΩ resistor and the current through the 2 μF capacitor as functions of time. The switch is closed at $t = 0$ with no initial charge on either capacitor. ECAP assumes initial charges to be zero unless specified otherwise. The closure of the switch at $t = 0$ is simulated simply by starting the solution with the switch closed. The program in Fig. 12.30 is designed to simulate the behavior of this circuit.

12.16 Initial Conditions in Transient Analysis

The transient behavior of an electric circuit is, in large measure, influenced by the initial conditions which prevail at the beginning of the study. The initial conditions which electrical engineers have come to recognize as significant are the initial charges on the capacitors and the initial currents in the inductors. These are the behavior characteristics of the circuit which cannot change instantaneously. Both the initial charges on capacitors and currents in inductors can be specified in the ECAP system. The initial charges are commonly specified indirectly in terms of

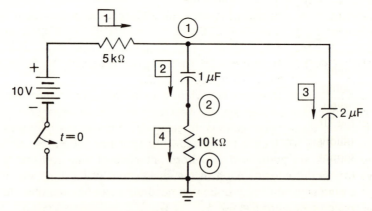

Figure 12.29 *A simple circuit for transient study.*

proportional initial voltages rather than directly in terms of charges themselves. The initial voltage on a capacitor is inserted into a transient solution by means of a data subgroup on the B-card which describes the branch containing the capacitor. This consists of the letters EO followed by an equal sign and the value of initial voltage in volts. These initial voltages may be positive or negative as required. For example, the B-card information

$$B10 \quad N(5,6), C=1E-6, EO=-15$$

indicates that branch 10 contains a 1 μF capacitor connected between nodes 5 and 6, where node 5 is the initial node and 6 is the final node. The initial charge on the capacitor is such that a voltage drop of 15 V occurs in the direction from node 5 to node 6.

In a similar way, we can specify the initial current in an inductor. The initial current is identified in a data subgroup by the letters IO followed by an equal sign and the value of initial current in amperes. For example, the B-card information

$$B20 \quad N(16,34), L=10E-3, IO=0.5$$

indicates that branch 20 contains a 10 mH inductance connected between nodes 16 and 34. Node 16 is the initial node and node 34 is the final node. The initial current in this inductor is 0.5 A directed from node 16 toward node 34. If the initial current was in the opposite direction, the sign would be negative.

12.17 Time-Dependent Sources

Earlier in our discussions, reference was made to a feature of ECAP transient analysis which permits the inclusion of time-dependent voltage sources and current sources as active elements in branches. The nature of these sources is of three kinds — sinusoidal, periodic, and arbitrary functions of time. For such sources to be most helpful, the user should have complete flexibility in describing the desired functions.

When using a sinusoidally varying source one may wish to start the function at any selected point on the sinusoidal wave. In other words, it may be desirable to have $t = 0$ occur at some time other than when the sinusoidally varying source passes through zero in the positive direction. Furthermore, one may wish to have a dc offset in the signal so that the axis of symmetry of the sinusoidal oscillations is not at zero magnitude. Also, the frequency and amplitude of the oscillating signal should be under the control of the user to achieve maximum utility. ECAP transient analysis is able to do all of these things. Figure 12.31 shows a graph of a typical sinusoidal time-dependent signal, along with its description and definition of symbols. The information of Fig. 12.31 is conveyed to the ECAP processor by means of an E-card if a voltage source is being described, or by means of an I-card if a current source is being described. This is in contrast to previous fixed voltage and current sources where the description of the source was an inherent part of the B-card describing the branch containing the source. When using time-dependent current or voltage sources, no mention is made of them in the B-card branch description. Only the nodal connections and the static element are described on the B-card. The time-dependent voltage or current source is described on an E-card or an I-card, respectively. These cards must follow the B-cards for the branch to which they refer. For example, if branch 3 is to contain a time-dependent sinusoidal current source its B-card branch description might be

B3   N(5,7),R=100

and the time-dependent current source described on an I-card which follows might be

I3   SIN(0.001),10,22,0.00015

The I3 must appear on the card in columns 1–5. The other information must appear in columns 7–72 and in the order shown. The current source here is sinusoidal having a period of 0.001 sec (corresponding to a frequency of 1000 Hz), an amplitude or peak value of oscillation of 10 A, a dc offset of +22 A, and a time offset of 0.00015 sec.

The E-card information shown below indicates a sinusoidal time-dependent voltage source in branch 17 having a frequency of 1 MHz, an amplitude of oscillation of 5 V, a dc offset of −10 V, and a time offset of 0.01 μsec:

E17   SIN(1E−6),5,−10,1E−8

C   A TRANSIENT SOLUTION WITH STATIC ELEMENTS
        TRANSIENT ANALYSIS
C
  B1   N(0,1),R=5E3,E=10
  B2   N(1,2),C=1E−6
  B3   N(1,0),C=2E−6
  B4   N(2,0),R=10E3
          TIME STEP = 1E−4
          OUTPUT INTERVAL = 10
          FINISH TIME = 50E−3
          PRINT,NV,EC
          EXECUTE

  T =   .0000000

                    VOLTAGES
NODES
  1 – 2   .19999939−04   .19999920−04
                    CURRENTS
BRANCHES
  1 – 4   .19999960−02   .19781510−08   .19999940−02   .19999919−08

  T =   .1000000−02

Figure 12.30   *A program and results for a transient analysis of Fig. 12.29.*

VOLTAGES

NODES

  1 – 2   .92320320+00   .87334634+00

CURRENTS

BRANCHES

  1 – 4   .18153594—02   .87334588—04   .17280243—02   .87334633—04

T =   .2000000—02

VOLTAGES

NODES

  1 – 2   .17230240+01   .15472886+01

CURRENTS

BRANCHES

  1 – 4   .16553952—02   .15472889—03   .15006652—02   .15472886—03

                   ⋮   ⋮   ⋮   ⋮

T =   .4899994—01

VOLTAGES

NODES

  1 – 2   .94209524+01   .57841182+00

CURRENTS

BRANCHES

  1 – 4   .11580951—03   .57840347—04   .57964325—04   .57841181—04

T =   .4999993—01

VOLTAGES

NODES

  1 – 2   .94491485+01   .55032444+00

CURRENTS

BRANCHES

  1 – 4   .11017029—03   .55030584—04   .55129528—04   .55032443—04

T =   .5009993—01

VOLTAGES

NODES

  1 – 2   .94518913+01   .54759133+00

CURRENTS

BRANCHES

  1 – 4   .10962174—03   .54758787—04   .54855347—04   .54759132—04

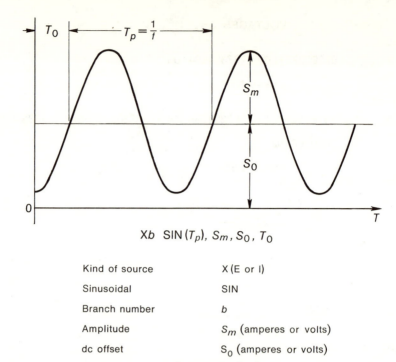

$Xb \; SIN(T_p), \; S_m, S_0, T_0$

Kind of source	X (E or I)
Sinusoidal	SIN
Branch number	b
Amplitude	S_m (amperes or volts)
dc offset	S_0 (amperes or volts)
Time offset	T_0 (sec)
Period	T_p (sec)

Figure 12.31 *A typical time-dependent source and its ECAP description.*

There is a limitation on the use of sinusoidal signals such as shown in Fig. 12.31. This limitation also applies to periodic sources which are described next. The period of sinusoidal or periodic sources must be such that the description of one full period does not require more than 126 entries.

Time-dependent periodic sources other than sinusoidal sources can also be included in an ECAP transient analysis, providing that they can be graphed as a combination of straight line segments. Functions having discontinuities are not allowed. As we mentioned above, we must be able to describe the function over a complete cycle by not more than 126 entries equally spaced in time. Furthermore, the time spacing of these entries must be some integral multiple of the time step, and one of these points must occur at each breakpoint where the slope of the function changes. For example, consider the periodic voltage function of Fig. 12.32 which has a period of 90 time steps. Suppose further that the voltage function is to be included as an active element in branch 22. The function would be described as follows:

$$E22 \quad P(5),0,0,2,4,6,6.5,7,7.5,8,8.5,9,9,9,9,9,4.5,0,0,0$$

In the description of the time-dependent source just presented, the E22 in columns 1–5 indicates a voltage source in branch 22. The other information in col-

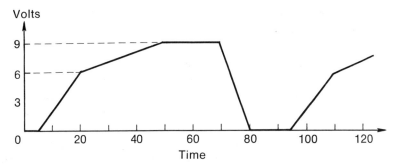

Figure 12.32 *A periodic function.*

umns 7–72 indicates a periodic source with five time steps between successive defining points, and with the magnitude of voltage at each of these points following in succession. Should the information on the periodic source description card exceed the amount which can be included in columns 7–72, any required number of continuation cards can be added by simply placing an asterisk in column 6 of each continuation card following the first. Each card to be continued should end with a comma separating one data subgroup from the next. The first and last magnitudes of a periodic source description should be the same since they describe a similar point one period apart.

Arbitrary sources which are nonperiodic can be included in an ECAP transient analysis by a process similar to that for periodic sources. The only difference is that the P in the periodic source description is omitted from the arbitrary source description and, of course, the first and last magnitudes may be equal or different as required by the function being described. The maximum number of points describing an arbitrary source is limited to 126 also.

12.18   The ECAP Switch

The switch is perhaps the single most important feature of ECAP transient analysis. It is by means of switches that transient analysis of complicated circuits having nonlinear elements can be implemented. Switches also permit functions with discontinuities to be simulated. These special features are in addition to the usual functions of switches—to close and open circuits at prescribed times—and yet, it is by this same action that the special functions are made possible.

The ECAP switch is a simulated switch that has rather unique properties. It is not manually operated. Neither is it time-dependent for its operation, although this can be simulated. Rather, its condition, OFF or ON, is current-dependent. Any branch in an ECAP transient analysis circuit can be designated as a switch. The current in every branch has an assumed positive current direction. If a branch has been designated as a switch, by a means yet to be described, the current in that branch is continuously monitored by the ECAP system throughout the transient analysis. If the element current is positive, according to the assumed positive element current direction, the switch controlled by that current is in the ON condition. If the element current is zero or negative, the switch is in the OFF condition. As a consequence of this, the condition of a switch will change if the element current changes direction in the branch designated as a switch.

We have already mentioned that the operation of an ECAP switch does more than open or close branches of a circuit. The actuation of an ECAP switch can cause the values of circuit elements in its own and/or other branches to change from one specified value to another. Each circuit element in every branch can be assigned two parameter values. Which value of branch circuit parameter is effective at any time depends on the condition of the switches controlling that branch. Not only is each branch capable of being designated as a switch, each branch is capable of being controlled by one or more switches.

In order that the value of a parameter can be changed from one value to another by the operation of a switch, the parameter must first be assigned two values on the B-card input data defining the branch containing the parameter to be changed. If only a single value of a parameter is given, the value of the parameter does not change. If a current controlling a switch changes direction, causing the switch to actuate, and later changes direction again so that the current direction is again back to its earlier direction, the switch will revert back to its earlier condition.

A two-step process is required to implement an ECAP switch. The first step indicates the identifying number of the switch, specifies the branch which is to be considered as a switch, indicates which branch or branches will be affected by the operation of the switch, and states whether the switch will be initially OFF or ON. This is accomplished by means of an S-card. Switches are numbered in sequence beginning with number S1. The second step indicates two values for each of the parameters to be controlled by the switch. This is done on the B-card which describes each of the affected branches.

For example, suppose that branches 17 and 22 are to be controlled by a switch in branch 30. Branch 17 connects from node 7 to node 10 and contains a resistor and a current source. Branch 22 contains a capacitor and a voltage source and connects from node 5 to 9. The resistance of the resistor in branch 17 is to have a value of 10^7 Ω when the current in branch 30 is negative or zero, and 10^2 Ω when the current in branch 30 is positive. The current source in branch 17 is to remain unchanged at 5 A. The capacitance and voltage in branch 22 are to both be changed by the switch action. The capacitance is to be 1 μF and the voltage source is to be 20 V when the current in branch 30 is negative or zero, and 10 μF and −20 V, respectively, when the current in branch 30 is positive. The necessary S-card and corresponding B-card information is shown below. Branch 30 connects from node 12 to node 4. Negative current in branch 30 is directed from node 4 toward node 12 while positive current is directed from node 12 toward node 4.

```
B17   N(7,10),R=(1E7,1E2),I=5
B22   N(5,9),C=(1E−6,10E−6),E=(+20,−20)
B30   N(12,4),R=1E−3
S1    B=30,(17,22),OFF
```

Examination of the preceding B-card and S-card information reveals that the two values of each parameter to be affected are enclosed in parentheses on the B-card and separated by a comma. The first of these values will be in effect when the controlling switch is in the designated condition — OFF in this case. The second value will be in effect when the current in branch 30 reverses and the switch turns ON. The S-card indicates that this is switch number 1 as shown by the S1 in columns 1 through 5. The other information is in columns 7 through 72 and indicates that branch 30 is to be the switch (B=30), that branches 17 and 22 are to be affected [(17,22)] and that the first stated values of each parameter in these branches is to be in effect when the switch is OFF (that is, when the current in branch 30 is negative or zero).

Another example will serve to clarify the use of the switch as a circuit element. Suppose that the circuit of Fig. 12.29 is modified by the addition of a branch between nodes 1 and 0 containing a resistor of 500 Ω, which is to be switched into the circuit at $t = 50$ msec. This modified circuit is shown in Fig. 12.33.

In order that the switch in branch 5 of Fig. 12.33 can be simulated, an additional auxiliary timing circuit must be implemented to control the switch. Such a timing circuit is shown in Fig. 12.34. The action of the timing circuit of Fig. 12.34 can best be understood by considering the following fundamental principles. The capacitance of a capacitor is defined by Eq. 12.7 as the ratio of charge to voltage on the capacitor. If the ratio is constant, the capacitor is said to be linear. Solving Eq. 12.7

$$C = \frac{q}{V} \qquad (12.7)$$

for voltage and differentiating with respect to time gives Eq. 12.8, providing that C is constant.

$$\frac{dV}{dt} = \frac{1}{C}\frac{dq}{dt} \qquad (12.8)$$

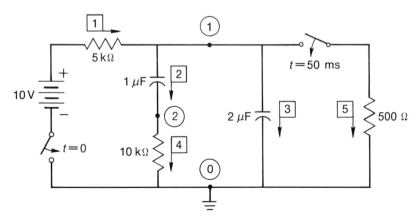

Figure 12.33 *A modification of Fig. 12.29.*

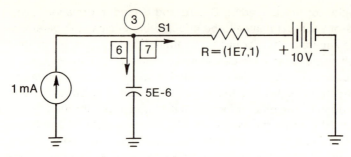

Figure 12.34 *An auxiliary timing circuit for switch control.*

Equation 12.8 reduces to Eq. 12.9 if $I = dq/dt$ is constant as it is in Fig. 12.34.

$$\frac{dV}{dt} = \frac{I}{C} \tag{12.9}$$

Equation 12.9 indicates that the slope of the graph of voltage versus time is constant. Such a graph is shown in Fig. 12.35. The voltage in this plot is the voltage on the capacitor, which is the node voltage at node 3 in Fig. 12.34.

At $t = 0$, the voltage across the capacitor in Fig. 12.34 is zero. Current will flow in branch 7 toward node 3 under the influence of the 10 V battery. If the switch S1 is initially OFF, this current will hold it in that condition. Meanwhile, the milli-ampere current source will be charging the capacitor and the voltage at node 3 will be rising toward 10 V. When the voltage at node 3 reaches 10 V, the current in branch 7 will become zero. The switch S1 will remain in the OFF condition. As soon as the voltage at node 3 exceeds 10 V, however, the current in branch 7 will flow away from node 7 and the switch S1 will assume the ON condition. The time re-

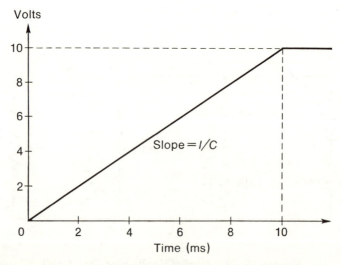

Figure 12.35 *The behavior of the timing circuit of Fig. 12.34.*

quired for this action to occur depends on the initial charge on the capacitor, the magnitude of the current source, and the capacitance of the capacitor.

The action of switch S1 can be used to control branch 7 as well as other branches in the circuit. The program of Fig. 12.36 incorporates the switch of Fig. 12.34 to provide the desired switching action in Fig. 12.33. The current of 1 mA and the capacitance of 5×10^{-6} F, with an initial condition of zero charge on the capacitor, cause the switching action to occur at $t = 50$ msec as desired. Varying these parameters will cause the switching action to occur at almost any other desired time.

In the program of Fig. 12.36, the switch S1 is used to change the resistance of branch 7 from 10^7 Ω to 1 Ω, and to change the resistance of branch 5 from 10^7 Ω to 5×10^2 Ω. The switching of branch 7 causes the voltage at node 3 to be clamped at 10.001 V. The switching of branch 5 simulates the action of the switch in that branch.

12.19 A Nonlinear Resistor

One application of the ECAP switch is in simulating a nonlinear resistor. This is an element whose resistance varies with current. An example of such an element is a diode whose forward resistance is low but finite, and whose backward resistance is high but also finite. Also, there is a smooth transition from the backward resistance to the forward resistance as the current increases in the forward direction. Figure 12.37 shows a typical voltage-current characteristic for a diode. The slope of the curve is the conductance of the diode at any point. As the current increases, the conductance also increases.

To construct a practical simulated model of the diode, we use a piecewise linear approximation. The piecewise linear approximation of Fig. 12.37 is shown in Fig.

```
              TRANSIENT ANALYSIS
        B1   N(0,1),R=5E3,E=10
        B2   N(1,2),C=1E−6
        B3   N(1,0),C=2E−6
        B4   N(2,0),R=10E3
        B5   N(1,0),R=(1E7,5E2)
        B6   N(3,0),C=5E−6,I=.001
        B7   N(3,0),R=(1E7,1E−3),E=−10
        S1   B=7,(7,5),OFF
             TIME STEP=1E−4
             OUTPUT INTERVAL=10
             FINISH TIME=100E−3
             PRINT,NV,EC
             EXECUTE
```

Figure 12.36 *A program to simulate Fig. 12.33.*

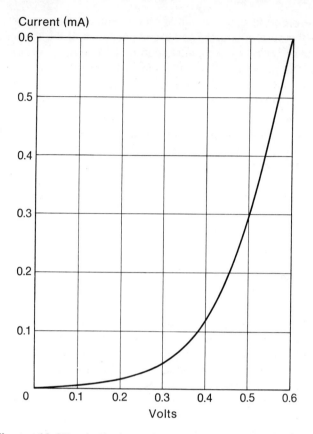

Current (mA)

Volts

Figure 12.37 *A diode voltage-current characteristic.*

12.38. Since the current is in milliamperes and the voltage is in volts, the slopes are in milimhos. The breakpoints are indicated with lower case letters.

When resistive elements are connected in parallel, the conductance of the combination is equal to the sum of the individual conductances. Hence, as more and more elements are placed in parallel the conductance of the combination becomes larger and larger. This is precisely what is needed to realize the piecewise linear resistor characteristic of Fig. 12.38.

Referring to Fig. 12.38, we see that a conductance of 0.05 millimhos could be used for the segment ab. Providing that proper switching can be achieved, the addition of an element in parallel with the first, having a conductance of 0.25 millimhos, would result in a combination conductance of 0.30 over the segment bc. An additional element of 0.4 millimhos added at the proper time would yield a total conductance of 0.7 over the segment cd. Then, adding conductances of 1.2 and 1.1 millimhos properly in sequence would result in total conductance of 1.9 and 3.0 millimhos over the intervals de and ef, respectively.

The ECAP switch is a means for automatically switching the elements in or out as needed to realize the simulated nonlinear resistor. In Fig. 12.39(a) there is a

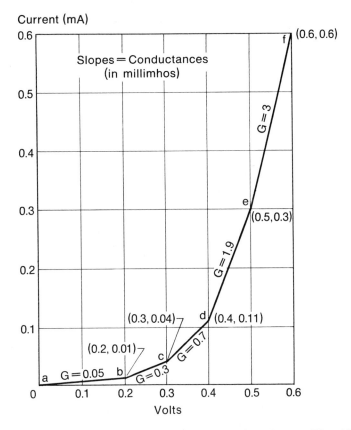

Figure 12.38 *A piecewise linear approximation to Fig. 12.37.*

nonlinear resistor connected between nodes 8 and 10. It is assumed that the voltage-current characteristic here is as graphed in Fig. 12.37. Figure 12.39(b) shows a circuit which will behave in a manner analogous to the circuit in part (a), providing that the switches operate correctly. The partial program of Fig. 12.40 defines the necessary switch action.

Notice that if the polarity of the voltage across the nonlinear resistor was reversed, the conductance would be very nearly 0.05 millimhos because of the negligible effects of the other elements when the switches are off.

12.20 Switches with T-Cards

Occasionally, it may be desirable to use a switch to modify the value of a dependent current source by changing the value of BETA or GM. When this is done, it is necessary that the two desired values of BETA (or GM) appear enclosed in parentheses on the T-card and separated by a comma as with any other parameter. The

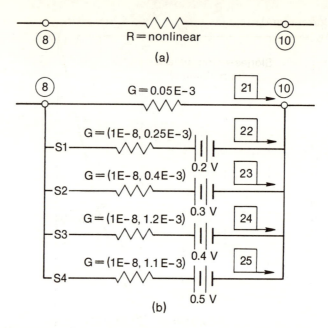

Figure 12.39 *A circuit to model a nonlinear resistor.*

branch affected by the actuation of the switch, as shown on the S-card, is the *from* branch that is associated with the dependent source rather than the *to* branch as might at first be expected. An example of an S-card and related B-cards and T-cards for modifying BETA are shown below:

```
B10   N(6,8),R=1E3
B13   N(7,9),R=50E3
T1    B(10,13),BETA=(50,10)
S1    B=12,(10),OFF
```

12.21 EQUILIBRIUM Solution

Earlier, we made reference to the *equilibrium solution* available in ECAP. Recall that equilibrium or steady state occurs in a circuit when all transients have decayed to zero. An equilibrium solution can therefore be obtained—although not very efficiently—by letting the ECAP transient solution proceed until steady state is reached. A more efficient method is to use an EQUILIBRIUM solution control card as part of an ECAP program.

At equilibrium, an inductor appears as a short circuit and a capacitor appears as an open circuit. The time rate of change of voltage across a capacitor is zero at equilibrium and, hence, the current is zero as it would be in an open circuit. Furthermore, the time rate of change of current through an inductor is zero at

```
        ⋮        ⋮
B21  N(8,10),G=0.05E−3
B22  N(8,10),G=(1E−8,0.25E−3),E=−.2
B23  N(8,10),G=(1E−8,0.4E−3),E=−.3
B24  N(8,10),G=(1E−8,1.2E−3),E=−.4
B25  N(8,10),G=(1E−8,1.1E−3),E=−.5
S1   B=22,(22),OFF
S2   B=23,(23),OFF
S3   B=24,(24),OFF
S4   B=25,(25),OFF
        ⋮        ⋮
```

Figure 12.40 *A partial program to simulate a nonlinear resistor.*

equilibrium and, hence, the voltage across the inductor is zero as it would be in a short circuit. The EQUILIBRIUM feature of ECAP takes advantage of both these facts in producing an equilibrium solution.

The equilibrium solution is a two-step automatic process. First, the inductors are replaced by resistors having very small resistance to simulate the short circuits at equilibrium, and the capacitors are replaced by resistors having very large resistance to simulate the open circuits at equilibrium. Next, a dc analysis of the circuit is obtained to find the resulting node voltages and element currents. This analysis is the equilibrium solution. All that the user must do to obtain an equilibrium solution is include an EQUILIBRIUM solution control card in the ECAP program.

For example, consider again the circuit of Fig. 12.29, and the program and results of Fig. 12.30. One can observe that the circuit had not yet reached equilibrium at a FINISH TIME of 50 msec. The addition of an EQUILIBRIUM solution control card to the ECAP program, as in Fig. 12.41, gives the equilibrium solution shown in that figure.

The low value of resistance used for short circuits during an equilibrium solution is assumed by the ECAP processor to be 0.01 Ω, and the high value of resistance used for open circuits is assumed to be 10^7 Ω. These values can be changed if necessary by the addition of two solution control cards. If, for example, we wanted the short circuit resistance to be 10^{-3} Ω, and the open circuit resistance to be 10^6 Ω, the following solution control cards would accomplish the desired changes when added to the program:

$$\text{SHORT} = 1\text{E}−3$$
$$\text{OPEN} \ = 1\text{E}6$$

The equilibrium solution applies only where fixed current and voltage sources are employed. Equilibrium solutions should not be tried if time-dependent sources are included in the circuit.

```
C   AN EQUILIBRIUM SOLUTION
        TRANSIENT ANALYSIS
    B1   N(0,1),R=5E3,E=10
    B2   N(1,2),C=1E−6
    B3   N(1,0),C=2E−6
    B4   N(2,0),R=10E3
        TIME STEP=1E−4
        OUTPUT INTERVAL=10
        FINISH TIME 50E−3
        PRINT NV,EC
        EQUILIBRIUM
        EXECUTE
STEADY STATE SOLUTION

                    VOLTAGES
NODES
    1 − 2        .99900149+01    .99800348−02
                    CURRENTS
BRANCHES
    1 − 4        .19970178−05   .99800349−06    .99900147−06    .99800346−06
```

Figure 12.41   *An equilibrium solution.*

12.22   Initial Condition Solution and Initial Time

The current flowing in an inductor and the voltage across a capacitor cannot change instantaneously from one value to another. Consequently, the first solution of a transient solution is an initial condition solution. For this calculation each inductor is replaced by a current source equal to the initial current and a parallel resistor having large resistance, and each capacitor is replaced by a voltage source equal to the initial voltage and a series resistor having small resistance. The value of these resistors are the OPEN and SHORT values discussed in the preceeding section.

The reader should note that the resistors substituted in place of inductors and capacitors for initial condition calculations are just the reverse of the substitutions used for equilibrium solution calculations. SHORT and OPEN control cards apply here also.

If an INITIAL TIME solution control card is used, the first solution will be labeled with the time indicated on the card, and time will proceed normally from this time until the FINAL TIME is reached at which point the solution will be terminated. None of the calculations are affected by this control card.

12.23 1ERROR and 2ERROR

Because of the limited precision of the calculation of the currents in each branch, the sum of currents flowing into a node and the sum of those flowing out of the same node might differ slightly, giving a small residual current unbalance. During the processing of a dc, ac, or transient solution, the ECAP processor keeps a running account of the current unbalance at each node.

In addition, the sum of these absolute current unbalances is also found. If the total residual current thus found exceeds a preselected maximum value, a printout of each nodal residual current is produced. The ECAP processor assumes this maximum allowable value to be 10^{-3} A unless specified otherwise. If the user wishes to make this limit something other than 10^{-3} A (for example, 0.1 A) he may do so by including a solution control card such as

$$1ERROR = 1E-1$$

If a large residual current is observed at any node as a result of the 1ERROR limit being exceeded, it indicates too wide a difference between the values of impedance connected to the node in question. As a general rule, the value of the smallest impedance connected to a given node should not be more than five orders of magnitude smaller than the value of the next larger impedance connected to the same node. When determining these values for transient analysis, a capacitor should be considered as a resistor having resistance equal to TIME STEP/C, and an inductor should be considered as a resistor having a resistance of 2L/TIME STEP.

The actuation time of any switch can be determined to within a very small part of a time step. The ECAP processor assumes this to be one-thousandth of a time step unless otherwise indicated. If a user wishes the actuation time of a switch to be other than one-thousandth of a time step, he may so indicate by including a solution control card such as

$$2ERROR = 0.01$$

which indicates that, in this case, the fraction of a time step to be used is one-hundredth. Immediately following the actuation of a switch, the affected parameters are changed and an initial condition calculation is made. The transient solution then proceeds normally until the next switch actuation occurs.

12.24 Parameter Modifications in Transient Analysis

More recent versions of ECAP include a parameter modification capability for transient analysis that is similar to the capability for dc analysis. Voltage and current sources as well as resistance, inductance, and capacitance values can be modified. The following features that are unique with transient analysis can also be modified:

TIME STEP
INITIAL TIME
OUTPUT INTERVAL
FINAL TIME
1ERROR
2ERROR
SHORT
OPEN

Up to 50 parameter values can be modified in a single modify routine after which a new solution is obtained. Parametric studies are not possible.

Transient analysis modifications are similar to ac and dc modifications in that the final values of any parameter in any solution carry over to the next solution, unless specifically reentered in their entirety in the modify routines. If no other provision is made, time-dependent sources retain their last value from the previous solution and appear as fixed sources thereafter. Switches retain their last states from the preceeding solution as well as the parameters they control unless a change is specified. The EQUILIBRIUM control does not carry over and must be reentered if needed.

12.25 Partial Derivatives and Sensitivity Coefficients

Indication of the relative effect of variations in each of the circuit parameters on each of the node voltages is given by the sensitivity coefficients. In some versions of ECAP only dc analysis provides for sensitivity coefficient determination while in other versions, ac analysis also has this feature.

Sensitivity coefficients exist only for node voltages. The sensitivity coefficient for a node voltage is defined as the change in node voltage for a 1% change in the branch parameter. In dc analysis these coefficients are found with respect to resistances, voltage sources, current sources, and transconductances. In ac analysis, in addition, coefficients are found with respect to inductances and capacitances. Also in ac analysis, since the node voltages have magnitude as well as phase, sensitivity coefficients are determined for both phase and magnitude of each node voltage.

To determine the sensitivity coefficients, we must know the partial derivatives of each node voltage with respect to each circuit parameter. These partial derivatives are determined and printed out along with the sensitivity coefficients. To obtain these printed outputs, a solution control card bearing the word SENSITIVITIES is all that is required, unless WORST CASE or STANDARD DEVIATION control cards are used. If WORST CASE or STANDARD DEVIATION cards are used then SE must be included in the PRINT control to get sensitivity coefficients and partial derivatives printed out.

To summarize, the sensitivity output includes the partial derivative of every node voltage with respect to every circuit parameter. It also includes the sensitivity of every node voltage to a 1% change in every circuit parameter.

12.26 Worst Case

The WORST CASE capability of ECAP yields the minimum and maximum values of node voltages for every node. These maximum and minimum values are calculated based on stated nominal, maximum, and minimum parameter values supplied by the user. These nominal maximum and minimum parameter values establish parameter tolerances. The positive parameter tolerance is the difference between the maximum and nominal parameter values. The negative parameter tolerance is the difference between the minimum and nominal parameter values.

Depending on the sign of the node voltage partial derivitives, determined for sensitivity coefficient calculations, the nominal values of the nonzero tolerance parameters are replaced by either the maximum or minimum parameter values in performing the worst-case calculations. If the sign of the partial derivative of a node voltage with respect to a particular parameter is positive, the nominal value of that parameter is replaced by the maximum parameter value for the worst-case maximum solution, and by the minimum parameter value for the worst-case minimum solution. Similarly, if the partial derivative of a node voltage with respect to a particular parameter is negative, the minimum parameter value is used to replace the nominal value for the worst-case maximum solution and the maximum parameter value is used for the worst-case minimum solution.

ECAP assumes that the signs of the partial derivatives of all node voltages do not change over the range of parameter variation from minimum to maximum value. The signs of the partial derivatives are determined after all parameters have been set to their indicated extremes. These signs are then compared with the signs obtained when nominal values are used. If any of these compared signs do not agree, a warning message is printed out indicating that a true worst case has not been found.

Parameter tolerances can be indicated on the appropriate B-cards by one of two methods—either explicitly or as a fraction of the nominal value. For example, if a resistor is to have a nominal value of 100 Ω with a maximum of 110 Ω and a minimum of 95 Ω, the B-card could be written

$$\text{B7} \quad \text{N(1,2),R=100(95,110)}$$

If the parameter was a current source having a nominal value of −5 A with a minimum of −10 and a maximum of +3, the B-card could appear as

$$\text{B16} \quad \text{N(3,7),R=500,I=−5(−10,+3)}$$

Alternatively, we can express tolerances as a nominal value and a fractional variation. For example, if a voltage source is to have a nominal value of 75 V and a variation of 10% above and below this value, the B-card could be written

$$\text{B27} \quad \text{N(5,12),R=50,E=75(.10)}$$

Hence, the maximum value used would be 82.5 V and the minimum value used would be 67.5 V. Worst-case output is obtained by simply including a solution control card containing the words WORST CASE. If this is done, the worst-case solutions for all nodes are determined. If the words WORST CASE are followed by a series of node numbers each separated by a comma, the worst-case solutions will be found only for those nodes mentioned. For example,

WORST CASE, 6, 7, 12, 18

would result in worst-case solutions for nodes 6, 7, 12, and 18.

Because of the complexity of calculations for worst-case solutions in the ac case, the signs of the partial derivatives are not compared as in the dc case. For this reason, extra care must be exercised when performing ac worst-case studies.

The circuit of Fig. 12.9 will serve as an example for WORST CASE analysis. Suppose that the program of Fig. 12.10 is modified to assign tolerances to some of the parameters so that a worst-case study can be made. The program shown in Fig. 12.42 could be used, in which worst-case behavior is determined only for nodes 1 and 2 since they are mentioned explicitly. Also, the PRINT statement asks for sensitivities to be printed out. This is sufficient since a SENSITIVITIES control card is not needed when a WORST CASE control card is used. Figure 12.43 shows the output resulting from the above program.

```
C   PROGRAM TO ILLUSTRATE WORST CASE AND SENSITIVITIES
        DC  ANALYSIS
    B1   N(0,1),R=100(90,105),E=50
    B2   N(1,2),R=20
    B3   N(2,0),R=45(0.1)
    B4   N(2,3),R=10
    B5   N(3,0),R=5,I=10(9,11)
        WORST CASE, 1, 2
        PRINT, NV,SE
        EXECUTE
```

Figure 12.42 *A program for worst-case determination.*

12.27 ECAP Program Arrangement

An orderly arrangement of ECAP program input information has proved to be desirable. The following arrangement will avoid difficulties which sometimes occur if proper order is not observed. The asterisks indicate required cards.

(1) Command Card
   *DC ANALYSIS
   *AC ANALYSIS   } (use only the one which is appropriate)
   *TRANSIENT ANALYSIS

(2) Data Cards
    *B-cards (dc, ac, and transient analyses)
    T-cards (dc, ac, and transient analyses)
    M-cards (ac analysis only)
    S-cards (transient analysis only)

(3) Solution Control Cards
    *FREQUENCY (ac analysis only)
    SENSITIVITIES ⎫
    WORST CASE ⎬ (dc and ac analyses only)

    *TIME STEP ⎫
    OUTPUT INTERVAL ⎪
    1ERROR ⎪
    2ERROR ⎪
    INITIAL TIME ⎬ (transient analysis only)
    FINAL TIME ⎪
    SHORT ⎪
    OPEN ⎪
    EQUILIBRIUM ⎭

(4) Output Control Cards
    NODE VOLTAGE   (NV) ⎫ (dc, ac, and transient analyses)
    ELEMENT CURRENT   (EC) ⎭

    ELEMENT VOLTAGE   (EV) ⎫
    BRANCH CURRENT   (BC) ⎪
    BRANCH VOLTAGE   (BV) ⎪
    ELEMENT POWER   (EP) ⎬ (dc and ac analyses only)
    MISCELLANEOUS   (MI) ⎪
    SENSITIVITIES   (SE) ⎭

(5) Command Card
    *EXECUTE   (dc, ac, and transient analyses)

12.28   Assumed Solution Controls

In order to avoid any confusion and to provide a convenient place of reference, the assumed solution controls are repeated below. Unless otherwise stated the ECAP processor assumes the values shown.

FINAL TIME	$= 10^{37}$ sec
INITIAL TIME	$= 0$ sec
SHORT	$= 10^{-2}\ \Omega$
OPEN	$= 10^{7}\ \Omega$
OUTPUT INTERVAL	$= 1$ time step
1ERROR	$= 10^{-3}$ A
2ERROR	$= 10^{-3}$ (time step)

NODES		NODE VOLTAGES	
1 – 3	.40476189+02	.38571426+02	.46190475+02

PARTIAL DERIVATIVES AND SENSITIVITIES OF NODE VOLTAGES
WITH RESPECT TO RESISTANCES

BRANCH	NODE	PARTIALS	SENSITIVITIES
1	1	−.22675739−01	−.22675739−01
1	2	−.81632660−02	−.81632660−02
1	3	−.27210886−02	−.27210886−02
2	1	.72562390−01	.14512478−01
2	2	−.81632682−02	−.16326536−02
2	3	−.27210894−02	−.54421787−03
3	1	.16326529+00	.73469377−01
3	2	.19591835+00	.88163254−01
3	3	.65306114−01	.29387751−01
4	1	−.43537419+00	−.43537418−01
4	2	−.52244903+00	−.52244902−01
4	3	.79818607−01	.79818605−02
5	1	.52789112+01	.26394555+00
5	2	.63346934+01	.31673466+00
5	3	.82702942+01	.41351470+00

WITH RESPECT TO VOLTAGE SOURCES

BRANCH	NODE	PARTIALS	SENSITIVITIES
1	1	.23809524+00	.11904762+00
1	2	.85714282−01	.42857140−01
1	3	.28571427−01	.14285713−01

WITH RESPECT TO CURRENT SOURCES

BRANCH	NODE	PARTIALS	SENSITIVITIES
5	1	.28571428+01	.28571427+00
5	2	.34285713+01	.34285713+00
5	3	.44761904+01	.44761903+00

WORST CASE SOLUTIONS FOR NODE VOLTAGES

NODE	WCMIN	NOMINAL	WCMAX
1	.36744531+02	.40476189+02	.44229664+02
2	.34219680+02	.38571426+02	.42947367+02

Figure 12.43   *The results of executing the program of Fig. 12.42.*

12.29   ECAP as a General Purpose Simulation Language

In the preceding sections of this chapter, we have described how ECAP can be
used with a digital computer to model and study the behavior of electric circuits.

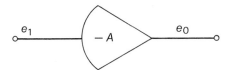

Figure 12.44 *An operational amplifier.*

When used in this way, the computer is a special purpose electric circuit simulator and ECAP is a special purpose simulation language. Certainly, ECAP is this, but it is more.

Earlier chapters described the use of the electronic analog computer as a general purpose simulator. In the final analysis, an analog computer, when assembled as a simulator, is nothing more than an electric circuit. Since this is the case, and since ECAP can be used to study the behavior of electric circuits, it follows that any system that can be studied with the aid of an electronic analog computer can also be studied using ECAP. Taking this point of view, we can therefore think of ECAP as a general purpose simulation language. To understand better this expanded concept of ECAP requires a more detailed consideration of analog computer circuits, which we now do.

The basis of most electronic analog computer elements is the operational amplifier diagrammed in Fig. 12.44. The output voltage of such an operational amplifier is

$$e_0 = -Ae_1 \qquad (12.10)$$

Figure 12.45 shows an equivalent circuit of the operational amplifier. The output voltage of such an equivalent circuit is

$$e_0 = -G_m e_1 R_0 \qquad (12.11)$$

The similarities between Eqs. 12.10 and 12.11 are obvious. If $R_0 = 1$, there is direct analogy between e_0 in both circuits, between e_1 in both circuits, and between amplifier gain A in Eq. 12.10 and transconductance G_m in Eq. 12.11.

The characteristics required of operational amplifiers when used in analog computers are high gain, high input impedance, and low output impedance. These characteristics are easily obtained in the equivalent circuit by making R_i and G_m large, and R_0 small.

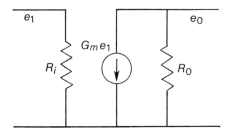

Figure 12.45 *An operational amplifier equivalent circuit.*

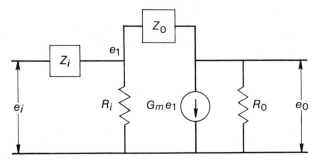

Figure 12.46 *The equivalent circuit with input and feedback impedances.*

If the equivalent circuit of the operational amplifier is supplied with appropriate input and feedback impedances, as shown in Fig. 12.46, the behavior of the resulting circuit is very close to the behavior of the operational amplifier circuit of Fig. 12.47.

The circuit of Fig. 12.47 is the basic circuit of analog adders, sign changers, integrators, and transfer function simulators. Typically, Z_i is a resistor; Z_0 is a resistor when the circuit is a sign changer or an adder. When the circuit is an integrator Z_0 is a capacitor, and both Z_0 and Z_i may be more complicated combinations of resistors and capacitors when the circuit is used for transfer function simulation. When the circuit is used as an adder or an adder integrator, Z_i is replaced by several resistors—one for each input. The analog computer circuits for these devices are described in considerably more detail in the Appendix.

Experience has shown that values of $R_i = 10^9 \ \Omega$, $G_m = 10^5$ mhos, and $R_0 = 1 \ \Omega$ in Fig. 12.45 give results with ECAP that are more accurate than those obtained with typical analog computers.

When using ECAP as a general purpose simulator one can proceed as follows:
(1) Develop an analog computer block diagram of the system to be simulated.
(2) Using the block diagram, develop a schematic circuit diagram showing all circuit elements including resistors and capacitors with their appropriate values and operational amplifiers.

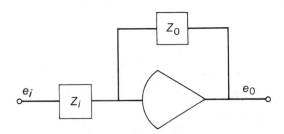

Figure 12.47 *The operational amplifier with input and feedback impedances.*

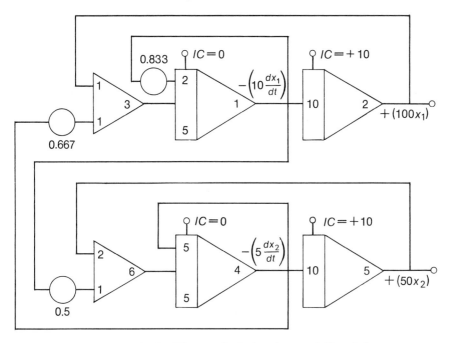

Figure 12.48 *The scaled simulator of Fig. 6.1.*

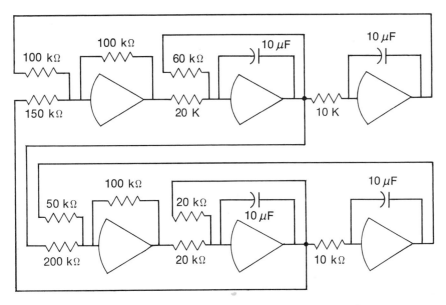

Figure 12.49 *An analog computer schematic.*

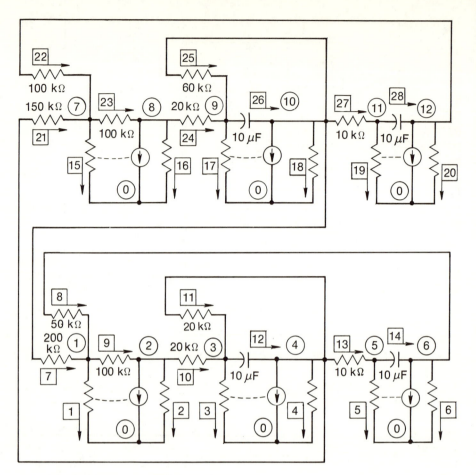

Figure 12.50 *The analog computer schematic ready for ECAP programming.*

(3) Replace each of the operational amplifiers with the equivalent circuit of Fig. 12.45, letting $R_i = 10^9\ \Omega$, $G_m = 10^5$ mhos, and $R_0 = 1\ \Omega$ in each case.

(4) Write an ECAP program to simulate the resulting circuit.

Some examples will help to make the procedure clear. Let us turn our attention back to Fig. 6.4 which is a simulator devised to study the system of Fig. 6.1. Figure 6.4 is repeated here as Fig. 12.48 for convenience.

The development of Fig. 12.48 constitutes the first step in the study of the system using ECAP.

Figure 12.49 shows the second step. In this figure, one possible choice of input and feedback elements for each operational amplifier is illustrated. The elements shown result in the proper multiplying constants. Other choices could also be made.

```
        TR
B1    N(1, 0), R = 1E9
B2    N(2, 0), R = 1
B3    N(3, 0), R = 1E9
B4    N(4, 0), R = 1
B5    N(5, 0), R = 1E9
B6    N(6, 0), R = 1
B7    N(10, 1), R = 200E3
B8    N(6, 1), R = 50E3
B9    N(1, 2), R = 100E3
B10   N(2, 3), R = 20E3
B11   N(4, 3), R = 20E3
B12   N(3, 4), C = 10E−6
B13   N(4, 5), R = 10E3
B14   N(5, 6), C = 10E−6, EO = 10
B15   N(7, 0), R = 1E9
B16   N(8, 0), R = 1
B17   N(9, 0), R = 1E9
B18   N(10, 0), R = 1
B19   N(11, 0), R = 1E9
B20   N(12, 0), R = 1
B21   N(4, 7), R = 150E3
B22   N(12, 7), R = 100E3
B23   N(7, 8), R = 100E3
B24   N(8, 9), R = 20E3
B25   N(10, 9), R = 60E3
B26   N(9, 10), C = 10E−6
B27   N(10, 11), R = 10E3
B28   N(11, 12), C = 10E−6, EO = 10
T1    B(1, 2), GM = 1E5
T2    B(3, 4), GM = 1E5
T3    B(5, 6), GM = 1E5
T4    B(15, 16), GM = 1E5
T5    B(17, 18), GM = 1E5
T6    B(19, 20), GM = 1E5
      TI = 0.01
      OU = 10
      F1 = 5.0
      SH = 1.
      PR, NV
      EX
```

Figure 12.51 *An ECAP program for simulating the system of Fig. 6.1.*

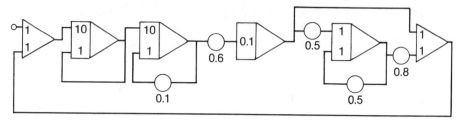

Figure 12.52 *A time-scaled simulator with stabilization.*

The third step in the procedure is shown in Fig. 12.50. Here each operational amplifier of Fig. 12.49 is replaced by the equivalent circuit of Fig. 12.45. The nodes and branches have been numbered in this figure, also. It should be noticed that the effects of the potentiometers in Fig. 12.49 are included in the input and feedback elements chosen for Fig. 12.50. We have thus eliminated the potentiometers. This is possible since for the ECAP model almost any appropriate values of resistance and capacitance can be used with very little restriction.

With the completed schematic of Fig. 12.50, we can now move on to the fourth step in the procedure. The resulting ECAP program for studying the system is contained in Fig. 12.51.

When writing the ECAP program, attention must be given to the TIME STEP, OUTPUT INTERVAL, and FINISH TIME, which are determined by the speed of response of the system. In Chapter 6, where the system being discussed was introduced, the natural frequencies were found to be 7 and 10 rad/sec or a little over 1 cps. A TIME INTERVAL = 0.01 was chosen to provide approximately 100 calculated data points per cycle so as to give good accuracy. Printing out of every tenth value is sufficient for most purposes, hence, we selected OUTPUT INTERVAL = 10. The two time constants for this system are 1.2 and 0.4 sec. If we let the solution run for four time constants then a FINAL TIME = 5. guarantees that the slowest transient response would be essentially complete.

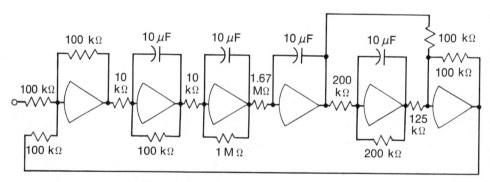

Figure 12.53 *A schematic of Fig. 12.52.*

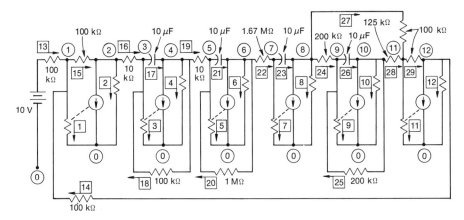

Figure 12.54 *An analog computer schematic ready for ECAP programming.*

Let us consider another example to further demonstrate the method. For this example we will refer to the analog computer diagram of Fig. 6.20, repeated here for convenience as Fig. 12.52. Figure 12.53 is the schematic diagram with appropriate input and feedback elements indicated.

In Fig. 12.54 we see a schematic diagram in which each operational amplifier of Fig. 12.53 has been replaced with an equivalent circuit and is ready for ECAP programming. The resulting ECAP program is shown in Fig. 12.55.

The constant voltage source introduced in branch 13 of Fig. 12.55 is the driving signal for the system being simulated, and is arbitrarily set equal to 10 V. This would simulate a step function disturbance on the system. The magnitude of this signal is of little importance since the system is linear and no saturation or other magnitude sensitive nonlinearity occurs anywhere. Hence, this driving signal could have any other value or form we wished. A repeating periodic arbitrary signal, a sinusoidal signal, or a nonrepeating arbitrary signal are all possible with ECAP.

12.30 Summary

ECAP is a special purpose digital computer programming language, whose specific function is the analysis and design of electric circuits. ECAP is capable of performing dc, ac, and transient analyses of circuits subject to rather minor restrictions. Proper ECAP programming allows for nonlinear circuit elements to be studied individually or included in other more complicated circuits. Worst-case and statistical studies can also be handled by the ECAP system.

ECAP programming is easy and straightforward. The designers of ECAP have

TR

B1	N(1, 0), R = 1E9
B2	N(2, 0), R = 1
B3	N(3, 0), R = 1E9
B4	N(4, 0), R = 1
B5	N(5, 0), R = 1E9
B6	N(6, 0), R = 1
B7	N(7, 0), R = 1E9
B8	N(8, 0), R = 1
B9	N(9, 0), R = 1E9
B10	N(10, 0), R = 1
B11	N(11, 0), R = 1E9
B12	N(12, 0), R = 1
B13	N(0, 1), R = 100E3, E = 10
B14	N(12, 1), R = 100E3
B15	N(1, 2), R = 100E3
B16	N(2, 3), R = 10E3
B17	N(3, 4), C = 10E−6
B18	N(4, 3), R = 100E3
B19	N(4, 5), R = 10E3
B20	N(6, 5), R = 1E6
B21	N(5, 6), C = 10E−6
B22	N(6, 7), R = 1.67E6
B23	N(7, 8), C = 10E−6
B24	N(8, 9), R = 200E3
B25	N(10, 9), R = 200E3
B26	N(9, 10), C = 10E−6
B27	N(8, 11), R = 100E3
B28	N(10, 11), R = 125E3
B29	N(11, 12), R = 100E3
T1	B(1, 2), GM = 1E5
T2	B(3, 4), GM = 1E5
T3	B(5, 6), GM = 1E5
T4	B(7, 8), GM = 1E5
T5	B(9, 10), GM = 1E5
T6	B(11, 12), GM = 1E5
	TI = 0.025
	OU = 40
	FI = 15
	PR, NV
	EX

Figure 12.55 *An ECAP program to simulate the system of Fig. 6.16.*

tried to anticipate the needs of the user and have incorporated most of the features that one would commonly require when studying electric circuits.

However, ECAP is more than just a special purpose electric circuit simulation language. Based on the analog computer simulator of a system, the resulting electric circuit can be studied using ECAP and the results can be interpreted in terms of system behavior. ECAP can, in this manner, be considered to be a general purpose simulation language with much broader application than just studies of electric circuit behavior.

EXERCISES

1. For the circuit in Fig. 12.56, find the current in each branch, the voltage across each branch, and the power in each branch. The resistances are given in ohms.

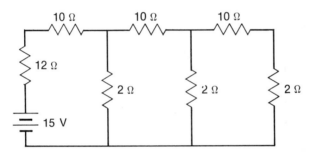

Figure 12.56

2. In Fig. 12.57, the resistances are given in kiloohms. Find the resistance between a and b.

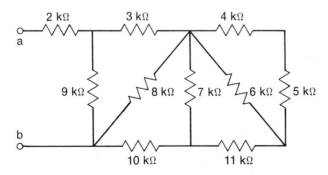

Figure 12.57

3. The circuit in Fig. 12.58 has a generator which delivers a constant current of 15 A. What is the voltage across the load L?

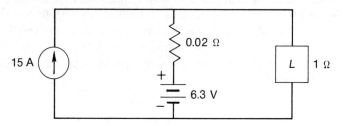

Figure 12.58

4. In Fig. 12.59, the switch is changed from position 1 to position 2 at $t=0$. It can be assumed that the switch has been in position 1 long enough for steady state to result. Find the maximum voltage across C. At what time does the maximum occur?

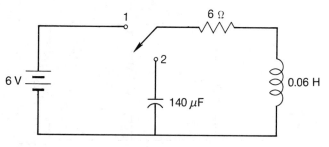

Figure 12.59

5. The circuit in Fig. 12.60 is in steady state with the switch in position 1. The switch is thrown to position 2 at $t=0$. Find the current at $t=0.007$ sec.

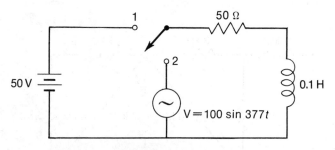

Figure 12.60

6. The circuit of Exercise 5 is modified as follows: Rather than leaving the switch in position 2, it is thrown back to position 1 at $t=0.005$ sec. Find the current at $t=0.007$ sec.

7. From electric network theory, it is known that the Thevenin equivalent circuit between any two terminals in the network can be formed by a voltage source in series with an impedance. The characteristic of the voltage source is that its voltage is equal to the open circuit voltage across the terminals and the impedance is equal to the open circuit voltage divided by the short circuit current flowing between the terminals when they are shorted together. Use this principle to find the Thevenin equivalent circuit between terminals a and b for the circuit in Fig. 12.61.

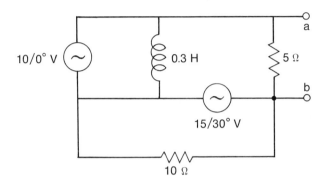

Figure 12.61

8. The Norton equivalent circuit between two terminals of a network consists of a current source in parallel with an impedance. The characteristic of the current source is given by the short circuit current which flows when the terminals are shorted together and the impedance is obtained as explained in Exercise 7. Find the Norton equivalent circuit for the network of Exercise 7.
9. If a circuit contains no voltage or current sources, the impedance to be used in Thevenin or Norton equivalent circuits can be obtained by connecting a $1/0°$ ampere source across the terminals for which the equivalent circuit is

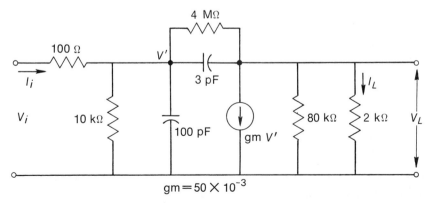

Figure 12.62

desired. All voltage sources must be shorted and all current sources must be opened for this study. The desired impedance is numerically equal to the resulting voltage across the terminals in question. Use this method to verify the results obtained in Exercises 7 and 8.

10. The circuit in Fig. 12.62 is a hybrid π equivalent circuit for a single transistor with resistive load.

Find the current gain $A_i = I_L/I_i$ at a frequency of 150 MHz.

11. The T-equivalent circuit for a single stage common emitter amplifier is shown in Fig. 12.63. Find the current gain $A_i = I_L/I_i$ at a frequency of 1000 Hz.

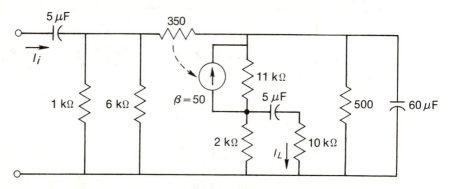

Figure 12.63

12. The circuit in Fig. 12.64 is a crude oscillator. The switch S_2 closes when the current in the coil reaches 0.5 A and opens when the current drops to 0.3 A. Find the period of oscillation in the steady state. How long is S_2 closed? How long is it open?

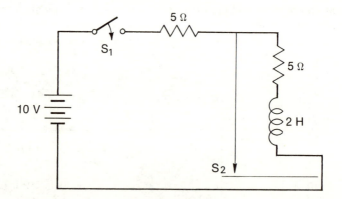

Figure 12.64

13. In Fig. 12.65, S_1 closes at $t=0$ and S_2 closes at $t=0.02$ sec. Find the current in the inductor as a function of time from $t=0$ to $t=0.04$ sec.

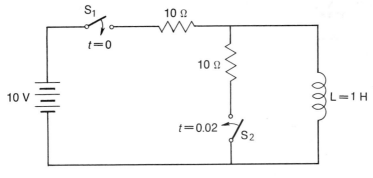

Figure 12.65

14. Use ECAP to find the current in each branch of the circuit in Fig. 12.66 and the power dissipated in the 0.01 Ω resistor.

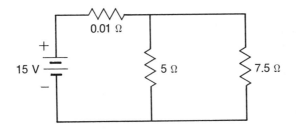

Figure 12.66

15. Use ECAP to find the node voltages, element currents branch voltages, and power dissipated in each resistor for the circuit in Fig. 12.67.

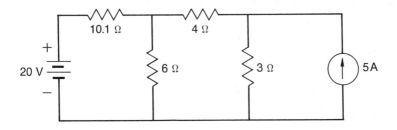

Figure 12.67

16. Use ECAP to find the nominal and worst case node voltage values for the circuit shown in Fig. 12.68.

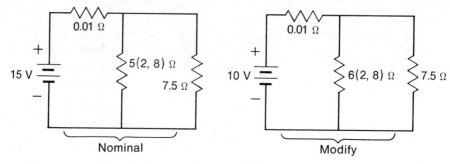

Nominal   Modify

Figure 12.68

17. Use ECAP to find the miscellaneous output for the circuit of Exercise 2.
18. Use ECAP to find the branch currents, element currents, node voltages and
    element powers throughout the circuit in Fig. 12.69. The voltage source has
    an effective value of 250 V.

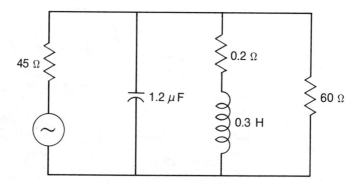

Figure 12.69

19. Use ECAP to find the magnitude and phase of the voltage across the 60 Ω
    resistor in the circuit of Exercise 5 as the frequency is varied from 100 Hz to
    2000 Hz in logarithmic fashion. Find additional data in the range from 180 Hz
    to 320 Hz as the frequency is varied linearly. Find sufficient points to plot
    smooth curves. Plot the curves of magnitude and phase versus frequency.
20. Find the error(s) in the following ECAP program, if any:

```
            DC CIRCUIT
        B1  N(1,2),R=3.,E=2400E−02
        B2  N(2,3),R=.004E3
        B3  N(3,1),G=0.2
            PRNT,EC,NV
            EXCUTE
```

21. Find the frequency response of the single-stage common-emitter amplifier
    shown in Fig. 12.70.

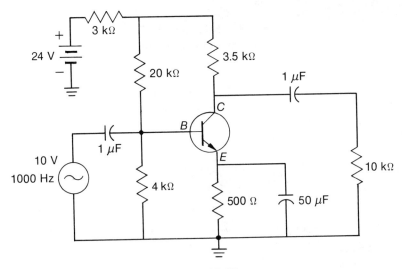

Figure 12.70

The transistor for this application can be replaced by the model in Fig. 12.71.

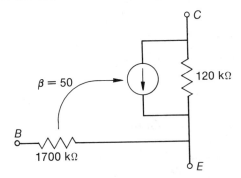

Figure 12.71

22. Find the response of the amplifier in Exercise 11 as the frequency varies between 500 Hz and 5000 Hz.
23. Find the error(s) in the following ECAP program, if any:

```
         TR
    B1   N(0,1),C=4,IO=2
    B2   N(2,1),L=20,EO=-4
    B3   N(2,0),R=4,E=5
         FR=1000
         PR=NV,EC
         END
         EX
```

24. Find the error(s) in the following ECAP program, if any:

```
          AC
      B1  N(0,1),C=1E−6
      B2  N(1,2),L=8E−3
      B3  N(2,3),R=200
      B4  N(2,3),G=1E−2
      B5  N(3,5),R=2(4)10
      T1  B(2,6),BETA=−5
          FREQ=0
          PRI=NV,EC,AC
          EXCUTE
          MODIFY
      B5  R=5,E=10/0
          EX
```

25. Use ECAP to simulate a half-wave rectifier. The half-sine wave voltage shown in Fig. 12.72(b) is to appear between nodes 1 and 0 in the circuit of Fig. 12.72(a). [*Hint:* Use an ECAP switch.]

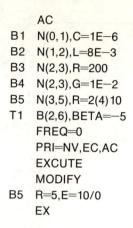

(a)   (b)

Figure 12.72

26. Use ECAP to find the Thevinin and Norton equivalent circuits for the circuit in Fig. 12.73. The equivalent circuits are to replace all but the 100 Ω load resistor.

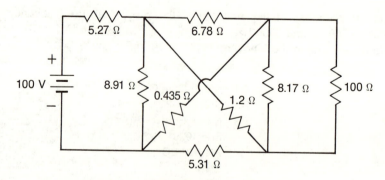

Figure 12.73

27. A low pass filter has been designed to meet the following specifications: cutoff frequency = 4000 Hz, match 500 Ω input and output circuits, attenuation 20 dB at all frequencies above 4400 Hz. The filter is shown in Fig. 12.74. Use ECAP to verify the design.

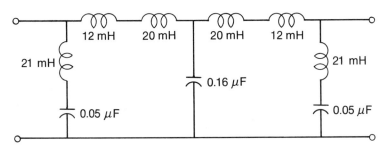

Figure 12.74

28. Figure 12.75 shows a low-pass filter which has been designed to have a cutoff frequency of 3000 Hz with very high attenuations at 3200, 3840, and 500 Hz. It is terminated in a 2000 Ω resistance load as shown. How well does this filter meet the specifications? The inductances are given in henrys and the capacitances are given in microfarads. Use ECAP to simulate the circuit and to obtain the performance of the filter.

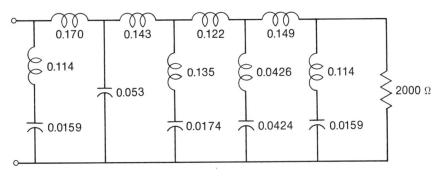

Figure 12.75

13

Coordinate Geometry (COGO)

13.1 Introduction

Some readers may feel that a discussion of the kind presented in this chapter is inappropriate in a book on simulation. The appropriateness is better appreciated, however, if one considers the subject from the broad general view that has been adopted throughout the book, that point of view being that a simulator has the appearance or behavior, without the reality, of the system being simulated. Furthermore, the systems with which we have previously dealt have not included human activities as part of the system behavior and yet, from a macroscopic consideration, humans and their activities are very much a part of many systems.

Such is the case with some of the systems with which civil engineers work. These systems do not behave in the same sense that mechanical or electrical systems behave, and yet they do have a kind of behavior when the human participant is included. That behavior can also be described and studied using a computer model.

For example, the activities of a surveyor such as measuring angles, distances, bearings, azimuths, and elevations, and performing calculations based on these measurements, are typical behavior characteristics of the systems in which civil engineers work. It is this kind of behavior that interests us here. The surveyor himself is part of the system. So, also, are the terrain with which he works, the instruments he uses, the records he keeps, and the calculations he performs. The elements of this system always relate to a set of geometric coordinates which may be one, two, or three dimensional. It is from this environment that the words *coordinate geometry* are drawn. These words, while descriptive, are lengthy, and from them the acronym COGO has been derived. This convenient name identifies a programming language for digital computers that is useful in studying problems in coordinate geometry.

COGO is a special purpose digital computer programming language. Its purpose is to make digital computers more easily accessible and, thus, more useful to civil engineers. Using words that are a part of the civil engineering vocabulary, COGO helps to break down the communication barrier that often frustrates potential digital computer users. Without a special purpose user-oriented language such as COGO, the civil engineer who uses computers is forced to abandon the familiar terminology of his profession, and adopt a less familiar computer-oriented language. This hinders the use of computers by such individuals and frequently obstructs it completely.

As we mentioned above, COGO is oriented toward the solution of geometric problems encountered in civil engineering. Such problems as land surveys, right-of-way surveys, highway design, layout of construction projects, and the design of bridges are typical of the problems to which COGO can be applied. Using COGO, computer programs can be written quickly; often only a few minutes are required to write a detailed and sophisticated program. This can be done by persons who are skilled as civil engineers, but who have had little or no experience in digital computer programming. Of course, the programs written in COGO can be of any length—short or long as the problem requires.

In a typical situation, where a general purpose language such as FORTRAN is employed, considerable effort is made to keep programs very general. This is done to achieve efficiency and economy. The investment in time, effort, and money that must be made to write such a program is often considerable. Theoretically at least, general programs can be filed away after their initial use and taken out again whenever the need arises. The practical difficulty with this concept is that frequently the new requirements, for reasons not anticipated when the original program was first written, cannot be met by the old program. The user then finds himself struggling to make the old program work. This requires cutting the program here, adding to it there, and sometimes outright faking of information needed by the program to make it run, but not needed to solve the problem. Fortunately, the situation is different with COGO. The time, money, and effort expended in the writing of a COGO program is so small that one can afford to write a new program for each problem. After a single use, the COGO programs are discarded.

A number of features have been designed into COGO by its creators to make it easy to learn and use. The instructions, and data pertaining to those instructions, are combined together in a free format arrangement. This eliminates complicated data reading instructions and frees the user from most of the rigid card-column positioning restrictions of some other languages. Also, the results of a computation are printed out immediately following the printout of the instructions that produced them. This makes the association of instructions, data, and results extremely easy.

13.2   The Structure of COGO Instructions

A COGO program consists of a series of instructions describing the operations to be performed. These instructions use words common to a civil engineer's vocabulary. Words such as AZIMUTH, BEARING, ALIGNMENT, OFFSET, ADJUST, AREA, INTERSECT, and so on, are used when writing these instructions. How well these instructions are used depends on the individual's skill as a civil engineer, and not on his skill as a programmer.

Each instruction is comprised of an instruction name and a set of pertinent data. One can almost think of the preparation of a set of COGO instructions for a computer as the preparation of a set of instructions for another engineer. However, COGO has also been designed to accept an abbreviated mnemonic form of each instruction. For example, instead of writing LOCATE/LINE, one can write LLN, or instead of writing EXTERNAL/TANGENT, ET will suffice. The long form and short form of each COGO instruction are given in Table 13.1, pages 362-408.

The instructions listed in Table 13.1 are in alphabetical order for convenient reference. Sometimes it is more convenient to refer to the various instructions in functional groupings. Table 13.2, pages 409-410, has been provided for this purpose.

The abbreviated forms of COGO instructions given in Table 13.1 are useful for one who is somewhat familiar with the language. When one is first learning to use COGO, he might find the long form is preferable, because the words are familiar. As one's acquaintance with COGO increases, however, the short form is more efficient and concise. At any stage, it is perfectly correct to intermix long form and short form instructions as desired.

13.3   An Example of the Use of COGO

Suppose that a surveyor has made a survey of a plot of ground, and now wishes to find the area of the plot, the lengths and azimuths of each straight side of the plot, and the arc length of the curved side. The plot is shown in Fig. 13.1. The surveyor has set up his transit at the corner point 25 and measured the azimuths to points 26, 27, and 28. He chained the distances from point 25 to each of the other points. (See Fig. 13.1.) He knows the coordinates of point 25 where he has his transit located.

Figure 13.2 is a COGO program to find the desired information concerning Fig. 13.1.

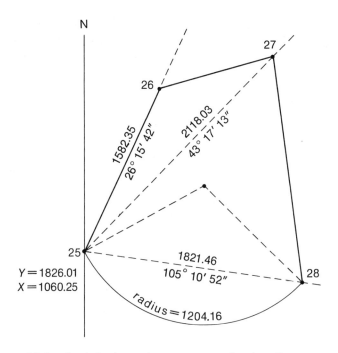

N

27

26

1582.35

26° 15' 42"

2118.03

43° 17' 13"

25

Y = 1826.01
X = 1060.25

1821.46
105° 10' 52"

28

radius = 1204.16

Figure 13.1 *A plot plan whose area and azimuths are needed.*

In Fig. 13.2, the numbers at the top of the figure represent card-column identification numbers. Columns 73 to 80 are not used in COGO and are used here
only for card identification purposes. Each line of information is punched on a
separate card. Card No. 1 contains the word START beginning in column 1. Any
other desired information can be written on this card starting in column 13 or
beyond and ending in or before column 72. Such information constitutes a page

1 INSTRUCTION 20	21 DATA 72	73 80
START	CALCULATION OF AREA AND AZIMUTHS	1
CLEAR	1 999	2
STORE	25 1826.01 1060.25	3
LOCATE/AZIMUTH	25 26 1582.35 26 15 42	4
LOCATE/AZIMUTH	25 27 2118.03 43 17 13	5
LOCATE/AZIMUTH	25 28 1821.46 105 10 52	6
AREA/AZIMUTHS	25 26 27 28 25	7
SEGMENT/PLUS	25 28 1204.16	8

Figure 13.2 *A COGO program to solve the problem of Fig. 13.1.*

heading and will be printed at the top of each page of output until the next START card is encountered. In this case CALCULATION OF AREA AND AZIMUTHS would be printed at the top of each page. The instruction on card No. 2 in Fig. 13.2 is CLEAR which causes the indicated locations in the coordinate table to be cleared of previous values. In this case locations 1 to 999 are cleared. Notice that COGO uses blanks to separate items of data, rather than commas as in other languages. At least one blank must terminate each instruction. Only the CLEAR instruction is printed out. Card No. 3, STORE, causes the coordinates of point 25 to be stored as $Y = 1826.01$, $X = 1060.25$. Cards No. 4, 5, and 6, LOCATE/AZIMUTH, compute the coordinates of points 26, 27, and 28, and store them in the corresponding locations in the coordinate table. The coordinates are also printed out. Card No. 7, AREA/AZIMUTHS, computes the area of the closed polygon having the corner points 25, 26, 27, and 28. Note that the first and last corner points must be the same to indicate the closed nature of the polygon. Card No. 7 also computes the azimuth and distance of each of the sides of the polygon and prints out a table of this information. Card No. 8, SEGMENT/PLUS, computes the area of the circular segment and adds it to the previously computed polygonal area which was found as a result of card No. 7.

This example, while admittedly simple, demonstrates the characteristics of COGO. Other instructions are available and can be used in much the same way as those illustrated in Fig. 13.2. There are additional details which also must be understood if COGO is to be used successfully.

Figure 13.3 is a reproduction of the printout resulting from running the program of instructions of Fig. 13.2. Observe that the printout lists each instruction and, wherever appropriate, the results of executing each instruction are printed immediately following the instruction itself. The reader should compare Figs. 13.2 and 13.3 to see this behavior.

13.4 Coordinate Tables

In the previous example use was made of the coordinate table. This can be thought of as a list of 999 locations in which the Y and X coordinates of an equal number of points can be stored for ready reference. The identifying number of a point, which must be between 1 and 999 inclusive, also identifies the location in the coordinate table where the coordinates of the particular point are to be found.

Any portion of the coordinate table can be cleared of previous coordinates by the CLEAR instruction. Whenever the coordinates of any point are found as a consequence of any instruction whatever, these coordinates are placed in the coordinate table and thereafter are available for whatever use the programmer may need of them. Coordinates can also be stored in the coordinate table by making use of the STORE instruction.

CLEAR   1 999

STORE   25 1826.01 1060.25

LOCATE/AZIMUTH   25 26 1582.35 26 15 42
PT= 26   YCOORD=3245.034   XCOORD=1760.394

LOCATE/AZIMUTH   25 27 2118.03 43 17 13
PT= 27   YCOORD=3367.786   XCOORD=2512.482

LOCATE/AZIMUTH   25 28 1821.46 105 10 52
PT= 28   YCOORD=1349.023   XCOORD=2818.146

AREA/AZIMUTHS   25 26 27 28 25
FROM POINT 25 TO POINT 26 DISTANCE=1582.350 AZIMUTH=26 15 41.984
FROM POINT 26 TO POINT 27 DISTANCE=762.040   AZIMUTH=80 43 48.860
FROM POINT 27 TO POINT 28 DISTANCE=2041.772 AZIMUTH=171 23 24.540
FROM POINT 28 TO POINT 25 DISTANCE=1821.460 AZIMUTH=285 10 51.915
AREA=2192132.500 SQ. FT. AND 50.324 ACRES

SEGMENT/PLUS   25 28 1204.16
CORD LENGTH=1821.460 ARC LENGTH=2065.541 SEGMENT AREA=526180.880
SQ.FT.
CUMULATIVE AREA=2718313.300 SQ. FT. AND 62.404 ACRES

Figure 13.3 *A reproduction of the printout resulting
from running the program of Fig. 13.2.*

13.5 Saving of Angles and Distances for Later Use

Angle tables and distance tables are also constructed as a part of a COGO program. In the case of the coordinate table, the coordinates of all points are saved
as they are found, but in the angle table and the distance table, only those
angles and distances that are specifically indicated to be saved are retained. The
ANGLE/SAVE instruction is used to identify the angle to be saved, cause it to be
computed, and to save its value at a specified location in the angle table. For example, the instruction

1 INSTRUCTION	21	DATA	72	
ANGLE/SAVE	25 35 29 17			

instructs the machine to compute the clockwise angle at point 35 from point 25
to point 29 and save the result in location 17 of the angle table.

In a similar way, the DISTANCE/SAVE instruction is used to compute and save
a distance. For example, the instruction

1 INSTRUCTION	21	DATA	73
DISTANCE/SAVE	25 35 14		

instructs the machine to compute the distance from point 25 to point 35 and store the result in the distance table at position 14.

These saved distances and angles can be used in other calculations by simply referring to them by their location in their respective tables, rather than specifying values of these distances and angles.

As an example, suppose a distance has been saved in location 14 in the distance table, as shown above, and is to be used in another instruction such as

1 INSTRUCTION	21	DATA	73
LOCATE/BEARING	72 197 D14 1 30 45 27		

This instruction tells the machine to locate point 197 at a distance from point 72 as given in the distance table at location 14, and at a bearing in quadrant 1 having a bearing of N30° 45′ 27″ E. The coordinates of point 197 would be stored in the coordinate table as a result of this instruction.

A similar procedure is followed to make use of a saved angle. Suppose an angle has been saved in the angle table at location 17, as explained earlier, and it is to be used in another instruction such as

1 INSTRUCTION	21	DATA	73
LOCATE/ANGLE	19 53 75 D14 A17		

This instruction tells the machine to backsight on point 19 from point 53 and locate point 75 at distance D14 and clockwise angle A17. D14 specifies a location in the distance table and A17 specifies a location in the angle table where the values of the respective distance and angle can be found.

13.6 Comments in a COGO Program

Regardless of the language in which computer programs are written, the programs have a tendency to become stale if not used for a long time. When one refers to such a program after an extended period of disuse, he finds that it often takes considerable effort to reorient his thinking to that of the program so that he can again make use of it.

The solution to this problem is to place a liberal number of comments scattered strategically throughout the program to assist the user in understanding and re-calling what the program is all about. There are two ways of inserting comments in a COGO program. If at least three blank spaces are left after the final data item of any instruction, a comment can then be added without disturbing the instruc-tion in any way. Such comments will then be printed out with the instruction listing. Also, any card with an asterisk (*) in column 1 will be treated as a comment. The comment itself can be placed anywhere in the field between columns 7 and 72 inclusive. Such comments cause no action but are merely listed at the time the program is run on the computer.

13.7 Errors in COGO Programs

One soon discovers that it is difficult, if not impossible, to write an error-free digital computer program of considerable length on the first try. The process of finding and correcting errors is called *debugging.* The programmer usually makes a first attempt to write a correct program and submits it to processing by the computer. More often than not this first attempt will contain errors, some of which will be obvious once they have been pointed out. However, other errors may be more subtle, and can result from incorrect coding or execution. The errors are corrected as they are found and repeated attempts are made until a solution is obtained.

Coding errors are easiest to find because the computer helps in locating them. As a COGO program is processed, it is scanned for coding errors and if any are found, error messages are printed out to indicate the nature and location of the errors. Checks are made to ensure proper command names are used, no misspellings are present, no improper characters are used, and so on.

Execution errors are much harder to locate. They cause incorrect results to be calculated and are often caused by incorrect numerical data. Usually these errors will only be found after a meticulous search of the program and data.

13.8 Rules for Writing COGO Programs

The beginning user of COGO has two main tasks which can be categorized as (a) learning what the various COGO instructions are, what they do, what data they require, how the data is supplied, and the output that can be expected; and (b) learning some details about the idiosyncracies of COGO that will allow convenient and rapid use of the language with a minimum of errors.

The information for the first of these tasks is contained in Table 13.1 which describes in detail the COGO instructions. The second task is simplified by observing the following rules:

(1) Each data processing card in a COGO program nominally contains a single instruction along with the data required to execute that instruction.

(2) The first letter of the instruction must be punched in column 1 of the card. The data can be punched beginning in column 21 and must not extend beyond column 72.

(3) If necessary, an instruction can extend to one or more continuation cards. This is accomplished by punching as much data information as possible on the first card of the instruction, including but not exceeding column 72, omitting all information from columns 1 through 20 of the continuation card, and continuing the data beginning in column 21 of the continuation

card. Items of data can be split with one part on the first card and another part on the continuation card. For example, the number 678.93 might appear with 67 in columns 71 and 72 of the first card and 8.93 in columns 21, 22, 23, and 24, respectively, of the continuation card.

(4) Blank spaces are used as delimiters in COGO instructions to separate items of data. Blanks must not, therefore, be used indiscriminately. Follow the arrangements shown in Table 13.1 to avoid difficulty. At least one blank and not more than six are needed.

(5) COGO has both a long form and a short form of each instruction name. Both forms can be used in any intermixed arrangement the programmer desires.

(6) Every COGO program must begin with the instruction START. Columns 13 to 72 of this instruction card can be used for a page heading which will then be printed at the top of each page until the job is finished or a new START instruction is encountered, at which time the information on the new START instruction will be printed as page headings.

(7) Comments can be inserted wherever desired in a COGO program by punching an asterisk in column 1 and punching the comment in columns 7 to 72.

(8) If three blanks are left following the last item of data of an instruction card, the remaining space on the card up to column 72 may be used for comments.

(9) The only way comments of any kind may be continued onto successive cards is by placing an asterisk (*) in column 1 of all continuation cards.

(10) If two or more consecutive cards contain the same instruction name, it is not necessary to punch the instruction name on any but the first card. Each succeeding card need only have the appropriate data in columns 21 to 72.

(11) Each item of data must contain from 1 to 8 digits and may also contain a decimal point and plus or minus sign. The plus sign is implied if omitted. The minus sign must be expressly stated.

(12) It is not necessary that all coordinates are positive. Any or all may be negative.

(13) Locations in the coordinate table are numbered from 1 to 999. These location numbers correspond to the respective point numbers in the problem for which coordinates are known or are to be determined.

(14) All COGO instruction cards must terminate with at least one blank column. Hence, if the last item of data ends in column 72, the next card must be blank to provide the necessary blank terminator for the instruction.

(15) Decimal points following the right-most digit in data items need not be punched.

(16) Zeros must always be punched as such because spaces are interpreted as delimiters, not as zeros.

(17) It is good practice to clear the coordinate table using the CLEAR instruction at the beginning of any COGO program. This avoids the possibility of inadvertently using values of coordinates left over from previous runs.

(18) The distance table and angle table each have storage locations numbered 1 to 50.

(19) If an instruction requires a distance as part of its data, the distance can be drawn from the distance table if it has been previously saved and its location in the table is known. This is done by placing DXX in place of the distance in the instruction, where XX represents the location (between 1 and 50) of the stored distance in the distance table. Any number of such saved distances can be used in a single instruction as needed.

(20) If an instruction requires an angle as a part of its data, the angle can be drawn from the angle table if it has been previously saved and its location in the table is known. This is done by placing AXX in place of the angle in the instruction, where XX represents the location (between 1 and 50) of the saved angle in the angle table. Only one such stored angle can be used in a single instruction.

(21) In all cases distances are measured in feet and may contain a whole number and a fractional part separated by a decimal point. Angles and azimuths are in degrees, minutes, and seconds. Bearings are in quadrant, degrees, minutes, and seconds. The seconds part of all angular measures may contain a whole number and fractional portion separated by a decimal point. All other numbers must contain no decimal points.

(22) Quadrants in bearings are identified as follows:

1 = northeast quadrant
2 = southeast quadrant
3 = southwest quadrant
4 = northwest quadrant

13.9 Summary

COGO is a language for communication with a digital computer, whose specific goal is to make computers easier to use by civil engineers. It does this by providing a set of instructions to carry out the calculations using identifiers that are drawn from the typical civil engineering vocabulary.

Subject only to minor restrictions, COGO permits the engineer to work quite freely and to concentrate his attention on the problem being solved rather than on the computer programming details.

COGO is easy to learn and use. Because this is so, the user finds it unnecessary to invest much time and effort towards making the programs elegant and sophisticated. It is quite practical to write programs using COGO that will be run one time only and then discarded.

The results of running a COGO program are printed out intermixed with the instructions. The results immediately follow the instruction that produced them. This makes it easy to relate the instructions and results in a very natural way.

Table 13.1

COGO Instructions

Name *Long and Short Form*	*Description*

ADJUST/ANG/LS
AAN
	
	Form
	
	ADJUST/ANG/LS P1 P5
	                 P1 P2 D1 A1
	                 P3 D2 A2
	                 P4 D3 A3
	                 P5 D4 A4
	
	Explanation
	
	Adjust the angle traverse starting at point P1 and ending at point P5. For the first course, P1 is the point back, P2 is the point ahead, D1 is the distance along the traverse, and A1 is the azimuth (degrees, minutes, seconds). For all other courses, the point ahead, the distance, and the clockwise angle (degrees, minutes, seconds) measured at the point back are given. Traverses of up to 200 courses are allowed. Corrections to angles or azimuths must be previously made.
	
	Output
	
	The error in North (or Y) direction, error in East (or X) direction, total error, azimuth of closure line, adjusted coordinates, adjusted distances, and adjusted azimuths.

ADJUST/AZ/LS
 AAZ

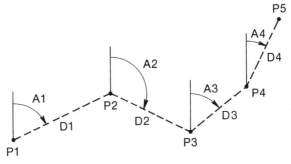

Form

ADJUST/AZ/LS   P1   P5
                  P1   P2   D1   A1
                  P2   P3   D2   A2
                  P3   P4   D3   A3
                  P4   P5   D4   A4

Explanation

Adjust the azimuth traverse starting at point P1 and ending at point P5. For each course, the point back, the point ahead, the distance, and the azimuth (degrees, minutes, seconds) must be given in that order.

Output

Same as for ADJUST/ANG/LS.

Table 13.1 *(Continued)*

Name *Long and Short Form*	*Description*
ALIGNMENT ALN	 *Form* ALIGNMENT SN P1 P2 P3 P4 P5 P6 D1 D2 SB D3 *Explanation* SN Identification number of the alignment section P1 Any known point on the back tangent (may be the same as P6 of the preceding curve) P2 Point of intersection of the tangents P3 Any known point on the ahead tangent P4 Point of tangency on the back tangent P5 Point at center of the curve P6 Point of tangency on the ahead tangent D1 Radius of the curve D2 The tangent distance from P4 to P2 or from P2 to P6 SB Station at the known point (P1) on the back tangent D3 Distance from the known point (P1) on the back tangent to the point of tangency (P4) on the back tangent *Note:* D1, D2, and/or D3 may be unknown. If so, their values must be entered as 0 (zero). If all are

entered as zero, and P4 of the new curve corresponds to P6 of the preceding curve, the new curve will be compounded or reversed with the preceding curve, whichever is appropriate. If D1 and D2 are entered as zero, and D3 is finite, the new curve will be located so that the point of tangency (P4) is this finite distance from the known point on the back tangent.

If SB is entered as −1, P1 for the new curve is taken to be the P6 of the preceding curve and SB for the new curve is taken to be the station of P6 of the preceding curve.

All points of intersection (P2) for all curves should be located before using the alignment instruction.

Output

The section number (SN), radius (D1), sign = +1 if curve is toward the right, −1 if toward the left, tangent distance (D2), deflection angle (A1) (degrees, minutes, seconds), length of curve (D4), tangent section length (D3), station at P4, station at P6, and the coordinates of P4, P6, and P5.

ANGLE
ANG

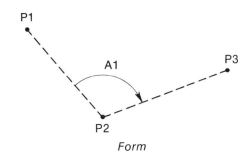

Form

ANGLE   P1   P2   P3

Explanation

Compute the clockwise angle A1 at P2 from P1 to P3.

Output

The clockwise angle A1 at P2 from P1 to P3.

Table 13.1 *(Continued)*

Name *Long and Short Form*	*Description*
ANGLE/SAVE ASV	*Form* ANGLE/SAVE P1 P2 P3 AN *Explanation* Compute the clockwise angle at P2 as in the ANGLE instruction, but in addition, save the angle in position AN of the angle table.
ARC/ARC/INTERSECT AAI	 *Form* ARC/ARC/INTERSECT P4 P1 D1 P2 D2 P3 *Explanation* Find the coordinates of the point P4 at the intersection of the circle having center at P1 and radius D1 with the circle having center at P2 and radius D2. If two points of intersection occur, P4 is the one closest to P3. P3 may be on or off the circles. If no point of intersection exists, a message to that effect is printed out. *Output* The coordinates of P4.

ARC/LINE/AZIMUTH ALA	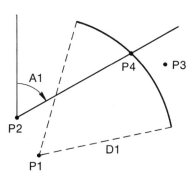
	Form
	ARC/LINE/AZIMUTH P4 P1 D1 P2 A1 P3
	Explanation
	Find the coordinates of the point P4 at the intersection of the circle having center at P1 and radius D1 with the line defined by point P2 and azimuth A1. If two points of intersection occur, P4 is the one closest to P3. P3 may be on or off the circle. If no point of intersection occurs, a message to that effect is printed out.
	Output
	The coordinates of P4.

Table 13.1 *(Continued)*

Name *Long and Short Form*	*Description*
ARC/LINE/POINTS ALP	 *Form* ARC/LINE/POINTS P4 P1 D1 P2 P3 P5 *Explanation* Find the coordinates of the point P4 at the intersection of the circle having center at P1 and radius D1 with the line defined by points P2 and P3. If two points of intersection occur, P4 is the one closest to P5. P5 may be on or off the circle. If no point of intersection occurs, a message to that effect is printed out. *Output* The coordinates of P4.

AREA
 AR
AREA/AZIMUTHS
 ARA
AREA/BEARINGS
 ARB

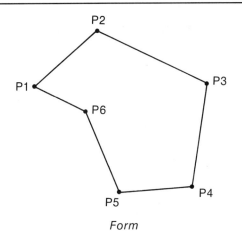

Form

AREA   P1 P2 P3 P4 P5 P6 P1
or AREA/AZIMUTHS   P1 P2 P3 P4 P5 P6 P1
or AREA/BEARINGS   P1 P2 P3 P4 P5 P6 P1

Explanation

The area enclosed by the polygon whose corner points are listed is computed. The first and last points in the list must be the same point to indicate the closed nature of the polygon.

AREA results in the enclosed area being computed in both square feet and in acres, as does AREA/AZIMUTHS and AREA/BEARINGS. Also, however, AREA/AZIMUTHS causes the azimuth of each side to be computed and AREA/BEARINGS causes the bearing of each side to be computed. Both instructions cause the length of each side of the closed polygon to be calculated.

Output

AREA   Enclosed area in square feet and in acres.
AREA/AZIMUTHS   Enclosed area in square feet and in acres, and a table of azimuths and distances of each side of the polygon.
AREA/BEARINGS   Enclosed area in square feet and in acres, and a table of bearings and distances of each side of the polygon.

Table 13.1 *(Continued)*

Name *Long and Short Form*	*Description*
AZ/INTERSECT AIN	 *Form* AZ/INTERSECT P3 P1 A1 P2 A2 *Explanation* Find the coordinates of the point P3 at the intersection of the line passing through point P1 with azimuth A1 and the line passing through point P2 with azimuth A2. Azimuths are in degrees, minutes, and seconds. *Output* The coordinates of P3.

BR/INTERSECT BIN	
	Form
	BR/INTERSECT P3 P1 B1 P2 B2
	Explanation
	Find the coordinates of the point P3 at the intersection of the line passing through point P1 with bearing B1 and the line passing through point P2 with bearing B2. Bearings are in quadrant, degrees, minutes, seconds.
	Output
	The coordinates of P3.
CLEAR CLR	*Form*
	CLEAR N1 N2
	Explanation
	The coordinate table is cleared of previously stored or saved values between locations N1–N2, inclusive. N1 and N2 must be numbers between 1 and 999, inclusive, and N1 must be less than N2.
	Output
	None.

Table 13.1 *(Continued)*

Name *Long and Short Form*	*Description*
COORD/EL/OFFSET CEO	 *Form* COORD/EL/OFFSET P1 S D1 SN *Explanation* Compute the coordinates and elevation of a point P1 with radial offset D1 from station S on the horizontal alignment section SN. D1 is negative if offset is to left, positive if to the right. The vertical curve used for this computation is the one defined by the last set of ORIGIN, PI, and TERMINUS instructions which is still in the computer. *Output* The coordinates and elevation of P1.

COORD/EL/POA CEP	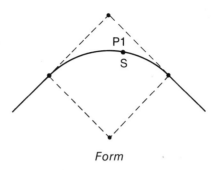
	Form
	COORD/EL/POA P1 S SN
	Explanation
	Compute the coordinates and elevation of the point P1 at station S on the horizontal alignment section SN. The vertical curve used for this computation is the one defined by the last set of ORIGIN, PI, and TERMINUS instructions which is still stored in the computer.
	Output
	The coordinates and elevation of P1.

Table 13.1 *(Continued)*

Name *Long and Short Form*	*Description*
COORDINATE/OFFSET COF	 *Form* COORDINATE/OFFSET P1 S D1 SN *Explanation* Compute the coordinates of P1 at station S and an offset radial distance D1 from the alignment section SN. D1 is entered as plus if to the right, and minus if to the left, of the alignment section. *Output* The coordinates of P1.

COORDINATE/POA CPA	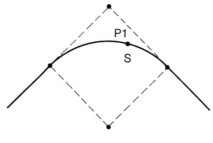 *Form* COORDINATE/POA P1 S SN *Explanation* Compute the coordinates of point P1 at station S on the alignment section SN. *Output* The coordinates of P1.

Table 13.1 *(Continued)*

Name *Long and Short Form*	*Description*
CROSS TANGENT CT	 *Form* CROSS TANGENT P1 P2 D1 P3 P4 D2 SIGN *Explanation* Find the coordinates of points P1 and P3 which are the two points of tangency of the cross tangent to the two circles having centers at points P2 and P4 and radii D1 and D2, respectively. There are two possible solutions. The desired solution is indicated by SIGN, which is either + or −. If the angle made by the extension of the line connecting the centers of the circles to the desired cross tangent is clockwise, SIGN is entered as +1. If the angle is counterclockwise, SIGN is entered as −1. P1, P2, D1 are associated with the larger of the two circles. *Output* The coordinates of P1 and P3, and the distance and azimuth of the cross tangent between P1 and P3.

CURVE/SPIRAL CS	
	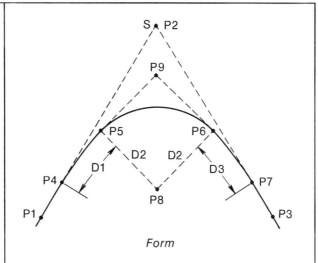

Form

CURVE/SPIRAL   SN P1 P2 P3 D1 D2 D3 S P4 P5
P6 P7 P8 P9

Explanation

A spiral curve having curve number SN is fitted to two tangents. P1 is any point on the back tangent, and P3 is any point on the ahead tangent. P2 is the point of intersection of the tangents. The station at P2 is S. A spiral of length D1 is inserted before the circular section and one of length D3 is inserted after the circular section. The radius of the circular section is D2. P4 is the point of tangency on the back tangent and P7 is the point of tangency on the ahead tangent. P5 and P6 are the ends of the circular section. P9 is the point of intersection of the tangents to the circular section. Any one of D1, D2, or D3 may be zero.

Output

The curve number, point of intersection number, angle at point of intersection, coordinates and station of P4, P5, P6, and P7, and the coordinates of P8 and P9. For both spirals: Spiral length, total spiral angle, short tangent distance, long tangent distance, length of spiral projection on tangent, distance from end of spiral to tangent, P, K, and total tangent distance.

Table 13.1 *(Continued)*

Name *Long and Short Form*	*Description*
DEFINE/CURVE DCV	 *Form* DEFINE/CURVE SN P1 S1 P2 P3 S3 P4 SIGN *Explanation* The DEFINE/CURVE instruction is used to store data concerning previously calculated horizontal alignment sections. Such stored descriptions can then be used with COORD/OFFSET, COORD/POA, STATION/POA, OFFSET/ALIGN, DIVIDE/STATION/LINE, COORD/EL/POA, STATION/EL/POA, COORD/EL/OFFSET, and OFFSET/EL/ALIGN instructions. SN is the alignment section number and P1 is the known point of tangency on the back tangent. P3 is the known point of tangency on the ahead tangent. P2 is the known point of intersection of the tangents. P4 is the known center of the alignment section. S1 is the station at P1. S3 is the station at P3. The sign is + if the curve is to the right of the back tangent, and − if the curve is to the left of the back tangent. *Output* None.

DISTANCE DST	P1 •⟍ ⟍ ⟍ ⟍• P2 *Form* DISTANCE P1 P2 *Explanation* The distance between points P1 and P2 is computed. *Output* The distance from P1 to P2 is printed out.
DISTANCE/SAVE DSV	*Form* DISTANCE/SAVE P1 P2 DN *Explanation* This instruction computes the distance between points P1 and P2, and saves this distance in location DN of the distance table. *Output* None.

Table 13.1 *(Continued)*

Name *Long and Short Form*	*Description*
DIVIDE/LINE DLN	 *Form* DIVIDE/LINE P1 P2 N *Explanation* The line between points P1 and P2 is divided into N equal parts. Numbers are assigned to these intermediate points as P1 + 1, P1 + 2, . . . , P1 + N − 1. *Output* The distance between the intermediate points and the coordinates of each point.

DIVIDE/STATION/LINE DSL	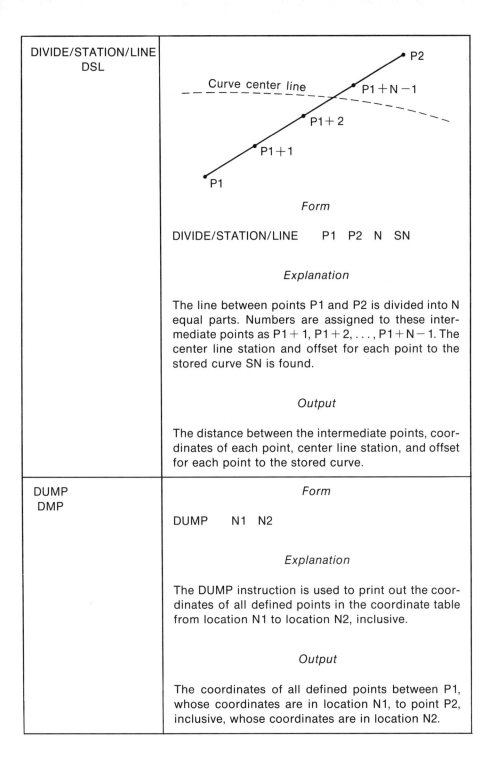 *Form* DIVIDE/STATION/LINE P1 P2 N SN *Explanation* The line between points P1 and P2 is divided into N equal parts. Numbers are assigned to these intermediate points as $P1 + 1, P1 + 2, \ldots, P1 + N - 1$. The center line station and offset for each point to the stored curve SN is found. *Output* The distance between the intermediate points, coordinates of each point, center line station, and offset for each point to the stored curve.
DUMP DMP	*Form* DUMP N1 N2 *Explanation* The DUMP instruction is used to print out the coordinates of all defined points in the coordinate table from location N1 to location N2, inclusive. *Output* The coordinates of all defined points between P1, whose coordinates are in location N1, to point P2, inclusive, whose coordinates are in location N2.

Table 13.1 *(Continued)*

Name *Long and Short Form*	*Description*
EVEN/STATIONS ES	 *Form* EVEN/STATIONS S1 D1 S2 *Explanation* A series of equally spaced points are located on the vertical curve presently stored in the computer, starting at station S1 and continuing until S2. The spacing between points is D1. S1 and S2 can be any stations on the vertical curve. *Output* For each station: The station, highway elevation, and grade in percent.

EXTERNAL/TANGENT ET	
	Form
	EXTERNAL/TANGENT P1 P2 D1 P3 P4 D2 SIGN
	Explanation
	Find the coordinates of points P1 and P3 which are the two points of tangency of the external tangent to the two circles having centers at P2 and P4 and radii D1 and D2, respectively. There are two possible solutions. The desired solution is indicated by SIGN, which is either + or −. If the angle made by the extension of the line connecting the centers of the circles to the desired external tangent is clockwise, SIGN is entered as +1. If the angle is counterclockwise, SIGN is entered as −1. P1, P2, and D1 are associated with the larger of the two circles.
	Output
	The coordinates of P1 and P3, and the distance and azimuth of the tangent from P1 to P3.
FINISH	*Form*
	FINISH
	Explanation
	This instruction terminates a COGO program. It is the last instruction in the program.
	Output
	None.

Table 13.1 *(Continued)*

Name *Long and Short Form*	*Description*
GIRDER/LENGTHS GRD	 *Form* GIRDER/LENGTHS P1 P2 N P3 P4 *Explanation* The line defined by points P1 and P2 has been divided into N parts by a previous DIVIDE/LINE instruction. The line defined by points P3 and P4 has been similarly divided. GIRDER/LENGTHS computes the distances between corresponding pairs of points. *Output* The distances between corresponding pairs of points.

INVERSE/AZIMUTH IAZ	 *Form* INVERSE/AZIMUTH P1 P2 *Explanation* This instruction computes the azimuth and distance of the line from P1 to P2. *Output* The azimuth and distance from P1 to P2.
INVERSE/BEARING IBR	*Form* INVERSE/BEARING P1 P2 *Explanation* The bearing and distance of the line from P1 to P2 are computed. *Output* The bearing and distance from P1 to P2.
LINES LN	*Form* LINES N *Explanation* This instruction results in N lines of output per page. If this instruction is not included in a COGO program, 55 lines per page will be printed out.

Table 13.1 *(Continued)*

Name *Long and Short Form*	*Description*
LOCATE/ANGLE LAN	 *Form* LOCATE/ANGLE P1 P2 P3 D1 A1 *Explanation* Compute the coordinates of point P3 which is located by backsighting on P1 and turning the angle A1 at P2 (+A1 for clockwise angle, −A1 for counterclockwise angle) and at a distance D1 from P2. Angle is in degrees, minutes, seconds. *Output* The coordinates of P3.

LOCATE/AZIMUTH LAZ	 *Form* LOCATE/AZIMUTH P1 P2 D1 A1 *Explanation* This instruction computes the coordinates of point P2 located at distance D1 and azimuth A1 from P1. Azimuth is in degrees, minutes, seconds. *Output* The coordinates of P2.
LOCATE/BEARING LBR	 *Form* LOCATE/BEARING P1 P2 D1 B1 *Explanation* The coordinates of point P2 located at distance D1 and bearing B1 from P1 are computed. Bearing is in quadrant, degrees, minutes, seconds. *Output* The coordinates of P2.

Table 13.1 *(Continued)*

Name *Long and Short Form*	*Description*
LOCATE/DEFLECTION LDF	 *Form* LOCATE/DEFLECTION P1 P2 P3 D1 A1 *Explanation* Compute the coordinates of point P3 which is located by backsighting on P1 and turning angle A1 at P2 to locate P3 at distance D1 from P2. A1 is in degrees, minutes, seconds. For clockwise angles, A1 is +; for counterclockwise angles, A1 is −. *Output* The coordinates of P3.

LOCATE/LINE
LLN

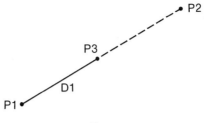

Form

LOCATE/LINE   P1   P2   P3   D1

Explanation

Compute the coordinates of P3 which is located by going D1 distance from P1 in the direction of P2. P3 may be beyond or short of P2. If D1 is negative, move away from P2 to locate P3.

Output

The coordinates of P3.

Table 13.1 *(Continued)*

Name *Long and Short Form*	*Description*
OFFSET/ALIGN OAL	 *Form* OFFSET/ALIGN P1 P2 SN *Explanation* This instruction computes the station and radial offset of point P1 from known point P2, where P1 is on the alignment section SN. *Output* The points P1, P2, station at P1, and offset from P1 to P2.

OFFSET/ELEV
OF

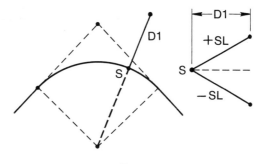

Form

OFFSET/ELEV   S   D1   SL

Explanation

This instruction locates a point offset distance D1 from station S and a cross slope SL from the vertical curve currently stored in the computer. SL is + if the slope is up from S, and SL is − if the slope is down from S.

Output

The station center line elevation, offset distance, cross slope, and offset elevation.

Table 13.1 *(Continued)*

Name *Long and Short Form*	*Description*
OFFSET/EL/ALIGN OEA	 *Form* OFFSET/EL/ALIGN P1 P2 SN *Explanation* Find the coordinates and elevation of the intersection of the horizontal alignment section SN with the radial offset through point P2. *Output* The coordinates and elevation of point P1.
ORIGIN ORG	See VERTICAL CURVE DEFINITION.

PARALLEL/LINE PLN	 *Form* PARALLEL/LINE P1 P2 D1 P3 P4 *Explanation* Find the coordinates of points P3 and P4 on a line parallel to another line through known points P1 and P2. The offset distance between the lines is D1. The point P3 is opposite P1, and P4 is opposite P2. Enter +D1 if the new line is to be to the right of the old line, and enter −D1 if the new line is to be to the left. *Output* The coordinates of P3 and P4.
PI	See VERTICAL CURVE DEFINITION.

Table 13.1 *(Continued)*

Name Long and Short Form	Description
POINTS/INTERSECT PIN	*Form* POINTS/INTERSECT P1 P2 P3 P4 P5 *Explanation* Find the coordinates of the point P1 at the intersection of the line passing through points P2 and P3, and the line passing through points P4 and P5. *Output* The coordinates of P1.
REDEFINE RDF	*Form* REDEFINE P1 P2 *Explanation* The point previously known as number P1 is assigned the new number P2. *Output* None.

RT/TRI/HYP RTH	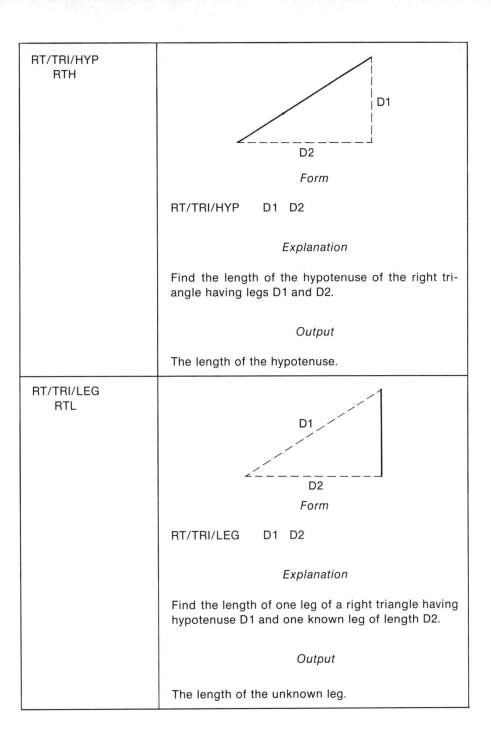 *Form* RT/TRI/HYP D1 D2 *Explanation* Find the length of the hypotenuse of the right triangle having legs D1 and D2. *Output* The length of the hypotenuse.
RT/TRI/LEG RTL	*Form* RT/TRI/LEG D1 D2 *Explanation* Find the length of one leg of a right triangle having hypotenuse D1 and one known leg of length D2. *Output* The length of the unknown leg.

Table 13.1 *(Continued)*

Name *Long and Short Form*	*Description*

SEGMENT
    S
SEGMENT/MINUS
    SMI
SEGMENT/PLUS
    SPL
	
	Form
	
	SEGMENT P1 P2 D1
	SEGMENT/MINUS P1 P2 D1
	SEGMENT/PLUS P1 P2 D1
	
	Explanation
	
	The area of the segment formed by the chord between points P1 and P2 having radius D1 is found. If SEGMENT/PLUS or SEGMENT/MINUS is used, the area of the segment is added to, or subtracted from, the cumulative area resulting from the last AREA, AREA/AZIMUTH, or AREA/BEARING instruction and any other intervening SEGMENT/PLUS or SEGMENT/MINUS instructions. The area of any number of segments may be added to, or subtracted from, the area of any polygon.
	
	Output
	
	After each SEGMENT, SEGMENT/PLUS, or SEGMENT/MINUS instruction, the chord length, arc length, and segment area are printed out. Also, after each SEGMENT/PLUS or SEGMENT/MINUS instruction, the net cumulative area is also printed out in square feet and acres.

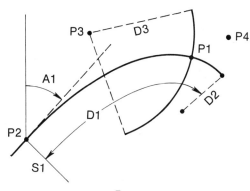

Form

SPIRAL/CURVE/INTER   P1 P2 A1 S1 D1 D2 P3 D3 P4

Explanation

Find the coordinates and station of point P1 at the intersection of a circular curve and a spiral curve. The point of tangency of the spiral with a line of azimuth A1 is P2. The station at P2 is S1. The length of the spiral from P2 is D1. The radius of the spiral at distance D1 from P2 is D2. D3 is the radius of the circular curve having a center at P3. The solution found is that closest to a known point P4.

Also, determine the spiral length from P2 to P1 and the radius of the curve at P1.

D2 is entered as +D2 if the spiral deflects toward the right, and −D2 if it deflects toward the left.

Output

The coordinates and station of P1, the spiral length from P2 to P1, and the spiral radius at P1.

Table 13.1 *(Continued)*

Name *Long and Short Form*	*Description*

SPIRAL/LINE/INTER
SLI
	
	Form
	
	SPIRAL/LINE/INTER P1 P2 A1 S1 D1 D2 P2 A2 P3
	
	Explanation
	
	Find the coordinates and station of point P1. This point is located at the intersection of the line passing through point P3 having azimuth A2 and a spiral curve. The point of tangency on the spiral is P2. The azimuth of the tangent at P2 is A1. The station at P2 is S1. The length of the spiral from P2 is D1. The radius of the spiral at distance D1 from P2 is D2.
	    Also, determine the spiral length from P2 to P1 and the radius of the curve at P1.
	    D2 is entered as +D2 if the spiral deflects toward the right, and as −D2 if it deflects toward the left.
	
	Output
	
	The coordinates and station of P1, the spiral length from P2 to P1, and the spiral radius at P1.

| SPIRAL/SPIRAL/INTER SSI | 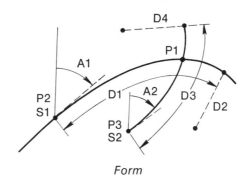 |

Form

SPIRAL/SPIRAL/INTER P1 P2 A1 S1 D1 D2 P3 A2 S2
D3 D4

Explanation

Find the coordinates and station of point P1. This point is located at the intersection of two spirals. On one spiral, P2 is the point of tangency, S1 is the station, and the tangent has an azimuth A1. D1 is the length of the spiral from P2 to a point where the spiral radius is D2. On the other spiral, P3 is the point of tangency, S2 is the station, and the tangent has an azimuth A2. D3 is the length of the spiral from P3 to a point where the spiral radius is D4.

Output

The coordinates and station at P1 relative to the first spiral, the distance from P2 to P1, the station at P1 relative to second spiral, and the distance from P3 to P1.

Table 13.1 *(Continued)*

Name *Long and Short Form*	*Description*
START	*Form* START ANY DESIRED HEADING *Explanation* The printout skips to the top of the next page. ANY DESIRED HEADING can be placed on the START instruction card between columns 13 and 72, inclusive, and this information will be printed at the top of all pages of printout until the next START instruction is encountered.
STATION/EL/POA SEP	 *Form* STATION/EL/POA P1 SN *Explanation* Find the station and elevation of known point P1 on the known alignment section SN and the vertical curve presently stored in the computer and defined by the last set of ORIGIN, PI, and TERMINUS instructions. *Output* The elevation, curve number, point number, and station of the known point P1.

STATION/POA SPA	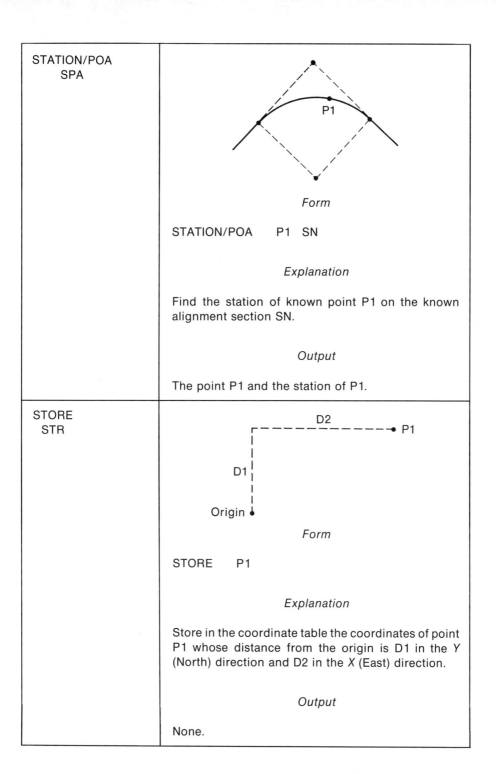 *Form* STATION/POA P1 SN *Explanation* Find the station of known point P1 on the known alignment section SN. *Output* The point P1 and the station of P1.
STORE STR	*Form* STORE P1 *Explanation* Store in the coordinate table the coordinates of point P1 whose distance from the origin is D1 in the *Y* (North) direction and D2 in the *X* (East) direction. *Output* None.

Table 13.1 *(Continued)*

Name *Long and Short Form*	*Description*
STORE/SUPER SUP	*Form* STORE/SUPER SA SB N *Explanation* The cross-section characteristics at stations SA and SB are stored. N is the number of segments describing the profile characteristics at each of the two stations. The maximum number of segments at any station is 10. There must be N VERTICAL/SEGMENT cards included, one for each segment, and these N cards must be placed immediately following the STORE/SUPER instruction card to which they refer. See VERTICAL/SEGMENT instruction for further details. *Output* None except as used with VERTICAL/SEGMENT, SUPER/SPECIAL, and SUPER/EVEN instructions.

SUBGRADE SUB	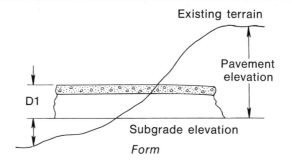
	SUBGRADE D1
	Explanation
	The pavement surface elevation minus the subgrade elevation is stored as D1. This value is then used in executing subsequent SURVEY/STATION instructions when computing D2 which is the subgrade elevation minus the terrain elevation.
	Output
	None except as used with SURVEY/STATION instructions.

Table 13.1 *(Continued)*

Name *Long and Short Form*	*Description*
SUPER/EVEN SE	 *Form* SUPER/EVEN S1 D1 S2 *Explanation* Compute the offset elevation at each of the offset profiles beginning at station S1 and advancing at equal intervals of length D1 until station S2 is reached. The profiles at each interval are defined by a preceding STORE/SUPER and VERTICAL/SEGMENT set of instructions. *Output* For each station the following is printed out: Line 1 contains station and center line elevation, followed by one line per segment, each giving segment number, segment width, cross slope, and elevation.

SUPER/SPECIAL SSP	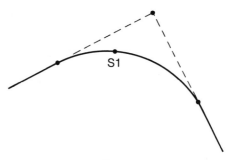
	Form
	SUPER/SPECIAL S1
	Explanation
	The offset elevation is computed at station S1 for each of the offset profiles as defined by the preceding STORE/SUPER and VERTICAL/SEGMENT set of instructions.
	Output
	Line 1 contains station and center line elevation, followed by one line per segment, each giving segment number, segment width, cross slope, and elevation.

Table 13.1 *(Continued)*

Name *Long and Short Form*	*Description*
SURVEY/STATION SS	 *Form* SURVEY/STATION S1 E1 *Explanation* Determine highway profile elevation and terrain elevation, the subgrade elevation minus the terrain elevation, and the grade at station S1 and elevation E1 on the vertical curve presently stored in the computer as defined by the most recent ORIGIN, PI, and TERMINUS instructions. Use is made of the preceding SUBGRADE instruction in executing this instruction. *Output* The station, highway profile elevation, terrain elevation, subgrade elevation minus terrain elevation, and grade.
TERMINUS TRM	See VERTICAL CURVE DEFINITION.

VERTICAL CURVE DEFINITION

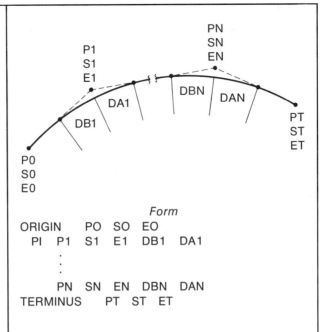

Form

```
ORIGIN    PO  SO  EO
    PI  P1  S1  E1  DB1  DA1
        ⋮

        PN  SN  EN  DBN  DAN
TERMINUS    PT  ST  ET
```

Explanation

Three instructions are required to define a vertical curve. These are ORIGIN, PI, and TERMINUS. The origin is located and defined as point PO at station SO and having elevation EO. The terminus is defined by point PT at station ST having elevation ET. Between the origin and terminus of the vertical curve may be up to 20 sections, each defined by a point of intersection of tangents to the curve. Each section has a point of intersection PN, having station SN, elevation EN, curve length back to point of tangency DBN, and curve length ahead to point of tangency DAN.

Output

For each PI card the computer will print out point of intersection number, station number at beginning of the section with corresponding elevation and grade ahead, station number at the point of intersection with corresponding elevation, elevation on the curve and grade on the curve, and station number at the end of the section with the elevation and grade ahead.

Table 13.1 *(Continued)*

Name *Long and Short Form*	*Description*
VERTICAL/SEGMENT SEG	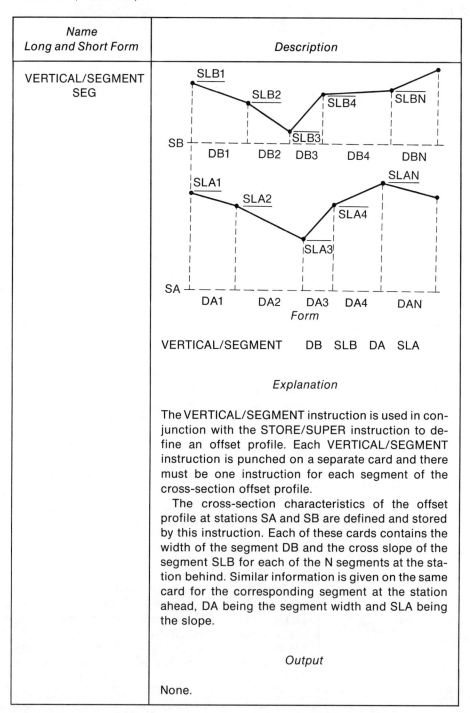 *Form* VERTICAL/SEGMENT DB SLB DA SLA *Explanation* The VERTICAL/SEGMENT instruction is used in conjunction with the STORE/SUPER instruction to define an offset profile. Each VERTICAL/SEGMENT instruction is punched on a separate card and there must be one instruction for each segment of the cross-section offset profile. The cross-section characteristics of the offset profile at stations SA and SB are defined and stored by this instruction. Each of these cards contains the width of the segment DB and the cross slope of the segment SLB for each of the N segments at the station behind. Similar information is given on the same card for the corresponding segment at the station ahead, DA being the segment width and SLA being the slope. *Output* None.

Table 13.2

Functional Groupings of Instructions

Function	Instructions	Page
Alignment Routines	ALIGNMENT	364
	DEFINE/CURVE	378
Alignment Offset Routines	COORD/OFFSET	374
	COORD/POA	375
	DIVIDE/STATION/LINE	381
	OFFSET/ALIGN	390
	STATION/POA	401
Angle and Distance Routines	ANGLE	365
	ANGLE/SAVE	366
	DISTANCE	379
	DISTANCE/SAVE	379
	INVERSE/AZIMUTH	385
	INVERSE/BEARING	385
	RT/TRI/HYP	395
	RT/TRI/LEG	395
Arc Intersection Routines	ARC/ARC/INTERSECT	366
	ARC/LINE/AZIMUTH	367
	ARC/LINE/POINTS	368
Area Routines	AREA	369
	AREA/AZIMUTHS	369
	AREA/BEARINGS	369
	SEGMENT	396
	SEGMENT/MINUS	396
	SEGMENT/PLUS	396
Bridge Routines	DIVIDE/LINE	380
	GIRDER/LENGTHS	384
Combined Horizontal and Vertical Routines	COORD/EL/OFFSET	372
	COORD/EL/POA	373
	OFFSET/EL/ALIGN	392
	STATION/EL/POA	400
Line Intersection Routines	AZ/INTERSECT	370
	BR/INTERSECT	371
	POINTS/INTERSECT	394

Table 13.2 *(Continued)*

Function	*Instructions*	*Page*
Locate Point Routines	LOCATE/ANGLE LOCATE/AZIMUTH LOCATE/BEARING LOCATE/DEFLECTION LOCATE/LINE PARALLEL/LINE	386 387 387 388 389 393
Offset Elevation Routines	OFFSET/ELEV	391
Offset Profile Definition Routines	STORE/SUPER VERTICAL/SEGMENT	402 408
Offset Profile Routines	SUPER/EVEN SUPER/SPECIAL	404 405
Service Routines	CLEAR DUMP FINISH LINES REDEFINE STORE	371 381 383 385 394 401
Spiral Routines	CURVE/SPIRAL SPIRAL/CURVE/INTER SPIRAL/LINE/INTER SPIRAL/SPIRAL/INTER	377 397 398 399
Tangent Routines	CROSS/TANGENT EXTERNAL/TANGENT	376 383
Traverse Adjustment Routines	ADJUST/ANG/LS ADJUST/AZ/LS	362 363
Vertical Curve Definition Routines	ORIGIN PI SUBGRADE TERMINUS	392 393 403 406
Vertical Curve Routines	EVEN/STATIONS SURVEY/STATION	382 406

1. The boundary of a parcel of land is made up of some straight-line sections and two circular sections as shown in Fig. 13.4. The coordinates of known points are also shown.

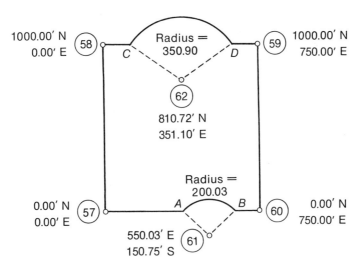

Figure 13.4

The coordinates of A, B, C, D are not known. Use COGO to find the coordinates of A, B, C, D; the distances 58–C, 59–D, 60–B and 57–A; the area enclosed.

2. The coordinates of the corners of a traverse are shown in Fig. 13.5.

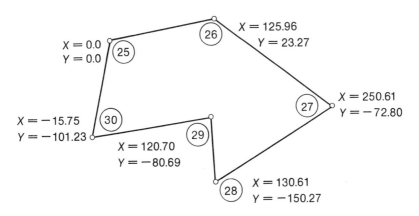

Figure 13.5

Use COGO to find the bearing of each boundary line, the length of each boundary line, the interior angle at each point, and the area enclosed by the traverse.

3. A highway is being built across an existing property as shown in Fig. 13.6. It is desired to find the area cut off by this highway (the shaded region in the figure). The distance along the curve from point 25 to point 26 is also needed. The coordinates of points 21, 22, and 27 are known, as are the azimuths of three of the existing boundaries (this information is given in the figure). The distance along the existing boundary from point 23 to 24 is 1525.27 ft. The radius of the curve is 1318.00 ft and its center is at point 27. Use COGO to solve this problem.

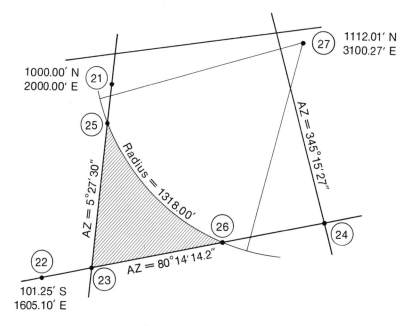

Figure 13.6

4. Three circular curves are to be fitted to the tangents shown in Fig. 13.7. Use COGO to accomplish this task. The known information is given in the figure.
5. Use COGO to find the coordinates of the point where the line drawn from point 102 to point 111 in Exercise 4 would intersect curve 51. Where would it intersect the line drawn between point 104 and point 105? Where would it intersect the line drawn between point 105 and point 106?
6. Use COGO to find the two points of intersection between the circle with center at coordinates 1052.27' N and 2573.68' E with radius 752.68, and the circle with center at coordinates 1560.75' N and 3520.00' E and with radius 1500.0. Find the area inside the first circle but outside the second circle.
7. Use COGO to find the points of intersection between the first circle of Exercise 6 and the line drawn through the point 1960.00' N, 1148.25' E with an

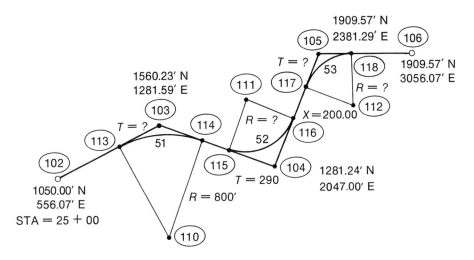

Figure 13.7

azimuth of 85°15'14". Where does the line intersect the second circle of Exercise 6?

8. Since the line of Exercise 7 does not pass through the center of either circle but does intersect both circles, it divides each circle into a smaller and a larger portion. Use COGO to find the area of the smaller portion of each circle cut off by the line.

9. Devise a COGO program for finding the area of the larger portion of each circle cut off by the line in Exercise 7.

10. Use COGO to adjust the closed traverse and find the area enclosed.

AB	N 26°10' W	285.1 ft
BC	S 75°25' W	610.4 ft
CD	S 15°30' E	720.5 ft
DE	N 1°40' E	203.0 ft
EA	N 53°06' E	647.03 ft

14

Structural Engineering
Systems Solver (STRESS)

14.1 Introduction

We have already mentioned that the use of digital computers for obtaining solutions to engineering problems is often obstructed by the difficulties of computer programming. Consider the case of the structural engineer. Professional programmers often do not understand the techniques or needs of these people, and the engineers often are unwilling to learn the details and procedures of digital computer programming. Another special computer language, STRESS, was developed to overcome these obstructions. STRESS is used primarily in the study of elastic, statically loaded, framed structures.

The acronym, STRESS, stands for Structural Engineering System Solver. STRESS is a digital computer program and programming language. It thus consists of two parts:

(1) A user-oriented language which simplifies the description of the system to be solved;

(2) A processor in the form of a program which accepts this user-generated description of the structural system as input, and performs the necessary processes to accomplish the desired analysis.

A similar point of view can be taken regarding STRESS, as a simulation language, as was taken in the preceding chapter regarding COGO. That is, the system being simulated consists not only of the structure itself, but also includes the engineer performing the analysis as well.

STRESS is a tool for the use of the structural engineer. From his point of view it is a digital computer programming language which he uses to describe the system he is studying. This language is easy for him to learn and use because it employs the words of his profession in a very natural way. In many ways, a STRESS program of instructions to a computer is similar to the instructions that a structural engineer might give to an engineering assistant. Using STRESS, the engineer specifies the nature and size of the structure being analyzed, the nature and location of loads, the procedure to be followed when performing the analysis, and the output results required.

As with COGO and ECAP, programs written in STRESS are simple enough that they can be used once and discarded. The procedures are also simple enough that previous programming experience is not needed for their effective use. This means that the small investment in programming effort used to write a STRESS program makes it quite practical to use the program once, obtain the desired results, and throw the program away. If the same system must be analyzed again at a later date, the program is simply rewritten.

Of course, programs can be saved if one wishes to do so. Furthermore, STRESS provides a means whereby portions of an existing program can be easily modified. This feature, in particular, makes STRESS a valuable tool for design. When STRESS is used in this manner, an engineer can program a proposed design, obtain the results of the analysis, modify the original proposal, and then try again. This can be repeated over and over, again and again, as often as necessary to perfect the design.

14.2   An Example of the Use of STRESS

Example 14.1   Suppose we wish to find the behavior of the structural system shown in Fig. 14.1. This is a plane truss structure with two concentrated loads at

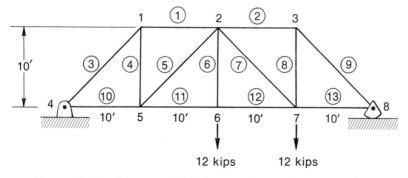

Figure 14.1   *A truss with joints and members identified.*

the joints 6 and 7 as shown. The problem is to determine the forces in members 7 and 12.

A STRESS program to accomplish this analysis is shown in Fig. 14.2. Each line of this program must be punched on a separate data processing card for reading by the computer. A detailed description of this program follows.

```
STRUCTURE EXAMPLE 14.1
NUMBER OF JOINTS 8
NUMBER OF SUPPORTS 2
NUMBER OF MEMBERS 13
NUMBER OF LOADINGS 1
TYPE PLANE TRUSS
METHOD STIFFNESS
TABULATE MEMBER FORCES
JOINT COORDINATES
1 X 120, Y 120, FREE
2 X 240, Y 120
3 X 360, Y 120
4 X 0, Y 0, SUPPORT
5 X 120, Y 0
6 X 240, Y 0
7 X 360, Y 0
8 X 480, Y 0, S
MEMBER INCIDENCES
1 1 2
2 2 3
3 4 1
4 5 1
5 5 2
6 6 2
7 7 2
8 7 3
9 8 3
10 4 5
11 5 6
12 6 7
13 7 8
MEMBER PROPERTIES, PRISMATIC
1 AX 20, IZ 200
2 AX 20, IZ 200
3 AX 20, IZ 200
4 AX 20, IZ 200
5 AX 20, IZ 200
```

Figure 14.2 A STRESS program to analyze the system in Fig. 14.1.

6 AX 20, IZ 200
7 AX 20, IZ 200
8 AX 20, IZ 200
9 AX 20, IZ 200
10 AX 20, IZ 200
11 AX 20, IZ 200
12 AX 20, IZ 200
13 AX 20, IZ 200
CONSTANTS E,30000, ALL
LOADING 1
JOINT LOADS
6 FORCE Y −12
7 FORCE Y −12
JOINT RELEASES
8 FORCE X
SOLVE THIS PART
LOADING 1
MEMBER FORCES

MEMBER	JOINT	AXIAL FORCE
1	1	8.9999945
1	2	−8.9999945
2	2	14.9999943
2	3	−14.9999943
3	4	12.7279165
3	1	−12.7279165
4	5	−8.9999981
4	1	8.9999981
5	5	12.7279200
5	2	−12.7279200
6	6	−12.0000005
6	2	12.0000005
7	7	4.2426373
7	2	−4.2426373
8	7	−14.9999966
8	3	14.9999966
9	8	21.2131940
9	3	−21.2131940
10	4	−8.9999896
10	5	8.9999896
11	5	−17.9999870
11	6	17.9999870
12	6	−17.9999900
12	7	17.9999900
13	7	−14.9999920
13	8	14.9999920

Figure 14.2 (Continued)

```
SELECTIVE OUTPUT
LOADING 1
PRINT FORCES 12, 7
LOADING 1
MEMBER FORCES
MEMBER   JOINT   AXIAL FORCE
   12       6     −17.9999900
   12       7      17.9999900
    7       7       4.2426373
    7       2      −4.2426373
FINISH
TIME USED: 1 SECOND
```

The first word of the program must be the word STRUCTURE. This is for control purposes. Likewise the last word must be FINISH to indicate the end of the program.

Following the word STRUCTURE are four statements which indicate the structure configuration: NUMBER OF JOINTS 8, NUMBER OF SUPPORTS 2, NUMBER OF MEMBERS 13, NUMBER OF LOADINGS 1. The next statement, TYPE PLANE TRUSS, indicates the type of structure being studied. Five different types of structures may be specified: TYPE PLANE TRUSS, TYPE PLANE FRAME, TYPE PLANE GRID, TYPE SPACE TRUSS, and TYPE SPACE FRAME.

The next card, METHOD STIFFNESS, indicates the method of analysis to be used in this program.

TABULATE MEMBER FORCES is a statement which calls for a printed tabulation of the force in each member. The results of executing this instruction appear toward the end of the program.

Following the JOINT COORDINATES statement are eight statements which locate each of the joints with respect to some coordinate system origin. In this case joint 4 is chosen as the origin and all joint coordinates are located with respect to this reference. Distances are in inches. For example, joint 1 is 120 in to the right and 120 in above the origin. The status of the joint is also indicated by the word FREE or the letter F meaning that it is not a support. If the word FREE or letter F is omitted, as in several following statements, the joint is assumed to be free. Hence, either the word FREE, or F, or nothing at all, indicates the status of an unsupported joint. Joints 4 and 8 are supports. This is indicated by the word SUPPORT for the status of joint 4, or the letter S for the status of joint 8. Either SUPPORT or S is an acceptable status indicator of a supported joint, but one or the other must appear.

MEMBER INCIDENCES followed by the next 13 statements define the structure of the truss. There is one statement for each member of the structure for a total of 13.

Each of these 13 statements contains three integer numbers. The first identifies the member itself by member number, and the other two identify the joints between which it connects by joint number. For example, member 9 connects from joint 8 to joint 3. Each member has its own local *x*, *y*, and *z* orthogonal coordinate system; *x* is taken along the length of the member, and *y* and *z* are at right angles to *x* and to each other. The member incidence information also specifies the positive *x* axis direction in this local coordinate system. In the case just mentioned for member 9, the local positive *x* direction would be from joint 8 to joint 3 because that is the order in which the joint numbers appear.

MEMBER PROPERTIES, PRISMATIC is a statement indicating that the structural properties of the members and the type of these properties follow. The next 13 statements show that all members have a cross-sectional area normal to its local *X* axis of 20 in² (AX 20) and a moment of inertia about the local member *Z* axis of 200 (IZ 200).

CONSTANTS E, 30000, ALL indicates that all members have a Young's Modulus of 30000 in kips.

LOADING 1 followed by JOINT LOADS specifies the loading for this analysis. Joint 6 is specified as having a load directed downward of 12 kips, and likewise joint 7 has a similar load.

JOINT RELEASES followed by 8 FORCE X indicates that joint 8 is free in the *X* direction.

SOLVE THIS PART terminates the description of the system and initiates the analysis.

The heading MEMBER FORCES and the 26 items of information that follow indicate the axial forces that exist on the members at each joint. Notice that this information is printed out immediately following the SOLVE THIS PART statement.

The statements SELECTIVE OUTPUT, LOADING 1, PRINT FORCES 12, 7 which immediately follow the SOLVE THIS PART statement in the program, are separated from that statement in the printed output by the member forces output. These three statements result in a listing of the forces exerted on members 12 and 7 by their end joints. Notice that the force on member 12 by joint 6 is in the negative *x* direction, and that at joint 7 the force is in the positive direction, giving rise to a tensile stress in member 12. The force on member 7 by joint 7 is in the positive direction, and that at joint 2 is in the negative direction causing a compressive stress in member 7.

The FINISH statement ends the program.

14.3   Units in STRESS

STRESS assumes a consistent set of units throughout for lengths, forces, moments, and so on. For example, all length or distance information may be in inches, areas in square inches, forces in kips (1000's of pounds), moments in inch-kips, distributed loads in kips/inch, etc.

14.4 STRESS Coordinate Systems

It is obvious that two coordinate systems must be used for structural problems. One coordinate system is associated with the structure itself. This is often referred to as the *global coordinate system.* It is an arbitrary system usually chosen so that its axes coincide with the principal dimensions of the structure being analyzed. This system is used to specify the locations of the joints in the system. Joint displacements and reactions are likewise computed in this global system.

The other coordinate system is in reality many coordinate systems because there is a separate system for each member in the structure. The data as it applies to each member is in terms of this second coordinate system. The *x* axis in this system ordinarily coincides with the member axis of each member. This is often referred to as a *local coordinate system.*

To differentiate between the global coordinate system and the local coordinate systems, upper-case letters *X, Y,* and *Z* are used for the three orthogonal directions in the global system, and lower-case letters *x, y,* and *z* are used similarly for the member system.

For plane structures, one of the member axes is assumed to be in the *XY* plane. Figure 14.3 shows the global and local coordinate systems for a structural member.

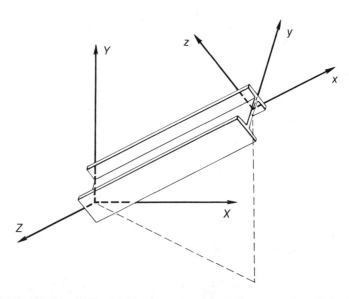

Figure 14.3 *Global and local coordinate systems in STRESS.*

14.5 Order of STRESS Statements

When writing a STRESS program, the programmer is permitted to place the statements in any order except for the following restrictions:

(1) The first statement must begin with the word STRUCTURE.

(2) The NUMBER OF JOINTS, NUMBER OF MEMBERS, and NUMBER OF LOADINGS must precede any joint data, member data, or loading data, respectively.

(3) The TYPE of structure must precede the input of member properties if member STIFFNESS or FLEXIBILITY matrices are included as member properties.

(4) TABULATE statements placed between the NUMBER OF LOADINGS statement and any loading headers apply to all loadings.

(5) Any TABULATE statement placed between a LOADING statement and the next loading header applies only to that loading situation.

(6) The last statement must be FINISH.

In accordance with the above restrictions, the following order of required statements will be acceptable:

```
STRUCTURE ___
NUMBER OF JOINTS ___
NUMBER OF SUPPORTS ___
NUMBER OF MEMBERS ___
NUMBER OF LOADINGS ___
TYPE ___
METHOD ___
JOINT COORDINATES
— — — ⎫
— — — ⎪
— — — ⎬ one card per joint
— — — ⎭

MEMBER INCIDENCES
— — — ⎫
— — — ⎪
— — — ⎬ one card per member
— — — ⎭

MEMBER PROPERTIES
— — — ⎫
— — — ⎬ one card per member
— — — ⎭

(LOADING DATA)
— — —
— — —
— — —

SOLVE
TABULATE or SELECTIVE OUTPUT and PRINT
FINISH
```

14.6 STRESS Statements

The basic order in which the statements should appear in a STRESS program was discussed in the preceding section. The STRESS statements, with explanations, are presented in this section in alphabetical order for easy reference.

ADDITIONS: This is a modification descriptor. It is used to indicate that a modification consisting of an addition is to be performed on the data by the statements immediately following the ADDITIONS statement.

ALL: This statement is used in conjunction with the TABULATE statement and the CONSTANTS statement as explained under those headings.

BETA: This specifies an angle of rotation in decimal degrees of a member about its x axis. Beta is zero when the y axis of the member lies in the plane formed by the local x axis and the global Y axis. BETA is measured in the counterclockwise direction. See Fig. 14.4.

CHANGES: This is a modification descriptor. It is used to indicate that a modification is to be performed by changing previously given data to some new data. The new data must be presented in the same form as was used to present the original data.

COMBINE: This statement is used following a LOADING COMBINATION header to indicate which independent loadings are to be combined. The form is

> COMBINE   N1   M1   N2   M2, . . .

where N1 and N2, . . . , are the sequential loading condition integer numbers and M1 and M2, . . . , are the decimal number coefficients to be used in combining the contributions of the respective loadings to form the total combined load.

CONCENTRATED: Used in conjunction with a MEMBER LOADS statement, it indicates the type of load on the member, its intensity and its location. This is described under MEMBER LOADS.

CONSTANTS: This statement is used to name and assign numerical values to Young's Modulus, E, and shear modulus, G. Three forms of this statement are allowed:

> CONSTANTS E, C1, N1, N2, . . . , C2, N3
> CONSTANTS E, C1, ALL
> CONSTANTS E, C1, ALL BUT C2, N1, N2, . . .

In the CONSTANTS statements, E indicates that values of Young's Modulus are to be given. In each case, a G could be given in place of E to indicate that values of shear modulus are being specified. C1, C2, . . . , indicate the numerical values of the modulus and N1, N2, . . . , indicate the identifying numbers of the members to which the given value of modulus applies. For example the statement

> CONSTANTS E, 30000, 1, 2, 3, 4, 5, 10000, 6, 7, 8

indicates that the Young's Modulus is 30000 for members 1, 2, 3, 4 and 5, and is 10000 for members 6, 7, and 8.

DELETIONS: This is a modification descriptor. It is used to indicate that a modification is to be performed by deleting previously given data. For example, the statements

```
CHANGES
LOADING 2
DELETIONS
JOINT 4 LOAD 3
```

would cause load 3 at joint 4 to be deleted. This is a part of LOADING 2.

DISPLACEMENTS: Displacements are prescribed joint motions at support joints. The form of this statement is

```
JOINT DISPLACEMENTS
J DISPLACEMENT X N1 Y N2 Z N3 ROTATION X N4 Y N5 Z N6
```

where J is the support joint number; X, Y, Z are the global axes; N1, N2, N3 are the respective displacements; and N4, N5, N6 are the rotations about X, Y, Z in radians. For example, the statements might appear as

```
JOINT DISPLACEMENTS
3 DISPLACEMENT X .2 Y .3 ROTATION Y .002 Z .01
```

Any displacement or rotation not specified is considered to be zero.

DISTORTIONS: Distortions are prescribed displacements between member ends. The sign of the distortion is positive if the displacement from member START to member END is in the positive local coordinate direction. The form of the statement is

```
MEMBER DISTORTIONS
M DISTORTION X N1 Y N2 Z N3 ROTATION X N4 Y N5 Z N6
```

where M is the identifying number of the member. Rotation distortion is the angle in radians between the tangents at the ends when the member is free and when it is distorted. For example, the statements might appear as

```
MEMBER DISTORTIONS
10 DISTORTION X .01 Y .02 ROTATION X .01 Z .01
```

E: This statement specifies Young's modulus or the modulus of elasticity, and it is used in conjunction with the CONSTANTS statement.

FINISH or FINISHED: This must be the last statement of a STRESS program.

FORCE: A FORCE statement is always used in conjunction with JOINT LOADS, MEMBER LOADS, PRINT, TABULATE, JOINT RELEASE, and MEMBER RELEASE statements.

FREE or F: Indicates that a joint is free or has no restraints. Used in conjunction with a JOINT COORDINATES statement.

G: This indicates the value for the shear modulus; it is used in conjunction with the CONSTANTS statement.

JOINT COORDINATES: This statement is used to indicate that data concerning the joints of the structure are to follow. The coordinates of the joints are specified in the arbitrary global orthogonal coordinate system. Each joint in the structure must be described by a separate statement of the form

J X D1 Y D2 Z D3 Status

where J is the identifying number of the joint, and X D1, Y D2, and Z D3 indicate the distances in the X, Y, and Z directions that the joint J is located with respect to the origin of the global coordinate system. The status of the joint is indicated by the word FREE or the letter F if the joint is unrestrained, and by the word SUPPORT or the letter S if the joint is supported. The FREE or F designation may be omitted except when the status of a joint is being changed to FREE from a previously SUPPORT status. For example,

7 X 120, Y 120, Z 100, FREE

indicates that joint number 7 is located 120 units in both the X and Y directions from the origin, and 100 units in the Z direction. The Z coordinate is omitted in plane structures.

JOINT DISPLACEMENTS: This statement followed by joint displacement data is used to specify joint motion with respect to some supporting structure. It can only be used at support joints. The form of the data is

J DISPLACEMENTS X N1 Y N2 Z N3 ROTATION X N4 Y N5 Z N6

where J is the joint number; N1, N2, and N3 are the displacements in the X, Y, and Z directions, respectively; N4, N5, and N6 are the rotations in radians about the X, Y, and Z axes, respectively.

JOINT LOADS: Used in conjunction with a LOADING header, concentrated forces are described by a JOINT LOADS statement, followed by a data card of the form

J FORCE X N1 Y N2 Z N3 MOMENT X N4 Y N5 Z N6

where J is the number of the JOINT; N1, N2, and N3 are the forces applied to the joint in the X, Y, and Z directions, respectively; N4, N5, and N6 are the moments about the X, Y, and Z axes at the joint J. Only the components present need to be specified. Any unspecified data is assumed to be zero. Notice that the coordinate system for this data is the global system.

JOINT RELEASES: This statement is used to indicate that a support joint is free to move in the specified direction or directions. Any release or freedom to move that is not specified is assumed to be fixed. The releases may be specified in a local orthogonal coordinate system—x' y' z'—other than the global system—X Y Z. The general form is

JOINT RELEASES
J FORCE X Y Z MOMENT X Y Z $\theta 1$ $\theta 2$ $\theta 3$

where J is the joint number; X Y Z are the axes of the local coordinate system along which forces are released, or the local axes about which moments are released; $\theta 1$, $\theta 2$, and $\theta 3$ are the angles in decimal degrees which specify the orientation of the local coordinate system with respect to the global system. $\theta 1$ is the angle by which the local x' axis has been rotated out of the XZ plane, $\theta2$ is the angle by which the local x' axis has been rotated out of the XY plane, and $\theta3$ is the angle by which the local z' axis has been rotated out of the $x'Z$ plane.

LINEAR: This is used in conjunction with a MEMBER LOADS statement to describe a type of member load that varies linearly.

LOADING N or LOADING Title: Load data is presented following a LOADING header which may be one of two types:

> LOADING N

or

> LOADING Title

The LOADING N type is used for designating different loading conditions, or when MODIFICATIONS are specified. Sequential numbers are assigned to N. The LOADING Title type is used to separate groups of loads into loading conditions and to provide headings for output listings. Examples of the use of the LOADING headers are illustrated in the worked examples.

The load data is of four types—joint loads, joint displacement, member loads, and member distortions. Each of these is described in a separate section.

MEMBER DISTORTIONS: This statement followed by member distortion data is used to specify displacements between member ends. The form is as follows:

> MEMBER DISTORTIONS
> M DISTORTION X N1 Y N2 Z N2 ROTATION X N4 Y N5 Z N6

where M is the member identifying number; X, Y, and Z are the local coordinate axes of the member being specified; N1, N2, and N3 are the distortions in the X, Y, and Z directions, respectively; N4, N5, and N6 are the rotation distortion angles in radians between the tangents at the member ends if the member were free.

MEMBER END LOADS: Whenever the member flexibility or stiffness matrix is given, or whenever the loading pattern is different from CONCENTRATED, LINEAR, or UNIFORM, it is necessary to compute separately the member end loads and supply them to the processor. The form is

> MEMBER END LOADS
> M END FORCE X N1 Y N2 Z N3 MOMENT X N4 Y N5 Z N6
> START FORCE X N7 Y N8 Z N9 MOMENT X N10 Y N11 Z N12

MEMBER INCIDENCES: This statement, along with the data which follows, indicates how the members connect together to form the structure. Each member has a joint at each end. Following the MEMBER INCIDENCES statement is a separate statement for each member of the structure of the type

> M JS JE

In these statements, M is the member identifying number; JS and JE are the joint numbers at the START and END of the member in the positive local x coordinate direction. M, JS, and JE are integers having no decimal points.

MEMBER LOADS: This statement, followed by other descriptors and data, describes loads applied to members. The form is

MEMBER LOADS
M Direction, Type, Labels, Data

A member load statement specifies one force or moment acting between the ends of the member. The direction of the force must be specified as one of the following:

FORCE X
FORCE Y
FORCE Z

The axis about which the moment acts must be specified as one of the following:

MOMENT X
MOMENT Y
MOMENT Z

Member loads may be CONCENTRATED, UNIFORM, or LINEAR. If the load is concentrated, the data is of the form

CONCENTRATED P N1 L N2

where N1 is the value of the concentrated load, N2 is the distance from member START to point where the load is applied. If the load is uniformly distributed between LA and LB, the data is given as

UNIFORM W N1 LA N2 LB N3

where N1 is the value of the uniformly distributed load, N2 is the distance from the member START to the point where the load begins, and N3 is the distance from the member START to the point where the load ends. If the load is linearly changing between LA and LB, the data is

LINEAR WA N1 WB N2 LA N3 LB N4

where WA is the value of load at the beginning point LA; WB is the value of load at the end point LB; N3 and N4 are the distances from member START to LA and LB, respectively, as in UNIFORM.

MEMBER DISTORTIONS: Followed by member distortion data, this instruction is used to specify displacements between the member ends.

MEMBER PROPERTIES: This statement indicates that data concerning the member are to follow. There must be one statement per member describing its properties. If many members have the same properties, they may be grouped together. For example, if all members are assumed to be prismatic, the above statement may be written MEMBER PROPERTIES, PRISMATIC, followed by the area and moment of inertia data for each member. Prismatic members have constant cross section throughout the length of the member. It is also possible to omit the type PRISMATIC from the MEMBER PROPERTIES statement and to include it with the data for each member.

Following the first approach, one may write, as was done in the example of Figs. 14.2 and 14.3,

> MEMBER PROPERTIES, PRISMATIC
> 1 AX 20, IZ 200
> .
> .
> .
> 13 AX 20, IZ 200

The above statements would be interpreted as meaning that all members are prismatic and that the cross-sectional area, AX, is 20 in^2 and the moment of inertia is 200. Of course, it is possible to have different properties for each member. Here they were simply assumed to be equal.

The same information could have been shown as follows:

> MEMBER PROPERTIES
> 1 PRISMATIC AX 20, IZ 200
> .
> .
> .
> 13 PRISMATIC AX 20, IZ 200

with the same interpretation and result.

Labels are used to identify area and moment of inertia data as can be seen in the above examples. These labels are

> AX for the normal cross-sectional area at right angles to x
> AY for the effective shearing area in the y direction
> AZ for the effective shearing area in the z direction
> IX for the torsional constant
> IY for the moment of inertia about the y axis
> IZ for the moment of inertia about the z axis

The typical data statement of member properties would, therefore, be of the form

> M PRISMATIC AX N1 AY N2 AZ N3 IX N4 IY N5 IZ N6 BETA N7

where M is the member number; AX, AY, . . . , have been previously explained; N1, N2, . . . , are the appropriate data associated with the labels. BETA N7 indicates that the member is rotated about the x axis by an amount N7 degrees in the counterclockwise direction from the position where the y axis of the member would normally lie in the plane formed by the x local axis and the Y global axis.

If any of the items of data information are omitted, STRESS assumes them to be zero or that they are not to be used in the analysis.

Members may have stepwise variation of section properties. If so, the word PRISMATIC is replaced by the word VARIABLE in the member data. The number of segments must be shown, and a set of cross-section data supplied for each segment and the length of each segment. BETA applies to the entire member and is, therefore, given first. The following data statement would be typical:

M VARIABLE N1 SEGMENTS, BETA N2 AX N3 AY N4 AZ N5 IX N6 IY N7 IZ N8 LN9

M identifies the member by number; N1 indicates the number of segments; BETA the angle of rotation; AX N3 . . . IZ N7 the cross-section data for the first segment; L the length of the first segment. The cross section and length of each succeeding section follows.

MEMBER RELEASE: This statement is used to indicate that specified components of force or moment at member ends are always zero. It is necessary not only to designate which components are released, but also whether or not it is at the START or the END of the member that is being specified. Member releases are in terms of the local member coordinate system. Since releases can only occur at member ends, releases at other points require the creation of new members by adding new joints. The form of the statement is

MEMBER RELEASE
M END FORCE X Y Z MOMENT X Y Z START FORCE X Y Z MOMENT X Y Z

Only those items specifically released are affected. If a force or moment is not mentioned, it is not released.

METHOD STIFFNESS: At the time of this writing the stiffness method is the only one implemented in STRESS. It is anticipated that other methods will be added and hence provision is made to include these as they become available. The statement must appear in this form:

METHOD STIFFNESS

MODIFICATION: This statement is used as an output title. It has two forms:

MODIFICATION OF FIRST PART, Title
MODIFICATION OF LAST PART, Title

When the problem, as initially specified, is being modified, the first form is used. When the modifications apply to the problem just completed, the last form is used.

MOMENT: This statement is used as a part of several other statements. JOINT RELEASES, MEMBER RELEASES, JOINT LOADS, MEMBER LOADS, and MEMBER END LOADS all make use of MOMENT.

NUMBER: Four of these statements must appear in each STRESS program to indicate the number of joints, members, loadings, and supports in the structure being studied. For example,

NUMBER OF JOINTS 8
NUMBER OF SUPPORTS 2
NUMBER OF MEMBERS 13
NUMBER OF LOADINGS 1

The above statements indicate 8 joints, 2 supports, 13 members, and 1 loading. These numbers are entered as integers with no decimal points. They were taken from Example 14.1.

PRINT: This is used with the SELECTIVE OUTPUT and LOADING statements to print out particular data. It can be written with descriptors in one of the following ways:

> PRINT FORCES N1, N2, N3, . . .
> PRINT REACTIONS N1, N2, N3, . . .
> PRINT DISTORTIONS N1, N2, N3, . . .
> PRINT DISPLACEMENTS N1, N2, N3, . . .

The descriptors can be shown singly or in a string. N1, N2, N3, . . . , represent the joint or member identifying numbers for which printed output is desired.

Also, the statement
> PRINT DATA

can be used to give a listing of all the current data in the system. This statement can be used without the SELECTIVE OUTPUT statement.

PRISMATIC: This is used with a MEMBER PROPERTIES statement to indicate that a member has the same section properties throughout its length. Consider this statement in contrast with the VARIABLE statement which is used when a member has stepwise changes in its section properties.

REACTIONS: This is used in conjunction with a TABULATE or PRINT statement to indicate that support reactions and joint loads are to be listed.

ROTATION: This is used in conjunction with the MEMBER DISTORTIONS statement as explained under that heading.

SELECTIVE OUTPUT: This is used when only selected items of output information are desired instead of all the information that is obtained with TABULATE. The form for using this statement is

> SELECTIVE OUTPUT
> LOADING N1
> PRINT FORCES N2 N3 . . . REACTIONS N4 N5, etc.

In addition to FORCES and REACTIONS, DISTORTIONS and DISPLACEMENTS can also be used with appropriate joint numbers or member numbers given for whatever output is desired.

SOLVE: This is a termination statement. When this statement is used, a solution will be obtained with the requested tabulation of results using the data given up to this statement. The problem is then terminated.

SOLVE THIS PART: This is the same as SOLVE except that after the solution has been found and results tabulated, selective output and modifications can be specified.

START: This is used in conjunction with MEMBER RELEASE and MEMBER END LOADS statements as explained under those headings. START specifies one end of a member and END the other end. The positive local *x* axis is directed from START to END. See the explanation of MEMBER INCIDENCES also.

STRUCTURE: This statement must appear as the first statement of any STRESS program. Additional title information may be added to the statement for identification purposes. This added information has no effect except to be printed at the top of each output page.

STOP: This terminates the processing. It is used after the final program in a series.

SUPPORT or S: This is used as a joint status indicator in conjunction with a JOINT COORDINATES statement as explained under that heading.

TABULATE: This statement is used to effect a tabulated output listing of forces, reactions, distortions, and/or displacements as they apply to all joints and members in the structural system. The TABULATE statement may be followed by the appropriate descriptor or descriptors. For example, valid statements could be

TABULATE FORCES
TABULATE MEMBER FORCES
TABULATE JOINT DISPLACEMENTS
TABULATE MEMBER DISTORTIONS, JOINT REACTIONS
TABULATE ALL

The words MEMBER and JOINT may be included or not as desired. The word FORCES in this application refers to the member forces at the START and END of each member. The word REACTIONS refers to the support reactions and joint loads. The word DISPLACEMENTS refers to the displacements occurring at joints. The word DISTORTIONS refers to member distortions, which is the sum of the strains between START and END of a member. Axial and shear distortions are tabulated as well as rotations between end tangents. The word ALL causes all of the forces, reactions, displacements, and distortions for all joints and members to be tabulated.

TYPE: One of five different TYPE statements must be included in every STRESS program. This statement must be selected as one of the following:

TYPE PLANE FRAME
TYPE PLANE TRUSS
TYPE PLANE GRID
TYPE SPACE TRUSS
TYPE SPACE FRAME

The word PLANE in the TYPE statement indicates a two-dimensional structure, while the word SPACE indicates a three-dimensional structure. The word FRAME indicates rigid joints between members, whereas the word TRUSS indicates hinged joints. Where a mixture of hinged and fixed joints occurs in a structure, the type of structure should be specified as a FRAME with the hinges introduced by means of RELEASES wherever applicable.

UNIFORM: This is used in conjunction with the MEMBER LOADS statement to indicate a uniformly distributed load. This is described under MEMBER LOADS.

VARIABLE: This is used in conjunction with the MEMBER PROPERTIES statement to indicate a member whose section properties are not constant. This is described under MEMBER PROPERTIES.

14.7 Examples of the Use of STRESS

Example 14.2 Figure 14.4 shows a linkage to be studied using STRESS. It is desired to find the resulting forces at joints 1 and 5 for the connected links under the action of the applied couple. The structure is considered as having four members and five joints as identified in the figure. The couple is applied to member 1 as shown. The STRESS program and results are shown in Fig. 14.5. Notice that the applied couple is 50 ft lb or 600 in lb or 0.6 in kips as specified in this program. The resulting forces are consequently in kips.

Example 14.3 The structure shown in Fig. 14.6 rests on a smooth horizontal plane. The connections at joints 4, 5, 6, 7, and 8 are ball and socket joints. It is desired to find the total force at joint 4 due to the 1000 lb load applied at joint 6.

The properties of the members are not specified; however, the example assumes values for these properties for illustrative purposes. The structure as given is unstable. There is no strut to prevent the leg consisting of members 8 and 9 from collapsing. The connection of member 8 and joint 8 was kept rigid to keep the frame stable. The results show the components of force at all joints. If the resultant of the forces at joint 4 is found, it is determined to be 513 lb. Figure 14.7 shows the program and results.

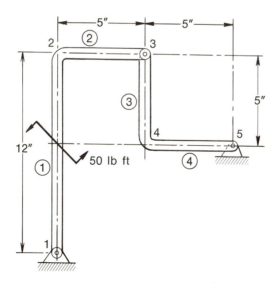

Figure 14.4 *A linkage for Example 14.2.*

STRUCTURE EXAMPLE 14.2
NUMBER OF JOINTS 5
NUMBER OF SUPPORTS 2
NUMBER OF MEMBERS 4
NUMBER OF LOADINGS 1
TYPE PLANE FRAME
METHOD STIFFNESS
JOINT COORDINATES
1 X 0, Y 0, S
2 X 0, Y 12
3 X 5, Y 12
4 X 5, Y 7
5 X 10, Y 7, S
MEMBER INCIDENCES
1 1 2
2 2 3
3 3 4
4 4 5
MEMBER PROPERTIES, PRISMATIC
1 AX 20, IZ 200
2 AX 20, IZ 200
3 AX 20, IZ 200
4 AX 20, IZ 200
CONSTANTS E, 30000, ALL
JOINT RELEASES
1 MOMENT Z
5 MOMENT Z
MEMBER RELEASES
2 END MOMENT Z
LOADING 1
MEMBER LOADS
1 MOMENT Z CONCENTRATED P, 6 L 7
SOLVE THIS PART
SELECTIVE OUTPUT
LOADING 1
PRINT REACTIONS 1, 5

JOINT	X FORCE	Y FORCE	BENDING MOMENT
		SUPPORT REACTIONS	
1	−.0352941	.0352941	.0000000
5	.0352941	−.0352941	−.0000000

FINISH
TIME USED: 1 SECOND

Figure 14.5 *The STRESS program for Example 14.2.*

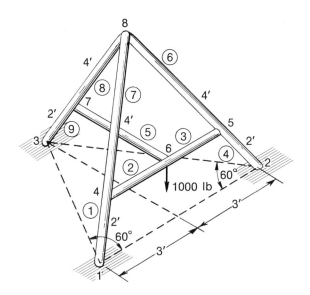

Figure 14.6 *A structure for Example 14.3.*

STRUCTURE EXAMPLE 14.3
NUMBER OF JOINTS 8
NUMBER OF SUPPORTS 3
NUMBER OF MEMBERS 9
NUMBER OF LOADINGS 1
TYPE SPACE FRAME
METHOD STIFFNESS
JOINT COORDINATES
1 X 0, Y 0, Z 0, S
2 X 72, Y 0, Z 0, S
3 X 36, Y 0, Z −62.3, S
4 X 12, Y 19.56, Z −6.93
5 X 60, Y 19.56, Z −6.93
6 X 36, Y 19.56, Z −6.93
7 X 36, Y 19.56, Z −48.7
8 X 36, Y 58.8, Z −20.8
MEMBER INCIDENCES
1 1 4
2 4 6
3 6 5
4 5 2
5 6 7
6 5 8

Figure 14.7 *The STRESS program for Example 14.3.*

Figure 14.7 *(Continued)*

7 4 8
8 7 8
9 7 3
MEMBER PROPERTIES, PRISMATIC
1 AX 2, AY 2, IX 4, IY .667, IZ .667, BETA 35
2 AX 2, AY 2, IX 4, IY .667, IZ .667, BETA 35
3 AX 2, AY 2, IX 4, IY .667, IZ .667, BETA 35
4 AX 2, AY 2, IX 4, IY .667, IZ .667, BETA 35
5 AX 2, AY 2, IX 4, IY .667, IZ .667, BETA 35
6 AX 2, AY 2, IX 4, IY .667, IZ .667, BETA 35
7 AX 2, AY 2, IX 4, IY .667, IZ .667, BETA 35
8 AX 2, AY 2, IX 4, IY .667, IZ .667, BETA 35
9 AX 2, AY 2, IX 4, IY .667, IZ .667, BETA 35
CONSTANTS E, 30000, 1, 2, 3, 4, 5, 10000, 6, 7, 8, 9
CONSTANTS G, 12000, ALL BUT 4000, 6, 7, 8, 9
JOINT RELEASES
1 FORCE X Z MOMENT X Y Z
2 FORCE X Z MOMENT X Y Z
3 FORCE X Z MOMENT X Y Z
MEMBER RELEASES
2 START MOMENT X Y Z
3 END MOMENT X Y Z
5 END MOMENT Z START MOMENT Z
6 END MOMENT X Y Z
7 END MOMENT X Y Z
LOADING 1
JOINT LOADS
6 FORCE Y −1
TABULATE FORCES, REACTIONS
SOLVE

			FORCES			MOMENTS	
MEMBER	JOINT	AXIAL	SHEAR Y	SHEAR Z	TORSIONAL	BENDING Y	BENDING Z
1	1	.3537880	.2056995	−.1440845	.0020830	−.0114979	−.0138268
1	4	−.3537880	−.2056995	.1440845	−.0020830	3.4653774	4.9446909
2	4	−.1015794	.4431992	−.2384224	.0000000	.0000916	.0000610
2	6	.1015794	−.4431992	.2384224	−.0000000	5.7220459	10.6367187
3	6	−.1024734	−.4437164	.2384522	.0000000	−5.7228526	−10.6491937
3	5	.1024734	.4437164	−.2384522	−.0000000	−.0000000	−.0000000
4	5	.3650878	−.2118929	.1483635	.0000355	−3.5563963	−5.0796417
4	2	−.3650878	.2118929	−.1483635	−.0000355	−.0000545	.0003142
5	6	−.1178537	.0000000	.0000193	−.0074962	.0000003	.0000000
5	7	.1178537	−.0000000	−.0000193	.0074962	−.0008081	.0000000
6	5	.0223087	−.1050950	.0735477	.0000000	−3.5334697	−5.0491060
6	8	−.0223087	.1050950	−.0735477	−.0000000	−.0000000	−.0000000
7	4	.0224568	−.1050001	.0750874	.0000000	−3.6074444	−5.0445474
7	8	−.0224568	.1050001	−.0750874	−.0000000	−.0000000	−.0000000
8	7	.1594377	−.0257931	.0180610	−.0000002	−.8695979	−1.2418822
8	8	−.1594377	.0257931	−.0180610	.0000002	.0000065	.0000094

JOINT							
9	7	.0915111	−.0521232	.0364975	−.0000000	−.8694896	−1.2417541
9	3	−.0915111	.0521232	−.0364975	.0000000	−.0000038	.0000026

JOINT	X FORCE	Y FORCE	Z FORCE	X MOMENT	Y MOMENT	Z MOMENT
		SUPPORT REACTIONS				
1	−.0003755	.4338645	.0001675	−.0068683	.0008396	−.0167285
2	.0000143	.4474365	.0000135	−.0002898	−.0001010	.0000938
3	−.0000003	.1114593	−.0000029	−.0000001	−.0000026	.0000038
		APPLIED JOINT LOADS				
4	.0019366	.0098031	.0006115	−.0425840	−.0357554	−.1638794
5	.0005873	−.0029843	.0003282	.0188025	.0010864	−.0332117
6	−.0008782	−1.0000538	−.0002274	.0000002	.0064948	−.0031853
7	−.0000159	.0002465	.0002008	−.0002965	−.0006747	−.0074785
8	−.0012682	.0002281	−.0010911	−.0000114	.0000001	.0000002

FINISH

TIME USED: 3 SECONDS

Example 14.4 This example is a repeat of Example 14.1, except that the type is specified here as TYPE PLANE FRAME, whereas in Example 14.1 it was specified as TYPE PLANE TRUSS. In a frame structure the joints are rigid and for that reason the results of this example are quite different from those of the earlier example. They include shear forces and bending moments. The STRESS program and results are shown in Fig. 14.8.

```
STRUCTURE EXAMPLE 14.4
NUMBER OF JOINTS 8
NUMBER OF SUPPORTS 2
NUMBER OF MEMBERS 13
NUMBER OF LOADINGS 1
TYPE PLANE FRAME
METHOD STIFFNESS
TABULATE MEMBER FORCES
JOINT COORDINATES
1 X 120, Y 120, FREE
2 X 240, Y 120
3 X 360, Y 120
4 X 0, Y 0, SUPPORT
5 X 120, Y 0
6 X 240, Y 0
7 X 360, Y 0
8 X 480, Y 0, S
MEMBER INCIDENCES
1 1 2
2 2 3
3 4 1
4 5 1
5 5 2
6 6 2
```

Figure 14.8 A program for Example 14.1 specifying frame structure.

Figure 14.8 *(Continued)*

7 7 2
8 7 3
9 8 3
10 4 5
11 5 6
12 6 7
13 7 8
MEMBER PROPERTIES, PRISMATIC
1 AX 20, IZ 200
2 AX 20, IZ 200
3 AX 20, IZ 200
4 AX 20, IZ 200
5 AX 20, IZ 200
6 AX 20, IZ 200
7 AX 20, IZ 200
8 AX 20, IZ 200
9 AX 20, IZ 200
10 AX 20, IZ 200
11 AX 20, IZ 200
12 AX 20, IZ 200
13 AX 20, IZ 200
CONSTANTS E, 30000, ALL
LOADING 1
JOINT LOADS
6 FORCE Y −12
7 FORCE Y −12
JOINT RELEASES
4 MOMENT Z
8 FORCE X MOMENT Z
SOLVE THIS PART
LOADING 1
MEMBER FORCES

MEMBER	JOINT	AXIAL FORCE	SHEAR FORCE	BENDING MOMENT
1	1	9.1301044	.2241492	10.3396298
1	2	−9.1301044	−.2241492	16.5582770
2	2	15.0147484	−.1750133	−14.5456782
2	3	−15.0147484	.1750133	−6.4559190
3	4	12.6395977	−.0263626	−3.6899534
3	1	−12.6395977	.0263626	−.7839289
4	5	−8.6947560	−.1739193	−11.3146098
4	1	8.6947560	.1739193	−9.5557014
5	5	12.1354493	.0032957	−2.5408400
5	2	−12.1354493	−.0032957	3.1001439
6	6	−11.7043009	−.0554702	−3.5841763

6	2	11.7043009	.0554702	−3.0722467
7	7	3.8687899	.0196657	5.3778746
7	2	−3.8687899	−.0196657	−2.0404973
8	7	−14.6483640	.1486924	10.1222445
8	3	14.6483640	−.1486924	7.7208422
9	8	20.9935940	.0301824	6.3870405
9	3	−20.9935940	−.0301824	−1.2649242
10	4	−8.9561786	.0810884	3.6898858
10	5	8.9561786	−.0810884	6.0407162
11	5	−17.7088270	.1924578	7.8146551
11	6	17.7088270	−.1924578	15.2802815
12	6	−17.7642990	−.1032426	−11.6961034
12	7	17.7642990	.1032426	−.6930120
13	7	−14.8660538	−.1766165	−14.8070462
13	8	14.8660538	.1766165	−6.3869369

```
SELECTIVE OUTPUT
LOADING 1
PRINT FORCES 12, 7
MEMBER FORCES
```

MEMBER	JOINT	AXIAL FORCE	SHEAR FORCE	BENDING MOMENT
12	6	−17.7642990	−.1032426	−11.6961034
12	7	17.7642990	.1032426	−.6930120
7	7	3.8687899	.0196657	5.3778746
7	2	−3.8687899	−.0196657	−2.0404973

```
FINISH
TIME USED: 4 SECONDS
```

Example 14.5 The structure shown in Fig. 14.9 is used as a basis for this example of STRESS. It is first studied as a TYPE PLANE TRUSS with only one loading condition and disregarding the distributed weights of the members comprising the structure. The problem is to find the forces in all members of the structure. Figure 14.10 contains the STRESS program and results.

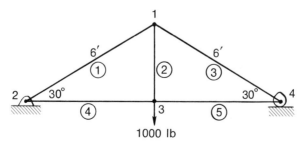

Figure 14.9 *A structure for Example 14.5.*

STRUCTURE EXAMPLE 14.5
NUMBER OF JOINTS 4
NUMBER OF SUPPORTS 2
NUMBER OF MEMBERS 5
NUMBER OF LOADINGS 1
TYPE PLANE TRUSS
METHOD STIFFNESS
TABULATE FORCES, REACTIONS, DISPLACEMENTS
JOINT COORDINATES
1 X 0, Y 36
2 X −62.352, Y 0, S
3 X 0, Y 0
4 X 62.352, Y 0, S
MEMBER INCIDENCES
1 2 1
2 3 1
3 1 4
4 2 3
5 3 4
MEMBER PROPERTIES, PRISMATIC
1 AX 20, IZ 200
2 AX 20, IZ 200
3 AX 20, IZ 200
4 AX 20, IZ 200
5 AX 20, IZ 200
CONSTANTS E, 30000, ALL
JOINT RELEASES
4 FORCE X
LOADING 1 WEIGHT AT CENTER
JOINT LOADS
3 FORCE Y −1
SOLVE
LOADING 1 WEIGHT AT CENTER
MEMBER FORCES

MEMBER	JOINT	AXIAL FORCE
1	2	.9999780
1	1	−.9999780
2	3	−1.0000000
2	1	1.0000000
3	1	.9999780
3	4	−.9999780
4	2	−.8659999
4	3	.8659999

Figure 14.10 *The STRESS program for Example 14.5.*

5	3	−.8659999
5	4	.8659999

LOADING 1 WEIGHT AT CENTER

JOINT	X FORCE	Y FORCE
		SUPPORT REACTIONS
2	.0000001	.5000000
4	−.0000000	.5000000
		APPLIED JOINT LOADS
1	.0000000	.0000000
3	−.0000000	−1.0000000

LOADING 1 WEIGHT AT CENTER

JOINT DISPLACEMENTS

JOINT	X DISPLACEMENT	Y DISPLACEMENT
		SUPPORT DISPLACEMENTS
2	−.0000000	−.0000000
4	.0001800	−.0000000
JOINT	X DISPLACEMENT	Y DISPLACEMENT
		FREE JOINT DISPLACEMENTS
1	.0000900	−.0003959
3	.0000900	−.0004559

FINISH

TIME USED: 4 SECONDS

Example 14.6 This example treats the same structure as that of Example 14.5 with three exceptions. Here, the structure is specified as TYPE PLANE FRAME, all joints are hinged, and the distributed weight of the members is included as 5 lb/ft of length (0.0004167 kips per inch). The STRESS program incorporating these changes and the results is shown in Fig. 14.11.

```
STRUCTURE EXAMPLE 14.6
NUMBER OF JOINTS 4
NUMBER OF SUPPORTS 2
NUMBER OF MEMBERS 5
NUMBER OF LOADINGS 2
TYPE PLANE FRAME
METHOD STIFFNESS
TABULATE FORCES, REACTIONS, DISPLACEMENTS
JOINT COORDINATES
1 X 0, Y 36
2 X −62.352, Y 0, S
3 X 0, Y 0
4 X 62.352, Y 0, S
MEMBER INCIDENCES
1 2 1
```

Figure 14.11 *The STRESS program for Example 14.6.*

Figure 14.11 *(Continued)*

2 3 1
3 1 4
4 2 3
5 3 4
MEMBER PROPERTIES, PRISMATIC
1 AX 20, IZ 200
2 AX 20, IZ 200
3 AX 20, IZ 200
4 AX 20, IZ 200
5 AX 20, IZ 200
CONSTANTS E, 30000, ALL
JOINT RELEASES
4 FORCE X
MEMBER RELEASES
1 END MOMENT Z START MOMENT Z
2 END MOMENT Z START MOMENT Z
3 END MOMENT Z START MOMENT Z
4 END MOMENT Z START MOMENT Z
5 END MOMENT Z START MOMENT Z
LOADING 1 WEIGHT AT CENTER
JOINT LOADS
3 FORCE Y −1
LOADING 2 UNIFORM WEIGHT OF MEMBERS
MEMBER LOADS
1 FORCE Y UNIFORM, −0.0004167
2 FORCE Y UNIFORM, −0.0004167
3 FORCE Y UNIFORM, −0.0004167
4 FORCE Y UNIFORM, −0.0004167
5 FORCE Y UNIFORM, −0.0004167
SOLVE
LOADING 1 WEIGHT AT CENTER
MEMBER FORCES

MEMBER	JOINT	AXIAL FORCE	SHEAR FORCE	BENDING MOMENT
1	2	.9999779	.0000000	.0000000
1	1	−.9999779	−.0000000	.0000000
2	3	−1.0000000	.0000000	−.0000000
2	1	1.0000000	−.0000000	.0000001
3	1	.9999780	−.0000000	.0000000
3	4	−.9999780	.0000000	−.0000000
4	2	−.8659999	.0000000	.0000000
4	3	.8659999	−.0000000	−.0000000
5	3	−.8659999	−.0000000	.0000000
5	4	.8659999	.0000000	−.0000000

LOADING 1 WEIGHT AT CENTER

JOINT	X FORCE	Y FORCE	BENDING MOMENT
		SUPPORT REACTIONS	
2	.0000000	.5000000	.0000000
4	−.0000000	.5000000	−.0000000
		APPLIED JOINT LOADS	
1	.0000000	.0000000	.0000001
3	−.0000000	−1.0000000	−.0000000

LOADING 1 WEIGHT AT CENTER
JOINT DISPLACEMENTS

JOINT	X DISPLACEMENT	Y DISPLACEMENT	ROTATION
		SUPPORT DISPLACEMENTS	
2	−.0000000	−.0000000	−.0000000
4	.0001800	−.0000000	−.0000000
		FREE JOINT DISPLACEMENTS	
1	.0000900	−.0003959	.0000115
3	.0000900	−.0004559	−.0000073

LOADING 2 UNIFORM WEIGHT OF MEMBERS
MEMBER FORCES

MEMBER	JOINT	AXIAL FORCE	SHEAR FORCE	BENDING MOMENT
1	2	.0425016	.0151449	−1.0800388
1	1	−.0425016	.0148568	1.0904103
2	3	−.0216515	.0080768	−.2700216
2	1	.0216515	.0069244	.2907654
3	1	.0635797	.0150009	−1.0800388
3	4	−.0635797	.0150009	1.0800388
4	2	−.0448841	.0173216	−.8100172
4	3	.0448841	.0086604	1.0800388
5	3	−.0368072	.0129910	−.8100172
5	4	.0368072	.0129910	.8100172

LOADING 2 UNIFORM WEIGHT OF MEMBERS

JOINT	X FORCE	Y FORCE	BENDING MOMENT
		SUPPORT REACTIONS	
2	−.0156494	.0516887	−1.8900560
4	−.0107534	.0577726	1.8900560
		APPLIED JOINT LOADS	
1	.0114016	−.0055330	.3011369
3	.0000000	−.0000000	−.0000000

LOADING 2 UNIFORM WEIGHT OF MEMBERS
JOINT DISPLACEMENTS

JOINT	X DISPLACEMENT	Y DISPLACEMENT	ROTATION
		SUPPORT DISPLACEMENTS	
2	−.0000000	−.0000000	−.0000000
4	.0000085	−.0000000	−.0000000

Figure 14.11 *(Continued)*

FREE JOINT DISPLACEMENTS

1	.0000055	−.0000197	4.1958905
3	.0000047	−.0000210	72.8278680

FINISH

TIME USED: 1 SECOND

Example 14.7 This example treats the same structure as that of Examples 14.5 and 14.6 with some exceptions. The structure is specified as TYPE PLANE FRAME as it was Example 14.6, but this time all joints are not hinged. Joint 2 is hinged and joint 4 is hinged and is released in the X direction. Loading 1 is for the concentrated load of 1 kip at joint 3. Loading 2 is for the uniform weight of the members. Loading 3 is a concentrated load of 20 kips on member 5. Loading 4 is linearly distributed loads on members 4 and 5. This system is shown in Fig. 14.12. The STRESS program and results are given in Fig. 14.13.

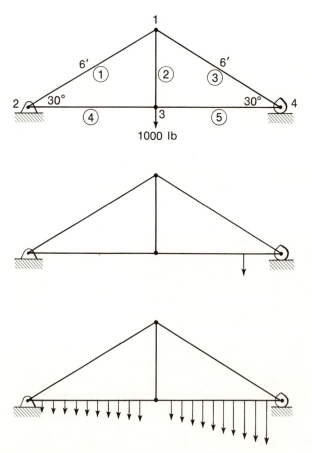

Figure 14.12 *A structure with loads for Example 14.7.*

STRUCTURE EXAMPLE 14.7
NUMBER OF JOINTS 4
NUMBER OF SUPPORTS 2
NUMBER OF MEMBERS 5
NUMBER OF LOADINGS 4
TYPE PLANE FRAME
METHOD STIFFNESS
TABULATE FORCES, REACTIONS, DISPLACEMENTS
JOINT COORDINATES
1 X 0, Y 36
2 X −62.352, Y 0, S
3 X 0, Y 0
4 X 62.352, Y 0, S
MEMBER INCIDENCES
1 2 1
2 3 1
3 1 4
4 2 3
5 3 4
MEMBER PROPERTIES, PRISMATIC
1 AX 20, IZ 200
2 AX 20, IZ 200
3 AX 20, IZ 200
4 AX 20, IZ 200
5 AX 20, IZ 200
CONSTANTS E, 30000, ALL
JOINT RELEASES
2 MOMENT Z
4 MOMENT Z FORCE X
LOADING 1 WEIGHT AT CENTER
JOINT LOADS
3 FORCE Y −1
LOADING 2 UNIFORM WEIGHT OF MEMBERS
MEMBER LOADS
1 FORCE Y UNIFORM, −0.0004167
2 FORCE Y UNIFORM, −0.0004167
3 FORCE Y UNIFORM, −0.0004167
4 FORCE Y UNIFORM, −0.0004167
5 FORCE Y UNIFORM, −0.0004167
LOADING 3 CONCENTRATED ON ONE MEMBER
MEMBER LOADS
5 FORCE Y CONCENTRATED P −20, L 40
LOADING 4 LINEAR ON TWO MEMBERS

Figure 14.13 *The STRESS program for Example 14.7.*

Figure 14.13 *(Continued)*

MEMBER LOADS
4 FORCE Y LINEAR −1, −2, 10, 50
5 FORCE Y LINEAR WA −2.0, WB −4.0, LA 10, LB 50
PRINT DATA
STRUCTURAL DATA
TYPE PLANE FRAME
METHOD STIFFNESS
NUMBER OF JOINTS 4
        MEMBERS 5
        SUPPORTS 3
        LOADINGS 4
JOINT COORDINATES

JOINT	X	Y	Z	STATUS
1	.000	36.000		
2	−62.352	.000		SUPPORT
3	.000	.000		
4	62.352	.000		SUPPORT

JOINT RELEASES

JOINT NUMBER	FORCE X Y Z	MOMENT X Y Z	THETA 1	2	3
2		*	.00	.00	.00
4	*	*	.00	.00	.00

MEMBER PROPERTIES

MEMBER	START	END	TYPE	SEGMENT	AX	AY	AZ	IX	IY	IZ	L BETA
1	2	1	PRISMATIC	1	20.000	.000	.000	.00	.00	200.00	
2	3	1	PRISMATIC	1	20.000	.000	.000	.00	.00	200.00	
3	1	4	PRISMATIC	1	20.000	.000	.000	.00	.00	200.00	
4	2	3	PRISMATIC	1	20.000	.000	.000	.00	.00	200.00	
5	3	4	PRISMATIC	1	20.000	.000	.000	.00	.00	200.00	

YOUNG'S MODULI
30000.00 VALUE FOR ALL MEMBERS
LOADING DATA
GIVEN IN TABULAR FORM WITHOUT LABELS
LOADING 1 WEIGHT AT CENTER
TABULATE
    FORCES
    REACTIONS
    DISPLACEMENTS
JOINT 3 LOADS   .00000 −1.0000 .0000 .0000 .0000 .0000
LOADING 2 UNIFORM WEIGHT OF MEMBERS
TABULATE
    FORCES
    REACTIONS
    DISPLACEMENTS

```
MEMBER 1 LOAD FORCE Y UNIFORM        −.0004    .0000 .0000 .0000
MEMBER 2 LOAD FORCE Y UNIFORM        −.0004    .0000 .0000 .0000
MEMBER 3 LOAD FORCE Y UNIFORM        −.0004    .0000 .0000 .0000
MEMBER 4 LOAD FORCE Y UNIFORM        −.0004    .0000 .0000 .0000
MEMBER 5 LOAD FORCE Y UNIFORM        −.0004    .0000 .0000 .0000
LOADING 3 CONCENTRATED ON ONE MEMBER
TABULATE
    FORCES
    REACTIONS
    DISPLACEMENTS
MEMBER 5 LOAD FORCE Y CONCENTRATED  −20.0000    .0000  40.000      .0000
LOADING 4 LINEAR ON ONE MEMBER
TABULATE
    FORCES
    REACTIONS
    DISPLACEMENTS
MEMBER 4 LOAD FORCE Y LINEAR         −1.0000 −2.0000  10.0000  50.0000
MEMBER 5 LOAD FORCE Y LINEAR         −2.0000 −4.0000  10.0000  50.0000
SOLVE
LOADING 1 WEIGHT AT CENTER
MEMBER FORCES
```

LOADING 1 WEIGHT AT CENTER
MEMBER FORCES

MEMBER	JOINT	AXIAL FORCE	SHEAR FORCE	BENDING MOMENT
1	2	.9039036	.0070936	−.4693146
1	1	−.9039036	−.0070936	.9800458
2	3	−.9162106	−.0000000	.0000002
2	1	.9162106	.0000000	−.0000003
3	1	.9039037	−.0070937	−.9800469
3	4	−.9039037	.0070937	.4693132
4	2	−.7792509	.0418946	.4693125
4	3	.7792509	−.0418946	2.1429022
5	3	−.7792509	−.0418947	−2.1429023
5	4	.7792509	.0418947	−.4693134

LOADING 1 WEIGHT AT CENTER

JOINT	X FORCE	Y FORCE	BENDING MOMENT
		SUPPORT REACTIONS	
2	.0000000	.4999996	−.0000020
4	−.0000000	.4999997	−.0000001
		APPLIED JOINT LOADS	
1	.0000000	.0000006	−.0000014
3	−.0000000	−.9999999	.0000001

LOADING 1 WEIGHT AT CENTER
JOINT DISPLACEMENTS

JOINT	X DISPLACEMENT	Y DISPLACEMENT	ROTATION
		SUPPORT DISPLACEMENTS	
2	−.0000000	−.0000000	−.0000087

Figure 14.13 *(Continued)*

4	.0001620		−.0000000	.0000087

FREE JOINT DISPLACEMENTS

1	.0000810		−.0003572	−.0000000
3	.0000810		−.0004122	.0000000

STRUCTURE PROBLEM 3
LOADING 2 UNIFORM WEIGHT OF MEMBERS
MEMBER FORCES

MEMBER	JOINT	AXIAL FORCE	SHEAR FORCE	BENDING MOMENT
1	2	.0552793	.0129213	.0193100
1	1	−.0552793	.0170805	−.1690384
2	3	−.0292232	.0076139	.0334426
2	1	.0292232	.0073873	−.0293651
3	1	.0634403	.0177200	.1984034
3	4	−.0634403	.0122817	−.0026293
4	2	−.0564133	.0109685	−.0193103
4	3	.0564133	.0150136	−.1067975
5	3	−.0487995	.0142097	.0733550
5	4	.0487995	.0117724	.0026293

LOADING 2 UNIFORM WEIGHT OF MEMBERS

JOINT	X FORCE	Y FORCE	BENDING MOMENT

SUPPORT REACTIONS

2	−.0150012	.0497988	−.0000003
4	−.0000000	.0541294	−.0000000

APPLIED JOINT LOADS

1	.0000000	.0000000	−.0000001
3	.0000000	.0000000	.0000000

LOADING 2 UNIFORM WEIGHT OF MEMBERS
JOINT DISPLACEMENTS

JOINT	X DISPLACEMENT	Y DISPLACEMENT	ROTATION

SUPPORT DISPLACEMENTS

2	−.0000000	−.0000000	−.0000010
4	.0000109	−.0000000	.0000010

FREE JOINT DISPLACEMENTS

1	.0000060	−.0000237	.0000000
3	.0000059	−.0000255	−.0000000

LOADING 3 CONCENTRATED ON ONE MEMBER
MEMBER FORCES

MEMBER	JOINT	AXIAL FORCE	SHEAR FORCE	BENDING MOMENT
1	2	7.5370197	.2070409	4.8777710
1	1	−7.5370197	−.2070409	10.0288454
2	3	−7.4409355	−3.2703125	−75.1739270
2	1	7.4409355	3.2703125	−42.5573210
3	1	10.1417378	1.8220681	32.5284480
3	4	−10.1417378	−1.8220681	98.6575660

4	2	−6.4236802	−.3630890	−4.8777778
4	3	6.4236802	.3630890	−17.7615440
5	3	−9.6939919	7.0778465	92.9354740
5	4	9.6939919	12.9221536	−98.6575750

LOADING 3 CONCENTRATED ON ONE MEMBER

JOINT	X FORCE	Y FORCE	BENDING MOMENT
		SUPPORT REACTIONS	
2	−.0000002	3.5848052	−.0000068
4	−.0000002	16.4151880	−.0000095
		APPLIED JOINT LOADS	
1	−.0000002	.0000065	−.0000281
3	.0000007	−.0000001	.0000029

STRUCTURE PROBLEM 3

LOADING 3 CONCENTRATED ON ONE MEMBER

JOINT DISPLACEMENTS

JOINT	X DISPLACEMENT	Y DISPLACEMENT	ROTATION
		SUPPORT DISPLACEMENTS	
2	−.0000000	−.0000000	−.0000506
4	.0016749	−.0000000	.0003771
JOINT	X DISPLACEMENT	Y DISPLACEMENT	ROTATION
		FREE JOINT DISPLACEMENTS	
1	.0010179	−.0035719	−.0000197
3	.0006675	−.0040183	−.0001175

LOADING 4 LINEAR ON TWO MEMBERS

MEMBER FORCES

MEMBER	JOINT	AXIAL FORCE	SHEAR FORCE	BENDING MOMENT
1	2	99.5774110	−2.3366090	−201.0877600
1	1	−99.5774110	2.3366090	32.8556170
2	3	−94.9186410	−9.7974818	−233.0837200
2	1	94.9186410	9.7974818	−119.6256130
3	1	107.7552440	7.7671287	86.7697900
3	4	−107.7552440	−7.7671287	472.4511700
4	2	−87.4042580	25.7235710	201.0873600
4	3	87.4042580	34.2764280	−404.9579300
5	3	−97.2017370	60.6422210	638.0416900
5	4	97.2017370	59.3577780	−472.4512300

LOADING 4 LINEAR ON TWO MEMBERS

JOINT	X FORCE	Y FORCE	BENDING MOMENT
		SUPPORT REACTIONS	
2	.0000076	73.4898240	−.0003929
4	−.0000067	106.5101040	−.0000687
		APPLIED JOINT LOADS	
1	−.0000029	.0000615	−.0002060
3	.0000019	.0000086	.0000381

LOADING 4 LINEAR ON TWO MEMBERS

Figure 14.13 *(Continued)*

JOINT DISPLACEMENTS

JOINT	X DISPLACEMENT	Y DISPLACEMENT	ROTATION
		SUPPORT DISPLACEMENTS	
2	−.0000000	−.0000000	−.0014397
4	.0191843	−.0000000	.0022780
		FREE JOINT DISPLACEMENTS	
1	.0101587	−.0414924	−.0000360
3	.0090831	−.0471875	−.0003764

FINISH

TIME USED: 3 SECONDS

Example 14.8   The structure for this example is shown in Fig. 14.14. It consists of two cylindrical members having circular cross sections and a common centroidal axis.

The structure is treated as a single member with variable properties. It is loaded, as shown in the figure, with two concentrated loads. The problem is to find the over-all extension of the structure under the influence of the loads. The STRESS program and results are given in Fig. 14.15, showing the extension to be 0.0123718 in.

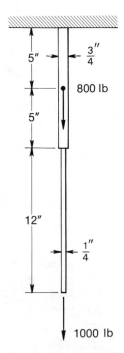

Figure 14.14   *A structure for Example 14.8.*

STRUCTURE EXAMPLE 14.8
NUMBER OF MEMBERS 1
NUMBER OF JOINTS 2
NUMBER OF SUPPORTS 1
NUMBER OF LOADINGS 1
TYPE PLANE FRAME
METHOD STIFFNESS
TABULATE ALL
JOINT COORDINATES
1 X 0.0, Y 0.0, S
2 X 22, Y 0.0
MEMBER INCIDENCES
1 1 2
MEMBER PROPERTIES
1 VARIABLE, 2 SEGMENTS, AX .11045, IZ .00871, L 10, .0491, .0040, 12
CONSTANTS E, 30000, ALL, G, 12000, ALL
LOADING 1
JOINT LOADS
2 FORCE X 1
MEMBER LOADS
1 FORCE X CONCENTRATED P .8, L 5
SOLVE
LOADING 1
MEMBER FORCES

MEMBER	JOINT	AXIAL FORCE	SHEAR FORCE	BENDING MOMENT
1	1	−1.8000000	.0000000	.0000000
1	2	1.0000000	−.0000000	−.0000000

LOADING 1

JOINT	X FORCE	Y FORCE	BENDING MOMENT
		SUPPORT REACTIONS	
1	−1.8000000	.0000000	.0000000
		APPLIED JOINT LOADS	
2	1.0000000	−.0000000	−.0000000

LOADING 1
MEMBER DISTORTIONS

MEMBER	AXIAL DISTORTION	SHEAR DISTORTION	BENDING ROTATION
1	.0123718	−.0000000	−.0000000

LOADING 1
JOINT DISPLACEMENTS

JOINT	X DISPLACEMENT	Y DISPLACEMENT	ROTATION
		FREE JOINT DISPLACEMENTS	
2	.0123718	.0000000	.0000000

FINISH
TIME USED: 1 SECOND

Figure 14.15 *The STRESS program for Example 14.8.*

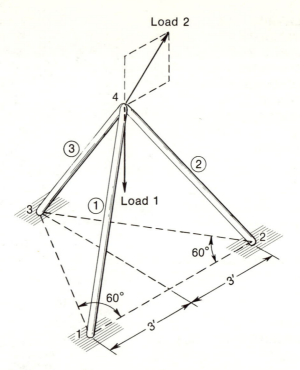

Figure 14.16   *A structure for Example 14.9.*

Example 14.9   Figure 14.16 shows the structure for this example, which is specified as a TYPE SPACE TRUSS consisting of three members. It is loaded in three different ways. Joint 4 is first loaded with a vertical load of 1 kip. The second load has components in both *X* and *Y* directions. The third load is a linear combination of 50% of the first load and 25% of the second. The STRESS program and results are given in Fig. 14.17.

```
STRUCTURE EXAMPLE 14.9
NUMBER OF JOINTS 4
NUMBER OF SUPPORTS 3
NUMBER OF MEMBERS 3
NUMBER OF LOADINGS 3
TYPE SPACE TRUSS
METHOD STIFFNESS
TABULATE ALL
JOINT COORDINATES
1 X 0.0, Y 0.0, Z 0.0, S
2 X 72, Y 0.0, Z 0.0, S
3 X 36, Y 0.0, Z −62.3, S
```

Figure 14.17   *The STRESS program for Example 14.9.*

4 X 36, Y 58.8, Z −20.8
MEMBER INCIDENCES
1 1 4
2 2 4
3 3 4
MEMBER PROPERTIES, PRISMATIC
1 AX 2, AY 2, IX 4, IY .667, IZ .667
2 AX 2, AY 2, IX 4, IY .667, IZ .667
3 AX 2, AY 2, IX 4, IY .667, IZ .667
CONSTANTS E, 30000, ALL
CONSTANTS G, 12000, ALL
LOADING AT JOINT 4
JOINT LOADS
4 FORCE Y −1.0
LOADING AT ANGLE AT JOINT 4
JOINT LOADS
4 FORCE X 1.0, Y 1.0
LOADING COMBINATION OF ABOVE LOADS
COMBINE 1 .5, 2 .25
SOLVE
LOADING AT JOINT 4
MEMBER FORCES

MEMBER	JOINT	AXIAL FORCE
1	1	.4079175
1	4	−.4079175
2	2	.4079175
2	4	−.4079175
3	3	.4086484
3	4	−.4086484

LOADING AT JOINT 4

JOINT	X FORCE	Y FORCE	Z FORCE
		SUPPORT REACTIONS	
1	.2039178	.3330658	−.1178192
2	−.2039178	.3330658	−.1178192
3	.0000000	.3338684	.2356384
		APPLIED JOINT LOADS	
4	−.0000000	−1.0000000	.0000000

LOADING AT JOINT 4
MEMBER DISTORTIONS

MEMBER	AXIAL DISTORTION
1	−.0004896
2	−.0004896
3	−.0004902

LOADING AT JOINT 4
JOINT DISPLACEMENTS

Figure 14.17 (Continued)

JOINT	X DISPLACEMENT	Y DISPLACEMENT	Z DISPLACEMENT
		FREE JOINT DISPLACEMENTS	
4	.0000000	0.0005997	−.0000003

LOADING AT ANGLE AT JOINT 4
MEMBER FORCES

MEMBER	JOINT	AXIAL FORCE
1	1	−1.4081181
1	4	1.4081181
2	2	.5922831
2	4	−.5922831
3	3	−.4086484
3	4	.4086484

LOADING AT ANGLE AT JOINT 4

JOINT	X FORCE	Y FORCE	Z FORCE
		SUPPORT REACTIONS	
1	−.7039178	−1.1497325	.4067081
2	−.2960822	.4836009	−.1710697
3	.0000000	−.3338684	−.2356384
		APPLIED JOINT LOADS	
4	1.0000000	1.0000000	−.0000000

LOADING AT ANGLE AT JOINT 4
MEMBER DISTORTIONS

MEMBER	AXIAL DISTORTION
1	.0016901
2	−.0007109
3	.0004902

LOADING AT ANGLE AT JOINT 4
JOINT DISPLACEMENTS

JOINT	X DISPLACEMENT	Y DISPLACEMENT	Z DISPLACEMENT
		FREE JOINT DISPLACEMENTS	
4	.0024014	.0005997	.0000003

LOADING COMBINATION OF ABOVE LOADS
MEMBER FORCES

MEMBER	JOINT	AXIAL FORCE
1	1	−.1480708
1	4	.1480708
2	2	.3520295
2	4	−.3520295
3	3	.1021621
3	4	−.1021621

LOADING COMBINATION OF ABOVE LOADS

JOINT	X FORCE	Y FORCE	Z FORCE
		SUPPORT REACTIONS	
1	−.0740205	−.1209002	.0427674
2	−.1759795	.2874331	−.1016770

3	.0000000	.0834671	.0589096

APPLIED JOINT LOADS

4	.2500000	−.2500000	.0000000

LOADING COMBINATION OF ABOVE LOADS
MEMBER DISTORTIONS

MEMBER	AXIAL DISTORTION
1	.0001777
2	−.0004225
3	−.0001225

LOADING COMBINATION OF ABOVE LOADS
JOINT DISPLACEMENTS

JOINT	X DISPLACEMENT	Y DISPLACEMENT	Z DISPLACEMENT

FREE JOINT DISPLACEMENTS

4	.0006004	−.0001499	−.0000001

FINISH
TIME USED: 3 SECONDS

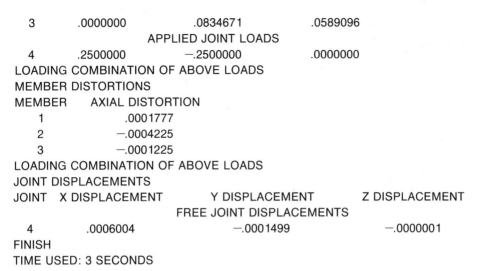

Figure 14.18   Three structures for Example 14.10.

Example 14.10   Figure 14.18(a) shows a 0.1 kip block hanging from a pair of cords, knotted so as to make angles of 30° and 60° with the horizontal. It is desired to find the tension in each cord. Two other configurations are also to be studied.

For purposes of this problem, the cords were replaced by steel rods whose distributed weight was neglected. The original program was modified to provide the other two solutions, which are shown in Figure 14.19.

STRUCTURE EXAMPLE 14.10
NUMBER OF JOINTS 3
NUMBER OF SUPPORTS 2
NUMBER OF MEMBERS 2
NUMBER OF LOADINGS 1
TYPE PLANE TRUSS

Figure 14.19   The STRESS program for Example 14.10.

Figure 14.19 (Continued)

METHOD STIFFNESS
JOINT COORDINATES
1 X 0.0, Y 10.0, S
2 X 23.09406, Y 10.0, S
3 X 17.32051, Y 0.0
MEMBER INCIDENCES
1 1 3
2 2 3
MEMBER PROPERTIES, PRISMATIC
1 AX 2.0, IZ .667
2 AX 2.0, IZ .667
CONSTANTS E, 30000, ALL
LOADING 1
JOINT LOADS
3 FORCE Y −.10
TABULATE FORCES, DISTORTIONS
SOLVE THIS PART
LOADING 1
MEMBER FORCES

MEMBER	JOINT	AXIAL FORCE
1	1	−.0500000
1	3	.0500000
2	2	−.0866666
2	3	.0866666

LOADING 1
MEMBER DISTORTIONS

MEMBER	AXIAL DISTORTION
1	−.0099020
2	.0094925

MODIFICATION OF FIRST PART
CHANGES
JOINT COORDINATES
2 X 20.0
3 X 10.0
SOLVE THIS PART
MODIFICATION OF FIRST PART
LOADING 1
MEMBER FORCES

MEMBER	JOINT	AXIAL FORCE
1	1	−.0707107
1	3	.0707107
2	2	−.0707107
2	3	.0707107

MODIFICATION OF FIRST PART

```
LOADING 1
MEMBER DISTORTIONS
MEMBER      AXIAL DISTORTION
    1             .0000167
    2             .0000167
MODIFICATION OF LAST PART
CHANGES
JOINT COORDINATES
1 Y 0.0
SOLVE THIS PART
MODIFICATION OF LAST PART
LOADING 1
MEMBER FORCES
MEMBER     JOINT    AXIAL FORCE
    1        1        −.1000000
    1        3         .1000000
    2        2        −.1414214
    2        3         .1414214
MODIFICATION OF LAST PART
LOADING 1
MEMBER DISTORTIONS
MEMBER      AXIAL DISTORTION
    1             .0000167
    2             .0000333
FINISH
TIME USED: 3 SECONDS
```

14.8 Restrictions in Using STRESS

(1) Normally one statement is placed on a single punched data processing card.

(2) Statements can be continued onto any number of successive cards by placing a $ in column 1 of these successive cards.

(3) Free format exists. No particular column restrictions apply except that columns 73 through 80 must not be used. Statements may begin anywhere in columns 1 through 72.

(4) In any statement, including those continued onto more than one card, not more than five blanks may be left between words and/or numbers. The letters of words must not be separated by blanks.

(5) An * in column 1 indicates a comment card. It has no effect on the processing.

(6) All numeric data which can attain noninteger values must have decimal points. Member numbers and joint numbers are integers and must not contain decimal points.

(7) Commas may be inserted as word separators or omitted as desired. Words must be separated by at least a comma or a blank or both.

14.9 Diagnostic Error Messages

STRESS has been written to contain a generous number of diagnostic error messages. These messages have been carefully chosen and are self-explanatory. For this reason they have not been presented in detail here.

14.10 Summary

STRESS is a convenient and powerful tool for the structural engineer. It enables an individual who is not skilled in computer programming to solve problems of considerable complexity. As with other tools, one will become skilled in the use of STRESS through practice. The worked examples presented in this chapter are admittedly simple, but they were chosen deliberately to illustrate the features of STRESS without obscuring them in the details of complicated problems. A skilled structural engineer should be able to extend these ideas from the simple examples presented here to more complicated structures of practical engineering.

EXERCISES

1. A Pratt roof truss is shown in Fig. 14.20. The snow load on the roof results in the forces shown. Use STRESS to find the forces in all members.

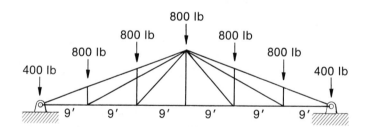

Figure 14.20

2. The Pratt truss of Exercise 1 is changed to a Howe truss as shown in Fig. 14.21. The dimensions and loadings remain the same as in Exercise 1. Use STRESS to find the forces in all members.

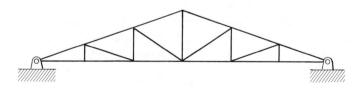

Figure 14.21

3. Figure 14.22 shows a truss in a structure used to support a signboard and experiencing a uniformly distributed wind load of 1000 lb. Use STRESS to find the forces in all members.

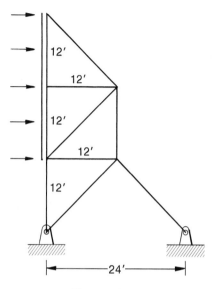

Figure 14.22

4. Use STRESS to analyze the Fink truss shown in Fig. 14.23.

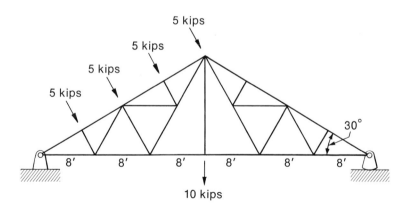

Figure 14.23

5. Use STRESS to find the forces in all members of the plane truss shown in Figure 14.24.

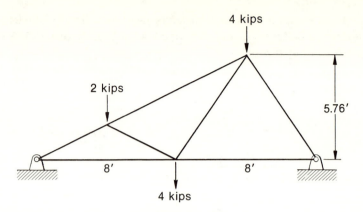

Figure 14.24

6. An equilateral tetrahedron, 5 ft on each side, rests on a horizontal surface and is subjected to a vertical force of 5 kips as shown in Fig. 14.25. Use STRESS to find the forces in all members.

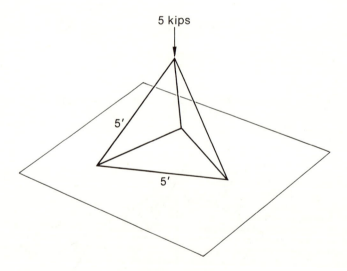

Figure 14.25

7. A space truss is in the form of a cube 10 ft on each side. To stiffen the structure, a diagonal member is connected across each face as shown in Fig. 14.26. A force $F = 1$ kip is applied to diagonally opposite corners AB on a line between these corners as shown. Use STRESS to find the forces in each member. Repeat with the force applied to corners CD.

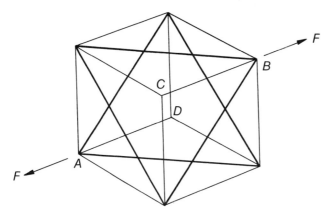

Figure 14.26

8. The diagonal members in Exercise 5 are rearranged as shown in Fig. 14.27. Analyze using STRESS for both conditions as in Exercise 7.

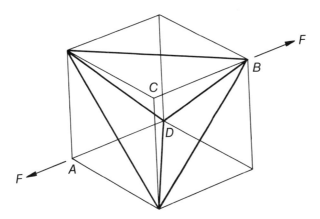

Figure 14.27

9. The space truss in Fig. 14.28 is one of a set of three proposed for a lunar land-ing module. The members *A*, *B*, *C*, and *D* are the same length and members *E* and *F* are also of equal length. Use STRESS to analyze the structure when the landing force *P* is 500 lb.

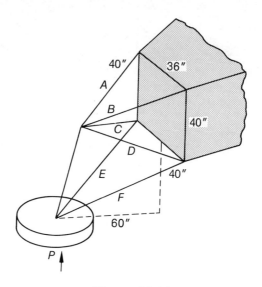

Figure 14.28

10. Figure 14.29 shows a vertical wall to which are connected three rods to form a non-symmetric tripod. Point O is the point on the wall where a perpendicular from P to the wall would strike the wall surface. The perpendicular distance from P to O is 15 ft. All distances shown are measured from point O. A vertical load of 1000 lb and a horizontal load of 500 lb are simultaneously applied to point P. Use STRESS to find the forces in all members.

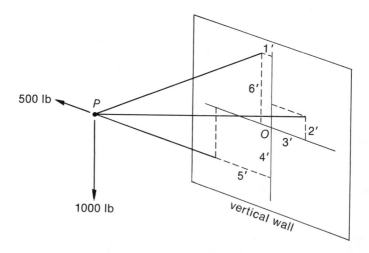

Figure 14.29

15

Hybrid Computers

15.1 Introduction

In preceding chapters we have looked at the use of both analog and digital computers as simulators of continuous systems. It was made apparent to the reader that each kind of computer suffers from certain disadvantages and enjoys certain advantages over the other. A rather obvious proposal immediately suggests itself. Why not combine both an analog and a digital computer together as a simulator to realize the advantages of both in a complementary way and thereby have a superior simulator? This has been tried and the resulting combination is called a *hybrid computer.* This concept is shown in block diagram form in Fig. 15.1.

Conceptually, at least, a hybrid computer can be thought of as a union of a stand-alone general purpose analog computer and a stand-alone general purpose digital computer. The union of these dissimilar machines requires an *interface.* This is a hardware device which provides for the conversion of analog to digital signals and for the conversion of digital to analog signals. It also provides logic capability and generates control signals to keep both machines synchronized. The interface, therefore, makes compatible machines out of otherwise incompatible ones. Most hybrid computers are formed in precisely this way. Sometimes both

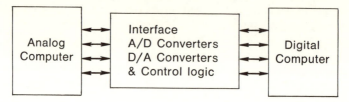

Figure 15.1   *The components of a hybrid computer.*

computers and interface hardware are supplied by a single manufacturer, while at other times all three are supplied by different makers. It is for reasons such as this that many hybrid computer installations are special, one-of-a-kind facilities, and their use is unique. Since it is more difficult to find a common area for discussion of hybrid computers than it is for either analog or digital computers, our discussion of hybrid computers will of necessity be quite general. The individual who is faced with the problem of working with a particular hybrid computer facility must look elsewhere for detailed information concerning his machine.

15.2   Advantages and Disadvantages Reviewed

As is true with most things, analog, digital, and hybrid computers are neither all good nor all bad. To help put the subject in proper perspective, and set the stage for our discussion, let us review briefly the characteristics and advantages and disadvantages of each type of computer.

The basic mechanism of analog computers is a set of electronic hardware in which variables are represented by time varying voltages. The advantages of this type of machine stem primarily from its inherent parallel nature. All tasks are performed simultaneously and this results in high speed performance which is unmatched by other computing methods. Also, the simultaneous action of all computing elements in the analog computer makes the run time independent of problem complexity. Furthermore, the inherent nature of analog computers provides excellent interaction between the user and the machine.

On the negative side, the scaling of analog computers is a tedious task which is always required and which no one enjoys. Also, the task of physically patching the plug board is a tiresome chore. Potentiometer setting is also disagreeable and none but the most sophisticated and expensive machines provide an automatic pot-set feature. Analog computers are simulators. This is their one special purpose for existing—their *raison d'etre*. Other types of computing tasks are not well suited to analog computers. The size of the problem that can be solved is frequently determined by the size of the analog computer available. Often skillful operators can find clever ways of getting by with less equipment, but the casual user does not ordinarily possess such skills.

Digital computers can be used as continuous system simulators as we have seen. When used in this fashion, the digital computer has a complement of functional elements similar to the analog computer, but the basic mechanism is a digital arithmetic unit which must be programmed to behave in the desired way.

It is easy to learn to use digital computers as simulators. Often the person who originates the problem can also do the required programming if the program is not too complex, and yet, the simulation languages available have appeal to professional programmers as well. A very real but often overlooked advantage of digital computers as simulators is their ready availability. Another often overlooked advantage is the somewhat self-documenting feature of digital computer printouts.

On the minus side is the fact that individual runs are slower on digital computers. This is not to say that total time required is longer — only that for individual runs. Also, there is frequently a lack of interaction between the man and the machine. Batch processing installations are particularly bad in this regard; the closed-shop effectively insulates the user from the machine. One does not get a "feel" for the system behavior by looking at a computer printout listing.

Hybrid computers try to combine what is good from both analog and digital computers. The problem being worked on is divided so as to take advantage of the capabilities of each. Those portions of a problem which require only modest accuracy or have high speed dynamics are assigned to the analog portion of the machine. Often if items of hardware from the system being simulated are included in the model, the interface between this hardware and the computer is best handled at the analog level. On the other hand, those portions of the problem which have low speed dynamics, require high accuracy, have decision-making elements or have nonlinear behavior are handled better in the digital portion of the machine. The digital computer memory has no analog competitor and is often used to advantage.

The advantage enjoyed by the hybrid computer lies entirely in its high speed capability. Because of this, it is frequently the only practical way of solving some types of large complicated problems. In such cases analog solutions would be too inaccurate and require too much skill on the part of the users, while digital computers would be too slow and thus too expensive.

Hybrid computers are not easy to use well. Considerable operator skill is required, and they are expensive to buy, operate, and maintain.

So we see that the choice — analog, digital, or hybrid — is not a simple one to make. Often the choice is made merely on the basis of availability. After all, any solution, even though obtained by less than ideal means, is better than no solution at all.

15.3 Why Use Hybrid Computers at All?

The hybrid computer comes under consideration whenever a problem has features, some of which are best satisfied by the capabilities of analog processing and others which are best satisfied by digital processing. Some examples are as follows:

(1) Hybrid computers are useful for studying dynamic systems described by simultaneous differential equations having widely differing parameters. Such systems give rise to both high and low frequency components in the solution.

(2) Some systems require the rapid solution of sets of simultaneous differential equations where the parameters or initial conditions are varied in some predictable way from one solution to the next. The solutions obtained from such a solution set might be used for optimization purposes.

(3) Some systems have combinations of both discretely changing and continuously changing variables. Sampled data control systems are of this type. The hybrid approach is ideal in such cases.

(4) Systems containing transport delays are nicely handled by hybrid computers. The system dynamics is assigned to the analog portion and the delays and associated controls to the digital portion.

15.4 Organization of a Hybrid Computer

A hybrid computer is not a machine which must be constructed along set lines. Considering the choice of available hardware, one sees that a number of different equipment combinations is possible. The type of problems to be solved has some bearing on what equipment is actually brought together, but any hybrid facility would be expected to contain some mixture of the following components:

(1) A digital section having arithmetic and logic capability with information storage provisions.

(2) An analog section having a complement of adders, high speed integrators, multipliers, and function generators which can all operate simultaneously or in parallel.

(3) An interface to provide communication between the analog and digital sections. This interface must convert analog voltage signals to equivalent digital information for transmission to the digital section. Conversely it must also convert digital information to analog form for transmission to the analog section.

(4) The device must be programmable. The timing of events in both analog and digital sections must be synchronized. This capacity ordinarily comes from the digital section.

(5) Input and output equipment must be provided. This is required for program checkout and debugging, as well as for communication with the outside world.

Typically, in use, the high speed analog section will be found doing integration of linear or nonlinear differential equations where accuracy is less important, while the digital section will be performing precise low speed calculations of slowly varying variables. Not all integration needs to be done rapidly. Numerical integration in the digital portion might be done more satisfactorily at slower speed if accuracy is important. It is not clear that function generation is best done one place or the other; either analog or digital might be used. The results of computed data will obviously be stored in the digital portion if such storage is required. Also, logical decisions based on computed results will be done in digital fashion.

It is obvious that a hybrid system does not require an expensive, highly sophisticated digital computer. Ordinarily the demands on it are relatively modest and a small low cost digital capability would be sufficient for most purposes.

The interface between the analog and digital sections requires, ordinarily, a capability to handle binary numbers of not more than 12 or 13 binary digits plus algebraic sign. This will equal or exceed the accuracy limitations of the analog section. Providing more capability than this would be wasteful and unnecessary.

Since the analog section operates in parallel, a number of analog to digital channels are required. This permits simultaneous sampling of many items of analog information, with the results stored in analog track and store units. The contents of these units can be converted sequentially by a multiplexer and one analog to digital converter into digital form and then stored sequentially in the digital memory. From another approach, separate analog to digital converters could be used on each channel with no need for analog storage.

The digital to analog conversion can also be accomplished in one of two ways. If separate digital to analog conversion channels are used, each with its own converter, the consecutive digital values of each variable are supplied to the particular converter input and converted to analog voltages with the output being updated at the converter operating rate. The other approach is to use a multiplexer to supply input signals to one digital to analog converter with the outputs stored in analog track-and-store devices between updating times.

The control feature of the hybrid computer must be able to provide rapid control over the mode of operation of the analog section based on computed results. This implies the use of electronic switching rather than relay switching to fully exploit the capabilities of the machine. Relay switching could, at times, cause unnecessary delays. The control should also permit automatic read-in and read-out of data and results. The need for rapid control of the analog computer section also suggests the need for automatic coefficient potentiometer setting under the control of the digital controller.

If the hybrid computer is comprised of a general purpose analog computer coupled to a general purpose digital computer by means of some interface hardware, the combination provides a really wide range of capability. A very large number of possible digital computers are available for such implementation. The choice determines the effectiveness of the resulting hybrid combination, and yet it is possible to select a more powerful digital machine than is actually needed to properly coordinate with and complement the analog computer. The interface and digital computer will together limit the over-all performance of the hybrid machine, and the selection and design of these elements must be done carefully.

At least one manufacturer has noted the difficulties of forming a hybrid computer by joining together a general purpose analog computer and a general purpose digital computer. As a result, special analog and digital computers have been built with associated interface hardware all designed for hybrid use. By specifically designing the equipment for hybrid operation, many of the difficulties of the separate computer concept are avoided. The resulting hybrid computer is a special purpose machine whose use is limited to hybrid simulation of continuous systems. This is accomplished with considerable efficiency, however.

15.5   Analog to Digital and Digital to Analog Converters

A detailed functional understanding of analog to digital (A/D) converters and digital to analog (D/A) converters requires more than a cursory inspection of the electric circuits of which they are contrived. Our policy, in the previous chapters of this book, has been not to present detailed circuit studies in the main body of the text, but rather to include information of this kind in the Appendix. We continue this policy again here, and assume that A/D and D/A converters have been designed and developed and are available. The required A/D and D/A conversions for hybrid operation can be achieved in such equipment. Some typical A/D and D/A conversion schemes are presented in the Appendix for those readers who wish more detailed information.

15.6   Planning for Hybrid Simulation

The individual who is accustomed to using either analog or digital computers might be somewhat surprised by the additional amount of planning required to effectively use hybrid computers. This need for increased planning stems from two sources. First, the size of problems simulated on hybrid computers, typically, are larger than those simulated on either analog computers or on digital computers. Second, the fact that hybrid simulation requires the joining together of two technologies—analog and digital—at both the machine level and at the human level also necessitates additional planning.

Analog computer users are accustomed to on-the-spot solutions to problems of implementation. This is the nature of this kind of work. In dealing with hybrid machines, programmers and operators both must abandon this impromptu approach for a preplanned approach. Digital computer programmers and users will also find a quite different set of problems than they customarily encounter, which must be given attention—scaling, for example.

For planning purposes, analog computer users have used symbolic function diagrams, as presented early in this book. Digital computer users have become accustomed to using logic flow diagrams to help them in their planning. Useful as these diagrams are, they are insufficient for hybrid computer planning. Some other type of planning diagram is needed.

Figure 15.2 shows a PERT type chart which has proved to be useful for hybrid planning purposes. The word PERT stands for "Program Evaluation and Review Technique." This chart shows the interaction that must occur between the various functional tasks needed to solve the problem.

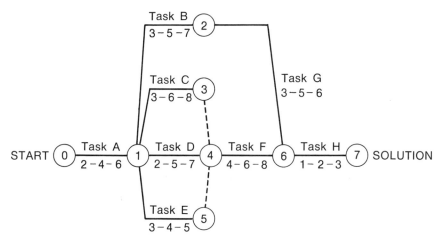

Figure 15.2 *A PERT chart for planning.*

In the PERT chart of Fig. 15.2 there are eight functional tasks that must be completed before a solution is obtained. These tasks must be completed in a particular way, and each task requires a certain expected time for completion. The problem solution begins with Task A, which must be completed before any other task can commence. Task A nominally requires 4 time units for completion, but may be finished in as little as 2 time units and may take as long as 6 time units. The numbers 2–4–6 on the chart alongside the task line represent this time information. Tasks C, D, and E may be done in parallel, but all must be completed before Task F may be started. Task B must precede Task G. Tasks F and G must precede Task H. The nominal, minimum, and maximum times expected to complete each task are shown alongside each task line as in Task A.

In a particular problem the required tasks must be identified and appropriate descriptive labels placed on the PERT diagram. This kind of planning chart will help the planner to organize his work so that the program objectives are met and so that the proper allocation of computing tasks to the analog section and digital section can be made.

Every problem to be solved on a computer will have general and specific objectives. As planning proceeds, these objectives must be kept in mind to be sure that they are not overlooked. The PERT chart will also help in this consideration.

It will not always be immediately apparent how much and what kind of equipment will be needed to effect a solution. After some consideration, the planner may decide that a hybrid solution is not required; perhaps only an analog solution or only a digital solution is sufficient. As another possibility, it may be determined that the problem can be segmented and solved separately—part being done in analog fashion and a separate part being done digitally—with no need for combined hybrid simulation. These conclusions can be drawn only after careful planning.

One should always be on the lookout for simpler ways of achieving the desired results. As a general rule, the simpler the simulator, the better it will be. Do not use a more complicated procedure than is necessary to accomplish the desired task within the allowable error.

The purpose of creating a simulator of a system on any kind of a computer is to be able to conduct experiments. Therefore, when planning a simulation study, the desired experiments should be kept in mind. Provision must be made to include the necessary features in the simulator that will permit the desired experiments to be performed. It would be unfortunate if a simulator were arranged so that necessary experiments were prevented.

Errors can arise in both the analog and the digital sections of a hybrid computer, and the planner of a hybrid computer simulator must be aware of these sources of error. In the analog section errors occur because of component imperfections. Both static and dynamic errors are introduced from this source. Accuracies of 0.01% are often claimed, but this is unusual; more typical accuracies are closer to 1%. In the digital section, errors also occur. The digital computer is thought of as being more accurate than an analog computer, and this is generally true. Digital devices are not error free, however. Errors occur due to truncation and round off. Moreover, errors also are introduced when a continuous system is represented discretely (sampling of continuous data at discrete time periods introduces such errors). Finally, there are errors which occur due to the inability of analysts to describe system behavior exactly. Inasmuch as any model can only represent a portion of a system, the model will, at best, be an approximation.

The user of a hybrid computer must assign computing tasks to the analog and digital sections of the machine. This assignment must be made with due consideration being given to the capabilities of the two sections, the errors associated with each, and the time required by each. Most often a compromise must be reached. The judgment of the planner is the best basis for making these assignments and judgment is best developed by experience. Alternate formulations of the mathematical description of system behavior should also be given consideration since one formulation may have decided advantages over another. For example, one formulation may be easier to implement, while another may provide more useful output information. Such subtleties should not be ignored.

Analog computers, operating in parallel as they do, perform their assigned tasks very quickly. Digital computers, operating serially, perform much more slowly from a real-time point of view. This incompatibility causes severe problems of coordination and stringent time restrictions are thus imposed. Input data lines to the digital section must be sampled, the desired calculations performed, and the results buffered to output data lines within definite periods of time. If the simulator must wait for these operations to be accomplished, valid results are not possible.

As has been indicated earlier, one cannot afford to consider every alternative before trying any of them. Every solution is a compromise in some way. A good analyst will conceive some procedures and give them a try. If they are successful, use them. If not, that is the time to spend further time looking for other ways to solve the problem. A truly optimum simulator is rarely achieved—an acceptable one is the goal to be sought. Good planning will always be done with this in mind.

15.7 Programming for Hybrid Simulation

The programming of a hybrid computer is a combination of analog computer programming and digital computer programming. The programming of the analog section is not significantly different in a hybrid computer than it is in an ordinary analog computer. There are a few differences that deserve mention, however.

The presence of a digital computer as a controller permits the time sharing of items of analog equipment. This is not possible in conventional analog computers, but it is possible in hybrid computers.

Decision making and other logical operations are usually better done in the digital section. Analog comparators, for example, have much poorer performance characteristics than digital comparators.

D/A and A/D converters must receive their input signals and deliver their output signals at restricted voltage levels. This imposes a magnitude scaling restriction on the analog section that is not present when using analog computers alone.

The inherent accuracy of the digital section can be lost by careless analog programming. Since this accuracy is one of the important reasons for considering hybrid simulation in the first place, it would be unfortunate if it were thrown away by the failure of the analog programmer to use proper care.

A feature of hybrid computers not available to the programmer of a conventional analog computer is the automatic control which the digital section provides. Variables can be automatically rescaled, parameters can be automatically reset, and initial conditions can be automatically modified.

In summary then, we can state that hybrid simulation provides additional capability to the analog programmer beyond that with which he is normally accustomed with only the imposition of modest restrictions. As we shall see, however, the digital computer programmer is much more significantly affected by hybrid simulation.

The typical digital computer programmer, accustomed to the wide dynamic range of floating point arithmetic capability and absence of timing restraints, finds himself in a quite new environment when performing hybrid computer programming. The effects of system errors are much more apparent than he is accustomed to seeing, and much more serious. Digital computer programs are to a large extent self-documenting. The analog section of a hybrid computer, at least, is not self-documenting and attention must be given to providing records of programming decisions.

The programming of a hybrid computer is often referred to as real-time programming. This term is used to refer to the fact that the programmer must constantly be aware of what is occurring in the computer as a function of time. When programming a digital computer, the programmer only pays attention to the elapsed time required to perform operations and pays no attention to the time sequencing of events. Not so in the hybrid computer. Often it is necessary to sample certain items of data at specific time intervals. Other items must be sampled as a function of the state of the simulated system. Branching is often introduced into a hybrid program, depending on the availability of certain items of data, doing one thing if data are available and something else if they are not.

In general, the timing problems of real-time programming are the ones that cause greatest difficulty. Subprograms must communicate with each other at proper times. When errors occur for such reasons, they are difficult to trace, to find, and to correct.

The interrelationships between subprograms, main program, and analog program require much more logical programming than is needed in non-real-time programs. Again errors occurring here are difficult to find and repair.

The programming of a hybrid computer must be approached from both the analog and the digital points of view. As has been indicated, the analog programming for a hybrid computer will not be greatly different from conventional analog programming. However, because of the timing restraints of real-time operation, the digital programming for a hybrid computer will be quite different from conventional digital computer programming. The digital programming can be done using machine language, symbolic assembly language, a problem oriented language such as FORTRAN, or a special simulation language such as CSSL. Machine language is numerical, difficult to learn, difficult to use, and awkward to debug. Assembly language is easier to use, but programs written in it require processing into equivalent machine language by the computer prior to running the simulation study. Likewise, programs written in problem oriented language require conversion into a machine language equivalent by the computer using a compiler program. Program oriented languages are easy to use because that is why they were devised. Some of these languages are very sophisticated in that they are capable of performing complicated programming tasks with little effort, and they contain error diagnosing capabilities. Problem oriented languages frequently resemble the technical language used by humans to describe problems to each other.

A special simulation language such as CSSL or MIMIC is extremely easy to use for digital computer programming. Some hybrid computer manufacturers have adapted special simulation languages for hybrid use. Electronic Associates, Inc., has developed a language called HYTRAN which is intended specifically for hybrid computer use. Such languages ease the programming burden considerably and should be considered seriously by anyone attempting hybrid programming.

15.8 Summary

Because of the unique nature of most hybrid computer installations, no attempt has been made to describe hybrid computers in detail. Furthermore, no attempt has been made to show how hybrid computers might be used to solve specific problems. Such a discussion or presentation would have very little value at this point. Each application is specific, with very little of a general nature that can be transferred to another problem or another installation. For these reasons this discussion has presented only the general principles, difficulties, and capabilities of hybrid computation.

It is possible that for a restricted class of problems, hybrid computation offers the most economical and efficient means for solving them. Hybrid computers are more difficult to use than either analog or digital computers alone. This difficulty stems primarily from the associated timing problems and related programming difficulties. Skilled persons, however, can often make effective use of hybrid computers. Sometimes hybrid computation offers the only practical means of solution to certain kinds of problems.

Hybrid computers have found numerous areas of usefulness. In the aerospace industry, studies have been made of space vehicle simulations, aircraft adaptive control systems, nose cone ablative behavior, and terrain avoidance systems. In the chemical process industry, studies have been made of chemical reactors, heat exchangers, and process control systems. Simulators have been built to optimize chemical plant operations. In bioengineering, EKG and EEG data analysis studies have been successfully conducted. In communication, studies of wave propagation, antenna pattern calculations, and learning and recognition have been effectively made.

Hybrid computers have their place in the array of simulation tools offered to the engineer and scientist. They will, no doubt, continue to find areas of application where they are clearly superior, as well as areas where they must yield to other competitors. The wise user will be aware of their capabilities and limitations.

Appendix

A.1   Introduction

While it is possible to use an electronic analog computer (EAC) effectively for simulating physical systems without understanding the operation of the individual components, some users will want a more complete explanation of how the various analog computer elements function. For this reason, the underlying theory of operation of some of the EAC elements is presented in this appendix.

A.2   The Potentiometer

A potentiometer actually consists of a resistor having a fixed contact available at each end and a sliding contact. The sliding contact can be moved from one extreme to the other. The resistance may be distributed linearly with distance along the length of the potentiometer, or it may be arranged in some prescribed non-linear fashion. Potentiometers are available having either rectilinear motion or rotary motion. Rotary types are arranged for either limited or continuous motion. Some limited-motion rotary potentiometers are of the multiple-turn type.

Potentiometers are simple, rugged, and dependable. They are commonly used for multiplying a time varying input voltage by a constant whose value is less than unity. The circuit for such multiplication is shown in Fig. A.1. In this figure, R represents the total fixed resistance of the potentiometer across which the variable input voltage e_i is impressed. R_v is the adjustable resistance across which the output terminals are connected and across which the output voltage e_o appears. One terminal is common to both input and output. The resistance of the load is R_o. Equation A.1 gives the relationship between e_o and e_i if R_o is assumed to be infinite.

$$e_o = \frac{R_v}{R} e_i = k e_i \qquad (A.1)$$

Equation A.1 shows that the voltage input e_i can be multiplied by a constant $\left(k = \frac{R_v}{R}\right)$ to give the output voltage e_o. Note particularly that this constant cannot exceed unity, but it may take on any value between zero and unity inclusive. If the load resistance R_o is finite so that the current i_o is not zero, Eq. A.1 does not accurately express the relationship between input and output voltages. The discrepancy between Eq. A.1 and the actual relationship between e_o and e_i is dependent upon the magnitudes of R_o, R, and the potentiometer setting R_v.

When potentiometers are used as multipliers as described above, steps must be taken to eliminate errors caused by loading effects. This can be accomplished in several ways. One method that is used to prevent these errors from entering the computer solution of a problem is to set the constant multiplying potentiometers with their loads attached and then to measure the actual resulting multiplying factor by some external null voltage measuring device such as a resistance bridge. Another method that is sometimes used is to employ an isolating amplifier on the output of each potentiometer. A cathode-follower tube amplifier or an emitter follower transistor amplifier having unity gain are two such isolating devices. Amplifiers of this type may be designed to have a low output impedance with a high input impedance and when used in this manner, they produce the desired isolating effect.

The foregoing discussion describes how a variable input voltage e_i can be multiplied by a constant multiplier $\left(k = \frac{R_v}{R}\right)$ to give a proportional but reduced output voltage e_o. If two varying inputs are to be multiplied to give a corresponding variable output, then it is necessary to use some sort of positioning system that will

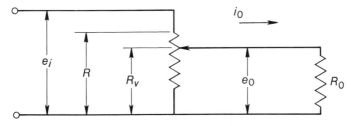

Figure A.1 *The potentiometer with load.*

position the potentiometer slider in such a way that its position is always proportional to one variable, while the input voltage e_i is always proportional to the other
variable. This is done in a device called a servo multiplier, which is described
below.

A.3 Analog Multipliers and Dividers

An analog computer multiplier can be thought of as a device by means of which
two input voltages (which may both be time varying) can be multiplied together
to give a voltage proportional to the product of the two input voltages. The resulting product should be correct both with respect to magnitude and algebraic sign.
If either of the two input voltages is negative but not both, the output is negative.
If both inputs are positive or both negative, then the output is positive. Multipliers
have been devised based on many different principles of operation. Two of these
will be described here — the *servo multiplier* and the *quarter square multiplier.*

Figure A.2 shows a diagram of a servo multiplier. We wish to have an output
voltage z which is proportional to the product of voltages x and y. Potentiometer A
is called the *follow-up potentiometer* and B is called the *multiplying potentiometer.*
The details of the servo positioning system are not pertinent to this discussion.
It is sufficient to say that it is a positioning device arranged so that the voltage
picked up by wiper A and fed back to the input of the servo system, when compared
with the voltage y, causes the servo system to operate in the direction that will
minimize the difference between the voltage at A and the voltage y. Neglecting the
time required for the servo system to adjust its position, the voltage picked up by
wiper A will be equal to the voltage y at all times. The dotted lines in the diagram
represent mechanical linkages. Potentiometers A and B are mechanically coupled

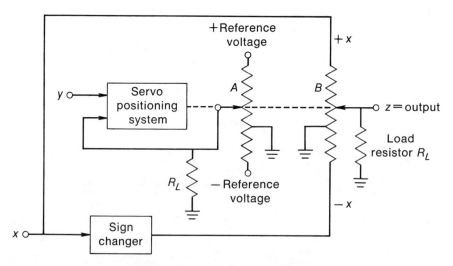

Figure A.2 *The servo multiplier.*

so that their wipers move together. All voltages are measured with respect to ground. The voltage x is applied to the upper end of potentiometer B and, with its sign changed, is applied to the lower end of B also. Both potentiometers are linear, that is, with negligible loading and constant applied voltage, the voltage at the wiper arm with respect to ground is proportional to the distance by which the wiper arm is displaced from the grounded midpoint. It can be shown that the output z of the servo multiplier of Fig. A.2 is given by

$$z = \frac{xy}{\text{Reference Voltage}} \qquad\qquad \text{(A.2)}$$

The resistor marked R_L has resistance equal to that of the load resistor so that errors due to loading will be eliminated. The load resistor of Fig. A.2 represents the total composite load on the multiplying potentiometer. With the resistor R_L equal to the load resistor, the follow-up potentiometer will be loaded in the same manner as the multiplying potentiometer. This loading will cause the position of wiper A to be slightly different than it would be if no loading were present. This difference in position is, of course, also present in the position of wiper B. Because of the loading caused by the load resistor, however, this difference in position is precisely what is needed to cause the output to be correct!

The servo multiplier can be used for dividing by rearranging and, as shown in Fig. A.3, the output is given by

$$z = \frac{(-\,\text{Reference Voltage})x}{y} \qquad\qquad \text{(A.3)}$$

Now let us suppose for purposes of discussion that two voltages are available and we wish to obtain their product. Figure A.4 shows a block diagram of the

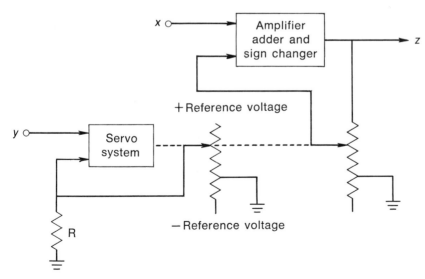

Figure A.3 A servo divider.

quarter square multiplier. An adder and a subtractor are shown; the output of the adder is $x + y$ and the output of the subtractor is $x - y$. If these results are each squared the output of one squarer is

$$(x + y)^2 = x^2 + y^2 + 2xy \qquad (A.4)$$

and the output of the other squarer is

$$(x - y)^2 = x^2 + y^2 - 2xy \qquad (A.5)$$

If the outputs of these two squarers are then subtracted, the final output is obtained. Therefore, subtracting Eq. A.5 from Eq. A.4 yields

$$(x^2 + y^2 + 2xy) - (x^2 + y^2 - 2xy) = 4xy \qquad (A.6)$$

Provided that this result is then divided by 4, the output voltage will be equal to the product of the two input voltages. This product has the correct algebraic sign for all combinations of input signs. The squaring operation is usually accomplished by some nonlinear function generator. The quarter square multiplier can also be used for dividing by proper modifications.

A.4 The Nonlinear Potentiometer

It is often convenient to have potentiometers available whose behavior is nonlinear. These devices can find considerable utility in simulating nonlinear systems and for generating nonlinear functions. Consider the potentiometer card shown in Fig. A.5. Wire is wrapped around this card to form a potentiometer of variable width. The wire is of uniform resistivity and cross section, and the card is uniformly wound with closely spaced wire. The output voltage e_o is measured with respect to ground and the potentiometer is energized with the battery E. The total resistance of the potentiometer is R and the variable portion of the potentiometer measured from the grounded end is R_v. Assume that there are n turns on the potentiometer card and the card has length l. The turns density is, therefore, n/l turns per unit length. Hence, in incremental length Δx there are $(n/l)\Delta x$ turns. As the slide moves through the distance Δx, there is a change in resistance R_v equal to ΔR_v. This change in resistance is given in Eq. A.7

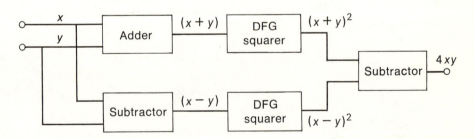

Figure A.4 *Block diagram of the quarter square multiplier.*

$$\Delta R_v = 2w(x)\rho \frac{n}{l} \Delta x \qquad (A.7)$$

where ρ is the resistance per unit length of wire and $w(x)$ is the width of the card at position x. Equation A.7 can be rewritten as

$$\frac{\Delta R_v}{\Delta x} = \frac{2w(x)\rho n}{l} \approx \frac{dR_v}{dx} \qquad (A.8)$$

The output voltage e_o will be a fraction of the total battery voltage E as shown in Eq. A.9 if we assume no loading effects. Equation A.9 is the same as Eq. A.1

$$e_o = \frac{R_v}{R} E \qquad (A.9)$$

Solving Eq. A.9 for R_v gives

$$R_v = \frac{R}{E} e_o \qquad (A.10)$$

If the output voltage e_o is to vary according to some function of x, then we may write

$$e_o = f(x)$$

Differentiating this with respect to x gives

$$\frac{de_o}{dx} = \frac{df(x)}{dx} \qquad (A.11)$$

Next, differentiating Eq. A.10 with respect to x to obtain

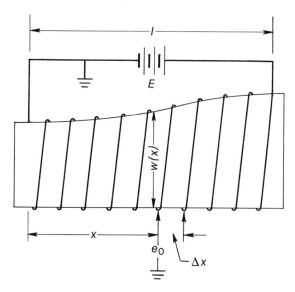

Figure A.5 *The nonlinear potentiometer.*

$$\frac{dR_v}{dx} = \frac{R}{E}\frac{de_o}{dx} \tag{A.12}$$

and then substituting Eqs. A.8 and A.11 into Eq. A.12 yields

$$\frac{2w(x)\rho n}{I} \approx \frac{R}{E}\frac{df(x)}{dx} \tag{A.13}$$

which when solved for w gives

$$w(x) \approx \frac{RI}{2\rho En}\frac{df(x)}{dx} \tag{A.14}$$

It can be seen from Eq. A.14 that the width of the card of Fig. A.5 as a function of x must be proportional to the derivative with respect to x of the desired function $e_o = f(x)$.

For example, if we are seeking an output voltage proportional to the sine of an angle, the potentiometer wire may be wound on a card shaped in such a fashion that its width is proportional to the derivative of the sine of the angle (see Fig. A.6). As the slider moves from the 0° position toward the 180° position, the voltage e_o will vary sinusoidally from zero volts to a maximum of $+E$ volts and back to zero. If the wiper continues to move from the 180° position to the 360° position, the voltage e_o will vary sinusoidally from zero volts to $-E$ volts and back to zero. In this manner, an output voltage is produced having a magnitude that is proportional to the sign of the angular displacement of the wiper arm from the zero position. Note that the algebraic sign is correct also, being positive between zero degrees and 180° and negative between 180° and 360°.

The same potentiometer can be used to generate the cosine of the angle by mechanically displacing the wiper by 90°. Commercially available potentiometers

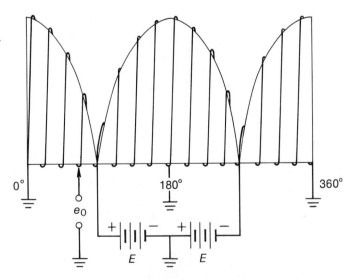

Figure A.6 *A tapered potentiometer.*

of this type generally carry two wiper arms that are mechanically displaced from each other by 90°. In this manner, voltages that are proportional to both the sine and the cosine of the input angle are available. In its actual construction, the sine-cosine potentiometer is built in circular fashion so that continuous rotation is possible. Following the same sort of reasoning, tapered potentiometers can be built to generate many other types of functions.

A.5 Operational Amplifiers

The development of high-gain dc amplifiers was a necessary precedent to the electronic analog computer that we know today. These high-gain dc amplifiers are generally called *operational amplifiers.* As we shall see, they are used in various electrical networks to produce high-accuracy mathematical operations. These operational amplifiers often incorporate internal positive feedback loops in order to achieve extremely high gain. In addition to having very high gain, these devices have very high input impedance and low output impedance. The features of very high gain and very high input impedance are basic to the developments that follow.

Ordinarily, operational amplifiers are employed in combination with some type of feedback impedance. The number of stages of gain in operational amplifiers is usually odd so that there is a sign reversal between input and output voltage. This means that through the feedback impedance, negative feedback is achieved. This negative feedback tends to produce stability. Figure A.7(a) is a block diagram of an operational amplifier with external input and feedback impedances. Figure A.7(b) illustrates the same device but with a conventional symbol used for the high-gain dc amplifier. When in use, operational amplifiers, such as the one shown in Fig. A.7, must be operated so that the output voltage does not exceed some specific limit. This insures that the amplifier will not saturate and the operation will be linear. This limit is called the *reference voltage* and is commonly 10, 50, or 100 V, depending upon the make of computer being used. If we limit the output voltage to be not more than 50 V and if the gain A of the amplifier is 100,000, then the input voltage e_1 cannot exceed 0.5 mV. This quantity is negligibly small compared with usual signal voltage magnitudes, and is called a *virtual zero.* Therefore,

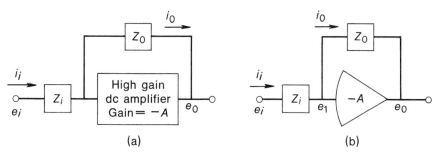

(a)   (b)

Figure A.7 *The operational amplifier.*

for simplicity, we shall assume that e_1 is zero and that the current entering the amplifier is also zero. Under these conditions $i_i = i_o$. From the circuit of Fig. A.7(b) we may write

$$i_i = \frac{e_i - e_1}{Z_i} \tag{A.15}$$

which reduces to

$$i_i = \frac{e_i}{Z_i} \tag{A.16}$$

since e_1 is assumed to be zero. In similar fashion, we may write

$$i_o = \frac{e_1 - e_o}{Z_o}$$

which reduces to

$$i_o = \frac{-e_o}{Z_o} \tag{A.17}$$

for the same reason as before. Substituting Eqs. A.16 and A.17 into Eq. A.15 gives

$$\frac{e_i}{Z_i} = \frac{-e_o}{Z_o} \tag{A.18}$$

Solving for e_o, we find

$$e_o = \frac{-Z_o}{Z_i} e_i \tag{A.19}$$

Equation A.19 is the general fundamental equation for the operation of the operational amplifier. This equation shows that the output voltage of the operational amplifier in Fig. A.7 is equal to the input voltage multiplied by the ratio of the feedback to input impedance and with the sign reversed.

Action of the operational amplifier is such that the output current i_o is forced to be the same as the input current i_i because of the extremely high input impedance of the amplifier. Furthermore, the voltage e_1 is forced to be zero by negative feedback action through the external impedance Z_o. Also, the output voltage is related to the input voltage by Eq. A.19.

A.6 Electrical Adders

In electrical adders the quantities that are usually added are voltages. The simplest form of voltage adder would be two batteries in series as shown in Fig. A.8. In this simple circuit the total voltage, E_o, is equal to the sum of E_1 and E_2. A more sophisticated and a much more useful adder would result if the batteries were replaced by potentiometers (see Fig. A.9). Figure A.9 shows a more flexible adder than Fig. A.8, but even this potentiometric adder is impractical for use in an actual computer.

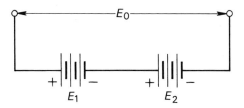

Figure A.8 *The addition of voltages in series.*

Consider the circuit of Fig. A.10. This figure shows a parallel resistor type of adder. It can be demonstrated that if, in Fig. A.10, $i_o = 0$ and if $R_1 = R_2 = R_n$, then the output voltage e_o is

$$e_o = (e_1 + e_2 + \cdots + e_n)\,\frac{1}{n} \qquad\qquad (A.20)$$

Now let us modify the circuit of Fig. A.10 to that of A.11, which includes an operational amplifier with feedback resistor. As in previous considerations, the input current to the amplifier and the input voltage to the amplifier are assumed to be zero. Under these conditions we may write

$$i_o = \frac{-e_o}{R_o}$$

$$i_1 = \frac{e_1}{R_1}$$

$$i_2 = \frac{e_2}{R_2} \qquad\qquad (A.21)$$

$$\vdots$$

$$i_n = \frac{e_n}{R_n}$$

We may also write

$$i_1 + i_2 + \cdots + i_n = i_o \qquad\qquad (A.22)$$

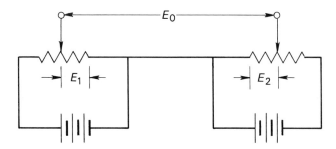

Figure A.9 *The potentiometric voltage adder.*

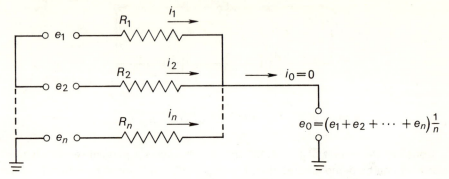

Figure A.10 *A parallel resistor voltage adder.*

When Eqs. A.21 are substituted into Eq. A.22, we get

$$\frac{e_1}{R_1} + \frac{e_2}{R_2} + \cdots + \frac{e_n}{R_n} = -\frac{e_o}{R_o} \tag{A.23}$$

and if all resistors are made equal, we see that

$$e_1 + e_2 + \cdots + e_n = -e_o \tag{A.24}$$

Comparing Eq. A.24 and Eq. A.20, we see that the adder of Fig. A.11 is a much more satisfactory one. In this latter case, the output is equal to the sum of the input voltages, where in the former case the output voltage was equal to the sum of the input voltages divided by the number of input voltages. In the adder of Fig. A.11 there is also a sign change, which is often a useful feature.

A.7   Integrators

Consider Fig. A.12, which shows a circuit containing a capacitor only. In this simple circuit the voltage developed across the capacitor, as a function of time, is given by

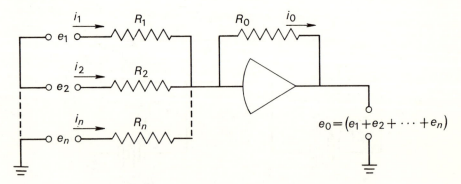

Figure A.11 *An adder with operational amplifier.*

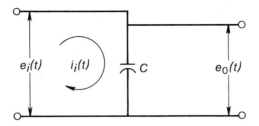

Figure A.12 *The capacitor integrator.*

$$e_o(t) = \frac{1}{C} \int i_i(t)\, dt \qquad\qquad \text{(A.25)}$$

If by some means the current $i_i(t)$ can be made proportional to the input voltage $e_i(t)$, then the output voltage will be proportional to the time integral of the input voltage. In other words, if

$$i_i(t) = Ke_i(t) \qquad\qquad \text{(A.26)}$$

then Eq. A.25 becomes

$$e_o(t) = \frac{K}{C} \int e_i(t)\, dt \qquad\qquad \text{(A.27)}$$

We know from our knowledge of dc electric circuit theory that current is proportional to voltage only when the circuit contains pure resistance. Neglecting all transient effects, we might try to make the integrator of Fig. A.12 practical by adding a resistor in series; this is shown in Fig. A.13. In order that the current in Fig. A.13 be proportional to the voltage $e_i(t)$, it is necessary that the voltage $e_o(t)$ be made very small because

$$i_i(t) = \frac{e_i(t) - e_o(t)}{R} \qquad\qquad \text{(A.28)}$$

This can be accomplished by changing the values of R and C. When this is at-

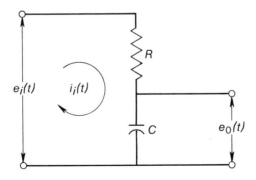

Figure A.13 *The R-C integrator.*

tempted, however, the useful signal $e_o(t)$ approaches zero and hence the R-C integrator of Fig. A.13 is impractical.

To improve the performance, we might consider adding an operational amplifier to the R-C integrator as shown in Fig. A.14. In this figure, the resistor R is the input element of the device and the capacitor C is the feedback element. The operation of the operational amplifier is such as to force the voltage at e_1 to be zero as described previously. This means that the current through resistor R is given by

$$i_i(t) = \frac{e_i(t)}{R} \tag{A.29}$$

Furthermore, the current $i_o(t)$ is forced by high input impedance of the operational amplifier to be equal to $i_i(t)$. The output voltage $e_o(t)$ is measured directly across the capacitor, and hence is given by

$$e_o(t) = \frac{-1}{C} \int i_o(t) \, dt = \frac{-1}{C} \int i_i(t) \, dt \tag{A.30}$$

Substituting Eq. A.29 into Eq. A.30 gives Eq. A.31

$$e_o(t) = -\frac{1}{RC} \int e_i(t) \, dt \tag{A.31}$$

which shows the output voltage to be proportional to the negative of the input voltage integrated with respect to time.

The results obtained above can also be obtained by a different approach using the concepts of operational impedance and the ideas developed earlier. In particular, we make use of Eq. A.19. Applying this equation to the integrator of Fig. A.14, we see that the input impedance is a resistor and the feedback impedance is a capacitor. In operational form,

$$Z_i(s) = R \quad \text{and} \quad Z_o(s) = \frac{1}{Cs} \tag{A.32}$$

Transforming Eq. A.19 into operational form and substituting Eq. A.32 into the transformed equation gives

$$e_o(s) = -\frac{1}{RCs} e_i(s) = -\frac{1}{RC} \frac{e_i(s)}{s} \tag{A.33}$$

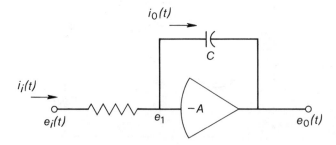

Figure A.14 The R-C integrator with operational amplifier.

in which the voltages e_o and e_i appear as functions of s. Taking the inverse Laplace transformation of Eq. A.33 yields

$$e_o(t) = -\frac{1}{RC} \int e_i(t) \, dt \qquad \text{(A.34)}$$

in which the input and output voltages appear as functions of time. Observe that Eq. A.34 is the same as Eq. A.31.

A.8 Nonlinear Function Generation

In the simulation of physical systems on electronic analog computers, it is sometimes necessary to simulate various nonlinearities. One common method for doing this is through the use of biased diodes. Consider the circuit of Fig. A.15. Notice in this figure that the voltages E_1 and E_2 act in a series-aiding counterclockwise direction around the closed loop, however, current cannot flow around this loop because of the blocking action of the two diodes. Assume that the input voltage e_i starts from zero and increases in a positive direction. This voltage tends to cause current to flow from left to right in the figure. When e_i is zero, no current will flow through either diode; however, when e_i becomes large enough to overcome the voltage E_1, the current will then commence to flow through the upper diode and through resistor R to ground. Before this current flows, the output terminal is connected to ground through the resistor R, and hence the voltage E_o is zero. When this current flows through R, a voltage drop occurs and e_o is then positive with respect to ground. If, on the other hand, e_i starts from zero and goes negative, no current will flow until e_i exceeds E_2, whereupon current will flow from ground through the resistor through the lower diode to the input terminal. Under these conditions, the output voltage e_o will be negative with respect to ground. This behavior is shown in the graph of Fig. A.16.

As before, the performance of devices such as the one shown in Fig. A.15 can be improved and additional flexibility can be obtained through the use of opera-

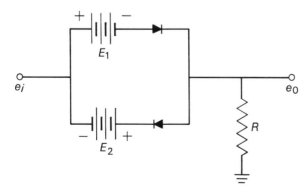

Figure A.15 *A biased diode circuit.*

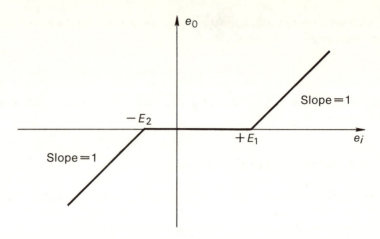

Figure A.16 *The behavior of the circuit of Fig. A.15.*

tional amplifiers. Consider the circuit of Fig. A.17. Observe again that the diodes block any current from flowing around the loop due to the action of the batteries E_1 and E_2. If e_i goes positive, the voltage e_1 also goes positive by the same amount until current begins to flow in one or the other of the diodes. The high gain of the amplifier causes e_o to go negative by a very much larger amount. As soon as e_o exceeds E_2 in magnitude, the lower diode will begin to conduct; current will flow then through the resistor and through the lower diode. This causes the voltage e_1 to stop rising, and the stable operating point is reached where e_o is equal to E_2 in magnitude. Because of the very high gain of the amplifier, the above action will occur for very small values of e_i. The resulting performance, therefore, is approximately as shown in Fig. A.18.

Figure A.19 is similar to Fig. A.17 except that resistors R_1 and R_2 have been added to the diode branches of the network. The performance of the circuit shown in Fig. A.19 is illustrated in Fig. A.20.

A.9 Simulation Based on Transfer Functions

Often, a system to be simulated on an analog computer such as a servomechanism or other feedback system is described in terms of transfer functions rather than in terms of differential equations. Under such circumstances, it is frequently desirable to work directly from the transfer functions themselves, rather than from the system-describing differential equations on which the transfer functions are based.

For example, suppose that in a particular system in which we have interest, the following transfer function expresses the relationship between the input quantity, X_2, and the output quantity, X_3,

$$\frac{X_3}{X_2} = \frac{10}{1 + 0.01s} \tag{A.35}$$

where X_2 and X_3 are functions of the Laplacian operator, s.

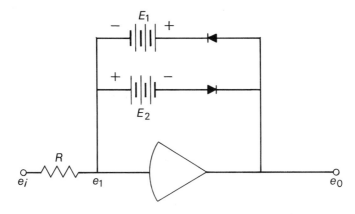

Figure A.17 *A biased diode-operational amplifier circuit.*

Manipulating Eq. A.35 gives

$$10X_2 = X_3 + 0.01s\, X_3 \tag{A.36}$$

which, when the inverse Laplace transform is taken, yields

$$10x_2 = x_3 + 0.01\frac{dx_3}{dt} \tag{A.37}$$

Equation A.37 can be rewritten as shown in Eq. A.38,

$$\frac{dx_3}{dt} + 100x_3 - 1000x_2 = 0 \tag{A.38}$$

which when solved for the highest derivative gives

$$\frac{dx_3}{dt} = 1000x_2 - 100x_3 \tag{A.39}$$

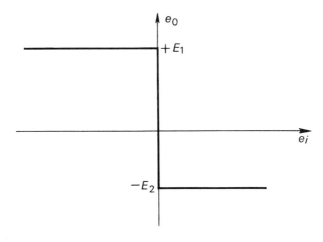

Figure A.18 *The performance of Fig. A.17.*

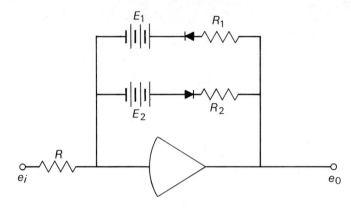

Figure A.19 *A modification of Fig. A.17.*

Equation A.39 is a differential equation which describes the behavior of the assumed system. Equation A.35 is a transfer function which describes the behavior of the same system. The basis of a simulation study of this system could be found either in the differential equation or in the transfer function. We will look at both approaches and draw some comparisons.

An analog simulator for simulating the behavior of the system described by Eq. A.39 could be accomplished by means of the circuit shown in Fig. A.21, using the techniques described in Chapter 4.

The simulator of Fig. A.21 can be redrawn as shown in Fig. A.22. The reader will observe that Fig. A.22 differs from Fig. A.21 only in the rearrangement of the components.

Let us now take the circuit of Fig. A.22 and substitute symbols for the numerical values as shown in Fig. A.23. The operational impedance of the input element is

$$Z_i = R_1 \tag{A.40}$$

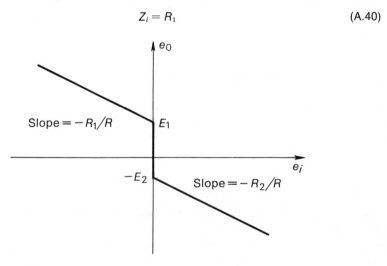

Figure A.20 *The performance of Fig. A.19.*

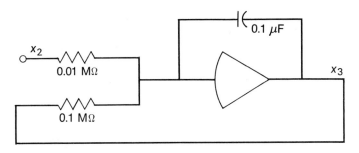

Figure A.21 *An analog simulator based on Eq. A.39.*

and that of the parallel feedback network is

$$Z_0 = \frac{\dfrac{R_2}{Cs}}{R_2 + \dfrac{1}{Cs}} = \frac{R_2}{R_2Cs + 1} \tag{A.41}$$

When Eqs. A.40 and A.41 are substituted into Eq. A.19 we get

$$-X_3 = \frac{-\dfrac{R_2}{R_2Cs + 1}}{R_1} X_2 = -\frac{R_2}{R_1} \frac{1}{1 + R_2Cs} X_2 \tag{A.42}$$

where X_3 is the output voltage and X_2 is the input voltage in Fig. A.23. If values of R_1, R_2, and C are chosen such that $R_1 = 0.1$ mΩ, $R_2 = 0.1$ mΩ, and $C = 0.01$ μF, Eq. A.42 reduces to

$$\frac{X_3}{X_2} = \frac{10}{1 + 0.01s} \tag{A.43}$$

Equation A.43 is exactly the form of Eq. A.35.

Having been through an analysis such as the above, one could hereafter recognize that a transfer function such as the one expressed in Eq. A.35 need not be changed to differential equation form for simulation studies. Rather, the circuit of

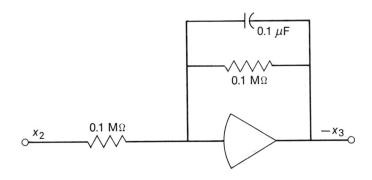

Figure A.22 *A rearranged version of Fig. A.21.*

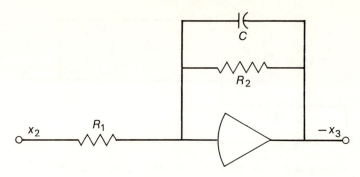

Figure A.23 *A general circuit diagram.*

Fig. A.23 can be used to generate the desired transfer function with proper values chosen for the resistors and capacitor to give the required numerical constants of the transfer function.

Many investigations have been made of other circuits and their equivalent transfer functions have been determined. Two of these are shown in Figs. A.24 and A.25 and Eqs. A.44 and A.45:

$$\frac{X_2}{X_1} = \frac{-R_2Cs}{1 + R_1Cs} = \frac{-T_1s}{1 + T_2s} \tag{A.44}$$

where $T_1 = R_2C$ and $T_2 = R_1C$, and

$$\frac{X_2}{X_1} = \frac{-R_2}{R_1} \frac{1 + T_1s}{1 + T_2s} \tag{A.45}$$

where $T_1 = R_1C_1$ and $T_2 = R_2C_2$. The reader is referred to other textbooks and articles where this subject is developed and cataloged to a much greater extent.

A.10 Digital to Analog Conversion

It is often necessary to make a conversion of information from digital form to analog form. This is accomplished in a device called a digital to analog converter (DAC). Such a device accepts digital representations of information as input and

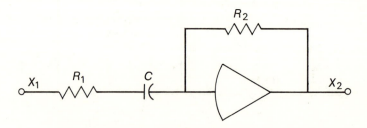

Figure A.24 *A circuit diagram for Eq. A.44.*

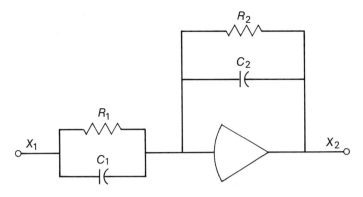

Figure A.25   *A circuit diagram for Eq. A.45.*

produces equivalent analog representations of the same information as output. Digital input information can be presented either in serial fashion or in parallel fashion. In serial fashion, signals representing the digits of a number are presented in time sequence, one digit at a time. In parallel fashion, signals representing all of the digits in a number are presented simultaneously. Many different coding schemes have been devised to represent information digitally. Throughout this discussion conventional binary representation of numbers is assumed.

Perhaps the most obvious way to handle digital information in serial form is to first convert it to parallel form by storing it in a shift register. Once this has been done, the number in the shift register is no longer dynamic and the digits of the number can be treated in parallel as though the information was in parallel form to begin with. The principle is illustrated in the block diagram of Fig. A.26.

The shift register in Fig. A.26 consists of an assembly of flip-flops with some associated logic circuits. The flip-flops are bistable electronic devices which can be switched electronically from one stable state to the other by appropriate control signals. The output voltage from the flip-flops will be at one of two levels corresponding to whatever state the flip-flop happens to be in. In our discussion we will assume the flip-flop to be on (in the one state) when the output voltage is positive, and off (in the zero state) when the output voltage is zero.

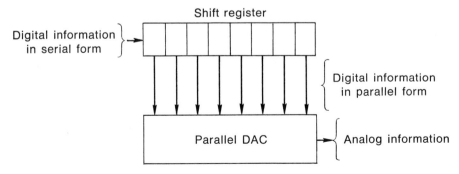

Figure A.26   *A serial DAC.*

The conversion begins when the lowest order or least significant digit (zero or one) of the serial binary number appears on the input line. This causes the left-most flip-flop in the shift register to be switched to a corresponding state—on or off, corresponding to the first digit in the series being either zero or one. The contents of each position of the shift register are then shifted one position to the right. The digit in the right-most position is lost. The digit in the left-most position moves to the next position to the right, and the left-most position assumes the condition corresponding to the second digit in the incoming binary series. This procedure continues until the shift register contains a static parallel representation of the original dynamic serial representation.

The information now in the static shift register can be converted to an equivalent analog form by means of an operational amplifier adder similar to the one de-scribed earlier and diagrammed in Fig. A.11. The input voltages to the DAC come from the flip-flops of the shift register as noted previously. These voltages will each have one of two possible values—a known positive voltage if the flip-flop is on and zero voltage if the flip-flop is off. These voltages have different weighted meaning, however, according to their positional significance in the corresponding binary number. Each digit, and hence each voltage, has twice the significance of the one on its right in the conventional binary manner. This difference in signifi-cance of equal voltages is accomplished in the operational amplifier adder by making the resistance of each input resistor one-half as large as the resistance of the resistor in the next position of lower significance. An eight input DAC is shown in Fig. A.27 with typical values of resistance.

A practical difficulty is encountered with the adder of Fig. A.27 which stems from the large number of precision input resistors required. This difficulty can be some-what offset by increasing the voltage and resistance of the higher-ordered inputs.

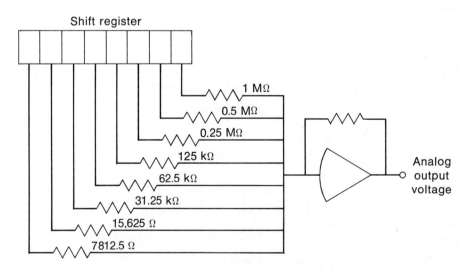

Figure A.27 *An eight input DAC adder.*

It is difficult to build a shift register where the flip-flops operate at different output voltage levels. For this reason, the contents of the shift register, whose flip-flops are all alike, are transferred to another auxiliary register where the higher-ordered positions operate at a higher output voltage level. Fig. A.28 shows how these ideas might be realized.

The adder of Fig. A.28 requires only four different sizes of input resistors while that of Fig. A.27 requires eight different sizes. This advantage is somewhat offset by the auxiliary register that is required, however.

The scheme shown in Fig. A.28 is typical of what might be done. Many other combinations of resistance are possible and have been successfully used.

A.11 Analog to Digital Conversion

Because of its rapid step response, the successive approximation scheme now to be described provides the most popular analog to digital converter (ADC). The

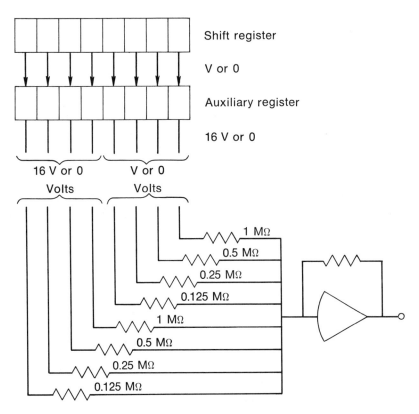

Figure A.28 *A modification of Fig. A.27.*

need for analog to digital conversion is no less common than the need for digital to analog conversion previously described.

Fig. A.29 shows a block diagram of a successive approximation or continuous balance ADC.

The principle upon which the ADC of Fig. A.29 operates is one of trial-and-error. The heart of the device is the up-down counter. This is a special counter that counts either up or down when a clock pulse occurs. Which way it counts depends on signals supplied by the logic circuitry. In turn, the logic circuitry receives signals from the comparator, the signal being negative if e_i is less than e_c and positive if e_i is greater than e_c. A positive signal causes the counter to count up and a negative one causes the counter to count down. The status of the counter is displayed in a register and the DAC converts this digital representation to a corresponding analog voltage e_c, which is fed back to supply one of the inputs to the comparator along with e_i as the other input. The digital representation in the register can be read out to give the desired digital output representation of the analog input e_i.

The up-down counter is special in yet another way. It does not count up from zero starting with the low-ordered digits first, but rather counts up or down from the high-ordered digits. A conversion is begun when a start signal is received. This start signal clears the counter register to zero in all positions and then turns on the highest ordered flip-flop in the counter register. A voltage e_c, corresponding to this highest-ordered or most significant binary digit, appears at the DAC output and is fed back to the comparator input. If e_c is greater than e_i the comparator output will be negative and the counter will count down by turning off the most significant flip-flop and by turning on the next most significant flip-flop. This process continues until e_c becomes less than e_i. When this occurs, the comparator output becomes positive and the counter counts upward by retaining the flip-flop then on in the on state for the duration of the conversion and turning on the next lower-ordered flip-flop. The process continues until all flip-flops in the register are on or off. The register can then be read to find the desired digital representation of the input.

An example will make this process clear. Consider an ADC having an eight binary digit register. Let us assume that the most significant digit position in this register causes an output voltage of 8 V to appear at the output of the DAC. Each successively lower ordered position causes a voltage of one-half the former voltage to

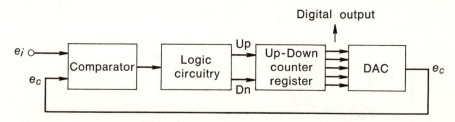

Figure A.29 *An analog to digital converter.*

appear at the output according to the following chart. Of course, two positions on causes the sum of the corresponding voltages to appear at the output.

MSG   LSG

8.0	4.0	2.0	1.0	0.5	0.25	0.125	0.0625
1	2	3	4	5	6	7	8

In the chart, MSG represents the most significant digit, and LSG the least significant digit. They are numbered 1 through 8 for convenient reference. If an input voltage e_i of 3.3 V is applied to the input terminal and a start signal is given, all but the MSG position (flip-flop 1) of the register will be turned off. The output voltage of the DAC will be 8 V and the output of the comparator will be negative. At the next clock pulse, flip-flop 1 will be turned off and the flip-flop 2 will be turned on. The DAC output will now be 4 V and the comparator output will still be negative. At the next clock pulse, flip-flop 2 will be turned off and flip-flop 3 will be turned on. The DAC output will now be 2 V and the comparator output will become positive. Flip-flop 3 will now stay on for the duration of the conversion and, at the next clock pulse, flip-flop 4 will also turn on. The DAC output will now be 3 V and the comparator output will remain positive and flip-flop 4 will hereafter remain on. At the next clock pulse, flip-flop 5 will turn on, the DAC output will be 3.5 V, and the comparator output will become negative. At the next clock pulse, flip-flop 5 will turn off, flip-flop 6 will turn on, the DAC output will be 3.25 V and the comparator output will become positive. This process continues until all register positions are either on or off. The following chart will help to clarify the procedure.

Pulse	Register	DAC Output	Comparator Output
Start	10000000	8.0	−
2	01000000	4.0	−
3	00100000	2.0	+
4	00110000	3.0	+
5	00111000	3.5	−
6	00110100	3.25	+
7	00110110	3.375	−
8	00110101	3.3125	−

In this example the trial voltages of each successive register position were one-half that of their predecessors. This results in a binary coded conversion. It is possible to use different voltage combinations by making appropriate compensating changes in the input resistors in the DAC adder.

So as to keep the preceding discussion as simple as possible, only positive inputs and outputs have been considered. The ideas presented here have been incorporated, however, into DAC's and ADC's that will accommodate signals of both polarities. More detailed treatments of these devices can be found in sources dealing exclusively with digital electronics.

References

Analog Computers

Ragazzini, J. R., R. H. Randall, and F. A. Russell: "Analysis of Problems in Dynamics by Electronic Circuits," *Proc. I.R.E.,* vol. 35, no. 5, pp. 444–452, May, 1947.

Goldberg, Edwin A.: "Stabilization of Wide-band Direct Current Amplifiers for Zero and Gain," *RCA Rev.,* vol. 11, no. 2, pp. 296–300, June, 1950.

Pickens, D. H.: "Electronic Analog Computer Fundamentals," *Proc. I.R.E.,* vol. 25, no. 3, pp. 144–147, August, 1952.

Korn, G. A., and T. M. Korn: *Electronic Analog Computers,* 2d ed., McGraw-Hill, New York, 1956.

Karplus, W. J., and W. W. Soroka: *Analog Methods: Computation and Simulation,* 2d ed., McGraw-Hill, New York, 1959.

Smith, G. W., and R. C. Wood: *Principles of Analog Computation,* McGraw-Hill, New York, 1959.

Warfield, J. N.: *Introduction to Electronic Analog Computers,* Prentice-Hall, Englewood Cliffs, New Jersey, 1959.

Jackson, A. S.: *Analog Computation,* McGraw-Hill, New York, 1960.

Rogers, A. E., and T. W. Connolly: *Analog Computation in Engineering Design,* McGraw-Hill, New York, 1960.

Truitt, T. D., and A. E. Rogers: *Basics of Analog Computers,* Rider, New York, 1960.

Fifer, S.: *Analogue Computation,* vols. I–IV, McGraw-Hill, New York, 1961.

Johnson, C. L.: *Analog Computer Techniques,* 2d ed., McGraw-Hill, New York, 1963.

James, M. L., G. M. Smith, and J. C. Wolford: *Analog and Digital Computer Methods in Engineering Analysis,* International Textbook Company, Scranton, Pennsylvania, 1964.

James, M. L., G. M. Smith, and J. C. Wolford: *Analog Computer Simulation of Engineering Systems,* International Textbook Company, Scranton, Pennsylvania, 1966.

Peterson, G. R.: *Basic Analog Computation,* Macmillan, New York, 1967.

Blum, Joseph J.: *Introduction to Analog Computation,* Harcourt Brace Jovanovich, New York, 1969.

Digital Computers

Selfridge, R. G.: "Coding a General Purpose Digital Computer to Operate as a Differential Analyzer," *Proc. Western Joint Computer Conf.,* pp. 82–84, 1955.

Hildebrand, B.: *Introduction to Numerical Analysis,* McGraw-Hill, New York, 1956.

Lesh, F.: "Methods of Simulating a Differential Analyzer on a Digital Computer," *J. ACM,* pp. 281–288, July, 1958.

Stein, M. L., J. Rose, and D. B. Parker: "A Compiler with an Analog-oriented Input Language," *Proc. Western Joint Computer Conf.,* pp. 92–102, 1959.

Hurley, J. R.: "DEPI 4 (Differential Equations Psuedo-code Interpreter): An Analog Computer Simulator for the IBM 704," Internal Memorandum, Allis Chalmers Mfg. Co., January 6, 1960.

Stein, M. L., and J. Rose: "Changing from Analog to Digital Programming by Digital Techniques," *J. ACM,* pp. 10–23, January, 1960.

Kelley, J. L., Jr., C. Lochbaum, and V. A. Vyssotsky: "A Block Diagram Compiler," *Bell System Tech. J.,* pp. 669–676, May, 1961.

Hamming, R. W.: *Numerical Methods for Scientists and Engineers,* McGraw-Hill, New York, 1962.

Gaskill, R. A., J. W. Harris, and A. L. McKnight: "DAS: A Digital Analog Simulator," *Proc. Spring Joint Computer Conf.,* pp. 83–90, 1963.

Hurley, J. R., and J. J. Skiles: "DYSAC, A Digitally Simulated Analog Computer," *Proc. Spring Joint Computer Conf.,* pp. 69–82, 1963.

Brennan, R. D., and R. N. Linebarger: "A Survey of Digital Simulation: Digital Analog Simulator Programs," *Simulation,* vol. 3, no. 6, pp. 22–36, December, 1964.

Brennan, R. D., and H. Sano: "Pactolus: A Digital Analog Simulator Program for IBM 1620," *Proc. Fall Joint Computer Conf.,* pp. 299–312, 1964.

Harnett, R. T., F. J. Sansom, and L. M. Warshawsky: *MIDAS Programming Guide,* Tech. Rept. SEG-TDR-64-1, Wright–Patterson Air Force Base, January, 1964.

Korn, G. A., and T. M. Korn: *Electronic Analog and Hybrid Computers,* McGraw-Hill, New York, 1964.

Petersen, H. E., F. J. Sansom, R. T. Harnett, and L. M. Warshawsky: "MIDAS: How

It Works and How It's Worked," *Proc. Fall Joint Computer Conf.*, pp. 313–324, 1964.

Clancy, J. J., and M. S. Fineberg: "Digital Simulation Languages: A Critique and a Guide," *Proc. Fall Joint Computer Conf.*, pp. 23–36, 1965.

Karafin, B. J.: "The New Block Diagram Compiler for Simulation of Sampled Data Systems," *Proc. Fall Joint Computer Conf.*, Part I, pp. 55–61, 1965.

Kuo, S. S.: *Numerical Methods and Computers,* Addison-Wesley, Reading, Massachusetts, 1965.

Sansom, F. J.: *MIMIC: Successor to MIDAS,* Conference Paper, Joint Meeting Central Midwestern Simulation Councils, May, 1965.

Southworth, R. W., and S. L. DeLeeuw: *Digital Computation and Numerical Methods,* McGraw-Hill, New York, 1965.

Syn, W. M., and D. G. Wyman: *DSL/90 Digital Simulation Language User's Guide,* Tech. Rept. TRO2.355, IBM Corporation, San Jose, California, July 1, 1965.

Syn, W. M., and D. G. Wyman: *DSL/90 Digital Simulation Language Systems Guide,* IBM Corporation, San Jose, California, July 15, 1965.

Syn, W. M., and R. N. Linebarger: "DSL/90: A Digital Simulation Program for Continuous System Modeling," *Proc. Spring Joint Computer Conf.*, pp. 165–187, 1966.

Burgin, G. H.: "MIDAS III: A Compiler Version of MIDAS," *Simulation,* pp. 160–168, March, 1966.

James, M. L., G. M. Smith, and J. C. Wolford: *Applied Numerical Methods for Digital Computation with FORTRAN,* International Textbook Company, Scranton, Pennsylvania, 1967.

Sansom, F. J.: *MIMIC Programming Manual,* Tech. Rept. SEG-TR-67-31, Wright–Patterson Air Force Base, July, 1967.

The SCI Simulation Software Committee, "The SCI Continuous System Simulation Language (CSSL)," *Simulation,* pp. 281–303, December, 1967.

Mathematics and Other Subjects

Brown, G. S., and D. P. Campbell: *Principles of Servomechanisms,* Wiley, New York, 1948.

Gardner, M. F., and J. L. Barnes: *Transients in Linear Systems,* Wiley, New York, 1952.

Howe, R. M., and V. S. Haneman: "The Solution of Partial Differential Equations by Difference Methods Using the Electronic Differential Analyzer," *Proc. I. R. E.* vol. 41, pp. 1497–1508, October, 1953.

Truxal, J. G.: *Automatic Feedback Control System Synthesis,* McGraw-Hill, New York, 1955.

Crandall, S. H.: *Engineering Analysis,* McGraw-Hill, New York, 1956.

Pipes, L. A.: *Applied Mathematics for Engineers and Physicists,* 2d ed., McGraw-Hill, New York, 1958.

Forsythe, G. E., and W. R. Wasow: *Finite-difference Methods for Partial Differential Equations,* Wiley, New York, 1960.

Wylie, C. R., Jr.: *Advanced Engineering Mathematics,* 2d ed., McGraw-Hill, New York, 1960.

Huskey, H. D., and G. A. Korn: *Computer Handbook,* McGraw-Hill, New York, 1961.

Salvadori, M. G., and M. L. Baron: *Numerical Methods in Engineering,* 2d ed., Prentice-Hall, Englewood Cliffs, New Jersey, 1961.

Dettman, J. W.: *Mathematical Methods in Physics and Engineering,* McGraw-Hill, New York, 1962.

Fox, L.: *Numerical Solution of Ordinary and Partial Differential Equations,* Pergamon Press, New York, 1962.

Froberg, C. E.: *Introduction to Numerical Analysis,* Addison-Wesley, Reading, Massachusetts, 1965.

Jenkins, W. M.: *Matrix and Digital Computer Methods in Structural Analysis,* McGraw-Hill, New York, 1969.

Hybrid Computers

Hurney, P. A.: "Combined Analog and Digital Technique for the Solution of Differential Equations," *Proc. Western Joint Computer Conf.,* pp. 64–66, February, 1956.

King, C. M., and R. Gelman: "Experience with Hybrid Computations," *Proc. AFIPS Fall Joint Computer Conf.,* pp. 36–43, 1962.

Electronic Associates, Inc.: *Introduction to Hybrid Computers,* Electronic Associates, Inc., Long Branch, New Jersey, 1963.

Korn, G. A., and T. M. Korn: *Electronic Analog and Hybrid Computers,* McGraw-Hill, New York, 1964.

Bekey, G. A., and W. J. Karplus: *Hybrid Computation,* Wiley, New York, 1968.

Index

Accuracy, 7, 8

Adder, 2, 4, 37, 480–82

Advantages: of analog, 7; of digital, 8

Analog computer: adder, 37, 480–82; control of, 41; cost, 33; function generator, 41, 485; functional blocks, 33; general procedure, 44; HOLD, 42; integrators, 38, 482–85; as a laboratory model, 51; multipliers, 39, 474–76; patch panel, 34; POT SET, 43; potentiometer, 35, 472–74; REPOP, 42; RESET, 42; sign changer, 37; size, 33; STANDBY, 42; static check, 43; symbols, 33; voltage signals, 33

Analog to digital conversion, 493–95

Analog versus digital, 160–63, 166

Analogies: algebraic, 10–12; involving integration and differentiation, 12–13

ASTRAL, 163

Block diagrams, 2, 142–54, 171

BLODI, 163

Brennan, R. D., 164

Capacitor: voltage drop across, 25, 52

Choice: analog or digital, 4, 7, 462–63

Circuit: analog simulation of, 52, 57–58, 64; digital simulation of, 283–351

COGO: comments in programs, 358; coordinate tables, 356; errors in, 359; instructions in alphabetical order, 362–408; instructions in functional groupings, 409–10; rules for writing programs, 359–61; saving angles and distances, 357; structure of instructions, 354

Comparison of analog and digital simulators, 166

Conversion: analog to digital, 493–95; digital to analog, 490–93

CSMP, 164–65

CSSL: arbitrary functions, 253–54; arithmetic operators, 230, 234–35; array dimensions, 256; assign, 274; band limited noise generator, 249; card read, 249; comments in programs, 225; communication interval, 255, 259; comparator, 240; conditional branch, 274; constants, 228–29; continue, 274; control statements, 254–62; data input, 251, 252, 256; dead space, 243; debug, 252; define variables, 257; derivative, 237; dynamic region, 265; error flag, 263; explicit mode, 223–24, 227–28; exponential function, 248; first-order transfer function, 238; free format, 232–34; FORTRAN operators, 232; function switch, 241; general description, 222–24; harmonic wave, 246; header, 252; hysteresis, 243; implicit iterative function, 240; implicit mode, 223–26; independent variable, 258; initial region, 264; initialization steps, 261; input switch, 241; integration method, 260; integrator, 239; integrator limiter, 245; label plots, 252; lead-lag, 238; limiter, 244; line spacing, 250; local termination, 275; logic gate operators, 231, 236–37; logical operators, 231, 236; macro call, 275; macro termination, 275; MERROR, 255, 261; minimum interval, 255, 262; number of calculation steps, 259; output switch, 241; page spacing, 250; parameters, 228–29; prepare for plot-

linear, 52; nonhomogeneous, 59–64; nonlinear, 52; variable coefficient, 52
Exponential decay, 23

Finite differences, 131–33
Frequency: actual, 22; natural, 14, 22
Function generators, 2, 3, 4, 41, 485

Gaskil, R. A., 164

Harnett, R. T., 164
Harris, J. W., 164
Heat conduction, 134
Hybrid computers: advantages and disadvantages, 462–63; importance of preplanning solutions, 466–68; organization, 464–66; programming, 7, 469–70; reasons for use, 463–64

Inductor voltage drop, 25
Initial conditions, 39
Integrators, 2, 3, 4, 25, 38, 39, 482–85

Laplace transformation, 111
Lesh, H. F., 163

McKnight, A. L., 164
MIDAS, 164
MIMIC: arbitrary functions, 185–94; arithmetic operators, 175, 178; block diagrams, 171; constant functions, 185–94; constants, 180–85; DT, 171, 173; DTMAX, 171, 173; DTMIN, 171, 173; expressions, 173; implicit statements, 203–05; input, 180–85; instruction format, 172; integration, 170, 205–10; logical variables, 194–99; mode control, 205; names, 172, 173; operator precedence, 176; output, 180–85; parameter functions, 185–94; parameters, 180–85; plotting, 212; programming efficiency, 170; result, 173; special functions, 206–12; sorting, 179–80; subprograms, 199–203; transcendental functions, 177–79
Models: analog, 4; digital, 4; mathematical, 1, 5; scale, 5
Multipliers: analog, 2, 3, 4, 39, 474–76; division by reference voltage, 40; sign of output, 40–41

Network analyzer, 5
Nonlinear potentiometer, 476–79

Nonlinearities, 6

Operational amplifier, 479–80
Oscillating systems, 13
Oscillations: damped, 14; electrical, 24; frequency of, 22; indicated frequency, 101; natural frequency, 100; undamped, 14

PACTOLUS, 164
Parker, D. B., 163
PARTNER, 164
Petersen, H. E., 164
Potentiometers, 35, 36, 472–74
Programming Services Corporation, 228

Resistor voltage drop, 25
Rose, J., 163
Runge-Kutta, 170, 260

Sansom, F. J., 164
Scale factors, 83, 90, 101
Scaled equations, 83, 102
Scaling: amplitude scale factor, 80; applied, 85; different point of view, 89; eased in digital simulation, 169; magnitude, 7, 80; need for, 76–79; procedure for, 89; scaled equations, 83, 103; time, 7; time scale, 92
Selfridge, R. G., 163
Sign changer, 2, 3, 4, 37
Simplification of analog simulators, 60–61
Simulation defined, 1, 4
Simulation Councils, Inc., 165
Simulation Software Committee, 222
State equations, 142, 145
State variables: advantages of, 147; defined, 142; and transfer functions, 147
Stein, M. L., 163
STRESS: constants, 419; coordinate systems, 420; finish, 418–19; global coordinates, 420; joint coordinates, 418; joint loads, 419; joint releases, 419; loading, 419; local coordinates, 420; member forces, 419; member incidences, 418; member properties, 419; method stiffness, 418; number of joints, 418; number of loadings, 418; number of members, 418; order of statements, 421; print forces, 419; restrictions in using, 455; selective output, 419; solve this part, 419;

STRESS (*cont.*)
statements in alphabetical order, 422–31; structure, 418; tabulate member forces, 418; type plane frame, 418; type plane grid, 418; type plane truss, 418; type space frame, 418; type space truss, 418; units, 419–20

System: brine tank, 53–54, 58–59; feedback control, 112–15; first-order simulation, 56; higher-order simulation, 25–26; mechanical, 53, 58, 64; nonlinear discontinuous, 105–10; of simultaneous equations, 98–105

Time constant, 23
Transfer functions, 110–12, 147, 486–90

Vibrating beams, 134
Vibrating shafts, 134
Vibrating strings, 133, 135

Warshawsky, L. M., 164

A	0
B	1
C	2
D	3
E	4
F	5
G	6
H	7
I	8
J	9